Defusing Default
Incentives and Institutions

Marco Pagano
Editor

Development Centre of the Organisation for Economic
Co-operation and Development

Distributed by the Johns Hopkins University Press
for the Inter-American Development Bank

Washington, D.C.
2001

© 2001   Inter-American Development Bank
1300 New York Avenue, N.W.
Washington, D.C. 20577

Produced by the IDB Publications Section.

To order this book, contact:
IDB Bookstore
Tel: 1-877-PUBS IDB/(202) 623-1753
Fax: (202) 623-1709
E-mail: *idb-books@iadb.org*
www.iadb.org/pub

The views and opinions expressed in this publication are those of the authors and do not necessarily reflect the official position of the Inter-American Development Bank.

Cover: Image @ 2001 PhotoDisc, Inc.

**Cataloging-in-Publication data provided by the
Inter-American Development Bank
Felipe Herrera Library**

Defusing default : incentives and institutions / Marco Pagano, editor.

p. cm.
Includes bibliographical references.
ISBN: 1886938989

1. Default (Finance)—Latin America—Case studies.   2. Debtor and creditors—Latin America.   3. Consumer credit—Latin America.   4. Bankruptcy—Latin America. I. Pagano, Marco.   II. Inter-American Development Bank.

332.75   P24—dc21   LCCN: 2001135436

TABLE OF CONTENTS

LATIN AMERICAN RESEARCH NETWORK
INTER-AMERICAN DEVELOPMENT BANK

The Inter-American Development Bank created the Latin American Research Network in 1991 in order to strengthen policy formulation and contribute to the development policy agenda in Latin America. Through a competitive bidding process, the Network provides grant funding to leading Latin American research centers to conduct studies on economic and social issues selected by the Bank in consultation with the region's development community. Most of the studies are comparative, which allows the Bank to build its knowledge base and draw on lessons from experiences in macroeconomic and financial policy, modernization of the state, regulation, poverty and income distribution, social services, and employment. Individual country studies are available as working papers and are also available in PDF format on the Internet at *http://www.iadb.org/res.*

ACKNOWLEDGMENTS

The studies in this book were financed by the Latin American Research Network of the Inter-American Development Bank (IDB) and the Development Centre of the Organisation for Economic Co-operation and Development (OECD). Although many friends and colleagues contributed to this volume, the editor would like to acknowledge Michael Gavin, Ricardo Hausmann, Tullio Jappelli, and Robert Townsend for their valuable input in defining the direction of the research project and for extensive comments on the individual studies. Special thanks also go to Norelis Betancourt and Raquel Gómez for managing the administrative and logistical details of the project. Emily Chalmers and John Dunn Smith provided excellent editorial assistance under the direction of Rita Funaro.

Introduction

Marco Pagano

In 1997 the average default rate in Paraguay was 13.1 percent. The differential between the average interest rate on loans and the banks' cost of funds ranged from 11 percent for commercial bank loans to 23 percent for loans made by finance companies and about 60 percent for credit to micro-enterprises. Largely because of the high credit risk, only a small fraction of firms and households had access to loans by "formal" lenders such as banks and finance companies (see chapter 8). While Paraguay is an extreme case, in many developing countries default risk is a major obstacle to the provision of credit, especially by "formal" credit intermediaries. As a result, a large portion of the economy is left starved of credit or remains at the mercy of informal lenders, who generally charge sky-high interest rates.[1]

The key to increasing credit market efficiency in these countries lies in a better understanding of what determines default and what can be done to reduce it. This book pursues precisely this objective, tackling the issue from several angles and with various analytical tools. The next three chapters use theoretical modeling as well as international and historical evidence to analyze how laws, enforcement, information sharing mechanisms and political intervention affect credit market performance. The six subsequent chapters analyze the same issues in the context of in-depth country studies. The case studies are Latin American economies, in whose credit markets the problem of debt repayment is particularly severe. Each of these six chapters summarizes the institutional arrangements affecting default in the corresponding country, and then zooms in on particular institutions or aspects for which the country's experience is particularly telling. The result is a balanced and informative picture—and a thought-provoking one.

The author is professor at the Department of Economics (University of Salerno, Italy), researcher at the Center for Studies in Economics and Finance (University of Salerno, Italy) and co-director of the Financial Economics Programme of the Centre for Economic Policy Research (London).
[1] For an excellent survey of the literature on the relationships between formal and informal credit markets in developing countries, see Besley (1995).

Why Do Borrowers Default?

Broadly speaking, there are two possible reasons why a borrower might default. The first is bad luck: the borrower cannot repay because his income is unexpectedly low due to accidental events such as a bad harvest, a health problem or a deep recession.

A second possible reason for default is opportunistic behavior. Some debtors end up short on cash to repay their debt because they have not taken sufficient care in managing their business or have embarked on excessively risky projects, knowing that the cost of failure was going to be borne by their creditors. Some may be unwilling to repay even though they have the money to do so. Though potentially solvent, they hide the proceeds of their project, and default strategically.

Default caused by opportunistic behavior is intrinsically different from accidental default because it is caused by the borrower's moral hazard. This is true irrespective of whether the moral hazard concerns the way the borrower has managed his project, his choice of the risk level, or his attempt to hide from creditors the cash flow generated by the project. In all these cases, the borrower rationally "chooses" to default, reckoning that the resulting benefit to him exceeds the expected sanctions associated with default.

The remedies against the two different types of defaults are as different as their motives. Lenders can reduce the frequency of accidental defaults by screening their customers more effectively. But better screening may be ineffective against borrowers' risk-shifting behavior or strategic default. Selecting borrowers carefully will be of little help if they have the incentive to increase the riskiness of their projects and can do so without the bank knowing it, or if they can hide from the bank the proceeds of their projects in case of success.

Of course, a bank can monitor borrowers to prevent such damaging behavior, and threaten sanctions in case of default. But monitoring may be expensive, and the threat of sanctions may be ineffective. After all, the perceived cost of sanctions to defaulting borrowers does not depend solely on the individual lender's willingness to inflict them, but on his ability to do so effectively. This, in turn, depends on the whole set of institutional arrangements that rule the credit market: the laws that regulate credit relationships in case of default or bankruptcy, the effectiveness of the judiciary, the degree of banking competition, the existence of private arrangements aimed at sanctioning default, etc. For instance, the threat of legal sanctions against default will not be credible if courts are so inefficient that lenders are unlikely to enforce their claims, and even more so if debtors expect to borrow easily from other lenders after defaulting on their current ones.

Institutional Arrangements Affecting Default

That default arising from borrowers' opportunism depends on the legal framework is increasingly recognized by the literature, especially following the influential contributions by La Porta, López-de-Silanes, Shleifer and Vishny (1997, 1998). This point is especially relevant to less developed countries (LDCs) and in particular to most of Latin America. In these countries, low protection of creditors' rights and poor enforcement of the law are prime candidates to blame for high default rates, for the low volumes intermediated by formal lenders, and for the presence of a large informal credit sector equipped with alternative enforcement mechanisms.

The role of the legal protection afforded to creditors provides a useful starting point for the analysis of default and credit market performance. However, stopping there would lead to a one-sided and misleading view of the effect of institutions on the credit market. This book contributes *three* basic insights that make the analysis more complete and balanced, and hopefully a better guide for policy.

First, the protection of creditor rights enshrined in the law and in contracts, though important, is a double-edged sword. It can raise borrowers' incentives to repay, but if pushed to the extreme it may become inefficient and counterproductive, for instance leading to a high default rate. Even the possibility of a debt moratorium or bailout, for all its negative effects on ex ante repayment incentives, in certain circumstances (such as aggregate adverse shock) can improve the efficiency of the credit market.

Second, the enforcement of contracts by the courts is at least as important as the formal protection provided by the law, and possibly more important. A theme that runs through the entire book—and one that is consonant with findings in related work—is that the cost of legal proceedings, their length, and in some cases the corruption of the judiciary are all key obstacles to the development of formal credit markets. Especially in Latin

American countries, removing them should be a top priority for any policymaker wishing to increase credit market efficiency.

Third, the institutional arrangements that determine the incentive to default extend far beyond the rules enshrined in the law and the efficiency of the judiciary in enforcing contracts and laws. They include several private arrangements, which in some cases compensate for, or at least temper, the lack of formal enforcement mechanisms or their inefficiency. Some of these arrangements are under the control of the contracting parties but others require a certain degree of collective coordination:

- Credit contracts can be structured so as to raise borrowers' incentives to repay by requiring collateral and other guarantees, and setting appropriate seniority rules and covenants.

- The borrower's incentives to repay can be further heightened by monitoring his behavior in the course of the contract; moreover, a stable lending relationship can provide incentives to repay that are absent in a one-shot setting.

- Private lenders may rely on nonstandard enforcement mechanisms such as peer pressure, as in the group lending arrangements common in rural communities, where joint liability may induce repayment in situations in which individual liability would lead to default.

- Lenders can discipline borrowers by exchanging information about their credit history: since access to future credit is affected by one's credit history, this information exchange provides an effective mechanism to punish defaulting borrowers.

What follows outlines how these three basic insights surface in different ways across the various essays of the book, and sets them against the backdrop of the literature.

Legal Protection of Creditor Rights

In the course of history, countries have developed different legal systems, which feature different degrees of protection of creditor rights. The law determines creditor rights at the repayment stage of a loan contract in case of controversy (i.e., sets the rules that judges use to "complete" the contract and enforce it). One of the main contributions made by La Porta *et al.* (1998) has been to propose a measure of the international differences in the degree of creditor rights' protection, and to show how widely this protection differs from country to country, and especially across legal systems with different historical origins. According to their evidence, common law countries, whose legal system derives from English law, give the best protection to creditors, while French civil law countries lie at the opposite end of the spectrum, with German and Scandinavian legal systems falling in between.

In a related paper (La Porta *et al.*, 1997), the same authors use these legal variables to explain the cross-country variation in the availability of external financing to the private sector. They relate measures of external debt (bank debt plus bonds) with their indicators of creditor protection, with country dummies capturing the origin of the legal system and with a survey-based measure of the respect for the law, while controlling for some macroeconomic variables. They find that the breadth of debt markets has a positive correlation with their creditor protection indicator. Moreover, French and Scandinavian civil law countries have less developed debt markets than common law countries, a difference not completely captured by their creditor rights index.

Even within the U.S. legal system, interstate differences in the rules governing the right to repossess collateral appear to affect the availability of credit. Gropp, Scholz and White (1997) analyze how cross-state differences in the U.S. personal bankruptcy rules affect the supply of and demand for household credit, using data from the 1983 Survey of Consumer Finances. They find that generous state-level bankruptcy exemptions reduce the amount of credit available to low-asset households (controlling for their observable characteristics) and increase their interest rates on automobile loans. Personal bankruptcy exemptions may be relevant also in the case of default on a business loan. This is always the case for unincorporated businesses, whose owners are not protected by limited liability. It applies also to small corporate firms whose debts are guaranteed by their shareholders. Berkowitz and White (2000) find that state-level personal bankruptcy exemptions decrease the supply of credit to noncorporate firms and raise their demand for credit. Small firms are 25 percent more likely to be denied credit if they are located in states with unlimited rather than low homestead bankruptcy exemptions.

A related piece of evidence is that credit flows abundantly when the legal sanction inflicted in case of default is extremely harsh, namely, it is a criminal penalty. This occurs even in countries where the judiciary is very inefficient, consistent with Becker's insight that the harshness of the penalty can substitute for the effectiveness of its enforcement. An instance of this is the story of postdated checks in Paraguay told by Straub and Sosa in chapter 8. Until 1996, in Paraguay the law treated the issuance of a postdated check as a criminal offense. In case of default by a debtor who had signed such a check, the creditor could initiate a criminal trial against him and obtain an arrest order to put him in jail. This threat was very effective, resulting in low default rates. As a result, postdated checks became widely used, also as collateral, to the point that they started trading in a large and liquid illegal secondary market. In 1995-96, Paraguay experienced a sharp recession and a banking crisis, which spread to check-based credit. The authorities attempted to revive check-based credit with a law that eliminated the criminal sanction against the issuance of checks without funds. Contrary to their intentions, this aggravated the credit crunch. The criminal sanction was precisely what made postdated checks a viable credit instrument. In chapter 6, Fuentes and Maquieira tell us a less colorful but equally telling story about criminal sanctions for bad checks in Chile. Issuing a bad check in Chile is punished with jail, while defaulting on a bill of exchange is not: correspondingly, the default rate is 1 percent for the former, and between 7 and 10 percent for the latter.

On the whole, the view that emerges from these empirical studies is that the protection of creditor rights granted by the law is an important prerequisite for the availability and cheap provision of credit. Does this imply that, if politically feasible, all countries should opt for steely legal protection of creditor rights? Padilla and Requejo provide a negative answer to this question in chapter 1. They suggest that, aside from moral and distributional concerns, efficiency considerations suggest that both creditor and debtor rights be given some weight in the legal rules governing credit relationships and bankruptcy procedures.

Strong legal protection of creditors, they argue, may be efficient ex ante, but creates inefficiencies ex post. For instance, it may exacerbate debt overhang problems. When any income earned after default must go to creditors, a debtor has little incentive to work, or, at least, to do any work that is legal. Other ex post inefficiencies may be associated with collateral liquidation. Being more interested in recovering their money than in the overall company's value, holders of collateral may strip the company of key assets and force its inefficient liquidation. Bolton and Scharfstein (1996) show that this arises particularly when there are many creditors, each of whom typically has less incentive to renegotiate the loan than a single lender. In addition, the liquidation of a firm can have negative externalities for third parties; for instance, it may inflict costs on employees who have invested in firm-specific human capital, or on suppliers or customers who have come to depend on the firm's operation.[2]

The tradeoff between ex ante efficiency and ex post inefficiency is particularly evident in the extreme case where the law punishes default as a criminal offense. Even a small probability of being eventually jailed is so appalling to most debtors as to eliminate or drastically reduce defaults caused by opportunistic behavior. But some defaults are not due to opportunism: they truly arise from bad luck. Even if the threat of jail were to eliminate all opportunistic defaults, this penalty would still be inflicted on the borrowers who truly cannot repay. This is a very high social cost to pay for an efficient credit market, as is again highlighted by the figures for Paraguay. According to Straub and Sosa's estimates, the issuance of unfunded checks was at the basis of 10 to 40 percent of all criminal proceedings in the 1990s, and of 10 percent of all convictions in 1990. The social cost of putting so many people behind bars can hardly match that of alternative routes to reducing defaults, such as improving the efficiency of civil courts or having banks improve their screening and monitoring practices. (Indeed, Paraguayan banks did precisely this once prison was no longer a threat against default.)

In some cases, strong protection of creditors may even cause ex ante inefficiencies. For instance, if their right to repossess collateral is granted very strong protection, creditors may feel so well cushioned from the effects of default as to be deterred from screening their borrowers' projects. Manove, Padilla and Pagano (1998) show that this may lead banks to effect less than the socially efficient amount of screening activity. In their model, a stronger

---

[2] Biais and Recasens (2001) argue that the socially optimal degree of creditor protection balances the ex post inefficiencies of the frequent liquidation of firms, including its diffused social costs, with the ex ante efficiency gains (especially more abundant credit) associated with strong creditor protection. They analyze how bankruptcy laws emerging from the political process can deviate from this social optimum, as each constituency fails to internalize the external effects of the law on the other constituencies.

protection of creditors' claims on collateral may paradoxically result in a higher frequency of defaults, due to less bank screening. By the same token, the Berkowitz-White empirical finding that larger bankruptcy exemptions are correlated with more frequent denials of credit may not imply that such denials are inefficient, since they may help borrowers avoid unwise investments.

Moreover, even the evidence on the effect of creditor protection is not completely clear-cut, at least at the cross-country level. Padilla and Requejo (chapter 1) produce estimates that qualify the results of La Porta *et al.* (1997), using the same basic data but controlling also for variables intended to capture the macroeconomic stability of the countries in the sample, such as the inflation rate and the government surplus. In these expanded specifications, the data fail to provide conclusive evidence on the sign and magnitude of the effect of creditor rights protection on credit market performance. Other variables appear to be empirically more relevant: "The efficiency of judicial enforcement and the stability of the macroeconomic scenario in which firms operate appear to have more significant effects on credit markets" (Padilla and Requejo, p. 52). These findings are extraordinarily consonant with the time-series evidence provided by the case studies in the last six chapters of this book. The degree of macroeconomic instability emerges as a key driver of the aggregate default rate and of the breadth of the credit market in virtually all the countries considered, as shown most graphically by the time-series evidence for Chile in chapter 6. The efficiency of judicial enforcement is equally prominent in several of the chapters, and warrants a separate discussion.

Efficiency of Judicial Enforcement

Even countries belonging to the same legal tradition and with similar laws may enforce those laws to different extents, depending on the efficiency and honesty of their judiciary. This is witnessed, for instance, by the impressive variation of the law-and-order indicator among civil law countries (see Table 1.3 in chapter 1). The indicator ranges from 10 in Belgium and 8.98 in France to an average of 5.18 for Latin American countries, whose legal systems are all equally rooted in the French civil law tradition. Even within Latin America, the law-and-order indicator ranges from 7.02 in Chile and 6.32 in Brazil to

2.50 in Peru and 2.08 in Colombia. The same applies to the measure of judicial efficiency reported in Table 5 of La Porta *et al.* (1998), which ranges from 9.50 in Belgium and 8.00 in France to a Latin American average of 6.47, registering a minimum of 5.75 in Brazil.

These enforcement variables have a robust direct correlation with the breadth of credit markets. This cross-country correlation, already documented by La Porta *et al.* (1997) and in this book by Padilla and Requejo, is consistent with other cross-country evidence. For instance, Bianco, Jappelli and Pagano (2001) document that mortgage lending is comparatively low in OECD countries where housing mortgage foreclosure procedures are comparatively lengthy and expensive.[3] Outstanding mortgage loans are 5.5 percent of GDP in Italy, where foreclosing a mortgage loan takes between 3 and 5 years. In contrast, mortgage lending is 22 percent of GDP in France and 51.9 percent in the United Kingdom, where the duration of housing mortgage foreclosure is about 1 year, and 43.6 percent of GDP in the United States, where foreclosing a mortgage takes 10 months. The length of the judicial procedure is a good proxy for its cost. Legal expenses range from 18-20 percent of the loan in Italy to 12-18 percent in France and 4.7 percent in the United Kingdom. Countries where mortgage foreclosures are lengthier and costlier also coincide with those where mortgagees must put up a larger fraction of the value of the house they want to buy. The down payment ratio is 42 percent in Italy, 20 percent in France, 9 percent in the United Kingdom and 15.5 percent in the United States.

The reason why the relationship between judicial enforcement and lending activity appears so starkly in the household lending market is likely to be the relatively small size of individual loans in this segment of the credit market. Judicial enforcement presumably has a large fixed cost component, which affects relatively more lending to households (and possibly to small firms) than lending to large companies.

Two essays in this book uncover within individual countries the same correlation between availability of credit and the effectiveness of enforcement that is present in cross-country data. Not surprisingly, the studies that perform this analysis concern the largest countries, Argentina and Brazil, where the number of jurisdictions and the variation in the efficiency of lo-

---

[3] Their data for mortage loans refer to 1986-96, and those for the length and cost of foreclosure procedures refer to 1990.

cal courts allow an econometric assessment of the latter's impact on local credit market conditions. Both studies are based on panel data: at the level of provinces in Argentina's case, and at the state level in Brazil's. Despite the differences in the proxies used to measure judicial inefficiency and in the specifications employed in the estimation, both studies report a statistically and economically meaningful correlation between enforcement variables and the breadth of the credit market. The advantage of this evidence over that offered by cross-country studies is that the legal rules applied by the various judicial districts of the same country are uniform by definition. Therefore, the coefficient of the enforcement variables is not clouded by differences in legal regimes, which in a cross-country regression may be imperfectly controlled for.

This evidence for Argentina and Brazil is consistent with that reported by similar studies for developed countries. Bianco, Jappelli and Pagano (2001) show that in Italian provinces with longer trials or large backlogs of pending trials, credit to nonfinancial enterprises is less widely available than elsewhere. Interest rates, instead, do not appear to have a robust correlation with judicial efficiency, if one controls for unobserved differences in credit quality across provinces. Similar results are reported for household credit in the United States and Italy. In Italy, Fabbri and Padula (2001) find that households located in less efficient judicial districts receive less credit, controlling for their characteristics. In the United States, Meador (1982) and Jaffee (1985) find that mortgage interest rates were generally higher in states where the law extended the length and expense of the foreclosure process. Consistent with these findings, in states that facilitate the foreclosure process the rate of foreclosure is higher (Clauretie 1987) and the losses incurred by lenders are lower (Clauretie and Herzog 1990).

Anyway, absent drastic sanctions, an inefficient and expensive judicial system will hardly ever be used. Lenders will try to find ways to avoid taking legal action against defaulting borrowers as much as possible. This emerges clearly from the country studies in this book. For instance, the Costa Rican banks interviewed by Monge-Naranjo, Cascante and Hall indicate that they generally do not take legal action for defaulted loans (see chapter 7). They prefer to renegotiate the loan in 95 percent of the unsecured loans extended to individuals and 97 percent of those extended to firms. The percentage is somewhat lower for secured loans, reaching the lowest value when the loan is assisted by fiduciary collateral: even in that case, however, they are willing to renegotiate 80 percent of households' defaulted loans and 87 percent of firms' defaulted loans. A similar figure is quoted by Chilean banks: due to the time required to settle a lawsuit and the costs involved, they take only 20 percent of defaulted loans to court and try to settle the others through private arrangements (see chapter 6). Of course, this implies that in these countries lenders must give serious thought to all the private mechanisms that can help them to avoid facing default, or else induce the borrower to behave well at the recontracting stage. As elaborated below, these private mechanisms are quite numerous, and range from appropriate contract design to intensive monitoring, and from relationship lending to information-sharing systems.

Design of Loan Contracts

Borrowers' incentives to repay can be crucially affected by features of loan contracts such as the posting of collateral or of fiduciary guarantees, the number of creditors and the allocation of rights on collateral among them, and the covenants describing contingencies in which the contract can be renegotiated. These features are under the direct control of the contracting parties, although the amount of collateral also depends on the type of firm applying for the loan (young and small firms seldom have large amounts of collateralizable assets).

Of course, the effectiveness of each of these features in ensuring repayment by solvent borrowers partly depends on the legal system and its enforcement. For instance, securing a loan with collateral is not very effective in raising borrowers' incentives to repay if the judicial procedure to seize and liquidate the collateral is lengthy and expensive. But all the country studies in this book highlight that, even where courts are inefficient, expensive and rarely used to enforce contracts, collateral is a key variable in granting a loan, and in determining both the likelihood of default and the amount recovered.

This is particularly clear in the case of Costa Rica, as shown by the results of the bank survey conducted by Monge-Naranjo, Cascante and Hall, and described in chapter 7. In Costa Rica, loans secured by real estate and fiduciary collateral are the most common credit contracts. All the banks interviewed consider the existence and value of collateral as important or crucial in extending loans, and 97 percent of them consider the value of collateral as important or crucial also in renegotiation or legal collection. These results support the theory that predicts that if tangible assets are pledged against the loan, the scope for default is reduced, and so is the borrower's ability to renegotiate the loan (Hart 1995). Fiduciary guarantees play a similar role, also when pledged by third parties: if the loan can be recovered at the expense of others, the latter will exert pressure on the borrower to avoid default.

An important limitation of contracts, however, may be their incompleteness. Some states of the world cannot be precisely described in a contract or verified by a court. In some cases, however, politically induced changes in the laws can "complete" private contracts. For instance, a loan contract may fail to specify what will happen if an adverse aggregate shock such as a bad harvest or a natural disaster hits the economy, making it very hard for borrowers to repay. Such a shock can, however, create a political majority in favor of a debt moratorium or of a bailout of insolvent borrowers. One may think that to secure the implied ex post efficiency gain, society is bound to incur an ex ante efficiency loss: anticipating this potential political intervention, creditors will be less willing to lend. While in certain cases this ex ante efficiency loss may arise,[4] Bolton and Rosenthal in chapter 3 show that this need not be the case. They propose a model where, in the presence of aggregate uncertainty, political intervention raises both ex ante and ex post efficiency, while bailouts do not affect the ex ante equilibrium and raise efficiency ex post. These surprising results derive from the fact that in their model political intervention occurs specifically in the contingencies that private contracts are unable to foresee.

Monitoring and Lending Relationships

Screening and monitoring by the lender can to a certain extent replace collateral in a credit contract: they can reduce default just as collateral does, not only by raising the borrower's incentives to perform, but also by preventing him from taking mistaken investment decisions. These activities, while ca-

---

[4] Indeed Alston (1984) reports that farm foreclosure moratorium legislation during the 1930s led both to fewer farm loans and to higher interest rates in states that enacted this legislation.

pable of generating a surplus to both of the parties involved in the credit contract, are obviously costly to the lender. The incentive to bear the cost of screening and monitoring activity is generally higher in the context of a repeated interaction, since this allows the bank to recoup it over the course of a lasting relationship. A moderate degree of banking competition is a necessary condition for such a relationship to arise and survive: if borrowers can easily switch to the competition, the payoff to a lender's screening and monitoring investment is likely to evaporate.

Besides enhancing lenders' incentive to screen and monitor, lending relationships provide them with an effective deterrent against borrowers' opportunism: default today can be sanctioned by less favorable terms of credit tomorrow. If default reduces the availability of credit and worsens interest rates in the future, the borrower typically has a greater incentive to perform. This may mitigate constraints on external financing for small firms, as confirmed by several empirical studies (Petersen and Rajan 1994; Berger and Udell 1995). However, firms relying on a single bank may face a higher cost of credit than other firms, because the private information generated in the banking relationship leads to an information monopoly that the bank can exploit later in the relationship, as pointed out by Rajan (1992).

In the study of Costa Rica presented in chapter 7, the role of long-term relationships between banks and borrowers appears on balance beneficial. Such relationships help facilitate companies' access to credit, even though they have little effect on interest rates and other terms of the contract (which is again consistent with the U.S. evidence). Relationships appear also to enhance the insurance role played by lenders, probably because they can better detect and sanction opportunistic defaults. The banks surveyed say they are willing to renegotiate loan contracts provided they are confident that the client is willing to repay, and they assess this willingness on the basis of their previous experience with the borrower and his reputation in the community.

Why does relationship lending seem to have a much more important role in Costa Rica than in any of the other countries studied in this book? A possible reason is that screening, monitoring and relationship lending require banks to acquire specialized skills and human capital that are not equally present in other Latin American countries (except possibly Chile). In this sense, an important role of microcredit programs may be precisely the development of these screening and monitoring skills by lenders, especially those dealing with borrowers who have little or no collateral to offer. The evidence offered on this score for Brazil, Paraguay and Peru (in chapters 5, 8 and 9) is particularly interesting. The studies of Brazil and Peru also illustrate that microcredit programs in some cases use successfully joint liability schemes to increase the chances of debt repayment. This agrees with the literature on group lending, which stresses that the members of a social group that is jointly liable for a loan can sometimes screen and monitor more effectively than the lender would.[5]

Information Sharing among Lenders

Sharing information about borrowers can be a very important mechanism to control defaults, especially in economies with poor judicial enforcement. In fact, as documented by Jappelli and Pagano in chapter 2, in most countries the exchange of information among lenders (banks, finance companies, credit card companies, retailers, suppliers, etc.) is massive. And even though in many cases it takes place via a publicly managed database (a central credit register), nothing prevents lenders themselves from arranging such an exchange of information—either cooperatively or by letting an entrepreneur do it for profit. The information exchanged generally concerns past defaults or arrears, but sometimes it also includes data about characteristics of the borrower and his overall debt exposure. The lenders that contribute their private information to these shared databases are granted exclusive access to them insofar as they provide timely and accurate data.

The effect of this exchange of information is fourfold. First, it allows banks to make a more accurate prediction of the solvency of credit applicants (partly overcoming adverse selection problems in the credit market: see Pagano and Jappelli 1993). Second, it reduces the rents that banks may

---

[5] Each individual in the group serves as another's guarantor, extending the collateral that the creditor can seize. This reduces the need for screening by the lender, since the group "self-selects" if its members are informed about the others' ability and honesty (Varian 1990). The lender can also economize on monitoring, because each debtor exerts "peer monitoring" within the group (Stiglitz 1990), and can punish default by other members via noneconomic sanctions, generally more effectively than the creditor (Arnott and Stiglitz 1991, and Besley and Coate 1995). Finally, group lending may also reduce defaults by pooling risks (Armendariz and Gollier 2000).

otherwise earn from their private information, forcing them to price their loans more aggressively, thereby raising borrowers' net profits and thus their incentive to perform (Padilla and Pagano 1997). Third, it works as a borrower discipline device: each borrower knows that if he defaults, his reputation will be spoiled with all the potential lenders in the market, cutting him off from credit or making it more expensive for him to raise external finance in the future. This boosts his incentive to repay, and raises the efficiency of the credit market (Padilla and Pagano 2000). Finally, information sharing makes each lender aware of a borrower's exposure to other lenders, thus eliminating the borrower's temptation to exploit opportunistically the lenders' ignorance of his total indebtedness (Bizer and DeMarzo 1992).

While chapter 2 provides cross-country evidence of the positive correlation between information sharing and credit market performance,[6] the individual country studies brim with very interesting descriptive evidence on the effect of information sharing on specific credit markets. The evidence highlights particularly its "disciplinary role." For instance, Castelar Pinheiro and Cabral (chapter 5) report that in Brazil the whole postdated check market (whose size is of the same order of magnitude as the stock of household credit) operates without collateral, without personal guarantees, and without legal sanctions of any type. Its only foundation is its information-sharing mechanism: a "black list" of people issuing checks without funds. This mechanism alone also explains why the interest rate charged by factoring companies that operate in this market is much lower than that charged by credit card companies. Similar evidence is reported for Chile, where department stores seeking to collect an unpaid loan send the relevant information both to a collection agency and to the main Chilean credit bureau, DICOM. Apparently, notifying DICOM is a very effective way of securing immediate repayment, since delinquent customers see their credit dry up with all the stores that they patronize.

Moreover, the degree and sophistication of information sharing arrangements appear to be correlated with those of the financial system as a whole. For instance, Costa Rica, which has one of the most sophisticated credit markets in the region, also has an impressive and keenly competing set of private credit bureaus covering the majority of the population of the country, with different bureaus specializing in different services. The devel-

---

[6] Jappelli and Pagano (1999) provide further evidence on this score.

opment of information sharing mechanisms appears in turn to prompt lenders to move toward more sophisticated screening and monitoring practices. This is witnessed by the central role that information-sharing systems have taken in borrower selection in Peru, especially after the development of a public rating register in that country. As Trivelli, Alvarado and Galarza explain in chapter 9, this has encouraged lenders to shift away from exclusive reliance on collateral and toward information-based lending.

A Summary of the Main Findings

The research collected in this book addresses three main issues. The first is the role that legal rules play in the efficient functioning of the credit market. Is a steely legal protection of creditor rights a prerequisite for an efficient credit market? Or are there potential drawbacks to be taken into account? Is the potential political decision of a debt moratorium or bailout always bad for efficiency? The answers that the book offers on this score are somewhat more balanced than those that might be drawn from the current literature. While several recent papers stress that strong creditor protection is a prerequisite for the provision of cheap and abundant credit, this book argues that efficiency demands that both creditor and debtor rights be given some weight in the legal rules governing credit relationships and bankruptcy procedures.

The second issue concerns the role of judicial enforcement in credit markets. How important is enforcement in determining the availability of credit? Here lies one of the most robust empirical findings of the book, and one that agrees with the thrust of other studies on this issue. Both cross-country evidence and individual country studies show that the quality of legal enforcement has a positive impact on the amount of lending available in the credit market, suggesting that more effective judicial enforcement improves the credit market's performance.

Third, to what extent can private contracting and other private mechanisms remedy the shortcomings of poor enforcement of the law, by reinstating private incentives to repay even in such circumstances? The answer to this question comes largely from the rich empirical evidence of the six country studies contained in the book, which exploit the variety of experiences and institutional settings that affect the operation of credit markets in Latin American countries.

Apart from two general features—relatively poor enforcement of the law by courts and a recent past of macroeconomic instability and poor prudential regulation—the variety of experiences is truly impressive. The law is not on the debtor's side in all countries: in Chile, creditors enjoy rather strong legal protection, even though courts are slow and cost-ineffective in enforcing it. Nor are banks unsophisticated and dormant in all countries: in Costa Rica they take a very active role in monitoring debtors and intervening when things go sour. Moreover, the degree of legal enforcement is generally far from uniform even within a given country. In Argentina and Brazil it varies so much from region to region that econometric evidence can be produced on the relationship between the effectiveness of judicial enforcement and the amount of credit extended by banks. Finally, a set of fascinating facts emerges about the remedial role of various institutional arrangements such as information sharing systems among lenders and microlending programs in different countries.

The resulting evidence is so rich and multi-dimensional that it is difficult to force it into a single conceptual mold. However, it is precisely this richness that discloses the complex and unexpected ways in which credit market institutions tend to adapt to the failure of the state enforcement mechanism and reestablish a certain amount of credit market activity. The evidence gathered here should provide considerable food for thought for policymakers intent on improving financial markets in Latin America and elsewhere.

Part One
Preventing Default: The Issues

CHAPTER 1

The Costs and Benefits of Protecting Creditor Rights: Theory and Evidence

Atilano Jorge Padilla and Alejandro Requejo

What are the efficiency implications of the laws and regulations that protect creditor rights? Many economists and legal experts argue that protecting creditor rights is crucial to the development and optimal performance of the credit market (see La Porta *et al.* 1997, 1998). These authors maintain not only that the credit market's primary economic function is to provide cheap funds but also that the market can perform this function only when creditor rights are protected and sanctions on defaulting debtors are enforced.

This orthodox view can be disputed on several grounds. First, important moral and distributional objections exist that economists often ignore. According to this thinking laws and regulations are needed to protect low-income households, small businesses, and entrepreneurs from the harsh consequences of default. Second, laws favorable to creditors may be efficient ex ante, as the proponents of the orthodox view suggest, but are likely to create serious inefficiencies ex post, once the uncertainty involved in the borrower's investment project is resolved (see, among many others, Gertner and Scharfstein 1991). This logic suggests that if creditors are protected against default, they may have little incentive to allow entrepreneurs to restructure their debt and reorganize their ventures, even when an investment project should be permitted to continue. And unless debtors are freed of all residual unpaid obligations at the end of a bankruptcy procedure, their incentives to work or invest in new creditworthy projects will necessarily be diminished.

Atilano Jorge Padilla is Associate Director at National Economic Research Associates (NERA) and a Professor of Economics at the Centro de Estudios Monetarios y Financieros (CEMFI) in Madrid, Spain. Alejandro Requejo, a Consultant at NERA, was Assistant Professor of Business at the Universidad Carlos III de Madrid when this work was conducted.

When things are examined from this viewpoint, then, a trade-off exists in the optimal protection of credit rights:

> ... [T]he easier it is for a borrower to escape from its obligations to pay interest and, ultimately, repay a loan, the more likely it is that creditors will lose some of the money they lend, and so the less willing they will be to extend credit. Less plentiful credit means less economic activity. . . . . When someone is too deeply in debt, he may have little incentive to work . . . Free him from his debts and his incentives to work (legally) are restored. In a sense, the right to go bust is an insurance policy against financial disaster [*The Economist* 1998].

Some authors also dispute the ex ante efficiency properties of legal arrangements that provide strong creditor protection. For instance Posner (1992, p. 400) argues that lenders may assume unjustified risks if protected against default:

> Some [U.S.] states have generous household [bankruptcy] exemptions for insolvent debtors, others chintzy ones. In the former states, the risk of entrepreneurship is reduced because the cost of failure is less, but interest rates are higher because default is more likely and the creditor's position in the event of default is weaker. And note that higher interest rates make default all the more likely. *Cutting the other way, however, is the fact that in the low-exemption states lenders' risk is less, which induces lenders to make more risky loans, i.e., loans likelier to end in bankruptcy. It is therefore unclear whether there will be more bankruptcies in the high-exemption states or in the low-exemption ones* [italics added].

Mitigating the cost of failure to entrepreneurs is likely to increase their willingness to take risks. Arguably in a legal environment in which creditor rights are strongly protected, forward-looking agents with bright but somewhat adventurous ideas may find it unattractive to go into business. Many analysts believe this situation exists in Europe. *The Economist* (January 25, 1997a) argues that to increase the rate of creation of new companies "requires a shift in Europe's laws and attitudes towards bankruptcy. If you start a company in London or Paris and go bust, you have just ruined your future. Do it in Silicon Valley, and you just completed your entrepreneurial training."

Manove and Padilla (1999) and Manove, Padilla and Pagano (1998) point out that the credit market serves economic functions other than the provision of cheap loans. These functions include screening projects, insuring risk-averse entrepreneurs who undertake high-risk investment projects, and protecting overconfident entrepreneurs and households from impulsive investment and purchasing decisions. The authors show that strong protection for creditor rights may lead to inefficient market equilibria because of imperfections in the banking industry, so that the provision of cheap credit is inappropriately emphasized over other functions of the market. The authors also show that imposing regulatory restrictions on collateral requirements and protecting debtors during bankruptcy proceedings may redress this imbalance and restore ex ante market efficiency.

None of these critical theories questions the need for an efficient judicial system that effectively enforces existing laws and regulations. These theories all reckon that in the absence of such a judicial system, economic activity is seriously hampered by all sorts of opportunistic behavior. What these theories dispute is the statement that laws and regulations favoring creditors are a prerequisite to efficient credit market performance.

This chapter discusses the theories that deal with the implications for efficiency of the various regulations that protect creditors. A cost-benefit analysis of strong creditor rights protection builds on the sample of 49 countries developed by La Porta *et al.* (1998). The analysis confirms the results obtained by La Porta *et al.* (1997, 1998) showing that an effective judicial system is crucial to the development and performance of the credit market. But unlike the previous studies, this analysis finds no conclusive evidence on the sign and magnitude of the effect of protecting creditor rights on credit market efficiency. The analysis does uncover the great importance of macroeconomic stability to credit market performance, finding in particular that countries with lower inflation have wider debt markets.

Although the chapter focuses on the legal prerequisites to the development of credit markets, the conclusions have far wider economic implications. Rajan and Zingales (1998) show that in a large sample of countries, industrial sectors needing external financing develop much faster in countries with well-functioning financial markets. This finding reveals the existence of a link between the development of the credit system and a country's growth potential. And it underscores the importance of determining which legal institutions best contribute to the development of the kind of wide, well-performing credit markets that will foster economic growth around the world.

Theories Concerning Creditor Rights and Economic Efficiency

A credit relationship usually involves three parties: a lender who provides the funds, a borrower who invests these funds and promises to pay principal plus interest, and a court of law that enforces the loan contract if a dispute arises between the lender and borrower. The lender and borrower have a common interest: capturing the gains from their transaction. Yet they are likely to disagree about the cost and size of the loan—that is, on how to split those gains. They are also likely to hold different views on how the funds should be invested and how to proceed in the event of default. These conflicting views result from the borrower's ability to behave opportunistically by taking excessive risks, behaving negligently, or just diverting the funds for personal uses, depriving the lender of an adequate return on the investment. These conflicts may become so severe that lenders stop making loans, hindering the ability of entrepreneurs and other potential borrowers to engage in business.

Courts can help remedy such problems by punishing opportunistic behavior. Generally, lenders will not provide financing in the absence of a third party (usually the courts) to effectively enforce repayment. Otherwise borrowers can simply refuse to repay, leaving lenders with huge losses.[1] Loan contracts often include collateral requirements that aim to protect lenders against default. Again, however, these requirements are effective only when third-party enforcement is available. Clearly, enforcement is instrumental to the development of the credit market. Further, the more efficient and predictable the third party's actions and proceedings are, the easier it is for lenders and borrowers to realize potential gains from trade. Hypothetically, then, external financing, and in particular debt, should be most widespread in countries with relatively efficient judicial systems that effectively enforce contracts.

---

[1] Obviously creditors can enforce their claims directly, precisely as organized crime does to support its lending activity. But private enforcement involves important private costs and substantial social distortions, making it an inferior alternative to public enforcement.

As Hart (1995) points out, in any lending relationship involving a single lender and a single borrower, courts should simply ensure that the terms of the loan contract are upheld. That is, the courts need only enforce repayment when default is not an option and oversee the transfer of ownership and control when default does occur. In reality when a judicial proceeding involves multiple creditors, the courts' role becomes more complicated. If a debtor cannot fully repay all debts, the creditors may engage in a socially inefficient race to repossess collateral or obtain a judgment to foreclose on any assets. This race may lead to the liquidation of individual assets—a practice that can reduce the overall value of the assets if they are worth more as a whole. Thus, in the presence of multiple creditors, the legal system must provide a bankruptcy procedure that disposes of borrowers' assets in an orderly and value-maximizing manner.[2] Bankruptcy laws and other credit regulations can be understood as standard contracts provided by the state that largely determine the extent of legal protection creditors enjoy within the lending relationship.

La Porta *et al.* (1998) show that bankruptcy laws and credit regulations differ vastly from country to country in the degree of protection they afford creditors. In most countries collateral requirements and restrictive loan covenants are legal. But some countries have significant limitations on collateral, bankruptcy exemptions, and discharge provisions built into their bankruptcy codes, while others do not. For example, in the United States "fresh-start" provisions in the 1978 Bankruptcy Code mandate the discharge of all debts remaining at the conclusion of bankruptcy proceedings, but such provisions do not exist in many European countries. And while some countries have absolute priority rules that give senior creditors the right to be paid in full before junior creditors and shareholders get anything, in other countries important deviations do occur. Finally, the degree of enforcement of creditor rights varies across countries. In some countries, for instance, court-supervised auctions of repossessed assets are manipulated by colluding bidders or, even worse, are run by corrupt officials. As a result the value of collateral in these countries is substantially reduced.

---

[2] Posner (1992) and Hart (1995) discuss several reasons why, in a world of costly contracting, bankruptcy processes are best governed by the state rather than by the parties themselves.

Given these differences, how can the optimal extent of creditor rights protection be determined? A review of the benefits and costs associated with strong protection for creditors provides some insight into this issue.

Benefits of Strong Creditor Rights Protection: The Orthodox View

One well-established strand of the literature claims that investor protection is central to the development of capital markets. In particular the argument holds that credit would not be extended if creditors were not legally entitled to repossess collateral. One theorist argues that "creditors are paid because they have the right to repossess collateral" and that absent such rights, "investors would not be paid, and therefore firms would not have the benefit of raising funds from these investors" (La Porta *et al.* 1998). This orthodox view originates from the idea that adverse selection and moral hazard are the main problems in credit relationships.

Adverse Selection

When a borrower applies for a loan, the lender generally does not know many of the personal and professional facts essential to an appropriate risk assessment. The borrower may be an honest entrepreneur with a creditworthy investment project or a dishonest individual whose only intention is to take the money and run. The lender may understand the dilemma but not be able to solve it. This problem is severe only if the borrower defaults and the lender cannot discern or verify in court a cause for the default. Honest entrepreneurs repay their debts unless forced to default by bad luck. Others never repay. How does a lender ascertain the borrower's level of risk?

Suppose that the loan contract can specify only an interest rate—that is, the lender cannot impose collateral requirements. Due to the lender's inability to discriminate between honest and dishonest entrepreneurs, the equilibrium interest rate will have to be high enough to compensate for the risk of lending to a crook. But while a crook is willing to borrow at any interest rate, an honest entrepreneur's demand for credit decreases as the loan's interest rate rises. The dishonest borrower does not intend to repay the loan at all, which explains why this type of demand is not sensitive to price. The honest entrepreneur will borrow only at interest rates at which the investment project has a positive net present value (NPV). Thus the high interest rates that can result from asymmetric information may end up excluding the honest entrepreneur from the credit market, a phenomenon known as adverse selection (see Stiglitz and Weiss 1981). With adverse selection the market outcome is highly inefficient, since investment projects put forth by honest entrepreneurs are not funded despite positive NPVs. In this example adverse selection produces market collapse, since the only borrowers willing to apply for loans at the prevailing rate have no intention of repaying. Lenders who understand these incentives will not lend to anyone in equilibrium.

In a credit market with asymmetric information, the optimal choice may be to allow parties to write contracts specifying collateral requirements, for two reasons. First, unlike intentions or luck, an entrepreneur's wealth is easily observable. Second, a borrower's willingness to post collateral conveys useful information about risk. An honest entrepreneur whose project has a positive NPV will be more willing to post collateral in order to obtain a low interest rate than a potential borrower who does not intend to repay. Bester (1985), Besanko and Thakor (1987a, 1987b) and Chan and Thakor (1987) show that such information can improve the allocation of credit in equilibrium, tempering the problems created by adverse selection. Lenders can discriminate among borrowers by offering a menu of contracts, each specifying a different interest repayment and collateral requirement. A contract with a large collateral requirement will carry a lower interest rate than a contract with a relatively small (or no) collateral requirement. Entrepreneurs with low-risk projects will be able to post collateral and thus take advantage of low interest rates.

Moral Hazard

Collateral requirements also mitigate problems of moral hazard. The borrower has the incentive to engage in opportunistic behavior at the creditor's expense because the lender cannot supervise them once the loan has been extended. The borrower may act in ways that affect the value of the loan—for instance by investing the funds in an undertaking other than the original project. If the new project is riskier, the interest rate in the original contract does not adequately compensate the lender, but the lender cannot punish such behavior unless the diversion of funds is observed and verified in a court of law. The borrower may engage in other kinds of asset substitution, including failure to manage a project appropriately, debt overhang, and outright fraud.

The right to repossess collateral gives the lender a means of ensuring that a borrower does not engage in such behaviors.[3] Opportunistic actions carry with them the danger that collateral will be repossessed, thus reducing the borrower's incentive to undertake such actions. In short, borrowers risk personal assets, not just the funds lent by the creditors. If the creditor cannot require collateral or effectively repossess it, interest rates will rise, and if anticipated repayments do not cover the opportunity cost of lending, the credit market may collapse. Strict protection of the creditor's right to repossess collateral leads to cheaper credit. Many valuable investment projects that would not be funded in the presence of moral hazard can be financed when debtors are allowed to use personal assets as collateral.

So far the arguments presented support the claim that strong creditor rights protection raises the credit market's efficiency ex ante. What about efficiency ex post—that is, once the uncertainty embedded in the investment project is resolved? Suppose the borrower defaults on a promise to repay at maturity. Two possible courses of action are generally available: either selling the assets comprising the investment project and using the money to repay the creditors, or reaching an agreement that allows the project to continue as an ongoing concern. Liquidation is efficient if the value of the assets once they are sold exceeds the value of the project as an ongoing concern. But if the bankruptcy procedure allows the borrower to file for reorganization without the creditor's consent, controls the reorganization process, and imposes an automatic stay on the firm's assets after reorganization, liquidation may not take place even if it is the most efficient option. This situation allegedly prevails in the United States and many other countries, including Spain. Protecting the creditor's right to repossess collateral and to be repaid according to absolute priority rules eliminates this ex post overinvestment problem (see Gertner and Scharfstein 1991).

---

[3] The right to repossess collateral is the most fundamental right awarded to creditors. Most other rights are intimately related to or even derived from it. These include the right to introduce restrictive covenants into the loan contract, the right to veto the reorganization of bankrupt firms, the right to take possession of their securities during such reorganizations, and the right to be repaid according to absolute priority in the event of bankruptcy.

The Cost of Strong Creditor Rights Protection: Critical Theories

Regulations favoring creditors over debtors can present the opposite problem: they may lead to underinvestment ex post. If creditors have strong protection against default, they have no incentive to allow debtors to restructure financially and continue their investment projects. Debtors' assets may be liquidated even when efficiency argues for keeping them in debtors' hands as part of ongoing investment projects.

The ex ante efficiency of creditor-friendly laws can also be disputed. These laws limit entrepreneurs' incentives to take risks, so that creditworthy projects may not be funded in equilibrium. Two scenarios illustrate this point. In the first, an entrepreneur obtains funds for an investment project of a fixed size at a given interest factor R_0 but is not required to post collateral. The entrepreneur's liability is thus limited to a promise to repay the principal plus interest from the returns to the investment project. In a competitive credit market, R_0 will be equal to R/p in equilibrium, where p is the probability of repayment and R is the opportunity cost of funds for the lender. If the project is successful, the entrepreneur earns the project's returns minus R_0. If the project fails, the entrepreneur loses nothing.

In the second scenario, the entrepreneur posts a house as collateral for the loan. In this situation the lender faces less risk, since the house can be liquidated to pay the debt. The lender is consequently willing to fund the investment project at a relatively low interest rate. In a competitive credit market, the total cost of funds to the entrepreneur (including the pecuniary cost associated with the potential loss of the house) is the same as it is for the first scenario, but the entrepreneur bears greater risk in the second. In this case the entrepreneur earns a large profit when the project succeeds (by paying a lower interest rate) but loses the house if the project ends in a fiasco. In the second scenario a risk-averse entrepreneur has fewer incentives to invest.

A creditor-friendly bankruptcy law, then, may act as a barrier to the creation of new businesses. As Arrow (1962) points out, this problem is particularly severe in a society with inadequate mechanisms to diversify risk and many risk-averse individuals. In such a society investment in risky but highly rewarding activities is inefficiently low, even in the absence of creditor-friendly regulations. Carr and Mathewson (1988) show that unlimited liability rules constitute barriers to entry even in the absence of risk aversion. Unlimited liability generates a problem of moral hazard because some shareholders can become free riders, letting others provide guarantees for insolvencies.

Creditor-oriented lending laws may also generate other ex ante inefficiencies. Bebchuk and Picker (1998) point out that deviations from absolute priority increase incentives for owner-managers to invest in managerial human capital and reduce incentives for these entrepreneurs to entrench themselves as managers (for instance by choosing projects that require their particular expertise). Likewise Berkovitch, Ronen, and Zender (1997) argue that in drawing up optimal bankruptcy laws, legislators must take into account the ex ante incentives of managers to invest in firm-specific human capital. Deviations from absolute priority may also discourage firms in financial distress from taking excessive risks prior to filing for bankruptcy (see Gertner and Scharfstein 1991) and facilitate the initiation of bankruptcy proceedings when bankruptcy is the most desirable option (see Baird 1991). Finally, Bebchuk and Fried (1996, p. 857) argue that "a borrower and a secured creditor may have incentives under full priority to expend resources inefficiently encumbering an asset merely to transfer value from nonadjusting creditors." These "nonadjusting" creditors include tort claimants, government tax and regulatory agencies, voluntary creditors with small claims, and voluntary creditors with large fixed claims.

Creditor-Friendly Laws and Credit Market Functions

As discussed above, one of the primary rationales for creditor-friendly laws is that they help reduce the cost of capital. In the models of Manove and Padilla (1999) and Manove, Padilla and Pagano (1998), when collateral requirements are unrestricted, competition among lenders leads to lower interest rates but not necessarily to an efficient allocation of credit. In the presence of bounded rationality or asymmetric information, creditors will not prevent borrowers from undertaking excessively risky projects or will invest very little effort in screening.

Jackson (1986) argues that banks may be more capable than entrepreneurs of assessing potential investment projects. Banks acquire valuable information in the course of dealing with entrepreneurs and thus develop useful yardsticks for evaluating new projects. Banks also have the best sectoral and cyclical information, which helps them predict the impact of macroeconomic trends on the profitability of specific investment projects. For these reasons banks are—or ought to be—in the business of evaluating projects. But a high level of collateral will weaken a bank's incentive to evaluate projects carefully. In the limiting case of a fully collateralized loan, the bank is shielded from default risk and is thus indifferent to the nature of the investment project being financed. Conversely, granting debtors some collateral exemptions (or discharges) restores the bank's incentive to screen and monitor. As Jackson (1986, p. 249) notes, "Discharge . . . heightens creditors' incentives to monitor: by providing for a right of discharge, society enlists creditors in the effort to oversee the individual's credit decisions."

Jackson makes clear that the incentive problem on the creditors' side is most important when borrowers are insured by a social safety net. In this case borrowers have an incentive to undertake excessively risky projects, and the banks—fully protected by collateral—have no incentive to restrain them. Jackson (1986, pp. 231-32) additionally states:

> If there were no right of discharge, an individual who lost his assets to creditors might rely instead on social welfare programs . . . [and] underestimate the true cost of his decisions to borrow. In contrast, discharge imposes much of the risk of ill-advised credit decisions . . . on creditors. The availability of an unlimited nonwaivable right of discharge in bankruptcy therefore encourages creditors to police extensions of credit and thus minimizes the moral hazard created to safety-net programs . . . . The importance of encouraging creditor monitoring in a society that provides other safety nets may explain why the right of discharge is not waivable.

Manove, Padilla and Pagano (1998) develop a model of credit market equilibrium to evaluate the robustness of Jackson's arguments. In this model entrepreneurs have privileged information on their ability to develop profitable investment projects. Entrepreneurs differ in this ability: some are better than others at identifying valuable investment projects. Banks know that entrepreneurs' abilities differ in this regard but cannot tell which potential borrowers are most capable. And entrepreneurs, irrespective of their abilities, may sometimes end up with a bad project. Consequently, ex ante screening of investment projects adds value to all entrepreneurs, even capable ones. Since banks are assumed to have an advantage in project evaluation, from a social standpoint they should undertake this activity.

Entrepreneurs must obtain loans in order to invest. Banks can discover the quality of a given project at a cost by screening, but since screening is neither an observable nor a contractible activity banks will use it only if the direct benefits of screening exceed the costs. When banks screen they approve only those loans likely to provide a return to the investment. Ultimately, then, entrepreneurs whose loan applications are approved end up paying not only their own screening costs, but also a prorated share of the screening costs of those applicants whose loans are denied.

In this setting entrepreneurial heterogeneity makes banks want to introduce collateral requirements into their loan contracts not only to protect themselves against default risk but also to discriminate among entrepreneurs. Collateral, however, reduces banks' incentives to screen projects before granting loans—sometimes to a level that is too low for social efficiency.

If screening costs are not too high, screening is socially efficient for all entrepreneurs. In any competitive pooling equilibrium in which no entrepreneur posts collateral, banks screen all projects and fund only sound investments. In this equilibrium no entrepreneurs default, but able entrepreneurs who secure loans pay a share not only of their own screening costs but also of the costs of screening less viable projects. Because the costs of screening the less viable projects are higher, capable entrepreneurs have an incentive to separate themselves from the screening process by posting collateral—but this move in turn removes banks' incentives to screen. Manove, Padilla, and Pagano (1998) show that for a range of screening costs, banks underinvest in project evaluation. Too many risky projects receive funding, and too many creditworthy entrepreneurs experience bankruptcy. This inefficiency can be partly corrected with collateral limitations, bankruptcy exemptions, and discharge provisions.

Bebchuk and Fried (1996) make a somewhat related argument, maintaining that "to the extent that the bank is insulated by a security interest from the effects of the borrower's misbehavior, the bank will have less incentive to control the borrower's behavior" (p. 903). This analysis, however, differs from that of Manove, Padilla, and Pagano (1998) in two respects. First, it focuses on ex post monitoring rather than ex ante screening. Second, and more important, in this analysis the inefficiencies associated with the creation of a security interest originate in the existence of creditors who cannot adjust their claims to take into account that any security interest subordinates their unsecured claims.

Limiting Creditor Rights to Protect against Overoptimism

Jackson (1986) identifies yet another reason why limiting creditor rights may increase value. He claims that these policy measures may help correct possible psychological biases that affect individual investment and consumption choices. That is, they may help limit the harmful decisions individuals make when they act impulsively or irrationally. Jackson points out that many individuals process available information in ways that consistently underestimate future risks. In the words of Adam Smith (1776, Book I, Chapter X):

> The overweening conceit which the greater part of men have of their abilities is an ancient evil remarked by the philosophers and moralists of all ages. Their absurd presumption in their own good fortune has been less taken notice of [but is], if possible, still more universal ... The chance of gain is by every man more or less overvalued, and the chance of loss is by most men undervalued.

The available empirical evidence seems to support these statements. De Bondt and Thaler (1995) review a large number of studies on behavioral economics written by economists, psychologists, and sociologists. The authors report that "perhaps the most robust finding in the psychology of judgment is that people are overconfident" (p. 389). People are unrealistically optimistic about their abilities and power and the outcome of their own actions. Psychologist Shelley E. Taylor (1989) concludes that the most important lesson from the existing evidence is that optimism is an essential characteristic of the healthy mind. Because individuals entertain optimistic expectations, many decisions they make in an uncertain context may not reflect their true subjective preferences for consumption, investment, or saving. The discrepancy between an individual's revealed and true preferences is rooted in the individual decisionmaking process, which is corrupted by misperceptions of which the individual is completely unaware.

Jackson argues that this psychological bias justifies the enactment of collateral limitations that cannot be waived. In the absence of such limits, overconfident entrepreneurs will commit large parts of their wealth in order to obtain low-cost loans. Optimistic entrepreneurs underestimate the likelihood of bankruptcy and thus the opportunity cost of collateral. Because of their optimism, these entrepreneurs may be willing to waive any discretionary protection—explaining why effective collateral limitations must not have provisions allowing them to be waived.

Many would argue that this position is paternalistic, and it is. Jackson considers that optimism does not constitute a reason for loyally fulfilling one's obligations. But for the very same reason, he maintains that optimists must be limited in their choices. Optimists need to be protected both from making mistakes themselves and from exploitation at the hands of individuals with superior information. This paternalistic intervention does not contradict the main tenets of economic and philosophic liberalism since, as Feinberg (1986) and Trebilcock (1993) point out, any choice based on ignorance or misperception is not truly free.

Arguably, a paternalistic intervention is not actually needed in a well-functioning credit market, because the market will have many institutions to deal with overconfidence and excessive boldness among entrepreneurs. Banks and other lending institutions serve as a first line of defense. But Manove and Padilla (1999) show that a competitive credit market does not afford enough protection against entrepreneurial optimism.

From a social viewpoint entrepreneurial optimism generates two kinds of distortions. First, optimists invest their borrowed funds in projects with returns that are less than the social cost of funds—that is, society as a whole would be better off if the funds were invested differently. Second, optimists may have less risky creditworthy alternatives, which they incorrectly tend to disregard. Society would be better off if they invested any borrowed funds in these safer (albeit less glamorous) projects.

Banks do internalize the opportunity cost of loans when fixing interest rates, raising rates to ensure sufficient returns and thus coping with the first distortion. But banks cannot cope with the second distortion because they cannot appropriate the returns to the more creditworthy projects. Interest rates do not incorporate this opportunity cost, and consequently the optimistic entrepreneur also neglects it. This outcome is the result of two factors: competition in the credit market, which in effect induces banks to maximize entrepreneurs' preferences, and the entrepreneurs' failure to realize that they hold unrealistic expectations.

Manove and Padilla (1999) show that if banks can require collateral to protect themselves from nonperforming loans, the relatively low interest rates that they will charge may serve only to encourage already overconfident entrepreneurs. Collateral requirements, which are efficient in other settings, are inefficient in this case. In short, Manove and Padilla provide a formal justification for the kind of paternalistic intervention suggested by Jackson by showing that the private sector alone cannot address the distortions generated by entrepreneurial optimism.

Measures of Credit Market Performance

Three direct though not fully comprehensive measures of credit market performance exist: lending volume, interest rates, and default rates. These three measures provide an indication of the effects of creditor protection according to the two theories discussed here—the orthodox and critical viewpoints (Table 1.1).

The orthodox view suggests that the strict protection of creditor rights will lead to cheaper credit because of the protection it confers to lenders. Further, this view argues that forcing entrepreneurs to risk their own wealth gives them the right incentives to perform, reducing the cost of credit. Reducing costs increases lending volumes and investment levels and results in fewer defaulted loans and insolvent enterprises.

The critical theories also predict that interest rates will fall in response to strong creditor rights protection. But these theories predict a larger proportion of defaulted loans and insolvent businesses. Too many unworthy projects are funded when creditors are protected against default, because incentives to screen projects and to discourage investment by overconfident entrepreneurs decline along with the risk of default. Predictions regarding lending volumes are mixed. On the one hand, cheaper funds should lead to larger lending volumes (the supply-side effect). On the other hand, creditor-friendly regulations may reduce demand for credit.

Table 1.1. The Impact of Strong Creditor Rights Protection

Theory	Lending volume	Interest rates	Default rates
Orthodox view	↑	↓	↓
Critical theories	↑↓	↓	↑

Empirical Evidence on Creditor Rights and Economic Efficiency

Few studies are available assessing the relationship between strong creditor rights protection and efficiency. Among them are La Porta *et al.* (1997, 1998), which use data from 49 countries to analyze the relationship between the strength of creditor rights protection and both the efficiency of the judicial system and lending volumes. The authors show that countries with the most efficient judicial systems and greatest respect for the law have the highest lending volumes. They also show that common-law countries, such as Japan, the United Kingdom, and the United States offer creditors better protection and have wider debt markets than civil law countries such as France, Germany, Italy, and Spain.

These last statements must be qualified, however, because important differences exist within each legal family. For instance among common-law countries the United Kingdom awards maximum protection to creditors, while the U.S. bankruptcy code has a marked bias in favor of debtors. Substantial differences also exist among countries belonging to the French civil law family. For example the degree of creditor protection in Spain is similar to that in Scandinavian countries and countries classified as falling within the German civil law tradition. In contrast France has a minimal degree of creditor protection.[4]

Gropp, Scholz and White (1997) also find a positive relationship between lending volume and the degree of protection of creditor rights. Using U.S. data they analyze the ways cross-state differences in personal bankruptcy rules affect the amount of credit available to low-asset households. They conclude, somewhat ironically, that bankruptcy exemptions divert credit toward relatively wealthier households.

Several other studies have confirmed the finding by La Porta *et al.* (1997) that more effective judicial systems sustain wider credit markets. Freixas (1991) shows that in Europe both the average cost and the duration of the judicial process required to repossess collateral are inversely related to the amount of funds available to finance consumption and house purchases.

---

[4] This fact cannot be attributed to the Napoleonic tradition that defines what is commonly called French civil law. The Napoleonic Commercial Code of 1807 treated debtors as criminals, even for defaults that were not fraudulent, and focused mainly on the repayment of unpaid debts. France reformed its bankruptcy law in 1984, turning it into the system most biased toward debtors among those in place in 1994 (see Espina 1998).

Meador (1982), Jaffee (1985), and Alston (1984) find evidence that interest rates also respond to judicial system efficiency. They find that interest rates in the U.S. mortgage market are highest in those states where the cost and duration of judicial interventions to repossess collateral are also high. Finally, Demirgüç-Kunt and Maksimovic (1998) show that in countries where legal systems score high on an efficiency index, a relatively large proportion of firms uses long-term external financing.

As shown by Demirgüç-Kunt and Maksimovic (1999), however, creditor rights are not significantly related to large firms' decisions on debt composition. The only exception is the right to seize collateral after default, which is associated with significantly shorter loan maturities for large firms. This right is not similarly correlated with the financing decisions of small firms, however. The authors have not been able to consistently relate specific investor protections with the financing decisions of firms.

Broadly speaking, the existing studies have focused on the impact of creditor rights protection on lending volume.[5] The studies show that the relationship between these two variables is negative and statistically significant. But as discussed earlier, this relationship alone is not enough for an evaluation of the relative merits of the various theories. Properly discriminating among them requires other measures of credit market performance, such as default rates.[6]

Another Look at the Effects of Creditor Rights Protection

This analysis builds on the sample developed and first used by La Porta et al. (1997, 1998) but introduces two new dependent variables, the default rate and the real interest rate, and two new explanatory variables, inflation and government surplus (Table 1.2). Like La Porta et al. (1997), this analysis measures the private sector's overall ability to access debt financing, using the ratio of the sum of private sector bank debt and the face value of corpo-

---

[5] A survey of this literature can be found in La Porta and López-de-Silanes (1998).

[6] No study has so far established a positive relationship between the filing rate and the generosity of the state property exemptions. For instance, Domowitz and Eovaldi (1993) conclude that the 1978 pro debtor amendment of the U.S. Bankruptcy Code cannot be established as the cause of the increase in nonbusiness bankruptcies that took place in the early 1980s. Business-cycle conditions and demographic trends seem to explain most of the increase.

Table 1.2. Description of the Variables

Variable	Description
Debt/GNP	Ratio of the sum of private sector bank debt and outstanding nonfinancial bonds to GNP in 1994, or last available. Source: La Porta *et al.* (1997).
Nonperforming loans/total loans	Ratio of total nonperforming loans to total loans in each country (1994-95 country average). Based on the BankScope bank-level data set produced by Fitch IBCA.
Bank provisions for loan losses/total loans	Ratio of bank provisions for loan losses to total loans in each country (1994-95 country average). Based on the BankScope bank-level data set produced by Fitch IBCA.
Real interest rate	Real prime lending rate in 1994, computed using 1994 inflation (consumer price index). Source: World Bank (1996); United Nations (1995).
GDP growth	Average annual percent growth of per capita GDP for 1970-93. Source: La Porta *et al.* (1997).
Log GNP	Logarithm of the 1994 GNP. Source: La Porta *et al.* (1997).
Inflation	1994 inflation (consumer price index). Source: United Nations (1995).
Government surplus (% GDP)	Ratio of current and capital revenue and official grants received, less total expenditure and lending minus repayments to 1994 GDP. Source: World Bank (1996).
Rule of law	Assessment of the law and order tradition in the country. Average of April and October from the monthly index for 1982-95. Scale from 0 to 10, with lower scores for less tradition for law and order. Source: La Porta *et al.* (1997).
Creditor rights	An index (0-4) aggregating creditor rights. Formed by adding 1 for each of the following: restrictions on filing for reorganization; provisions allowing secured creditors to claim their security once a reorganization petition is approved (no automatic stay); provisions preventing debtor administration of property pending reorganization; and first-place ranking for secured creditors in the distribution of proceeds from assets. Source: La Porta *et al.* (1997).

rate bonds to gross national product (GNP) in each country. As is standard the real interest rate is measured as the real prime lending rate. Two different proxies are used for the default rate. The first is the ratio of nonperforming loans to total loans in each country. Given that few observations are available for this variable, the analysis also uses the ratio of bank provisions for loan losses to total loans in each country.[7]

The macroeconomic controls used here include gross domestic product (GDP) growth and the logarithm of real GNP, as in La Porta *et al.* (1997), plus two indicators of the government's macroeconomic policy: the inflation rate and the size of the government's fiscal surplus (deficit). GDP growth is included because of its likely impact on valuations and also because it may constitute an appropriate indicator of the financing needs of firms. The log of real GNP is introduced because large economies may have correspondingly large credit markets simply as a result of economies of scale (see La Porta *et al.* 1997 and Demirgüç-Kunt and Maksimovic 1999).

The inflation rate and the size of the government's fiscal surplus (deficit) provide valuable indicators of the government's ability to manage the economy and of the stability of the macroeconomic context within which firms operate. The inflation rate also indicates the extent to which the local currency provides a stable measure for debt contracts (Demirgüç-Kunt and Maksimovic 1999). A higher inflation rate should have a negative impact on debt volume. The size of the fiscal surplus affects the amount and cost of funds available to the private sector. A larger (smaller) surplus (deficit) improves the private sector's access to debt financing.

The measure of creditor protection is taken from La Porta *et al.* (1997 and 1998) and is an aggregate index of various creditor rights during liquidation and reorganization procedures. The efficiency of the legal system in each country is denominated by the variable "rule of law," which is an assessment of the law and order tradition in the country (see La Porta *et al.* 1997, 1998), as shown in Table 1.3.

---

[7] Note that both variables may be subject to severe accounting problems and measurement errors. They may also be deeply affected by differences in banking regulatory practices in other countries. Furthermore, the variables may be distorted by the discretionary nature of the provisions for the loan loss ratio.

Table 1.3. Raw Data for Construction of the Variables

Country	Debt/ GNP	Non-performing loans/total loans	Bank provisions for loan losses/total loans	Real interest rate	GDP growth	Log GNP	Inflation	Government surplus (% GDP)	Rule of law	Creditor rights
OECD countries										
Australia	0.76	3.7	0.34	9.92	3.06	12.64	1.89	-2.9	10	1
Austria	0.79	—	0.9	—	2.74	12.13	3.05	-5.1	10	3
Belgium	0.38	—	0.26	6.84	2.46	12.29	2.4	-6.1	10	2
Canada	0.72	2.34	0.79	6.61	3.36	13.26	0.27	-4.5	10	1
Denmark	0.34	—	1.37	6.2	2.09	11.84	1.98	-5.7	10	3
Finland	0.75	3.3	2.51	6.74	2.4	11.49	1.09	-14.1	10	1
France	0.96	8.81	0.95	6.13	2.54	14.07	1.67	-5.5	8.98	0
Germany	1.12	—	0.6	8.54	2.6	14.46	2.73	-2.5	9.23	3
Greece	0.23	—	1.2	14.86	2.46	11.25	10.92	-15.6	6.18	1
Ireland	0.38	—	—	3.7	4.25	10.73	2.31	-2.3	7.8	1
Italy	0.55	5.21	1.74	6.89	2.82	13.94	4.03	-10.6	8.33	2
Japan	1.22	1.66	0.53	3.42	4.13	15.18	0.66	-1.6	8.98	2
Mexico*	0.47	7.09	2.89	—	3.07	12.69	6.95	—	5.35	0
Netherlands	1.08	—	0.05	5.4	2.55	12.68	2.75	-0.5	10	2
New Zealand	0.9	—	—	7.86	1.67	10.69	1.71	0.8	10	3
Norway	0.64	4.6	-0.06	6.91	3.43	11.62	1.39	-7.5	10	2
Portugal	0.64	5.56	1.56	9.25	3.52	11.41	5.26	-2.2	8.68	1
Spain	0.75	4.74	0.98	3.94	3.27	13.19	4.77	-4.8	7.8	2
Sweden	0.55	7.02	1.12	8.2	1.79	12.28	2.22	-13.4	10	2
Switzerland	—	—	0.75	4.58	1.18	12.44	0.88	—	10	1
Turkey	0.15	6.11	2.26	—	5.05	12.08	106.27	-4	5.18	2
United Kingdom	1.13	—	0.16	3.01	2.27	13.86	2.42	-6.6	8.57	4
United States	0.81	1.65	0.56	4.46	2.74	15.67	2.53	-3	10	1

Non-OECD countries

Argentina*	0.19	—	3.79	5.68	1.4	12.4	4.18	—	5.35	1
Brazil*	0.39	6.31	3.63	—	3.95	13.03	2502.5	-4	6.32	1
Chile*	0.63	0.93	0.34	7.97	3.35	10.69	11.42	1.7	7.02	2
Colombia*	0.19	7.34	1.74	14.03	4.38	10.82	23.21	-0.6	2.08	0
Ecuador*	—	4.64	1.99	13.09	4.55	9.49	27.33	0	6.67	4
Egypt	—	—	2.63	7.74	6.13	10.53	8.13	2.1	4.17	4
Hong Kong	—	—	0.28	—	7.57	11.56	8.08	—	8.22	4
India	0.29	—	3.87	5.41	4.34	12.5	10.33	-6	4.17	4
Indonesia	0.42	—	0.84	10.83	6.38	11.84	8.45	0.6	3.98	4
Israel	0.66	—	0.85	4.47	4.39	11.19	12.38	-3	4.82	4
Jordan	0.7	5.54	0.86	6.64	1.2	8.49	2.21	1.9	4.35	—
Kenya	—	—	—	—	4.79	8.83	29.04	-3.6	5.42	4
Malaysia	0.84	—	0.63	3.75	6.9	11	3.71	4.1	6.78	4
Nigeria	—	—	—	-23.25	3.43	10.36	57.01	—	2.73	4
Pakistan	0.27	—	—	—	5.5	10.88	12.47	-6.9	3.03	4
Peru*	0.27	8.93	3.45	24.14	2.82	10.92	23.73	3.1	2.5	0
Philippines	0.1	3.05	0.38	5.54	0.3	10.44	9.06	-1.4	2.73	0
Singapore	0.6	—	—	2.31	1.68	11.68	3.51	15.7	8.57	3
South Africa	0.93	—	0.73	6.1	7.48	10.92	8.95	-9.2	4.42	4
South Korea	0.74	—	0.79	—	9.52	12.73	—	0.3	5.35	3
Sri Lanka	0.25	—	0.83	4.2	4.04	9.28	8.45	-8.7	1.9	3
Taiwan	—	—	0.32	—	11.56	12.34	—	—	8.52	2
Thailand	0.93	—	0.49	8.28	7.7	11.72	5.65	1.9	6.25	3
Uruguay*	0.26	3.52	1.47	34.78	1.96	9.4	44.75	-3	5	2
Venezuela*	0.1	—	8.11	-8.85	2.65	10.99	60.84	-4.3	6.37	—
Zimbabwe	—	—	—	10.33	2.17	8.63	22.27	—	3.68	4

* Latin American country.
— Not available.
Source: See Table 1.2.

Table 1.4a. Summary Statistics

Variable	Number of observations	Mean	Standard deviation	Minimum	Maximum
Debt/GNP	41	0.59	0.31	0.10	1.22
Nonperforming loans/total loans	21	4.86	2.28	0.93	8.93
Bank provisions for loan losses/total loans	42	1.42	1.50	−0.06	8.11
Real interest rate	40	6.92	8.08	−23.25	34.78
GDP growth	49	3.79	2.23	0.30	11.56
Log GNP	49	11.73	1.58	8.49	15.67
Inflation	47	65.49	363.73	0.27	2,502.50
Government surplus (% GDP)	42	−3.26	5.43	−15.60	15.70
Rule of law	49	6.85	2.63	1.90	10.00
Creditor rights	47	2.30	1.37	0.00	4.00

Note: See Table 1.2 for variable descriptions and sources; see Table 1.3 for countries.

Summary Statistics

The sample contains substantial cross-sectional variability for each of the variables being considered (Table 1.4a). In Table 1.4b countries are grouped according to membership in the Organization for Economic Cooperation and Development (OECD). Latin American countries are then separated from the rest. Membership in the OECD is interpreted as an indicator of macroeconomic stability and sound macroeconomic policy management.[8]

Table 1.4b reveals a number of interesting results. OECD economies have significantly wider debt markets and lower default rates (measured by the ratio of provisions for loan losses to total loans) than non-OECD economies. On average the OECD countries also have lower (real) interest rates, but this difference is not statistically significant. The wider debt markets and lower default rates can be explained in part by the macroeconomic poli-

---

[8] "Under the terms of Article 2 of the [OECD] Convention, OECD countries undertake to ensure growth and external and internal stability" (see www.oecd.org.).

Table 1.4b. Summary Statistics for Selected Groups of Countries

Variable	Mean		Test of means t-statistic	Mean		Test of means t-statistic
	OECD country	Non-OECD country		Latin American country	Non-Latin American country	
Debt/GNP	0.69	0.46	–2.60	0.31	0.65	4.23
Nonperforming loans/total loans	4.75	5.03	0.26	5.53	4.52	–0.88
Bank provisions for loan losses/total loans	1.02	1.81	1.75	3.04	0.97	–2.75
Real interest rate	6.67	7.16	0.19	12.98	5.63	–1.38
GDP growth	2.84	4.62	3.16	3.12	3.93	1.56
Log GNP	12.69	10.87	–4.86	11.15	11.85	1.37
Inflation	7.39	121.15	1.10	300.54	9.81	–1.06
Government surplus (% GDP)	–5.60	–0.91	3.07	–1.01	–3.71	–1.86
Rule of law	8.91	5.01	–7.85	5.18	7.22	2.80
Creditor rights	1.73	2.83	2.99	1.25	2.51	2.37

Note: See Table 1.2 for variable descriptions and sources; see Table 1.3 for countries.

cies OECD countries pursue and in part by the high degree of respect for the law. The rule of law variable equals 8.91 for OECD countries and 5.01 for non-OECD countries—a statistically significant difference that may help to explain why OECD countries also have better access to debt financing. OECD countries do have a lower creditor rights index than non-OECD countries, a highly significant difference that is at odds with the orthodox claim that strong creditor rights protection increases the availability of credit.

Latin American countries have narrower debt markets and higher default rates (again measured by the ratio of provisions for loan losses to total loans) than the other countries in the sample. They also have a lower index of legal enforcement and, supporting the orthodox view discussed in previous sections, a lower index of creditor rights protection. Despite a significant positive correlation between the debt/GNP ratio and the variable rule of law, the debt/GNP ratio is not significantly correlated with the measure of creditor rights protection. While this finding again casts some doubt on the validity of the orthodox view of creditor rights, the puzzle may be partly resolved by considering the macroeconomic context. Indeed, in Latin America, wide debt markets appear to be inversely correlated with inflation and positively correlated with government surpluses. (For the Latin American countries in the sample, the correlations between inflation and the debt/GNP ratio and between government surplus and the debt/GNP ratio equal –0.56 and 0.42, respectively.[9])

Table 1.5 confirms these impressions and indicates the absence of severe multicollinearity problems in the sample. A more systematic analysis of the data requires a regression framework.

Regression Analysis

The ordinary least squares regressions (with robust standard errors) undertaken for this analysis cover a number of variables (Tables 1.6-1.10). These include private debt financing, default rates and real interest rates on several macroeconomic controls, a measure of the legal protection of creditor rights, and an index of the quality of legal enforcement and respect for the law.[10]

Creditor Rights and Debt Financing

The regressions reported in Table 1.6 include all countries in the original sample for which data were available on every variable. The first column reproduces the first regression from Table 7 in La Porta *et al.* (1997), who find a positive relationship between the aggregate measure of indebtedness and both GDP growth and the log of GNP.[11] More importantly, they find a positive and statistically significant association between debt finance and the variables describing the legal institutions in place: rule of law and creditor rights. The effect of the rule of law is large and robust to alternative

---

[9] Calculations of the correlation coefficient between inflation and the debt/GNP ratio exclude Brazil, because its inflation rate in this year was several standard deviations away from the sample mean.

[10] Table 1.10 also shows weighted least squares results for the default rates regressions.

[11] The differences in the point estimates between La Porta *et al.* and the present regressions are minimal and may be due to differences in the use of decimals. The different values of the standard errors may arise because a robust regression framework is employed, which is appropriate given potential heteroskedasticity. The qualitative results are identical.

Table 1.5. Correlation Matrix

Variable	Debt/GNP	Non-performing loans/total loans	Bank provisions for loan losses/total loans	Real interest rate	GDP growth	Log GNP	Inflation	Government surplus (% GDP)	Rule of law	Creditor rights
Debt/GNP	1									
Nonperforming loans/total loans	-0.3369 (0.1464)	1								
Bank provisions for loan losses/total loans	-0.5434 (0.0005)	0.5656 (0.0075)	1							
Real interest rate	-0.2163 (0.2121)	0.2563 (0.3046)	-0.1562 (0.3701)	1						
GDP growth	0.1425 (0.3743)	0.0591 (0.7990)	-0.1480 (0.3496)	-0.0333 (0.8385)	1					
Log GNP	0.4871 (0.0012)	-0.1252 (0.5887)	-0.1373 (0.3858)	-0.1553 (0.3385)	-0.0066 (0.9641)	1				
Inflation	-0.1241 (0.4455)	0.1536 (0.5063)	0.2544 (0.1132)	-0.1339 (0.4100)	0.0446 (0.7660)	0.1078 (0.4706)	1			
Government surplus (% of GDP)	0.1262 (0.4440)	-0.0446 (0.8519)	-0.0387 (0.8203)	0.0126 (0.9418)	0.1348 (0.3945)	-0.1525 (0.3349)	-0.0179 (0.9115)	1		
Rule of law	0.5711 (0.0001)	-0.3678 (0.1009)	-0.3123 (0.0441)	-0.0649 (0.6906)	-0.1956 (0.1781)	0.5638 (0.0000)	-0.0519 (0.7291)	-0.1480 (0.3495)	1	
Creditor rights	0.2693 (0.0973)	-0.3600 (0.1190)	-0.1993 (0.2176)	-0.2799 (0.0888)	0.3923 (0.0064)	-0.3086 (0.0348)	-0.1354 (0.375)	0.1319 (0.4173)	-0.1780 (0.2314)	1

Note: p-values are in parentheses. See Table 1.2 for variable descriptions; see Table 1.3 for countries.
Source: Authors' calculations.

Table 1.6. Debt/GNP Regressions, Total Sample

Independent variable	(1)	(2)
GDP growth	0.0438**	0.0464**
	(0.0186)	(0.0246)
Log GNP	0.0637**	0.0737**
	(0.0272)	(0.0280)
Inflation		−0.0001***
		(0.0000)
Government surplus/GNP		0.0084
		(0.0052)
Rule of law	0.0633***	0.0597***
	(0.0142)	(0.0140)
Creditor rights	0.0475*	0.0395
	(0.0280)	(0.0298)
Intercept	−0.8753***	−0.9184***
	(0.2686)	(0.2666)
Number of observations	39	36
Adjusted R^2	0.5325	0.5261

* Significant at 10 percent.

** Significant at 5 percent.

*** Significant at 1 percent.

Note: Regression results are from ordinary least squares; the dependent variable is debt/GNP. Robust standard errors are shown in parentheses. See Table 1.2 for variable descriptions and Table 1.3 for countries.

Source: Authors' calculations.

specifications indicating legal origin dummies. The same is not true for the creditor rights index, which loses significance when the legal origin dummies are introduced.

The second column presents an alternative specification that includes two additional macroeconomic controls: inflation and the size of the government fiscal surplus. Both have the expected signs, but only inflation has a statistically significant effect. The regression results indicate that a high inflation rate and a small (large) government surplus (deficit) limit private sector access to debt financing. The introduction of these new controls does not affect the size and statistical significance of the rule of law variable by very much, but the creditor rights index loses its significance under the new specification. The correlation between the creditor rights index and the two additional macroeconomic controls is low and not significant (see Table 1.5). For this reason multicollinearity alone cannot explain the loss of significance of the creditor rights variable. Another specification attempted to check whether a stricter protection of creditor rights has differential effects in countries with disparate law-and-order traditions by interacting creditor rights and the rule of law. This interaction term turned out not to be significant, further confirming previous results on the irrelevance of creditor rights for debt volume.[12]

Table 1.7 presents the results of ordinary least squares regressions like those in the second column of Table 1.6 for different subsamples. The first column reports the results for the subsample of OECD countries. Whereas the macroeconomic controls (inflation and budget surplus) are both significant and have the theoretically expected signs, the effects of the legal variables (rule of law and creditor rights) are not statistically significant. The second column focuses on the non-OECD countries in the sample. The results are qualitatively identical to those for the whole sample: among the two legal indicators, only rule of law has a large and significant impact on indebtedness.

Finally, Table 1.8 presents the results of the regression for Latin American countries only. Inflation and government surplus are dropped as explanatory variables because of the lack of sufficient degrees of freedom. The number of observations is very small, suggesting that these results should be taken with great caution. Yet this regression, which includes the same explanatory variables as the first column in Table 1.6, provides an interesting result: a higher creditor rights index leads to a lower debt/GNP ratio. This result is puzzling from an orthodox viewpoint, although it is consistent with some of the critical views. Owing to the limited size of the Latin American sample, only simple regressions are estimated for the macroeconomic policy controls (inflation and budget surplus). In both cases the estimated coefficients (not reported) carry the expected signs: inflation is negatively associ-

---

[12] The regression including the interaction between the creditor rights index and the rule of law variable is available from the authors.

Table 1.7. Debt/GNP Regressions, OECD and Non-OECD Countries

Independent variable	OECD countries	Non-OECD countries
GDP growth	–0.0287	0.0877***
	(0.0591)	(0.0150)
Log GNP	0.0995***	–0.0193
	(0.0295)	(0.0350)
Inflation	–0.0045**	–0.0001**
	(0.0018)	(0.0001)
Government surplus/GNP	0.0231*	–0.0087
	(0.0113)	(0.0079)
Rule of law	0.0108	0.1210***
	(0.0385)	(0.0230)
Creditor rights	0.0468	–0.0415
	(0.0463)	(0.0260)
Intercept	–0.4936	–0.1411
	(0.4905)	(0.3665)
Number of observations	21	15
Adjusted R²	0.4791	0.7544

* Significant at 10 percent.

** Significant at 5 percent.

*** Significant at 1 percent.

Note: Regression results are from ordinary least squares; the dependent variable is debt/GNP. Robust standard errors are shown in parentheses. See Table 1.2 for variable descriptions and Table 1.3 for countries.

Source: Authors' calculations.

ated with the debt/GNP ratio, and the relationship between this ratio and the government surplus is positive.[13] But only inflation seems to have a statistically significant effect on the size of the debt market.

These results suggest that the availability of external financing for private firms is significantly greater if inflation is low and laws and regulations

---

[13] Again Brazil is excluded from this regression for the reasons outlined in footnote 9.

Table 1.8. Debt/GNP Regressions, Latin American Countries

Independent variable	Coefficient
GDP growth	0.0485*
	(0.0118)
Log GNP	–0.1555**
	(0.0229)
Rule of law	0.1980**
	(0.0234)
Creditor rights	–0.2924**
	(0.0496)
Intercept	1.2737**
	(0.2322)
Number of observations	7
Adjusted R²	0.7832

* Significant at 10 percent.
** Significant at 5 percent.

Note: Regression results are from ordinary least squares; the dependent variable is debt/GNP. Robust standard errors are shown in parentheses. See Table 1.2 for variable descriptions and Table 1.3 for countries.

Source: Authors' calculations.

are widely respected. Macroeconomic stability and law enforcement are the main determinants of debt volume. The degree of protection of creditor rights appears to be irrelevant in this respect.

Creditor Rights and the Real Interest Rate

Table 1.9 empirically investigates the determinants of interest rates using the same explanatory variables employed in the analysis of debt volume. The real interest rate in each country is influenced by a combination of factors, including the country's monetary and fiscal policy, its position in the business cycle (which, in turn, determines the demand for credit), and the structure and conduct of its lending and legal institutions. The explanatory variables can be understood as proxies for these determinants of the real interest rate.

Table 1.9. Real Interest Rate Regressions, Total Sample

Independent variable	Coefficient
GDP growth	0.2455
	(0.2772)
Log GNP	−0.0665
	(0.3589)
Inflation	0.6725***
	(0.0916)
Government surplus/GNP	−0.0782
	(0.0636)
Rule of law	0.6247**
	(0.2995)
Creditor rights	−1.0358**
	(0.4674)
Intercept	0.5396
	(4.4495)
Number of observations	34
Adjusted R²	0.7638

** Significant at 5 percent.

*** Significant at 1 percent.

Note: Regression results are from ordinary least squares; the dependent variable is the real interest rate. Robust standard errors are shown in parentheses. See Table 1.2 for variable descriptions and Table 1.3 for countries.

Source: Authors' calculations.

Of the macroeconomic controls, only the inflation rate has a statistically significant effect on the real interest rate. A relatively high inflation rate is associated with a relatively high real interest rate. The other macroeconomic variables have the expected signs but are not statistically significant. Overall the regression results confirm the standard view that high real interest rates correlate with a rapidly expanding economy and high budget deficits.

The results also show that the real interest rate is significantly related to the legal variables. A high value on the creditor rights index is associated with a low interest rate. This sign is consistent with both the orthodox and critical theories presented here and therefore does not discriminate between them. Surprisingly—and inexplicably—the relationship between the rule of law and the real interest rate is positive and significant, although Table 1.5 shows that both variables are negatively but not significantly correlated. This result is a puzzle that requires further research.

Creditor Rights and Defaults

Finally, the analysis considers the empirical determinants of the default rate in each country. As explained above, two variables serve as proxies for the default rate: the ratio of nonperforming loans to total loans in each country and the ratio of provisions for loan losses to total loans. The first two columns of Table 1.10 present the regression results for the frequency of nonperforming loans. The first column shows ordinary least squares regression results; the second column, the same regression estimated by weighted least squares, using as weights the number of banks for which Fitch IBCA reports nonperforming loans. In principle using weighted least squares should yield better results, given that the number of banks available to compute the country averages differs markedly across countries. However, because the total number of banks per country is unknown, the weights employed may not appropriately capture the actual statistical significance of the various country averages.

The ratio of nonperforming loans is higher for expanding economies, possibly because buoyant economic growth often leads to lending booms during which lenders fail to properly assess the underlying quality of projects they fund (Gavin and Hausmann 1996). The ratio is also higher for countries with lax fiscal policies. In terms of the legal indicators, the results are different for the two estimation methods. With ordinary least squares a high value of the rule of law index is associated with a low incidence of nonperforming loans (the relationship is significant at the 5 percent level). In contrast, stronger creditor rights protection does not seem to have a significant effect on this ratio. With weighted least squares, however, exactly the opposite picture emerges: creditor rights protection has a negative and highly significant impact on the ratio of nonperforming loans, while rule of law appears to be statistically irrelevant.

The number of observations for the frequency of nonperforming loans is quite small, possibly explaining the ambiguity in the legal determinants of

Table 1.10. Default Rate Regressions, Total Sample

	Dependent variable			
	Nonperforming loans/total loans		Bank provisions for loan losses/total loans	
Independent variable	Ordinary least squares	Weighted least squares	Ordinary least squares	Weighted least squares
GDP growth	0.8515**	1.2233*	0.0016	0.0171
	(0.3871)	(0.5945)	(0.1263)	(0.1054)
Log GNP	−0.1333	−0.8351**	0.0064	0.0178
	(0.2736)	(0.3195)	(0.1231)	(0.0737)
Inflation	0.0001	−0.0002	0.0009***	0.0009***
	(0.0002)	(0.0004)	(0.0001)	(0.0001)
Government surplus/GNP	−0.2689*	−0.4888***	−0.0284	−0.0884***
	(0.1303)	(0.1026)	(0.0383)	(0.0286)
Rule of law	−0.4008**	−0.1558	−0.1542	−0.2620**
	(0.1817)	(0.3002)	(0.1018)	(0.1000)
Creditor rights	−0.9352	−2.3234**	−0.0292	0.0054
	(0.5631)	(0.8585)	(0.1554)	(0.0612)
Intercept	6.7814**	14.1525***	2.1031	2.5047**
	(2.9521)	(3.2864)	(1.3665)	(1.1418)
Number of observations	19	19	34	34
Adjusted R^2	0.0702	0.6771	0.1871	0.6275

* Significant at 10 percent.

** Significant at 5 percent.

*** Significant at 1 percent.

Note: Robust standard errors are shown in parentheses. The weighted least squares regression is weighted by the number of banks for which Fitch IBCA reports nonperforming loans in each country. The regression in the fourth column is weighted by the number of banks for which Fitch ICBA reports provisions for loan losses in each country.

Source: Authors' calculations.

default rates. The second pair of columns in Table 1.10 repeats the analysis using a different proxy for the default rate: the ratio of provisions for loan losses to total loans. The number of observations is larger for this variable, which is a worse proxy for the default rate (see footnote 7 above). Roughly speaking, estimating this regression using ordinary least squares produces the same signs as in the previous two columns, although now only inflation has a statistically significant impact on defaults. High inflation translates into a large ratio of provisions for loan losses to total loans. None of the legal indicators is significant in this regression. The weighted least squares results confirm the statistical significance of inflation. But in this last regression, the default rate is also significantly related to the tightness of fiscal policy and the rule of law. A lax fiscal policy increases this ratio, which in turn is low in countries with a sound tradition of law and order. In both regressions, however, the protection awarded to creditor rights appears to be of no importance in determining the dependent variable.

Implications for the Theoretical Debate

How can these empirical findings be reconciled with the theories described here? Table 1.11 expands on Table 1.1, incorporating regression results for the impact of stronger creditor rights protection on lending volumes and interest and default rates. The empirical analysis does not allow for complete discrimination between the orthodox views and the critical theories. If anything, the results suggest that elements of both theories are needed to understand the credit market.

As both sets of theories predict, strong creditor rights protection significantly reduces the cost of external financing. In contrast, strengthening

Table 1.11. The Impact of Strong Creditor Rights Protection: Theory and Evidence

Theory	Lending volume	Interest rates	Default rates
Orthodox view	↑	↓	↓
Critical theories	↑↓	↓	↑
This chapter	No effect	↓	?

the protection awarded to creditors has no significant effect on lending volume. This result is consistent with the critical theories, which emphasize the ex ante benefits as well as the costs of protecting creditor rights. But it contradicts the orthodox view as well as previous results by La Porta *et al.* (1997).

The regression results do not present a clear picture regarding default rates. In three of the four regressions on default rates, creditor rights protection has no significant impact on the incidence of default. In only one of these exercises does stronger creditor rights protection lead to a statistically significant lower proportion of defaults. The orthodox view on the efficiency implications of protecting creditor rights argues that stronger protection should lead unambiguously to fewer defaults by solving several problems of adverse selection and moral hazard on the borrower's side. Other authors take the opposite stance, remarking on the importance of moral hazard among lenders. In practice credit markets may be subject to both types of information asymmetries and noncontractability problems, possibly explaining these ambiguous findings.

The inconclusive results can reasonably be interpreted as suggestive of the practical irrelevance of the degree of protection awarded to creditors. The efficiency of judicial enforcement and the stability of the macroeconomic scenario in which firms operate appear to have more significant effects on credit markets. Further empirical investigations are needed, however, to reach more definitive conclusions. Controlling for differences in the degree of competitiveness of credit markets around the world, for instance, could be done using proxies of the structure and conduct of financial intermediaries in various countries. Most important is the development of panel data to enlarge the current data in terms of time. Panel data would control for possible fixed effects and obvious endogeneity problems that may be distorting current estimates.

Some Conclusions and Policy Implications

This chapter has reviewed the existing theories on the efficiency implications of the various regulations that protect the rights of creditors. It has investigated the impact of stronger creditor rights protection and a more efficient judicial system on debt volume and interest and default rates. The results confirm those of a previous analysis by La Porta *et al.* (1997) showing that an effective judicial system is an essential prerequisite to the development and optimal performance of the credit market. But in contrast to that study, this chapter finds no conclusive evidence on the sign and magnitude of the effect of creditor rights on credit market efficiency. Most important, it documents the fact that macroeconomic developments significantly contribute to credit market efficiency. In particular, countries with high inflation have narrow debt markets.

The results for Latin America concur with those of La Porta and López-de-Silanes (1998), who find that the region "offers investors a rather unattractive legal environment" (p. 25). The present findings, like theirs, show that reforms to improve the efficiency of judicial enforcement in Latin America are crucial. But the findings diverge from theirs on the need to enhance creditor rights. The regression results show that this policy recommendation is, at best, unwarranted; rather, a stable macroeconomic framework would actively promote well-functioning debt markets.

A comparison of the situation in Chile, Mexico, and Uruguay illustrates these claims. In 1994 Chile and Uruguay both had a creditor rights index equal to 2, while Mexico's was 0. Chile had a higher debt/GNP ratio than Mexico (0.63 compared with 0.47). But Mexico had a higher debt/GNP ratio than Uruguay, whose ratio was 0.26. The measure of legal enforcement and macroeconomic policy variables, such as inflation and government surplus/deficit, offer a better explanation of these credit market ratios. Chile's rule of law index exceeded Mexico's, which was larger than the corresponding value for Uruguay (7.02, 5.35 and 5, respectively). In 1994 inflation in Mexico (6.95 percent) was far lower than in Uruguay (44.75 percent). Chile had a surplus of 1.7 percent of GNP, while Uruguay had a budget deficit equal to 3 percent of GNP.

This analysis has treated legal code and law enforcement traditions as exogenous. In a recent and thought-provoking paper, Svensson (1998), discussing the importance of adequate legal institutions to economic development, asks the question "Why does not a rational, forward-looking government choose to reform the legal code, or alternatively invest in legal infrastructures?" (p. 1318). The answer he provides (in the spirit of North 1981) is based on rent seeking and lobbying by interest groups. Svensson's theory constitutes an interesting, though partial, answer to his question, which clearly requires further consideration.

CHAPTER 2

Information Sharing in Credit Markets: Theory and Evidence

Tullio Jappelli and Marco Pagano

Money and information are the two basic inputs of banks. The very survival of a bank in the marketplace depends critically on its ability to collect and process information efficiently as it screens credit applicants and monitors their performance. At the screening stage, lenders need information about borrowers' characteristics, including the riskiness of their investment projects. After credit is granted, lenders need information to control borrowers' actions. For instance, a borrower may relax his effort to avoid default or try to hide the proceeds of his business to avoid repaying his debts.

Unfortunately, in general banks do not have free access to the data needed to screen credit applications and monitor borrowers. To the extent that a bank does not have such information, it faces "adverse selection" or "moral hazard" problems in its lending activity. Adverse selection arises when lenders do not have adequate information about borrowers' characteristics (hidden information), which can lead to an inefficient allocation of credit, including rationing.[1] Moral hazard arises instead when lenders cannot observe the actions of borrowers that may affect the probability of repayment; for example, lenders do not see how much effort a borrower expends to manage his project and avoid default on his debt (hidden action). This creates the danger of opportunistic behavior, or moral hazard. The borrower may either invest too little effort to ensure the project's success or, if the project succeeds, may hide its proceeds from creditors to avoid repayment

Tullio Jappelli and Marco Pagano are professors in the Department of Economics at the University of Salerno, Italy; researchers with the Center for Studies in Economics and Finance at the University of Salerno, Italy; and research fellows at the Centre for Economic Policy Research, London.
[1] As shown in the classic paper by Stiglitz and Weiss (1981).

(strategic default). This type of informational disadvantage can lead banks to allocate credit inefficiently and may even result in credit rationing.

These adverse selection and moral hazard problems can be mitigated if the borrower can pledge collateral that the lender can seize in case of default, has a large equity stake in the project, or has a good reputation to safeguard in the business community. In these cases, the borrower and his creditors share similar incentives, and in some cases his intrinsic characteristics can be credibly communicated to lenders. But these mitigating factors are of no avail to many credit applicants, especially young and small firms that typically lack sufficient collateral and equity capital and have a short track record.

Another useful route for a bank to follow, especially when these mitigating mechanisms are unavailable or insufficient, is to attack the problem at its root by acquiring the missing information it needs about customers. It can do so by collecting first-hand information about them. At the screening stage, lenders can visit credit applicants' plants, talk to their managers, and study their business plans. At the monitoring stage, lenders can require a constant flow of information from borrowers, verify and analyze it, and take action when the project or the company shows signs of being mismanaged.

But it is often cheaper and more effective to acquire information by exchanging it with other lenders. Many borrowers apply for credit with different intermediaries during their life, and in so doing they leave a trail of information behind them. For instance, they may accumulate a record of punctuality in repayment or one of constant arrears and defaults. Their credit history may indicate that they often change residence, employment or line of business, or that they operate in a high-risk business. Finally, over time they may accumulate a large amount of debt, possibly by borrowing small amounts from a multitude of banks and credit card companies. Each bank typically has only some elements of this overall picture, and it may be able to discover the others only at a very high cost, if at all. But if all the lenders who have interacted with a specific individual or firm pool their data, the overall picture will emerge; each lender will have a much clearer idea about the credit risk implied by lending to that individual or firm.

In practice, there is considerable exchange of information among lenders. Sometimes they pass on information through informal contacts—for instance, with other local bank managers or loan officers. In this case, the need to preserve reputations presumably ensures the truthfulness of the information. But this exchange of information also takes place through formal mechanisms, some voluntary and others imposed by regulation.

Credit bureaus (sometimes called credit reference agencies) are typical voluntary mechanisms. They are information brokers that operate on the principle of reciprocity, collecting, filing and distributing the information supplied voluntarily by their members. Credit bureaus have a built-in enforcement mechanism that ensures the timeliness and accuracy of the data: the threat of being denied access to the common database. The initiative of setting up a credit bureau has historically come from various sectors. Some are profit-oriented ventures created by entrepreneurs; others are set up by coalitions of lenders as cooperative arrangements. Credit rating agencies such as the U.S. firm Dun & Bradstreet are also voluntary information-sharing mechanisms since they draw a large portion of their data from lenders and suppliers who in return obtain preferential access to the firm's data.

Public credit registers, instead, are databases created by public authorities and managed by central banks. Their records are based on information compulsorily reported by lenders, who then obtain a return flow of data to use in their lending decisions. Sometimes, special public registers exist for specific classes of debt contracts or securities. For instance, in many countries lease registers record the real collateral underlying housing mortgage loans; similarly, in many civil law countries negotiable promissory notes are recorded upon default in a public register. Typically, these registers for special classes of debt existed long before modern public credit registers managed by central banks, which record bank loans and lines of credit.

The distinctive feature of public credit registers, besides the fact that lender participation is compulsory, is their universal coverage of banking institutions. Where such a register exists, all the financial intermediaries under the regulatory authority of the central bank are required to file information there. In contrast, a credit bureau's information is limited to the data supplied by the subset of banks that patronize it. However, even the database of public credit registers is far from being universal; typically, it fails to include records by financial companies, credit card companies, department stores and retail stores, which are instead often reported to credit bureaus. Moreover, public credit registers seldom impose reporting requirements for all loans. In most countries, loans below a statutory threshold size need not be reported.

As a result, public and private information sharing mechanisms tend to specialize in different segments of the credit market. Public credit registers often provide a rather complete picture of corporate bank loans, especially large ones, but almost completely neglect loans to households and small companies. Conversely, private credit bureaus tend to provide reliable data, especially on consumer loans and small business loans.

The type of information pooled by lenders is at least as important as the mechanism they adopt to exchange it. The most basic form of data that lenders share is *black* or *negative* information, which consists of defaults and arrears. In more sophisticated arrangements, lenders also share *white* or *positive* information, including debtors' current overall loan exposure and guarantees, data from past credit histories (other than defaults and arrears), and debtor characteristics such as employment, income or line of business. For companies, balance sheet information and data about directors are often provided. Often information received from borrowers is merged with data from other sources such as official registers and criminal and tax records. In some cases, credit bureaus process this wealth of information upon customers' requests, assigning a credit score to borrowers based on statistical risk analysis.

This exchange of information is useful because it allows lenders to overcome their inherent information disadvantage vis-à-vis borrowers. But this is still a vague proposition, and the rest of this chapter is devoted to clarifying the benefits and shortcomings of information sharing, and its actual effects on the operation of credit markets.

The Role of Credit Information Systems

Information sharing can play various roles in credit markets and predictions can be drawn from models that have formalized them. Can these effects be expected to increase social welfare and, if so, can one expect information-sharing mechanisms to emerge spontaneously in a decentralized equilibrium?

In principle, exchanging information about borrowers can have four effects:

- First, credit bureaus improve a bank's knowledge of an applicant's characteristics and therefore allow it to more accurately predict the probability of repayment. This allows lenders to target and price their loans better, easing adverse selection problems.

- Second, credit bureaus reduce the informational rents banks can extract from their customers. When a bank knows more about a borrower, it can charge him interest rates just slightly below those offered by an uninformed competitor and earn a rent from its information. Pooling information with other banks reduces this advantage and the implied rent by forcing each lender to price loans more competitively. Lower interest rates increase borrowers' net return and, therefore, their incentive to perform.

- Third, credit bureaus serve as a means of disciplining borrowers: every borrower knows that if he defaults his reputation with all other potential lenders is ruined, cutting him off from credit or making it more expensive. This mechanism also heightens a borrower's incentive to repay, reducing moral hazard.

- Finally, borrowers have the incentive to become overindebted if they can draw credit simultaneously from many banks without any of them realizing it. Credit bureaus and public credit registers disclose to lenders the overall indebtedness of borrowers, thereby eliminating this incentive and the implied inefficiency in the provision of credit.

Reducing Adverse Selection

In the pure adverse selection model developed by Pagano and Jappelli (1993), information sharing improves the pool of borrowers, decreases the frequency of default, and reduces the average interest rate. In the model, each bank has private information about the creditworthiness of credit applicants who reside in its market area but has no information about credit applicants who have recently moved into its market area ("movers").

Therefore, banks face an adverse selection problem when lending to movers. However, another bank may have information about them. If they borrowed before moving, banks at their former location may know their creditworthiness. If all banks exchange private information about their clients, they can identify which of the movers who seek credit are creditworthy and lend to them as safely as they do with long-standing clients. As a result, the default rate decreases.

However, the effect on lending is ambiguous. The volume of lending may increase or decrease, because when banks exchange information about borrowers, the implied increase in lending to safe borrowers may fail to compensate for the reduction in lending to high-risk applicants. Banking competition strengthens the positive effect of information sharing on lending. When credit markets are contestable, information sharing reduces informational rents and increases banking competition, which in turn leads to greater lending.[2]

Reducing Borrowers' Hold-Up

The exchange of information between banks reduces the informational rents that banks can extract from their clients within lending relationships. Padilla and Pagano (1997) make this point in the context of a two-period model in which banks are endowed with private information about their borrowers. This informational advantage offers banks some market power over their customers and thereby generates a hold-up problem: anticipating that banks will charge predatory rates in the future, borrowers exert little effort to perform. This leads to high default and interest rates, and possibly to a collapse of the credit market.

If they commit to exchanging information about borrowers, however, banks restrain their own future ability to extract informational rents. Arguably, then, a larger portion of the total surplus generated by the financed projects will be left to entrepreneurs. As a result, these borrowers will have a greater incentive to invest the effort needed to ensure the success of their projects. This reduces the probability of default on their loans. The interest rate that banks charge will decline in step with the default rate, and total lending will be larger than in a regime without information sharing.

---

[2] This model also provides predictions about lenders' incentives to create a credit bureau. Lenders have a greater incentive to share information when the mobility of credit seekers is high and the potential demand for loans is large. Technical innovations that reduce the cost of filing, organizing and distributing information should foster credit bureaus' activity. Banking competition, in contrast, may inhibit the appearance of credit bureaus; with free entry, a bank that supplies information about its customers to a credit bureau is in effect helping other lenders to compete more aggressively. Pagano and Jappelli (1993) bring international and historical evidence to bear on these predictions.

Disciplinary Effect of Default Disclosure

Incentives are affected even when there is no hold-up problem, provided banks share information about past defaults instead of information about a borrower's quality. Padilla and Pagano (2000) show that this creates a disciplinary effect. When banks share default information, default becomes a signal of bad quality for outside banks, which penalize borrowers with higher interest rates. To avoid this penalty, entrepreneurs work harder to repay loans, leading to lower default and interest rates and ultimately to more lending.[3]

In contrast with the findings of Padilla and Pagano (1997), in this model disclosing information about the quality of prospective borrowers has no effect on default and interest rates. Ex ante competition is assumed to eliminate the informational rents of banks so that their customers' overall interest burden cannot be reduced further. As a result, when information about their quality is shared, borrowers have no reason to try harder to repay their loans, and equilibrium default and interest rates stay unchanged. Information sharing about borrowers' quality can even reduce lending. When they share such information, banks lose all future informational rents and therefore require a higher probability of repayment to be willing to lend. Thus, the credit market may collapse in situations in which it would be viable if no information sharing existed.

This suggests that communicating default data and disclosing borrowers' characteristics can have quite different effects on the probability of default. The disciplinary effect arises only from the exchange of default information. To the extent that banks also share data on borrowers' characteristics, however, they actually reduce the disciplinary effect of information sharing: a high-quality borrower will not be concerned about his default being reported to outside banks if these are also told that he is a high-quality client. But information about borrowers' characteristics may reduce adverse selection or temper hold-up problems in credit markets, thereby reducing default rates.

---

[3] In this model there is no hold-up problem because initially banks have no private information about credit seekers, and ex ante competition dissipates any rents from information acquired in the lending relation.

Eliminating Incentives to Overborrow from Multiple Lenders

The previous three effects have been analyzed under the assumption that households and firms cannot borrow from several lenders at the same time. All the models mentioned so far assume "exclusive lending." But in practice credit seekers may apply simultaneously for credit from several lenders and often manage to get loans and lines of credit from more than one institution. As shown by Ongena and Smith (2000), multiple bank relationships are common, especially among large companies, but the number of relationships varies across countries. In Norway, Sweden and the United Kingdom, the average is relatively low at less than three, and is between three and four in Finland, Ireland, Hungary, the Netherlands, Poland, and Switzerland. But it can be very large in other countries; for instance, in Belgium, France, Italy, Portugal, and Spain the average is 10 or more.

Maintaining multiple bank relationships has several advantages from the standpoint of a borrower. First, it may help reduce the cost of credit by forcing the various providers of credit to compete. Second, by lending a small amount to each client, lenders can diversify their loan portfolios more than they would under exclusive lending. This should also reduce interest rates by lowering the risk premium required by each lender. Third, a borrower who can obtain credit from several lenders is insured against the risk of problems with a single lender—for instance, having a loan or credit line withdrawn if that single lender suffers a liquidity shock (Detragiache, Garella and Guiso 2000).

Multiple bank relationships also have costs, however. They discourage each bank from monitoring the borrower closely (since lenders free ride on each others' monitoring efforts) and prevent the intertemporal sharing of rent surplus that would be possible within an exclusive bank-firm relationship (Petersen and Rajan 1994). The costs of multiple lending relationships escalate if potential lenders do not have clear information about how much credit the borrower has already obtained or will be able to obtain from other lenders. Default risk, from the viewpoint of a given lender, depends on the overall indebtedness of the borrower when his obligation to that lender will mature. If this information is unavailable to the lender, however, the borrower has the incentive to overborrow. To understand why, consider a borrower seeking credit from two banks that do not tell each other how much he borrows from each. Assume that his probability of default is an increasing function of his total indebtedness. When he applies for a loan from each of the two banks, each additional dollar he borrows reduces the probability of both capital and interest repayment to the other bank, which cannot modify the terms of its loan contract in response to such behavior. Thus, his expected interest burden per dollar of total debt is a decreasing function of his total debt and he has the incentive to overborrow. Anticipating this moral hazard, lenders will require a higher interest rate, or may even deny credit without collateral or covenants restricting total debt. Notice that a lender is threatened not only by the borrower's prior debt commitments, but also by those that he may contract in the future (Bizer and DeMarzo 1992).[4]

Lenders can reduce this particular form of moral hazard by agreeing to reveal to each other the magnitude of the loans and lines of credit that they have extended to each client. This suggests that when lenders share information about outstanding loans they can be expected to increase the supply of lending and/or improve the interest rates offered to credit seekers. Borrowers will, therefore, prefer these lenders to those who do not agree to share such information. This explains why competing banks may want to pool data about the amount lent to each client (Bennardo and Pagano 2001).

A side effect of this type of information sharing is to reduce the implied cost of entertaining a large number of credit relationships, and therefore make them more attractive to borrowers. This may partly explain why firms have a relatively large number of credit relationships in Italy, France, Spain, Portugal, and Belgium, where public credit registers provide very accurate information about the overall indebtedness of firms. Banks operating in these countries may feel confident providing credit to companies that are also served by many other lenders, since they can easily keep tabs on those companies' overall indebtedness.

Summary of Theoretical Predictions

The models mentioned so far not only highlight different channels through which information sharing affects the credit market, but also show that by exchanging different types of information, lenders can control different in-

---

[4] Indeed, the available evidence suggests that the number of bank relationships is negatively correlated with the availability of credit, although its impact on interest rates is ambiguous (Ongena and Smith 2000).

formational problems. Exchanging information about borrowers' characteristics relieves adverse selection and hold-up problems. Pooling default information tends to correct moral hazard problems, although its ability to do so is actually reduced if borrowers' characteristics are also disclosed. Finally, exchanging information about borrowers' debt exposure eliminates the particular form of moral hazard associated with the ability to borrow from several lenders.

Despite the variety of the informational problems considered, on the whole some of the predicted effects of information sharing are similar. All the models predict that information sharing (in one form or another) reduces default rates, while the prediction concerning its effect on lending is less clear-cut.

However, the prediction that information sharing reduces the default rate is unambiguous only if it refers to individual borrowers. When one considers the average default rate, composition effects may overturn the prediction. Suppose that information sharing gives relatively risky borrowers access to credit. Even if each borrower's probability of default is reduced, the aggregate default rate may increase because the relative weight of lower-grade borrowers increases in the total pool. If empirical tests rely on aggregate measures of the default rate, this composition effect may introduce a bias against the models' prediction.

Empirical Evidence

To gather information about the operations of credit bureaus and public credit registers around the world, questionnaires were sent to both types of institutions in 47 countries.[5] Credit bureaus in 39 countries responded to the questionnaire and data for four more came from other sources (Internet sites, published information, etc.). The questionnaire concerning public credit registers was submitted to the central banks of the respective countries, and 46 responded. Table 2.1 summarizes the data obtained, which are organized

---

[5] The list of countries used is the same as in La Porta *et al.* (1997). This choice was dictated by the need to merge data on information sharing with data on other institutional determinants of lending and default.

Table 2.1. Private Credit Bureaus and Public Credit Registers around the World

Country	Private credit bureaus		Public credit registers	
	Starting date	Information shared	Starting date	Data reported by participating institutions
Argentina	1950	B-W	1991	D, A, L, G
Australia	1930	B	none	
Austria	1860	B-W	1986	L, G
Belgium	1987	B	1985	D, A (consumer and mortgage loans)
Bolivia	—	—	1989	D, A, L, R, G, repayments
Brazil	1996	B	1997	D, A, L
Canada	1919	B-W	none	
Chile	1990	B-W	1975	D, A, L, G, risk class, sector, debt type
Colombia	—	—	1994	—
Denmark	1971	B	none	
Finland	1900	B	none	
France	none	—	1984	D, A for households L, G, undrawn credit facilities for firms
Germany	1927	B-W	1934	L, G
Greece	none	—	none	
Egypt	none	—	none	
Hong Kong	1982	B	none	
India	—	—	none	
Ireland	1963	B-W	none	
Israel	none	—	1975	D,L
Italy	1990	B-W	1964	D, A, L, G
Japan	1965	B-W	none	
Jordan	none	—	1966	A, L
Kenya	none	—	none	
Mexico	1997	—	1964	D, A, L, economic activity of debtor, type of credit
Netherlands	1965	B-W	none	
New Zealand	—	B	none	
Nigeria	none	—	none	
Norway	1987	B	none	
Pakistan	none	—	–	—
Peru	1995	B-W	1968	D, A, L, G
Philippines	1982	B	none	
Portugal	—	B-W	1977	D, A, L, G, undrawn credit facilities
Singapore	1978	B	none	
South Africa	1901	B-W	none	
South Korea	1985	B-W	none	
Spain	1994	B	1983	D, A, L, G

(Table continues on following page.)

Table 2.1. *(Continued)*

	Private credit bureaus		Public credit registers	
Country	Starting date	Information shared	Starting date	Data reported by participating institutions
Sri Lanka	none	—	1990	D, A, G
Sweden	1890	B-W	none	
Switzerland	1968	B-W	none	
Taiwan	1975	B-W	none	
Thailand	none	—	none	
Turkey	none	—	none	
United Kingdom	1960	B-W	none	
Uruguay	1950	B	1984	D, A, L
United States	1890	B-W	none	
Venezuela	—	—	1980s	D, A, L
Zimbabwe	none	—	none	

— Not available.

Note: Figures for private credit bureaus are based on questionnaires sent to the main credit bureaus in each country. When two or more credit bureaus responded in one country, we used the start-up date of the oldest bureau. Data for information shared are from the 1990s and include black information on defaults and arrears (B) and white information (W), such as debt exposure. Data for public credit registers are based on questionnaires sent to central banks. The data reported to the register are defaulted loans (D), arrears (A), total loan exposure (L), interest rates (R), and guarantees (G).

by country, the year in which credit bureaus and public credit registers were first established, and the type of information exchanged by them.

Of the 47 countries surveyed, 31 have at least one credit bureau, while 12 do not (in four countries the data are not available). But credit bureaus have been established at different times in different economies. In several countries, lenders have exchanged information via credit bureaus for decades and in some cases (e.g., the United States and Sweden) for more than a century. In other countries, credit bureaus are a relatively new phenomenon. In particular, in some Latin American and Asian countries, credit bureaus are in their infancy and exchange mainly black information.

Public credit registers are less commonly found than credit bureaus: 19 countries have a public credit register and 27 do not (the figure for Pakistan is missing). These registers are common in continental Europe and Latin America, but are absent in Anglo-Saxon countries (the United States, the United Kingdom, Canada, Australia, and South Africa). Most have been created in the last two decades, except for those in Germany (1934), Italy (1964) and Mexico (1964). The newcomers are located primarily in Latin America. The scope of information-sharing systems is narrower in less developed countries than in industrial economies because informal lending is much more widespread in the developing world. Typically, both credit bureaus and public credit registers collect only data reported by formal lenders, thereby limiting their utility in developing countries.[6]

The table also shows that the data reported vary considerably across countries. For instance, in Argentina lenders are required to report data on defaults, arrears, loan exposure, interest rates and guarantees. In Germany, only loan exposure and guarantees are reported and in Belgium, only defaults and arrears. Furthermore, the data distributed by public credit registers differ considerably from those available in private credit bureaus' files. While private credit bureaus almost invariably distribute data on individual loans, public credit registers provide data for aggregate indebtedness. The data in Table 2.1 can be used to relate bank lending to measures of the activity of credit bureaus and public credit registers, such as their presence, the quality of information collected, and the number of years they have been in operation.

Table 2.2 relates indicators of credit market performance in 1994-95 to the presence and type of information sharing prior to 1994. The countries are divided into three groups, depending on whether they (i) had no private credit bureaus or public credit register prior to 1994, (ii) had private or public arrangements to exchange only black information, or (iii) had both black and white information-sharing arrangements. Due to missing data, complete records are observed for only 40 countries.

The table shows that the ratio between *bank lending* to the private sector and gross domestic product (GDP) is about twice as large in countries where information is shared, regardless of the type of information exchanged.

---

[6] This shortcoming of information-sharing systems could be overcome by providing the public credit register access to informal lenders such as the nongovernmental organizations (NGOs) that manage microcredit programs. For instance, Trivelli, Alvarado and Galarza (in chapter 9 of this book) report that one of the main limitations of the Peruvian public credit register is its insufficient coverage of loans extended by informal and rural lenders: "The majority of the clients [such lenders] work with have never had any connection with the formal credit system and generally have taken out only small loans (less than US$ 5,000)", and therefore they are not registered in the credit register (p. 341).

Table 2.2. Information Sharing and Credit Market Performance

Variable	Total sample	No information sharing	Black information only	Black and white information
Bank lending / GDP (%)[a]	60.53	31.10	67.57	66.42
	(37.15)	(28.43)	(36.88)	(36.55)
Loan loss provisions / total loans[b]	1.21	1.65	0.74	1.30
	(1.05)	(0.98)	(0.68)	(1.12)
Credit risk[c]	7.77	15.20	5.11	7.14
	(5.84)	(6.53)	(3.37)	(5.24)
Rule of law[d]	7.24	4.80	8.14	7.59
	(2.60)	(1.32)	(3.15)	(2.25)
Creditor rights[e]	2.15	3.14	2.20	1.83
	(1.29)	(1.21)	(1.23)	(1.83)
Number of observations	40	7	10	23

a. Ratio of bank claims on the private sector to GDP in 1994-95 (from IMF 1995, line 32d).

b. Values for loan loss provisions are 1994-95 averages of nonperforming loans to total loans in each country and are based on the BankScope data set produced by Fitch IBCA. There are 34 observations in the total sample.

c. Credit risk is based on the International Country Risk Guide financial indicator (ICRGF). It is calculated for October 1995 and ranges from 0 to 50 (maximum risk). The indicator is based on a survey of leading international bankers that rates each country on a scale of 0-10 for each of five risks: default or unfavorable loan restructuring, delayed payment of suppliers' credits, repudiation of contracts by governments, losses from exchange controls, and expropriation of private investments. There are 35 observations in the total sample.

d. Rule of law is based on an index of the law-and-order tradition in each country. It is the average for 1982-95 and ranges from 0-10, with lower scores for relative lawlessness.

e. Creditor rights is an aggregate of various rights that secured creditors might have during bankruptcy, liquidation, and reorganization proceedings. The index range is 0-4.

Note: Countries are divided according to the type of information private credit bureaus or public credit registers exchange (Table 2.1). Black information only is 1 if private credit bureaus, public credit registers, or both exchanged such information before 1994, and 0 otherwise. Black and white information is 1 if credit bureaus or public credit registers exchanged black and white information before 1994. Standard errors of means are reported in parentheses.

Source: IMF (1995) for ratio of bank claims to GDP; Padilla and Requejo (chapter 1 in this book) for loan loss provisions and country averages; Erb et al. (1996) for credit risk; and La Porta et al. (1998) for rule of law.

The means reported in columns 2 and 4 of Table 2.2 are statistically differ-ent from each other at the 1 percent significance level. Jappelli and Pagano (1999) report that the positive correlation between bank lending and the presence of information sharing persists in cross-country regressions, con-trolling for the variables used by La Porta *et al.* (1997): the growth rate of output, the log of GDP, and measures of the rule of law, creditor rights and the legal origin of the commercial code of each country. The point estimates of the relevant coefficients indicate that information sharing increases bank lending by more than 20 percent of GDP. In principle, private credit bu-reaus may impact credit markets differently than public credit registers. But the evidence also suggests that private and public information-sharing ar-rangements are close substitutes for one another.

The other two indicators in Table 2.2 are proxies for default rates. Measurement problems complicate efforts to apply to the data the theoreti-cal prediction that information sharing lowers default rates. The proportion of *loan loss provisions* can be a distorted and noisy measure of the default rate, owing to international differences in accounting standards and pru-dential banking regulations, and to the discretion that banks have concern-ing this accounting item. An alternative proxy for default rates is the credit risk indicator produced by the International Country Risk Guide (ICRG). This survey-based measure of *credit risk* is obtained from a homogeneous sample of leading international bankers and is therefore internationally com-parable. In addition, this indicator has the advantage of being based on ex ante attitudes of potential lenders. The shortcoming of this proxy is that it is imperfectly correlated with the likelihood of default on bank loans, since it also reflects other risks. It is an equal-weighted indicator of five types of financial risk: the risk of loan default or restructuring, delayed payment of suppliers' credits, repudiation of contracts by governments, losses from ex-change controls, and expropriation of private investments.

Table 2.2 reveals that loan loss provisions in countries where informa-tion is not shared are about 50 percent higher than in countries where it is. Similarly, credit risk is at least twice as high as with information sharing. Jappelli and Pagano (1999) relate the ICRG indicator of credit risk to the presence of information sharing and the same set of controls used for bank lending. The regression results indicate that information sharing is inversely correlated with credit risk. However, the evidence is weaker than for bank lending, perhaps owing to the poor quality of the proxy for default rates.

An additional prediction of the theory discussed in the previous section is that public credit registers are needed most where creditor rights receive relatively poor protection and the law is less effectively enforced. In these situations debtors' opportunistic behavior is most likely to cripple the credit market. In this sense, public credit registers can act as a partial substitute for the lack of good judicial enforcement of creditors' rights. Interestingly, the international evidence shows that public credit registers are more likely to be established in countries where creditors' interests are least protected by the law and by courts (Jappelli and Pagano 1999). But credit bureaus can also play this role. The disciplinary effect of black information can be particularly effective for this purpose, as has been argued. For instance, in Brazil information-sharing mechanisms allow widespread reliance on postdated checks as a debt instrument. In chapter 5 of this book, Castelar Pinheiro and Cabral report that the "easy, low-cost access to information on the person writing the check and the high cost to the consumer of being placed on a 'black list' for writing a check without funds have made postdated checks the most widely used form of consumption financing" (p. 175).

When Is Public Intervention Useful?

It has been shown that communication among lenders corrects the problems deriving from information asymmetries in credit markets, and the evidence indicates that such arrangements are indeed correlated with more abundant lending and a lower default rate. One might be tempted to conclude that information sharing also improves social welfare and wonder why market forces do not spontaneously produce it in all countries. In fact, both the desirability of information-sharing arrangements and the need for public intervention in this area deserve closer scrutiny.

Several models show that information sharing is socially beneficial. For instance, the Padilla and Pagano (1997) model demonstrates that a regime with information sharing about borrowers' characteristics is Pareto superior. Lenders gain because they are able to lend more and earn larger profits; borrowers gain because they get access to valuable credit opportunities that would be precluded otherwise.

But this need not always be the case. Padilla and Pagano (2000), for instance, highlight that information sharing may increase or reduce efficiency depending on the level of effort to repay elicited by the disciplinary effect. In some situations, sharing information about defaults may elicit an equilibrium level of effort that exceeds the socially efficient level. In other situations, the effort that information sharing evokes may fall far short of what is socially optimal.[7] However, they also show that in some instances careful design can ensure that information-sharing mechanisms elicit the first-best level of effort as an equilibrium outcome. For instance, sharing only default information induces an excessive level of effort relative to the social optimum. In this case, sharing a certain amount of data about borrowers' characteristics can temper the disciplinary effect of default disclosure. One can thereby "fine-tune" the system to achieve the most efficient outcome. This indicates that the social efficiency of information exchange between lenders also depends on the type of information shared and, more generally, on the design of the sharing mechanism.

Another reason why a compulsory information-sharing mechanism such as a public credit register may be damaging is that it may discourage banks from searching for information on their own and thereby reduce their screening and monitoring activities. Banks may find it cheaper to free ride on the information collected by others, but all banks will have a disincentive to expend costly resources searching for information that others may then easily exploit. Compulsory information sharing may, therefore, kill relationship lending, which by its very nature rests on a high level of screening and monitoring activity by the lender.

However intuitively appealing, this argument should be considered with great caution. First, it does not apply to spontaneous information sharing, such as that taking place via private credit bureaus. In that case, banks can refrain from becoming part of the agreement, and keep their data for themselves; alternatively, they can choose to share certain data and not others. Second, the free-riding problem could be solved or attenuated if the information that banks contribute to bureaus were appropriately priced. Banks that are net suppliers of information to the system should be compensated, and banks that are net buyers of data should pay. If the access fees of the information system can be designed so as to implement such transfer payments, even a public credit register will not discourage banks from gen-

---

[7] The situation is complicated further by the multiplicity of equilibria, characterized by different levels of effort and therefore by a different probability of default.

erating and sharing information. But of course if such a system is not (or cannot be) engineered, forced communication between lenders can reduce their information production. This can be socially damaging, insofar as it leads to a misallocation of credit.

Thus, information sharing among lenders is not always efficient. It would be a comforting thought, however, to conclude that whenever inefficiency prevails, market forces will spontaneously produce an information-sharing arrangement designed to maximize efficiency. Unfortunately, it is impossible to be sure of this.

In some cases, information sharing might be efficient but generate winners and losers (i.e., fail the Pareto criterion), and still not be introduced because the relevant initiative can only be taken by the would-be losers. In the adverse selection model by Pagano and Jappelli (1993), for instance, if banks have no other source of market power except their superior information about their local clients, they will never want to share information. Doing so would eliminate their profits and transform the market into a perfectly competitive one. This would be socially efficient and, in principle, consumers could compensate banks for the profits they lose, but it is hard to imagine a private scheme through which this could happen. Alternatively, one could ask why potential borrowers themselves do not set up an arrangement to certify and publicly disclose their credit-relevant information. The answer is that most likely they cannot easily coordinate such a scheme, because they are too dispersed and individually have little incentive to create one. Therefore, if information sharing depends on the banks' initiative, it may not become a reality despite its social efficiency.

One can, however, imagine a policy intervention capable of introducing an information-sharing mechanism and compensating banks with adequate transfers. Transfers are not even necessary to the extent that the households that gain from a more competitive credit market coincide with the shareholders that lose from the banks' lower profits. Therefore, the introduction of a public credit register could be justified on exactly the same grounds as any antitrust policy: as an act designed to stimulate competition and attain the associated efficiency gains.

Another reason why the creation of a public credit register may be justified is to enhance the stability of the banking system. Bank managers may take an inefficiently high level of risk (for instance, because of the moral hazard caused by public deposit insurance or by the implicit public bailout promise of the government). In this respect, a public register may help indirectly by making real-time data on the lending policies of banks available to the central bank for supervision and prudential intervention. In practice, this may have been decisive in establishing public credit registers in many countries.

A public credit register may also help directly by reducing banks' mistakes in the evaluation of credit risks. This can help banks stay out of distress. Moreover, better information may in some cases lead banks to expand credit by shifting from a collateral-based lending policy to an information-based policy. Formal lenders, especially in developing countries, are often criticized for requiring collateral that often greatly exceeds the loan and for paying little attention to the cash flows that can be generated by the project they are financing. The availability of better and readily usable information may foster a shift in this lending strategy, as shown by Trivelli, Alvarado and Galarza in chapter 9 of this book.

Conclusions

This chapter draws together theory and empirical evidence to offer a comprehensive overview of the economic effects of information-sharing systems. It illustrates why lenders may want to share credit data and the effect that exchanging information has on credit market performance. One of the key insights is that the type of information exchanged matters at least as much as the decision to set up an information-sharing mechanism. The empirical evidence shows that, where private credit bureaus or public credit registers operate, bank lending is greater and default rates are lower.

From the normative viewpoint, information sharing among lenders is not always efficient. But there are instances in which some information-sharing mechanisms can increase social welfare if the winners compensate the losers. However, the marketplace cannot always be expected to provide these redistributive mechanisms spontaneously. In this case, public intervention is needed, in the form of a public credit register.

CHAPTER 3

The Political Economy of Debt Moratoria, Bailouts and Bankruptcy

Patrick Bolton and Howard Rosenthal

Throughout much of the history of the United States, states passed laws providing for debt moratoria and for other forms of debtor relief (Rothbard 1962; Domowitz and Tamer 1997). During the Great Depression, for instance, states passed laws permitting debt moratoria for farm mortgages. To further improve farm income, the Roosevelt administration moved to devalue the dollar against gold. Devaluation would have triggered clauses giving creditors the option of demanding repayment in gold then present in almost US$100 billion of outstanding private debt and most likely would have triggered a wave of corporate bankruptcies. Congress, however, abrogated all gold payment clauses, relieving debtors of $69 billion in additional payments generated by the devaluation (Kroszner 1998). More recently, bankrupt industrial firms and financial institutions have been the beneficiaries of similar government actions, this time in the form of bailouts and takeovers. This chapter models such ex post political intervention in debt contracts in a democracy.

Two types of factors can cause firms to fail and individuals to default: firm-specific factors such as incompetent management and poor product design, and macroeconomic factors that are correlated across firms. The motivation for ex post political intervention is to correct for incomplete contracts and to remedy possible externalities that arise when there are many simultaneous failures during a downturn in the economy. The presence of ex post intervention, however, influences interest rates and the volume of lending ex ante. Ex ante, are there benefits to having political institutions that permit ex post intervention in debt contracts?

Patrick Bolton is the John H. Scully 1966 Professor of Finance and Professor of Economics, and Howard Rosenthal is the Roger Williams Straus Professor of Social Sciences and Professor of Politics at Princeton University.

This chapter addresses that question in a two-period model and considers in turn the case of an economy without and with aggregate shocks. In each case, equilibrium in the economy is first characterized in the absence of political institutions that permit ex post intervention. The properties of the equilibrium are then analyzed when debt moratoria or bailouts can be declared by a majority or supermajority vote of the citizens. It is found not only that political intervention can improve the allocation of resources in the second period but also that the anticipation of intervention can, surprisingly, increase lending and improve the allocation of resources in the first period. Finally the model is confronted with the historical evidence from the Panic of 1819, a major economic downturn in the United States.

The Model

Three periods are required to model debt and default: $t = 0, 1, 2$.

- At $t = 0$, borrowing, lending, and investment occur.
- At $t = 1$, a first set of production flows is realized. Borrowers repay or default. In the case of default, lenders make a continuation or liquidation decision. At the end of period 1, some borrowers may become laborers and enter into labor contracts for production at $t = 2$.
- At $t = 2$, a second set of production flows is realized. All accumulated production is consumed.

Technology, Preferences, and Markets

To keep things as simple as possible, the model considers a one-commodity economy in which, to fix ideas, the commodity is wheat. To produce wheat, farmers need labor and wheat (land is not a scarce resource). On any given farm there can be at most two wheat crops, one at date $t = 1$ and the other at date $t = 2$.

Technological Assumptions

The production function on any given farm is given by:

$$x^t = \theta f(k^{t-1}, (1 + l^{t-1}))$$

where:

- x^t is period t wheat output;

- θ is a farmer-specific productivity shock (it can be interpreted as the result of either the farmer's ability or the land's fertility);

- k^{t-1} is the amount of wheat planted (or invested) in the farm in period $t-1$ (alternatively, k^{t-1} could represent the amount of tilled land); and

- $1 + l^{t-1}$ is the quantity of labor employed in period $t-1$; it includes the farmer's labor plus the labor from l^{t-1} workers.

Note that the only relevant productivity parameter is the farmer's productivity type. Laborers' productivity types are irrelevant. This feature captures in a stark way the idea that what matters most is organizational and entrepreneurial talent.

Again for simplicity the analysis uses the following piecewise-linear production function:

$$\theta f(k^{t-1},(1+l^{t-1})) = \begin{bmatrix} \theta\{\min[k^{t-1},1+l^{t-1}]+\alpha(\max[0,1+l^{t-1}-k^{t-1}])\} \\ \text{for } k^{t-1} \leq \bar{k}, \text{ where } \bar{k} > 1 \\ \theta\{\min[\bar{k},1+l^{t-1}]+\alpha(\max[0,1+l^{t-1}-\bar{k}])\} \\ \text{for } k^{t-1} > \bar{k} \end{bmatrix}.$$

This is the simplest function with diminishing marginal productivity of labor (on any given farm). This production function models a competitive agricultural economy. To obtain strictly positive profits in equilibrium, at least one scarce factor is needed (here it is wheat) and diminishing marginal productivity with respect to one of the more abundant factors.

The function above exhibits diminishing marginal productivity of labor whenever $a < 1$, for then a marginal increase in labor produces an increase in output of only $\alpha\theta$ when

$$1 + l^{t-1} \geq k^{t-1}, \text{ as opposed to } \theta \text{ when } 1 + l^{t-1} < k^{t-1}.$$

This production function also exhibits decreasing returns to scale (or more precisely, none) beyond the level of wheat investment $\bar{k} > 1$ so that there is no benefit to investing more than $\bar{k}$ on a farm. As will become clear below, decreasing returns to scale are essential to inducing wealthy farmers to lend wheat to poor farmers. The production function is illustrated in Figure 3.1, assuming that $\alpha = 0.5$ and $\bar{k} = 3.5$.

Farmer-specific productivity shocks are independently and identically distributed and take the values $0 \leq \theta_b < \theta_a < \theta_g$ with probabilities m_b, m_a, $m_g \equiv 1 - m_a - m_b$. Three types of farmers are introduced to provide a potential role for political intervention. The good type (θ_g) may always remain solvent. The bad type (θ_b) will always go bankrupt if he or she borrows wheat, and the average type (θ_a) may go bankrupt only if an unfavorable macroeconomic shock occurs.

It is assumed that farmers do not know their type at date $t = 0$. They are all equally ignorant about their talents and expect an average productivity of $\bar{\theta} = m_b \theta_b + m_a \theta_a + m_g \theta_g$. That is, not only are lenders unable to screen borrowers according to type, but also borrowers cannot use information about their own type in deciding whether to borrow. At date $t = 1$ farmers do learn their individual types, but this information remains private to each farmer. It is also assumed that the total population of farmers is large enough to make the proportions of farmer types in the population approximately the same as the probabilities m_a, m_b, m_g.

Besides farm-specific productivity shocks, the model also introduces a common macroeconomic shock such as weather conditions. This shock shifts the values of the farm-specific productivity shocks. This shock is de-

Figure 3.1. The Production Function

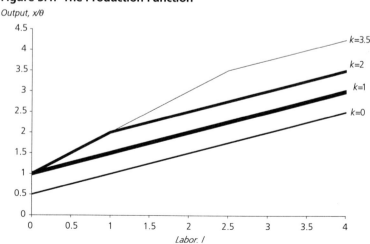

Output, x/θ

noted as $v \in \{H, L\}$, with state H occurring with probability λ and state L occurring with probability $1 - \lambda$. The productivity shocks are then fully described as θ_i^v with $\theta_i^H > \theta_i^L$.

The production function and productivity shocks completely describe the technological structure of the economy.

Assumptions on Preferences and Endowments

The model assumes identical risk-neutral preferences, mostly for technical convenience. But risk neutrality combined with limited liability induces behavior, contracting arrangements, and qualitative features similar to those common to risk aversion. For simplicity all consumption is assumed to take place at the end of the second period. Consequently each farmer maximizes expected lifetime wealth.

The model assumes M farmers, each able to supply costlessly one unit of labor in each period. Farmers differ only in their endowments of wheat. Some rich farmers are potential lenders or employers; poorer farmers are borrowers or laborers. There are N wealthy farmers with a per capita endowment of wheat $\overline{W} > 1$ and $M - N$ poor farmers with 0 endowment. Farmers know their endowments at $t = 0$. The poor are substantially more numerous than the rich—specifically, $M > N(1 + \overline{W})$. In addition:

$$0 \leq \frac{\alpha \theta_g (M - N)}{N(\overline{W} - 1)} < \theta_b < 1 < \theta_a < 1 + \alpha \theta_g < \theta_g.$$

Under the given technology, this assumption guarantees that:

- Bad types, if they do not default, will continue farming rather than work for wage $\alpha \theta_g$.

- Bad types will never make any additional investment at $t = 1$.

- Only good types will hire additional labor.

Assumptions on Contracts and Markets

Rich farmers face the following decision at date $t = 0$: should they use their wheat to hire poor farmers as laborers, or should they invest it, either in lending to poor farmers or in adding capital to their farm via increased k?

Reciprocally, poor farmers must make an occupational choice: should they borrow and remain independent farmers, or should they become laborers?

Although both markets could be open in equilibrium, the model demonstrates the existence of an equilibrium in which only the credit market is open at $t = 0$.[1] Such situations arise when all poor farmers prefer to borrow and work on their own farm rather than work as laborers, and all rich farmers prefer to lend rather than to hire workers at the prevailing equilibrium market terms. At date $t = 1$ the same two markets might be open. But under the contractual assumptions made in the model, only the agricultural labor market is open at this interim stage. There is no market for land, because the economy considered is one where land is abundant but wheat and labor are relatively scarce. Such an economy is a fairly realistic representation of much of North and South America around 1800. A model with a market for land would be more realistic, but the basic economics of the more elaborate model would be essentially the same as in the simpler setup.

The model is based on the following assumptions about the enforceability of these contracts.

Credit Contracts

A farmer can lend wheat in exchange for repayment at date $t = 1$. It is assumed that the macroeconomic shock cannot be described in a contract or verified by the courts, so that the repayment cannot be conditioned on the realization of the shock. In addition, wheat output on any given farm is not observable, let alone verifiable. These two assumptions immediately imply that a debt contract is simply the borrower's promise to make a unit repayment of D at $t = 1$ and the creditor's right to foreclose on the farm in case of default (Hart and Moore 1994, 1998; Bolton and Scharfstein 1990, 1996). In addition at $t = 1$ it is not legally possible for a farmer to acquire some other piece of land and continue to produce there unless he or she has repaid all debts. Thus by foreclosing on the debtor's land a creditor can prevent the debtor from continuing production.

This threat will induce the farmer to repay his debts when he can. The borrower has an incentive to repay, for otherwise he would lose his second-period output. For the debtor then the unit repayment D at date $t = 1$ is

---

[1] This chapter does not discuss uniqueness.

almost like purchasing the right to continue producing wheat on the land. Because there is no production beyond date $t = 2$, the borrower has no incentive to repay a loan at that date. In anticipation the creditor insists that repayments take place only at date $t = 1$. If the debtor does not produce enough wheat to repay D at date $t = 1$, default occurs and the creditor forecloses. At that point the debtor simply runs away with whatever wheat is available and becomes an agricultural laborer. As will become clear, in equilibrium the creditor does not gain by renegotiating the debt contract and allowing the debtor to stay and produce on the land.

Employment Contracts

The question of enforcement is an issue with labor contracts as well as with debt contracts. In this analysis wage contracts are enforceable because they require a simultaneous exchange of work for wages. Laborers are paid when, figuratively, the seeds are sown or the soil tilled—that is, the workers are paid before the farmer has output to show.

    This completes the description of the economy with no political institutions. As will be seen below, such an economy may give rise to excessively high bankruptcies at date $t = 1$, when the economy is hit by a large negative macroeconomic shock. This outcome results from the contractual incompleteness of debt contracts, a factor that precludes state-contingent repayments. To overcome this inefficiency the farmers in this economy may be willing to set up political institutions that can intervene ex post to suspend, delay, or cancel debt repayments. Because political decisions are made ex post, after the macro shock is realized and the individual farmers learn their types, political institutions can serve as a mechanism to remedy the contractual incompleteness of debt contracts. A potential drawback of such institutions, however, is that they may undermine the proper enforcement of debt contracts ex post.

Political Institutions

The political institution considered here is majority voting on either debt moratoria or bailouts financed with proportional consumption taxes. The vote takes place at $t = 1$, after production is realized but before debt repayment or default takes place. The model considers the effects of restricting the franchise to those with invested capital and of allowing the size of the majority needed to enact a moratorium or a bailout to be larger than a simple majority. Both moratoria and bailouts have adverse selection problems. For example as a farmer's wheat production is private information, good farmers may choose not to repay during a moratorium. Consequently alternative institutions that reduce adverse selection may be preferable. Specifically individual debtors may apply to an independent authority (say a bankruptcy court) for leniency. The bankruptcy court can learn, at a cost, the type of debtor and the nature of the macroeconomic shock. Repayment would be adjusted to reflect the severity of the macro shock. Bankruptcy courts were notoriously costly mechanisms in the 19th century and remain somewhat so today (Balleisen 1996). In any event, this chapter leaves the analysis of bankruptcy and other institutions to future researchers.

In addition to investigating equilibrium under moratoria, bailouts, and the base case of no political intervention, the model compares the relative efficiency of the institutions. This comparison suggests which institutions might be chosen ex ante, behind a so-called veil of ignorance where endowments, productivity types, and the nature of the macroeconomic shock are all unknowns. Also considered is the institutional choice at an interim level where endowments are known but not productivity or the macroeconomic shock.

No Aggregate Uncertainty

This section assumes that $v = L$ with probability 1 ($\lambda = 0$), so that there are no aggregate shocks. With no aggregate uncertainty, there is no role for ex post majority voting on debt moratoria (or bailouts) as a way of completing debt contracts. At best, voting on debt moratoria may help correct an ex post pecuniary externality in the labor market at $t = 1$. At worst, majority voting on debt moratoria undermines the efficient enforcement of debt contracts and introduces time inconsistency problems. Anticipation of majority voting on debt moratoria may improve ex post efficiency by limiting indebtedness and therefore the number of bankruptcies. Similarly anticipated bailouts can improve efficiency (both ex ante and ex post) by reducing the extent of credit rationing at date $t = 0$.

To show the effect of these two forms of political intervention, the model first considers the benchmark economy with no political institutions.

Economy without Political Intervention

The equilibrium being solved for is driven by technological assumptions of diminishing returns. It has the following characteristics:

- At $t = 0$, rich farmers invest $k = 1$ on their own farms and lend $\overline{W} - 1$ to poor farmers.

- The labor market shuts down at date $t = 0$, as it is more profitable not only for the rich to lend than to hire laborers at the going market rate, but also for the poor to borrow wheat and till their own land than to become laborers.

- The equilibrium repayment rate in the loan contract is such that bad and average types cannot repay. Thus at date $t = 1$, both bad and average poor farmers become laborers. Rich farmers get a unit repayment of $m_g D$. To simplify the analysis, it is supposed that rich farmers have a well-diversified loan portfolio so that $m_g D$ can be taken as a sure repayment. This assumption is not entirely realistic, but it is innocuous and convenient.

- At $t = 1$ bad and average rich farmers remain as farmers, but neither group increases its investment or hires laborers. Good poor farmers plow back all their net earnings to increase investment to $k_{pg} < \overline{k}$. They hire $k_{pg} - 1$ laborers. Good rich farmers increase investment to $\overline{k}$ and hire all remaining laborers.

- Laborers at $t = 1$ work on θ_g type rich and poor farms and earn equilibrium wage $r_1 = \alpha \theta_g$. That is, laborers earn their marginal product on good farms.

- At $t = 0$, a poor farmer borrows:

$$k_p = \frac{N(\overline{W} - 1)}{M - N}.$$

Note that, since $M > N(1 + \overline{W})$, $k_p < 1$.

- The equilibrium repayment rate is given by the maximum incentive compatible repayment at $t = 1$.

The rest of this section determines the conditions under which such an equilibrium holds. The section begins by considering good poor farmers' incentives to repay their debt, then proceeds to determine conditions under which average and bad farmers default, addressing the issue of renegotiation. Subsequently, it considers rich farmers' decision to lend to poor farmers or employ them as agricultural laborers. The section ends by deriving the aggregate wheat output in equilibrium.

Good Farmers' Incentives to Repay

In the equilibrium being solved for, poor farmers borrow k_p for a repayment Dk_p at date $t = 1$. They repay only if they turn out to be good farmers. These good-type borrowers derive output $\theta_g k_p + \alpha\theta_g(1 - k_p)$ from their initial investment at date $t = 0$. They can possibly expand production further by increasing their capital investment and hiring labor at date $t = 1$. They can also choose to default on their loans, keep their first period output, and work as laborers in the next period. The repayment terms D must be incentive-compatible with their not defaulting.

To see the intuition of the following analysis, consider the special case of $\alpha = 0$. In this case the good poor farmer cannot earn anything as a laborer in the second period. Thus the lender can demand all of the first-period output, so $D = \theta_g$. Now for $\alpha > 0$, the borrower's ability to earn wage income in the second period forces the lender to lower D and leave the borrower some surplus, which is reinvested in the farm. For sufficiently large α, the surplus is large enough for the borrower to hire labor.

Specifically, under the technological assumptions used here, second-period output for good poor farmers for sufficiently low D is:

$$\theta_g + \theta_g\left[\frac{(\theta_g - D)k_p - (1 - \alpha\theta_g)(1 - k_p)}{1 + \alpha\theta_g}\right].$$

The first term in the expression above represents the output obtained by increasing capital to 1, at which point the capital fully matches the farmer's own labor. The numerator of the bracketed portion of the second term is the amount of wheat available for investment after the debt has been repaid and capital increased to 1. Beyond one unit of capital, the farmer will match capital and labor.[2] The cost of a unit of capital and a unit of labor is the denominator. To keep things as simple as possible attention is restricted to parameter values such that:

$$\alpha \geq \frac{1-k_p}{2-k_p}.$$

Under this assumption Bolton and Rosenthal (1999) show that the equilibrium repayment D^*, for which the good farmer's incentive constraint binds is such that:

$$D^* = \theta_g - \frac{(1-k_p)(1-\alpha\theta_g)}{k_p} - \Delta$$

for Δ given by:

$$\theta_g\left(1+\left[\frac{\Delta k_p}{1+\alpha\theta_g}\right]\right) = \theta_g k_p + \alpha\theta_g(2-k_p).$$

This repayment is the one in this equilibrium, as at date $t = 0$ there is excess demand for loans at that rate. Poor farmers would like to expand investment beyond $k_p < 1$, but not enough funds are available to cover their investment demand. Repayment rates cannot increase to clear the market, as any higher repayment would not be incentive compatible.

Average and Bad Farmers' Incentives to Default and Debt Renegotiation

Bolton and Rosenthal (1999) show that average farmers will default unless the repayment rate is below $\hat{D}$, where:

$$\hat{D} \leq \frac{\theta_a - (1-k_p) - \alpha\theta_g}{k_p}.$$

---

[2] The bracketed expression indicates that good poor farmers are so constrained financially that they cannot expand capital beyond $\bar{k}$. Satisfying this constraint may require additional restrictions on the model's parameters.

In addition, bad farmers will default unless the repayment rate is below $\tilde{D}$, where[3]

$$\tilde{D} \leq \frac{\theta_b \left[k_p + \alpha(1 - k_p) \right] - \alpha \theta_g}{k_p}.$$

Thus it is not in the creditors' interest to forgive debt at date $t = 1$ if

$$m_g D \geq (m_g + m_a)\hat{D} \text{ and } m_g D \geq \tilde{D}.$$

It is therefore assumed that the θ_i and α are such that

(3.1)
$$D^* \geq \max\left[\left(1 + \frac{m_a}{m_g}\right)\hat{D}, \left(\frac{1}{m_g}\right)\tilde{D} \right].$$

Note that this necessary condition for equilibrium is satisfied when θ_g is large relative to θ_a and θ_b.

Borrowers' Ex Ante Expected Payoff

Because bad and average types default at date $t = 1$, run away with their first-period wheat production, and earn wage $\alpha\theta_g$ by working as agricultural laborers in the second period, a poor farmer's expected payoff at date $t = 0$, denoted R_p, is:

$$R_p = m_g \theta_g \left(1 + \left[\frac{\Delta k_p}{1 + \alpha\theta_g} \right]\right) + m_a(\theta_a k_a + \alpha\theta(1 - k_p) +$$
$$\alpha\theta_g) + m_b(\theta_b k_p + \alpha\theta_b(1 - k_p) + \alpha\theta_g)$$

Rich Farmers' Investment and Employment Decisions

Consider next the rich farmers' investment decisions. Note first that rich farmers never want to lend more than $\overline{W} - 1$, because the marginal return

---

[3] This inequality differs from the previous one since, by assumption, $\theta_b < 1$, and "bad" types do not increase their capital.

on capital $k < 1$ invested on their own farm is at least $\bar{\theta} > m_g D$. But they want to lend $\overline{W} - 1$ if they cannot hire any additional labor, because the first-period marginal return on capital $k > 1$ would be 0 (by the present assumptions). They would not want to expand investment on their farms and hire additional labor if by lending k_p they could expect a higher net return than they could expect from investing an additional k_p on their own farm. That is:

$$(m_g D - 1)k_p \geq \bar{\theta} \frac{k_p}{1 + w}$$

or

$$w \geq \frac{\bar{\theta}}{(m_g D - 1)} - 1$$

where w denotes the minimum wage at which a rich farmer can hire a poor farmer. Note that the rich farmer's second-period production decision is the same whether or not laborers are hired in the first period. Therefore the first-period decision to employ or lend is determined entirely by the relative first-period return of the two contracts.

Given that poor farmers can borrow and work on their own farms, they will consider working as agricultural laborers instead only if the wage exceeds the payoff from borrowing, or

$$w + \alpha \theta_g \geq R_p.$$

Assuming the lowest possible equilibrium wage prevails, then

$$w = R_p - \alpha \theta_g.$$

Substituting for R_p and w and substituting D^* for D, a rich farmer prefers a credit contract to an employment contract if and only if:

(3.2)

$$\frac{\bar{\theta} k_p}{m_g((\theta_g - \Delta)k_p - (1 - k_p)(1 - \alpha \theta_g)) - k_p} \leq$$

$$1 + \bar{\theta} k_p + m_g \theta_g \left[(1 - k_p) + \frac{\Delta k_p}{1 + \alpha \theta_g} \right] +$$

$$(m_a \alpha \theta_a + m_b \alpha \theta_b)(1 - k_p) + (1 - m_g)\alpha \theta_g.$$

Note that conditions (3.1) and (3.2) are mutually compatible for a subset of the parameter space. Both hold when $(\theta_g - \theta_a)$ is large enough (and α is commensurately small), so that the equilibrium exists for this subset of parameters.

Equilibrium Wheat Production

The economy's total wheat output in this equilibrium is then given by the following expression (see Bolton and Rosenthal 1999 for details):

$$(3.3) \qquad (M - N)(\overline{\theta}k_p + \alpha\overline{\theta}(1 - k_p)) + N\overline{\theta}$$

at date $t + 1$, and

$$(3.4) \quad (M - N)m_g\theta_g\left(1 + \left[\frac{(\theta_g - D^*)k_p - (1 - \alpha\theta_g)(1 - k_p)}{1 + \alpha\theta_g}\right]\right) + Nm_g\theta_g\overline{k} +$$

$$\alpha\theta_g\left((M - N)\left[(1 - m_g) - m_g\left(\frac{(\theta_g - D^*)k_p - (1 - \alpha\theta_g)(1 - k_p)}{1 + \alpha\theta_g}\right)\right] - Nm_g(\overline{k} - 1)\right)$$

$$+N(m_a\theta_a + m_b\theta_b)$$

at date $t = 2$.

In this equilibrium the good poor farmers plow all their first-period surplus back into their farms, and the good rich farmers take up the remaining labor supply. There may be a misallocation of labor ex post, as a fraction of laborers produce only $\alpha\theta_g$ when they can produce more elsewhere. This misallocation is partly due to the liquidity constraints of good poor farmers, which result in those rich farmers with the highest ability to pay crowding out the poor farmers with the highest marginal returns from labor. Moreover, if the number of defaulted farmers is so large that not all can be used efficiently on good farms, the most efficient option is to allow some defaulted farmers to remain independent farmers.

Yet this equilibrium results in the efficient allocation of resources ex ante, as all available capital is used at the highest expected marginal (and average) productivity $\overline{\theta}$. (Although poor farmers have less capital than rich ones, capital cannot be reallocated in a way that increases total expected output. This outcome is a consequence of the production function. With other production functions, the possibility of default leads to an inefficiently small transfer of capital from rich farmers to poor.)

Economy with Political Intervention

The equilibrium without political intervention produces potentially massive defaults by average and bad poor farmers. With a large number of defaults, political pressure builds to introduce some form of relief for the unfortunate. This relief can be in the form of additional subsidies or tax breaks, government guarantees on new loans (or possibly even new government loans), debt moratoria, and bailouts. This section covers the last two forms of government relief for debtors.

The main difference between a moratorium and a bailout is that a moratorium does not require government transfers and a bailout does. A moratorium is simply a form of debt cancellation that amounts to a direct ex post transfer from creditors to debtors. Under a bailout the government aims to repay existing debts—in this case those of poor farmers—by raising taxes on all citizens, both creditors and debtors. In this model a bailout amounts to an indirect ex post transfer from solvent debtors to creditors.[4]

Relief can be introduced if a majority of voters support it. The relief granted is nonselective—that is, it cannot be conditioned on the productivity type of the farmer. All farmers can vote on whether to introduce some form of debt relief at date $t = 1$, following the realization of crops and each farmer's acquisition of private information about his or her own type. The analysis focuses on simple majority rule, with brief comments on the effect of supramajority rule.

Debt Moratoria

For economic efficiency, debt moratoria are best targeted only to certain types of farmers and should be limited to the amount of debt these farmers cannot repay. In practice both discriminating between types and limiting the scope of debt forgiveness are difficult. Once a moratorium is proposed,

---

[4] In equilibrium, all agents have positive pre-tax returns. This model posits a proportional tax on consumption, so all agents have strictly positive final consumption in equilibrium.

proponents can maximize political support for the initiative by including all debtors in the scheme and by forgiving 100 percent of their debts. More precisely, farmers who will vote for partial cancellation of the debt prefer total to partial cancellation. Accordingly the analysis begins by considering a vote on 100 percent debt relief for all poor farmers. It starts with the case where a debt moratorium is unanticipated at date $t = 0$. A second step solves for equilibrium at date $t = 0$ when debt moratoria are anticipated.

Winners and Losers from a Moratorium

Identifying potential supporters of such an initiative requires first considering the effects of the moratorium on the labor market equilibrium at date $t = 1$. Suppose that the population of bad poor farmers is relatively high, so that:

$$m_b(M - N) > Z \equiv (\bar{k} - 1)Nm_g + (M - N)m_g \left(\frac{\theta_g k_p - (1 - \alpha\theta_g)(1 - k_p))}{1 + \theta_b k_p + \alpha\theta_b(1 - k_p)} \right).$$

Bolton and Rosenthal (1999) show that the labor market equilibrium following a moratorium will be such that Z bad poor farmers become laborers for good (rich and poor) types at equilibrium wage $\theta_b k_p + \alpha\theta_b(1 - k_p)$ and the remainder stay on their farms. At that wage all average poor farmers remain on their land and expand investment to $k = 1$. Average and bad rich types do not expand investment. No average or bad type hires labor. Good rich types expand investment to $\bar{k}$, but liquidity problems constrain good poor types who want to expand.

Under this scenario the moratorium creates a positive pecuniary externality for bad and average poor farmers, who see their second-period wheat income increase from $\alpha\theta_g$ to, respectively, $\theta_b k_p + \alpha\theta_b(1 - k_p)$ and θ_a. These farmers therefore clearly favor a moratorium. Note that this pecuniary externality comes at the expense of good farmers. Therefore all good rich farmers oppose this initiative even if the moratorium is limited only to bad and average poor farmers and therefore does not involve a direct loss in debt repayments. All rich farmers, a fortiori, oppose a moratorium that also includes the solvent good poor farmers. These farmers support a moratorium if the gain in debt forgiveness is greater than the increase in the wage bill, or if:

$$\frac{(\theta_g D^*)k_p - (1-\alpha\theta_g)(1-k_p)}{1+\alpha\theta_g} \le \frac{\theta_g k_p - (1-\alpha\theta_g)(1-k_p)}{1+\theta_g k_p + \alpha\theta_b(1-k_p)}.$$

This inequality holds for sufficiently large θ_g. In this case $(M - N)$ voters favor a moratorium, and a majority favors the moratorium ex post.

Ex Post Efficiency of Moratoria

Moratoria always increase ex post efficiency, as measured by total wheat output. Indeed, by allowing defaulting farmers to stay on their farms, moratoria improve the allocation of labor at date $t = 1$. Under the assumptions used here, it is efficient to have all bad farmers in excess of $(\bar{k} - 1)Mm_g$ as well as all average defaulting farmers remain on their farms. An unanticipated moratorium equilibrium achieves this. The only remaining inefficiency is that good poor farmers are liquidity constrained and cannot expand to $\bar{k}$. The general observation here is simply that the moratorium eliminates any distortions on the real economy resulting from nominal debt obligations. In other words, moratoria increase aggregate production by redistributing funds from rich creditors to poor borrowers. Thus the main (potential) problem with moratoria is not ex post efficiency but ex ante efficiency when moratoria are anticipated.

Ex Ante Equilibrium with Anticipated Moratoria

When moratoria are anticipated, they give rise to credit rationing. Indeed, rich farmers never lend if they expect a moratorium. Now, by lending to fewer poor farmers, rich farmers may guarantee that the number of debtors will not exceed the number of creditors, so that in a vote comprising only debtors and creditors, rich farmers have a majority to defeat any moratorium. But voting is not restricted to debtors and creditors, and the outcome of the vote depends on how the remaining agricultural laborers vote.

From the laborer's perspective, a moratorium is always good news, since it reduces the supply of labor. Thus laborers always weakly favor moratoria. If they vote in favor when they are indifferent, there will always be a winning majority for a moratorium, so that the credit market shuts down at $t = 0$. In that case the economy achieves a lower aggregate output in both periods. This output is:

$$N\theta\left[\overline{k}+\alpha(1+\frac{M-N}{N}-\overline{k})\right]$$

at date $t = 1$.[5] It is

$$N\overline{\theta}\overline{k}+\alpha\theta_g(M-N\overline{k})$$

at date $t = 2$.[6]

If laborers who are indifferent vote against moratoria, an equilibrium with credit rationing obtains at date $t = 1$, where $n < M - N$ poor farmers get credit of $k_p = 1$ (the efficient scale for a poor farmer working on his own). The number n is such that a majority against debt moratoria exists at date $t = 1$ (that is, $2n \le M$).

This equilibrium obtains only if laborers are indifferent. They are indifferent only if the equilibrium wage at date $t = 1$ is unaffected by an increase in the supply of labor as poor farmers default. In other words this equilibrium obtains only if $w = \alpha\theta_g$, whether a moratorium is approved or not. Consequently the equilibrium with credit rationing is extremely fragile and depends entirely on the assumed piecewise-linear structure of the production technology. Any small change in equilibrium wage resulting from a change in the supply of labor results in a majority that favors moratoria ex post and leads to a shutdown of the credit market.

An alternative way of ensuring that a majority against moratoria exists ex post is to lower the repayment for some farmers to $D^{\#}$ so that the cost of repayment is less important than the increased labor costs under a moratorium. In other words $D^{\#}$ solves:

$$\frac{(\theta_g - D^{\#})k_p - (1-\alpha\theta_g)(1-k_p)}{1+\alpha\theta_g} = \frac{\theta_g k_p - (1-\alpha\theta_g)(1-k_p)}{1+\theta_b k_p + \alpha\theta_b(1-k_p)}.$$

Good farmers borrowing at $D^{\#}$ also oppose the moratorium. If this group is large enough, a majority can emerge to oppose a moratorium. Under this scenario an ex post moratorium imposes a constraint on the terms

---

[5] Note, in particular, that $N(\overline{W} - \overline{k})$ of the initial endowment is not invested at date $t = 0$.

[6] At date $t = 1$, all bad and average rich farmers hire $(\overline{k} - 1)$ laborers at wage $\alpha\theta_g$ to produce additional output of (respectively) $\theta_b(\overline{k} - 1)$ and $\theta_a(\overline{k} - 1)$. Because they need to increase the labor force to reach maximum efficient scale, and because by assumption $\theta_b > \alpha\theta_g$, this choice is profitable. All other laborers are employed on good rich farms.

of lending but does not necessarily mean that credit rationing will be inefficient ex ante.

Implementing a two-tier loan structure is not feasible with decentralized lending and uncertainty about the number of borrowers who will be good types. Free riding will cause a two-tier structure to unravel. A two-tier structure could be supported if there were a single financial intermediary who would make the appropriate trade-off between increasing the probability of a moratorium and the benefit of obtaining D^* rather than $D^{\#}$ from borrowers at the margin. The solution to the maximization problem of the intermediary is provided in Bolton and Rosenthal (1999). When M is large, the probability of a moratorium will be close to, but not exactly, 0. Thus, a small chance exists of observing a moratorium on the equilibrium path.

The equilibrium with an intermediary leads to greater ex post efficiency even when the effects of a moratorium are fully anticipated and the moratorium does not occur. The gain comes from good poor farmers who have borrowed relatively cheaply; they can use retained earnings to expand at $t = 1$.

Interestingly, if the threat of a moratorium results in $D^{\#} < \theta_a$, then even average types would repay their loans ex post.[7] In this case, there is an additional ex post efficiency gain with the political institution of a moratorium. The threat of a moratorium allows average poor farmers to keep their farms.

Restricting Voting Rights

When repayment rates that are low enough to produce a majority opposed to a moratorium are not profitable for the rich, and when credit rationing is infeasible, credit markets collapse when moratoria are anticipated. To avoid a complete shutdown of the credit market at date $t = 0$, the authorities must restrict voting rights in some way. In fact voting rights were generally restricted at the beginning of the nineteenth century. Only landowners and men deemed sufficiently wealthy were allowed to vote. In this model re-

---

[7] The fact that average types will repay for low values of $D^{\#}$ makes reduced terms more feasible for creditors. If only good types repay, then $m_g D^{\#} > 1$. But if both good and average types repay, it suffices that $(m_g + m_a)D^{\#} > 1$.

stricting the franchise to those having capital, either endowed or borrowed, improves ex ante efficiency. This restriction eliminates the votes of agricultural laborers altogether and thus makes lending to a maximum number of poor farmers possible, where $\hat{n}(1 - 2m_g) = N$.

Another way to make moratoria more difficult is to require more than a simple majority in voting for enactment (under direct democracy). This approach can also be used in a representative democracy with a bicameral legislature in which property interests are overrepresented in one chamber. Measures to make a moratorium more difficult, however, are not desirable when the threat of a moratorium leads to an equilibrium with an interest rate that is lower than interest rates in an environment with no political intervention.

When there is no aggregate uncertainty, a debt moratorium will always improve ex post efficiency. But allowing for voting on a moratorium causes lenders to adopt strategies that always result in a majority that opposes a moratorium. Moratoria do not occur on the equilibrium path. The threat of a moratorium undermines credit markets, and ex ante efficiency is reduced if credit rationing occurs. The threat of a moratorium may lead to lower repayment rates, however, leaving ex ante efficiency unchanged and ex post efficiency improved.

Bailouts

Suppose again that farmers vote on whether to bail out defaulting debtors at date $t = 1$, following the realization of crops and the revelation of farmer types. Like moratoria, bailouts are difficult to target only to average and bad poor farmers. Accordingly, the analysis considers a vote on a bailout of D for all poor farmers financed with a proportional tax on consumption at date $t = 2$. That is, the government is able to run a deficit at date $t = 1$ by borrowing against receipts from a tax on accumulated consumption in the second period.

A consumption tax is a logical choice because consumption is easier to monitor than income. Just like any creditor, a government has difficulty observing or verifying the actual revenues individual farms generate, so an income tax gives rise to widespread evasion. This analysis assumes that all consumers are taxed at tax rate τ, with a maximum tax of $\bar{\tau} < 1$.

If taxing consumption were as difficult as taxing income, the tax base might be too small to finance a bailout—one reason debt moratoria appeared to be the preferred choice of relief in the Panic of 1819. Nevertheless suppose that an efficient consumption tax (or an inflation tax) is available, and consider who would support or oppose such a tax ex post.

Winners and Losers in a Bailout

Ignoring the tax implications of a bailout, average and bad poor farmers benefit to the extent that they both receive higher wages and have the option of remaining on their farms. Similarly, good poor farmers may oppose a bailout if it raises wages too sharply. But poor farmers have another more basic reason to oppose it: the extra tax burden. Rich farmers, however, now have a reason to favor bailouts: their loans are repaid. As long as the amount of repayment rich farmers receive exceeds the additional tax burden and wage bill, they will support a bailout.

Because the tax burden is spread over the entire population, creditors always end up getting more from a bailout than they pay out in the additional tax burden on their own consumption. The rich thus favor a bailout if it does not entail an overly steep wage hike. As the technological assumptions used here maintain that only good types hire labor, only these types would be likely, among the rich, to oppose a bailout. These types bear a disproportionate share of the bailout.

Thus if the wage effects of a bailout are relatively minor, rich creditors favor it, and some if not all poor farmers oppose it. The bad poor farmers, who would have defaulted and become agricultural laborers anyway, mainly see their tax bill increase and therefore oppose a bailout. Average poor farmers oppose a bailout if they value the option of staying on their land less than the increase in taxes. Finally good poor farmers oppose it because their tax burden is likely to exceed the nominal value of their debts. If a bailout has relatively strong effects on wages, all good farmers may oppose it and all average and bad types may support it. Thus the political coalitions that form to support or oppose a bailout are very different from those formed in support of or opposition to a moratorium.

Ex Post Efficiency of Bailouts

An unanticipated bailout has efficiency properties very similar to those of a moratorium. By removing the nominal debt overhang, a bailout allows bad poor farmers and average farmers to make efficient economic decisions. Following a bailout these farmers decide to become laborers only if they are more productive somewhere other than on their farm. As for the other farmers, their investment decisions are unaffected at date $t = 1$ because they get taxed only at date $t = 2$ and because a consumption tax is neutral with respect to investment decisions. Admittedly the ex post efficiency of a bailout depends to a large extent on the method of taxation used to finance them. If taxes are sufficiently distortionary, then a moratorium will likely be preferred.

Ex Ante Equilibrium with Anticipated Bailouts

To fix ideas suppose that wage effects are small so that all rich lenders and average poor farmers favor a bailout, but bad and good poor farmers oppose it. Suppose, in addition, that a majority favors a bailout, or $N > \frac{1}{2}M(1 - m_a)$. This implies that lenders are always fully repaid ex post and have every incentive to lend ex ante. In other words the ex ante response to a bailout is the opposite of the ex ante response to a moratorium. A bailout gives rise to more rather than less investment.

In fact, an anticipated bailout raises issues involving the existence of equilibrium. To see this, note that all poor farmers seek to borrow $\bar{k}$ no matter how high the required repayment D, because they know they will not have to repay out of their own money anyway. Now if $D > \bar{\theta}$ the rich prefer to lend all their endowment rather than invest in their own farms. But even if rich farmers lend everything, aggregate demand for loans exceeds supply, for by assumption $N(1 + \overline{W}) < M$. Consequently an equilibrium may obtain only at the maximum rate $\overline{D}$ that the government can actually repay. Such an equilibrium is sustainable, however, only if the bailout rule gives priority to bailing out debts of lower denominated interest rates. In that case no lender will sign a lending contract with $D > \overline{D}$ when all other contracts specify repayment $\overline{D}$.

To characterize this equilibrium further, suppose that all poor farmers borrow:

$$k_p^B = \frac{N\overline{W}}{M - N} < 1$$

in exchange for a unit repayment of $\overline{D} > \bar{\theta}$ at date $t = 1$. Then the total bailout bill for the government at date $t = 1$ is:

$$\overline{D}k_p^B(M-N) = \overline{D}N\overline{W}.$$

Denote by x the total accumulated output at date $t = 2$. In equilibrium, then:

$$\overline{D}N\overline{W} = \overline{\tau}x$$

or

$$\overline{D} = \frac{\overline{\tau}x}{N\overline{W}}$$

(assuming that the government can costlessly tax all private consumption at date $t = 2$ as well as borrow costlessly on international markets).

As long as equilibrium lending terms $\overline{D}$ are greater than $\overline{\theta}$ rich farmers prefer to lend all their wheat rather than invest in their farms. At these terms poor farmers obtain a strictly positive total expected before-tax payoff of:

$$\overline{\theta}k_p^B + m_g[\overline{k}\theta_g - (\overline{k} - k_p^B) - (\overline{k} - 1)\theta_b k_p^B] + m_a[\theta_a - (1 - k_p^B)] + m_b\theta_b k_p^B,$$

which is more than anything they can hope to get by working as agricultural laborers in both periods. (Indeed they would prefer to borrow more at these terms.)

Bolton and Rosenthal (1999) characterize in more detail the existence of this ex ante equilibrium with maximum lending. Note that ex ante efficiency follows from $k_p^B < 1$. An ex post bailout may improve both ex post and ex ante efficiency because the debt contract is inefficient under no bailout. The inefficiency stems from the fact that creditors are unable to appropriate ex post all the output produced with their investment on poor farms. A bailout allows for potentially superior collection technology ex post by complementing the creditors' debt-collection technology with the government's taxation technology.

In a world with costless tax collection, then, bailouts are more desirable than moratoria. Bailouts here occur along the equilibrium path, whereas moratoria are almost always an off-the-path possibility that constrains the equilibrium outcome. But with aggregate uncertainty moratoria can occur on the equilibrium path. Perhaps more interestingly, with aggregate uncertainty the equilibrium with bailouts may be such that with bad macroeconomic shocks total accumulated debts are too high for a government bailout that rescues everybody. In other words, anticipating a bailout in some states may trigger massive defaults in others.

Aggregate and Individual Uncertainty

This section extends the model by assuming that $0 < \lambda < 1$. Recall that λ denotes the probability that state H occurs, and $1 - \lambda$ denotes the probability that state L is realized. In state H the productivity of all farmers is higher than in state L. With aggregate uncertainty, ex post majority voting on debt relief may complete debt contracts, which are constrained to be independent of the state of nature. To keep the analysis tractable, the extreme assumption is made in this section that $\alpha = 0$ (and that $\theta_a^j > 1$ for $j = H, L$).[8] Although this assumption eliminates many interesting effects, it helps highlight the main observation of this section: that ex post political intervention can play a beneficial role in completing debt contracts.

Economy without Political Intervention

As in the case without aggregate uncertainty, the focus is on an equilibrium where:

- Rich farmers invest 1 on their own farms and lend the remainder,

  $\overline{W} - 1$, to poor farmers, and each borrows $k_p = \dfrac{N(\overline{W} - 1)}{M - N}$.

- The labor market shuts down at $t = 0$.

- Because $\alpha = 0$ there is only limited demand for labor at date $t = 1$.

Moreover, with aggregate uncertainty:

- The two states are distinguished by deriving an equilibrium repayment rate in the loan contract D such that bad and average types cannot repay in state L, but only bad types default in state H.

---

[8] In the previous section, with $\alpha > 0$, it was assumed that $1 < \theta_a < \alpha\theta_g$. Clearly with $\alpha = 0$ one of the inequalities has to be dropped. It is most natural to drop the second one.

With the restriction that $\alpha = 0$, deriving the conditions for such an equilibrium to obtain is straightforward. Poor farmers are considered first.

Poor Farmers' Ex Ante Expected Payoff and Ex Post Default Decisions

In state L good farmers repay their loans if and only if $\theta_g^L \geq D$, and average and bad farmers cannot repay if $D > \theta_a^L$. Similarly in state H good and average farmers repay their loans if and only if $\theta_a^H \geq D$ and poor farmers cannot repay if $D > \theta_b^H$. If good poor farmers retain some earnings after repaying their debts, they invest to expand capacity and possibly to hire labor. Because $\alpha = 0$, labor is essentially free and good farmers want to expand up to $\bar{k}$. Thus, assuming that:

$$\theta_g^H > \theta_g^L \geq \theta_a^H = D^* > \theta_a^L,$$

a poor farmer's ex ante payoff from borrowing k_p is given by:

$$R_p = [\lambda\bar{\theta}^H + (1-\lambda)\bar{\theta}^L]k_p + m_g[\lambda(\theta_g^H - \theta_a^H)\theta_g^H + (1-\lambda)(\theta_g^L - \theta_a^H)\theta_g^L].$$

To ensure that lenders do not wish to renegotiate the debt contract in either state, it is now assumed that:

1. In state L the θ_i^L are such that:

(3.5)
$$\theta_a^H \geq \max\left[\left(1 + \frac{m_a}{m_g}\right)\theta_a^L, \left(\frac{1}{m_g}\right)\theta_b^L\right].$$

2. In state H the θ_i^H are such that:

(3.6)
$$\theta_a^H \geq \left(\frac{1}{1-m_b}\right)\theta_b^H.$$

Rich Farmers' Lending Decisions

As in the case with no aggregate uncertainty, rich farmers never want to lend more than $\overline{W} - 1$. Bolton and Rosenthal (1999) show that a rich farmer prefers credit contracts lending $\overline{W} - 1$ to a labor contract if and only if:

$$k_p \geq \frac{1}{[(\lambda(m_g + m_a) + (1-\lambda)m_g)\theta_a^H - 1} - \frac{1}{[\lambda\overline{\theta}^H + (1-\lambda)\overline{\theta}^L]}$$
$$- \frac{m_g[\lambda(\theta_g^H - \theta_a^H)\theta_g^H + (1-\lambda)(\theta_g^L - \theta_a^H)\theta_g^L]}{[\lambda\overline{\theta}^H + (1-\lambda)\overline{\theta}^L]}.$$

Again, this condition is jointly satisfied with the renegotiation-proofness conditions 3.5 and 3.6 for a nonempty subset of the parameter space (e.g., for m_g, θ_a^H, and θ_g^H large enough).

Equilibrium Wheat Production in Each State of Nature

In state L the total equilibrium output is now simply:

$$(M - N)\overline{\theta}^L k_p + N\overline{\theta}^L$$

at date $t = 1$, and:

$$(M - N)m_g\theta_g^L(k_p + \theta_g^L - \theta_a^H) + N\overline{\theta}^L + N(\overline{k} - 1)(m_g\theta_g^L + m_a\theta_a^L)$$

at date $t = 2$. In state H total output is:

$$(M - N)\overline{\theta}^H k_p + N\overline{\theta}^H$$

at date $t = 1$, and:

$$(M - N)[m_g 2\theta_g^H k_p \left(1 + \theta_g^H - \frac{\theta_a^H}{k_p}\right) + m_a\theta_a^H k_p] + N\overline{\theta}^H$$
$$+ N(\overline{k} - 1)(m_g\theta_g^H + m_a\theta_a^H)$$

at date $t = 2$. Recall that $\alpha = 0$ (and labor is essentially free), so both good and average rich farmers now find it worthwhile to expand their farm capital up to $\overline{k}$ at date $t = 1$. Similarly, good poor farmers expand capacity by max $[(\theta_g^H k_p - \theta_a^H); \overline{k} - k_p]$ (assuming that $\overline{k} > (\theta_g^H + 1)k_p - \theta_a^H$, the expression above is obtained).

Economy with Political Intervention

This section considers, in turn, debt moratoria and bailouts.

Debt Moratoria

The analysis is restricted to parameter values that allow for a majority in favor of moratoria only in state L. More precisely, it determines an equilibrium repayment D such that good poor farmers oppose a moratorium in state H to get L. Then as long as $(M-N)m_g + N > (M-N)(1-m_g)$, there will be a majority against moratoria in state H and a majority in favor of moratoria in state L (as by assumption $(M-N) > N$).

In state H, a good poor farmer opposes a moratorium if the benefit in cheap labor outweighs the cost of repaying the loan. Assuming that the population of bad poor farmers is relatively high, so that:[9]

$$(M-N)m_b > M(\bar{k} - k_p)(m_g + m_a),$$

the equilibrium wage following a moratorium will equal $\theta_b k_p$. Therefore good poor farmers oppose a moratorium if:

$$(\theta_g^H - D)k_p \theta_g^H \geq \theta_g^H \left[(1-k_p) + \frac{\theta_g^H k_p - (1-k_p)}{1 + \theta_b^H k_p}\right]$$

or:

$$D \leq \theta_g^H - \frac{1-k_p}{k_p} - \frac{\theta_g^H}{1 + \theta_b^L k_p} + \frac{(1-k_p)}{(1 + \theta_b^L k_p)k_p}.$$

Thus, assuming that:

(3.7)

$$\theta_g^L - \frac{1-k_p}{k_p} - \frac{\theta_g^L}{1 + \theta_b^L k_p} + \frac{(1-k_p)}{(1 + \theta_b^L k_p)k_p} \leq \theta_a^H$$

$$\leq \theta_g^H - \frac{1-k_p}{k_p} - \frac{\theta_g^H}{1 + \theta_b^H k_p} + \frac{(1-k_p)}{(1 + \theta_b^H k_p)k_p},$$

an equilibrium repayment of $D^* = \theta_a^H$ gives rise to no moratorium in state H and a moratorium in state L. In the moratorium equilibrium, poor farmers' ex ante expected payoff is then:[10]

---

[9] A weaker, necessary and sufficient condition is straightforward but algebraically messy.

[10] Note that an implicit assumption here is that $(\theta_g^L + 1) k_p \leq \bar{k}$.

$$R_p^m = \lambda[\overline{\theta}^H k_p + m_g(\theta_g^H - \theta_a^H)\theta_g^H] +$$
$$(1-\lambda)[m_b 2\theta_b^L k_p + m_a(\theta_a^L + 1)k_p\theta_a^L + m_g(\theta_g^L + 1)k_p\theta_g^L].$$

Rich farmers prefer to lend ($\overline{W} - 1$) instead of hiring laborers if and only if:

$$(3.8) \qquad\qquad R_p^m \geq \frac{\lambda\overline{\theta}^H + (1-\lambda)\overline{\theta}^L}{(\lambda m_g \theta_a^H - 1)} - 1.$$

Thus as long as $(M - N)m_g + N > (M - N)(1 - m_g)$ and conditions (3.7) and (3.8) hold, the equilibrium with moratoria is such that:

1. Rich farmers continue to lend at repayment terms $D^* = \theta_a^H$.

2. No moratorium is voted in state H, with good and average types repaying their loans.

3. A moratorium is voted in state L.

This equilibrium dominates the equilibrium without political intervention in both ex ante and ex post efficiency. Ex post efficiency is improved in state L by allowing average and bad poor farmers to stay on their farms and thus remain productive. Ex ante, the likelihood of state L occurring $(1- \lambda)$ is sufficiently small that it does not affect rich farmers' lending decisions, so that efficiency is not impaired. Interestingly, the possibility of an ex post moratorium involves a transfer of rents to poor farmers both ex ante and ex post. The reason that poor farmers also benefit ex ante has to do with the threat of default or a moratorium in state H, which can be avoided only by giving poor farmers better lending terms ex ante. As suggested earlier, political intervention plays a critical role here in completing financial contracts that are constrained to be state independent.[11]

---

[11] Recall that repayments cannot be made contingent on aggregate shocks because courts cannot verify whether state H or L has occurred. The state of nature is certified only by the outcome of majority voting on debt moratoria. If no majority in favor materializes, it becomes common knowledge that state H has occurred (or that state L has occurred if a majority in favor of a moratorium is formed).

Bailouts

The most interesting case here is where a majority is in favor of a bailout in state L and a majority is opposed to one in state H. In this case the equilibrium with a bailout is similar to the equilibrium with a debt moratorium as long as λ is small. To see why, note first that the ex ante equilibrium outcome with anticipated bailout in state L is then the same as the equilibrium outcome with no bailout—that is, rich farmers continue to lend ($\overline{W} - 1$) at equilibrium repayment terms $D^* = \theta_a^H$. The reason that equilibrium terms do not exceed θ_a^H is simply that higher terms would trigger default by average poor farmers in state H and therefore would not be profitable. More precisely, if λ is large the anticipated increase in repayments in state L (through bailouts) is outweighed by the anticipated fall in expected repayments in state H.

In sum, anticipated bailouts in state L do not affect the ex ante equilibrium and lead to an ex post welfare improvement in state L, just like moratoria. In this case the sharp distinctions between the effects of bailouts and moratoria observed in the previous section disappear with the introduction of aggregate uncertainty.

The Political Economy of Debt Relief in the Panic of 1819

The empirical motivation for the model came from the observation that state legislatures in the United States frequently voted for debt moratoria in the late 19th and early 20th centuries. Most notably, many states intervened in private debt contracts as a result of the severe downturn known as the Panic of 1819. Between October 1818 and April 1822, Illinois, Kentucky, Louisiana, Maryland, Missouri, Pennsylvania, Tennessee, and Vermont passed stay laws imposing debt moratoria. Rhode Island made seizing the assets of debtors more difficult by repealing "summary process." Minimum appraisal laws in Indiana, Kentucky, and Pennsylvania made auctioning debtors' assets more difficult (Rothbard 1962). At the same time Congress delayed repayments of land debts to the federal government. But proponents of federal relief for private debts lost. Although the United States constitution explicitly gives bankruptcy powers to the federal government, no bankruptcy law existed between 1803 and 1842.

This section analyzes the politics of the Panic in light of the model, which closely approximates the economy of the United States in the period around 1820, particularly in the South and West. The frontier states, where new settlers borrowed to finance agricultural investment, were much more likely to provide debt relief than the older states, and congressional preferences on relief of land debts paralleled those leading to debt moratoria at the state level. Most of the data used here are political—either state legislation or congressional roll-call votes. As Domowitz and Tamer (1997) point out, there does not appear to be economic data before 1830 that would provide evidence of private defaults. However, there are ample data on political outcomes, which can be informative about the preferences of economic agents and their reaction to macro shocks.

The Economy at the Time of the Panic

The major cause of the Panic, according to North (1961, pp. 182-83), was the collapse of the world price for cotton. Between January 1918 and June 1919, cotton prices fell by more than 50 percent. Cotton dominated both American exports and the economy of the South. The decline of cotton prices also affected the West, as the economy there was driven largely by sales of wheat and livestock to the South. Bulk commodities were transported to the South on the Mississippi and its tributaries, as neither canals nor railroads crossed the Appalachians before 1825. The Northeast provided nonbulk manufactured goods as well as banking, shipping, and other services to the various regions.[12]

Both the South and the West correspond roughly to the technological structure of the model. In a nation that was still almost entirely rural, the West and western portions of the South were particularly so (99 percent in 1820). The Atlantic seaboard portion of the South was also 95 percent rural. What little urban population existed was concentrated mainly in the New England and Middle Atlantic states (10.5 and 11.3 percent, respectively). In a national labor force of 2,900,000 people, more than two-thirds worked on farms (United States Bureau of the Census 1975). Given the low technologi-

---

[12] North (1961) defines the South at this time as Alabama, Georgia, Louisiana, Mississippi, North Carolina, South Carolina, and Virginia; the West as Illinois, Indiana, Kentucky, Missouri, Ohio, and Tennessee; and the Northeast as all other states.

cal level of agriculture at this time, it is not too far-fetched to regard the South and West as single-commodity regions with labor (often slaves) as the major input factor.

Commodity prices are made endogenous when new land is brought into cultivation. Some of the drop in cotton prices reflects an expansion in production from 157,000 bales in 1812 to 377,000 in 1821. But over a longer period, cotton production was able to expand tremendously as whites prospered in the so-called Cotton Kingdom. In 1859 some 5,337,000 bales were being produced. Clearly the world market price was also determined by shifts in foreign demand. (World price shocks from that time are similar to the macroeconomic shock in the model.)

An important omission from the model is a market for land. The 13 former colonies had ceded all their western land claims to the federal government. Almost all of the Louisiana Purchase was government land. Sale prices and property rights for government-controlled virgin land were then and are today (as in Brazil) an important issue of economic policy. One argument maintained that the government should charge a zero price and regulate only quantities. But until 1860 the government sold land, and rising prices for cotton and other sources of prosperity stimulated land sales at the end of the Napoleonic Wars. Receipts from land sales in the South increased from $332,000 in 1815 to $9,063,000 in 1818. In the West, the jump was from $2,078,000 to $4,556,000 (North 1961).

With the Panic, land sales fell abruptly, never regaining their 1818 level in the South and passing it in the West only in 1835. The receipts were in large part only down payments, and some of this money was borrowed in private markets. Private debt was also used to finance investment on the land, including slave purchases.[13] In addition many citizens in the South and West were in debt to the federal government, with payments due on the outstanding balance of land purchases. Before the passage of the Land Act

---

[13] In the model there is no market for land (there is an abundance of land), so this story does not quite fit these events. It is innocuous, however, to introduce a market for land in the model. At date $t = 0$ all such a market will mean is a higher investment outlay for farmers. As for date $t = 1$, default will give rise to an excess supply of land, and consequently property prices will collapse, as seen in the Panic of 1819. But the main complication with introducing land in the model is the possibility of strategic behavior by rich buyers, such as waiting for panics to buy land on the cheap. Addressing these somewhat peripheral issues is beyond the scope of this chapter.

of 1821, such debtors owed the federal government some $23,000,000 (Rohrbough 1968). The land debt to the government exceeded annual federal expenditures (around $20,000,000 in 1820) and was an appreciable fraction of the government debt of $90,000,000 in 1821 (United States Bureau of the Census 1975).

When the Panic occurred the frontier branches of the privately owned Second Bank of the United States had been extending easy private credit. Credit tightening by the Philadelphia headquarters led to substantial resentment on the frontier.

Debt Relief at the State Level

The pressure to provide debtors with some relief generated a legislative response, but mainly in frontier states: Alabama, Illinois, Indiana, Kentucky, Louisiana, Missouri, Mississippi, Ohio, and Tennessee. (These states are distinguished from the states on the Atlantic seaboard that were once British colonies.) Six of these nine frontier states were listed by Rothbard (1962) as providing some form of relief for debtors in response to the Panic. In contrast, only four of the remaining 15 states passed a "stay law" or some other measure ($\chi_1^2 = 3.70$, p-value < 0.10). This chi-square statistic and those later refer to the 2 x 2 contingency table of, for example, ([frontier, nonfrontier] x [law, no law]).

Because the great preponderance of new agricultural investment was taking place in frontier states, and because these states were overwhelmingly rural, debtors were likely to dominate the electorate there. In addition, the frontier was more likely than the older states to have universal male suffrage rather than suffrage restricted on the basis of property holding or wealth (McCoy 1989). It is thus not surprising that most ex post intervention occurred on the frontier.

However, debt relief was largely a northern and border state matter. Of the eight states in North's (1961) southern region, only two, Louisiana and Tennessee, both on the frontier, granted debt relief, as opposed to eight of the 16 other states. Indeed, debt relief measures were passed in four of the nine New England and Middle Atlantic states, which in many historical accounts are regarded as pro-creditor.

The absence of debt relief in the South may have been the expression of a reaction to stay laws that were passed by southern state legislatures immediately preceding the formation of the United States. McCoy (1989, p. 41) notes, referring to James Madison,

> Madison vehemently condemned . . . popular legislation . . . in the wake of a commercial depression that overtook much of the country in the mid-1780s. Paper money laws, so-called "stay" laws that offered relief to debtors, laws that impugned the sanctity of contracts; all may have expressed the immediate will of a people suffering the consequences of economic hard times, but they just as clearly violated the rights of both individuals and minorities. And in Madison's judgment, he and other critics of this debtor legislation were defending much more than the specific interest of creditors . . . . By wantonly disregarding the rules of property and justice that raised men from savagery to civilized order, these laws threatened to bring republican government in America into profound disrepute.

Madison's economic conservatism may have carried over to state legislatures in the South, which were dominated by property owners in the older regions of the states, the high-endowment types in the model. Within the South, the one-white-man, one-vote ideology applied only in the four frontier states (Freehling 1989). In Virginia, for instance, about half the white males were disenfranchised by a property requirement. Moreover, the legislature was not reapportioned to reflect greater population growth beyond the Tidewater. South Carolina had universal white male suffrage, but severe property qualifications for office holding, and the state Senate was malapportioned to give control to the older coastal region.

Suffrage and apportionment may be an important reason stay laws and other forms of debt relief were most prevalent in frontier states. A larger fraction of the population may have been in default in those states, and those debtors may have had a relatively strong political voice.

Relief for Purchasers of Land

A national consensus emerged that the Panic required a policy adjustment for land debtors. Despite this consensus there was a sharp debate over the degree of leniency, with close roll-call votes in 1821 on amendments defining the terms of the new policy. Disappointed in 1820, the thinly populated frontier obtained better terms in 1821.

The initial federal reaction to the massive defaults by those buying land on credit was the Land Law of April 24, 1820. The law eliminated future sales on credit but reduced the minimum purchase price from $2 to $1.25 per acre. At the same time forfeiture on outstanding debt was delayed until March 21, 1821. Just before this deadline (March 2), another act was passed. Debtors could either repay at a 37.5 percent discount (the price reduction of 1820), give up part of their land as payment for the remainder, or extend the time required to pay. This bailout or moratorium was, like the savings and loan bailout of the 1980s, a substantial transfer between regions. The beneficiaries were concentrated on the frontier, but the entire nation bore the costs to the Treasury.

There were many roll-call votes on the floor of Congress on the 1820 and 1821 land bills. The 1820 bill was largely uncontroversial in the Senate, passing on a 31-7 vote. Although the bill granted a one-year moratorium on outstanding debt, its provisions banning future sales on credit were not to the liking of the frontier states. Amendments were introduced to make the law more lenient; one, by Senator Ninian Edwards (Illinois), reduced the purchase price to $1 an acre.[14] It failed 24-11, and of the 11 favorable votes, 10 came from the frontier (only five frontier senators cast negative votes). All eight of the frontier states (Missouri had not yet been admitted) had one senator voting for cheaper purchase prices. This voting pattern was repeated on other votes. For example, amendments by Edwards to give purchase preferences to squatters and by Senator James Noble (Indiana) to eliminate the cash payment requirement both failed 28-8. Of the eight favorable votes, seven came from the frontier. Of the seven votes cast against final passage of the bill, six came from frontier senators dissatisfied with its lack of leniency.

The House of Representatives also had a lopsided majority in favor of the 1820 bill. Only one amendment led to a recorded roll call. As in the Senate, frontier representatives wanted the cash payment provision eliminated. The nonfrontier states voted overwhelmingly (123-7) to maintain the cash payment, and they were joined by all six members of the Ohio delegation. Elsewhere on the frontier representatives sought, 12-6, to eliminate the new requirement for cash payment. The bill then passed. The bill won

---

[14] Vote #119, 2/18/19. All roll-call data are taken from VOTEVIEW at http://voteview.UH.edu.

overwhelming support in the older states (122-10), but lost on the frontier (13-11). The frontier won a temporary reprieve for its debtors as well as lower prices, but the terms of future purchases became much stricter.

The 1821 bill was more lenient. In the Senate, Walter Lowrie (Pennsylvania) failed by only one vote to reduce the discount for prompt payment from 37.5 to 25 percent. All 15 senators from the frontier voted against the amendment, which was supported by the older states 20-6 ($\chi_1^2 = 22.52$, p-value < 0.001). Although the amendment vote clearly delineates the frontier's desire for leniency, the passage of this bill—like the 1820 bill—was largely uncontroversial. On February 27, 1821 the House also voted on the 37.5 percent discount provided in the amendment offered by Richard C. Anderson, Jr. (Kentucky).[15] The amendment passed 72-62; the 20-4 margin from the frontier states was pivotal. The bill itself passed 97-40, winning 21 of the 24 votes from the frontier.

No Federal Relief for Private Debt: The Failure to Pass a Bankruptcy Bill

Although the federal government provided relief to those in debt to the government, Washington failed to provide a fresh start or even a breathing spell for those in default on private debts (in contrast to stay laws at the state level). The federal government's inaction is somewhat surprising. As noted earlier, the Constitution adopted in 1787 clearly gave the federal government power to pass bankruptcy laws. Moreover, in contrast to many other aspects of the Constitution, the bankruptcy clause was not in controversy during the ratification process. Before the enactment of a stable, permanent law, bankruptcy legislation tended to be short-lived and generally served to write off severe downturns in the economy. Creditors obtained very little in court proceedings (Balleisen 1996). Bankruptcy in the nineteenth century therefore resembled a moratorium, subject to the inefficiency of court costs. If bankruptcy is perceived as a moratorium, however, it is not surprising that an interim conflict over federal bankruptcy law developed despite the initial consensus that Congress could indeed enact such legislation.[16]

---

[15] VOTEVIEW #135.

[16] See Berglöf and Rosenthal (1998) for details of the congressional politics of bankruptcy legislation in the 1840s and 1890s.

The Panic of 1819 occurred during the so-called Era of Good Feelings, when the United States was virtually a one-party state. The Jeffersonian Democrat-Republicans were in control and, despite the Panic, the Electoral College reelected President Monroe in 1820 with only one dissenting vote. With the political ascendancy of the "left," it is not surprising that no bankruptcy law was passed, although the Jeffersonians were particularly strong on the debt-ridden frontier. The bill under consideration in 1822, for example, was, in the view of Representative James Blair (South Carolina), very similar to the 1800 law that the Jeffersonians had repealed on taking control of both the executive and legislative branches in 1803.[17]

In the 15th Congress, the Senate held no recorded floor votes on bankruptcy. The House held just one, voting in February 1818 to postpone consideration of a bill indefinitely. The 16th Senate did pass a bankruptcy bill by the narrow margin of 23-19 on February 19, 1821. Floor votes took place over ending the imprisonment of bankrupt individuals, including classes of debtors other than merchants, and applying the bill to contracts written before the legislation was passed. The Senate bill was reported unamended to the floor of the House by the Judiciary Committee but was tabled in seven procedural votes between February 28 and March 2, 1821.[18] The 17th House had amendment voting on the treatment of debtors other than merchants and on whether creditor majorities would be needed to approve voluntary bankruptcies. No action took place in the Senate. Substantive votes did occur in the 18th and 19th Senates on earlier issues and on the treatment of banks, but in these sessions the House took no action.

The voting patterns on bankruptcy did not match those on the land debt, so there was no clear conflict between frontier states and the older part of the country. The old South was as opposed to a federal bankruptcy law as the frontier South. House votes indicate that the main trading centers— Boston, Charleston, New York, and Philadelphia—voted together, frequently in opposition to rural districts in their own states. Representatives of these trading centers argued that it was especially necessary to provide a fresh start for merchants who, unlike farmers, were subject to circumstances beyond their control, including domestic and foreign political changes that involved uninsurable risk.[19]

---

[17] History of Congress (HC), 1822, 663. Information is for the House of Representatives.
[18] HC, 1821, 1193.
[19] Bureau of the Census (1975).

Merchants, it was argued, were also heavily engaged in interstate commerce and thus required a uniform national law.[20] A national law would give geographically distant creditors the same protection as creditors nearer the debtor.[21] Those opposed to a national law objected strongly to the "fresh-start" provision, in large part because they foresaw substantial opportunities for fraud.[22] The arguments for a bankruptcy law made in 1818 were remade, to no avail, in the 1821 and 1822 debates.[23] Why, then, did no bill materialize? Several explanations are possible.

First, amendments were offered that provided differential treatment for various classes of debtors, merchants, manufacturers, and banks or that set a debt threshold for declaring bankruptcy. For example, during the 1818 debate in the House a proposal was put forward that included merchants. But the proposal also set a threshold of $5,000 in debt—a measure designed to deter very small artisan manufacturers from taking advantage of bankruptcy. The threshold in fact turned small merchants against the proposal. But the most divisive item was a provision that required two-thirds of creditors to agree on a bankruptcy before the debtor could file, as some representatives preferred to allow debtors to declare bankruptcy on their own. The final House bill had 64 sections in all.[24] As Speaker Henry Clay remarked, "It was very probable the bill would be lost by the variance of opinion on some of its important details."[25]

In such a setting, it can be difficult to construct a stable majority combining a diverse set of groups. To take a more recent example, the modern underpinning of the banking industry in the United States, the Glass-Steagall Act, was not changed legislatively between 1933 and 1999. Kroszner and Strattman (1998) have recently argued that the legislative status quo prevailed because banks, insurance companies, and securities firms had distinct interests in any changes, and each group vetoed detrimental changes. In economies more diverse than that of this simple model, then, forming majorities to change the status quo on bankruptcy may be difficult.

---

[20] HC, 1818, 1018.
[21] HC, 1818, 1019.
[22] HC, 1818, 1023.
[23] HC, 1822, 967, 986.
[24] HC, 1818, 1010-1011.
[25] HC, 1818, 1011.

Second, one way to maintain the status quo is to use one house of Congress to block a bill that has majority support in the other house. While New York, Massachusetts, Pennsylvania, and Virginia had 25, 22, 23, and 25 representatives, respectively, the five frontier states of Indiana, Illinois, Alabama, Mississippi, and Louisiana each had only a single representative. Under these circumstances crafting legislation that would win a majority in both chambers was often difficult.

Third, the Supreme Court began ruling on the constitutionality of stay laws only in the late 1820s. In states where most of the debt was owed to foreigners or lenders residing in other states, debtors may have had a preference for maintaining state institutions. States' rights arguments were invoked frequently in the congressional debate.[26] Part of the argument was that the bankruptcy clause in the Constitution was intended not to extinguish contracts but to prevent debtors from evading payment by moving assets across state lines.

Fourth, if interstate or foreign debtors in a state had an interest in resisting federal intervention, intrastate creditors may also have wanted to avoid federal intervention if they believed that a federal bankruptcy law would be more debtor-friendly on intrastate debt. In particular, creditors in the old South may have had greater confidence in their gentry-controlled state legislatures.

Finally, the issue of states' rights was connected to slavery. Concerns about federal intervention on slave issues may have led to a preference for limiting federal intervention on other issues. Representative Samuel H. Woodson (Kentucky) did not mention slavery explicitly but did indicate that the bankruptcy issue was bound up with a much broader debate about states' rights.[27]

In addition to the long-term concern over slavery, the role of the federal government in economic matters was open to debate. The federal government was extremely small in 1820, with only 6,900 employees, most of them in the military.[28] The government provided defense and conducted foreign affairs, collected taxes through tariffs, managed the western lands,

---

[26] Representative Andrew Stevenson (Virginia), HC, 1822, 770, Representative Alexander Smyth (Virginia), HC, 1822, 792.

[27] HC, 1822, 1120.

[28] Bureau of the Census (1975).

and ran the post office. Federal bankruptcy courts would have represented an important expansion in federal regulation. In particular, a federal role in bankruptcy would have reduced the rents enjoyed by local assignees, receivers, sheriffs, and auctioneers (Balleisen 1996). In contrast, when a stable bankruptcy law was finally passed in 1898, a number of events had changed the overall situation. The Civil War had resulted in the abolition of slavery and the acceptance of federal predominance over state governments, one national and no state currencies existed, and federal economic regulation had been accepted through the Interstate Commerce Act of 1887 and the Sherman Anti-Trust Act of 1893.

Some Final Thoughts

With incomplete contracts there is an obvious case for governmental intervention in markets. Contracts cannot be contingent on individual productivity. Consequently, there will be excessive defaults. In this setup the total output of the economy is higher if average-type defaulting farmers are allowed to remain on their land. Contracts also cannot be conditioned on the state of the economy. In the equilibrium with uncertainty about the state of the economy, average farmers remain on their land in good times but default in bad times. With state-contingent contracts, average farmers are able, for some sets of parameters, to remain on their land in both states. Political intervention can remedy the inefficiencies that arise from both sources of contractual incompleteness. Not only is aggregate production increased ex post but, ex ante, the total output of the economy is increased by allowing for debt relief. The stay laws observed in the Panic of 1819 might well have been an anticipated response to aggregate uncertainty rather than an inefficient form of expropriation that would deter future lending.

Part Two
How Countries Cope: Case Studies

CHAPTER 4

The Importance of an Effective Legal System for Credit Markets: The Case of Argentina

Marcela Cristini, Ramiro A. Moya and Andrew Powell

In the 1990s Argentina set in motion a wide-ranging program of structural reform that involved privatization, economic liberalization, and deregulation (including the establishment of a currency board). These reforms resulted in tremendous achievements in terms of macroeconomic stability, economic activity and new investment, and encouraged the development of the credit market. Credit has grown substantially in Argentina, albeit from a very low base, and is once again an important mechanism for allocating capital to the private sector.

Yet Argentina's financial system remains small relative to gross domestic product (GDP), largely because of the gap between the many modern, market-oriented sectors of the economy and the country's legal institutions. This disparity hinders further development of the credit market. Other factors that help keep the market small include the slow pace of judicial proceedings, high legal costs (for procedures, lawyers, and expert witnesses), and an ambiguous system of judicial penalties that lends itself to corruption.

The literature on law and economics and, more recently, the literature on law and finance, emphasize the importance of effective contract enforcement to economic performance (Cooter and Ulen 1988; La Porta *et al.* 1996). This chapter shares much with the literature. One concept that is particularly important for the present purpose is the notion that legal systems have important implications for the development of the credit market and, more

Marcela Cristini is a senior economist with the Foundation of Latin American Economic Research (FIEL). Ramiro A. Moya is an economist with FIEL. Andrew Powell is the Chief Economist of the Central Bank of Argentina.

generally, for the economy as a whole. The chapter discusses this notion in terms of the performance of Argentina's legal system.

Argentina's 24 provinces have their own constitutions, governments, and independent judicial systems with judges, appeals courts, and supreme courts (Table 4.1). However, the majority of the provincial constitutions and laws are patterned on the legal principles of the national Constitution and laws, thus assuring the country's legal and political integration. The banking operations of each province are also guided by relatively uniform laws, which the local judiciary interprets and enforces. All banks in Argentina are subject to the Central Bank's prudential regulations and thus operate within a common regulatory framework with homogeneous information. But while the laws and legal codes themselves do not differ across provinces, the speed and cost of judicial enforcement do. This scenario makes Argentina a useful case study for analyzing the effect of institutions on the credit market. Because the laws and banking regulations are essentially national and the legal institutions are provincial, it is possible to identify the implications of legal enforcement separately from the effects of the laws themselves.

The analysis focuses in particular on two hypotheses:

- That a negative association exists between judicial effectiveness and the size of the loan market in each province (after controlling for other effects), since differences in judicial effectiveness translate into differences in transaction costs across provinces.

- That levels of arrears are highest in provinces with poor judicial performance, since inefficient judicial systems negatively affect debtors' willingness to repay or discourage banks from making legal claims (or both).

The results are strong. Legal effectiveness appears to be a very significant determinant of both the development of provincial credit markets and the level of nonperforming loans. These results support the recent literature, which advocates the importance of reforming the judicial system in order to enhance credit market performance and thus economic growth.[1]

---

[1] See, for instance, Sherwood, Shepherd, and de Souza (1994) and Weder (1995).

Table 4.1. Argentina: Provincial Structure, Selected Variables

Provinces	Judicial index ranking 1997	Per capita GDP (dollars)	Provincial GDP (% total GDP)	Unsatisfied basic needs index (NBI)	Deposits (% total deposits)	Loans (% total loans)	Nonperforming loans (% total non-performing loans)
Capital Federal	1	25,211	24.9	7.0	51.9	59.4	38.8
Tierra del Fuego	2	13,936	0.5	25.5	0.5	0.5	1.4
Buenos Aires	3	8,184	36.5	14.7	22.3	14.6	18.8
Chubut	4	9,474	1.3	19.4	0.7	0.7	1.0
Chaco	5	3,498	1.0	33.2	0.8	1.0	1.4
Santa Fé	6	7,762	7.6	14.0	5.0	5.1	7.8
Córdoba	7	7,639	7.4	12.8	6.2	6.0	11.5
Mendoza	8	4,699	2.4	15.3	2.5	2.4	2.9
Entre Ríos	9	5,718	2.0	17.2	1.3	1.3	1.7
Formosa	10	2,355	0.4	34.3	0.2	0.3	0.4
Neuquen	11	12,337	2.0	19.1	0.8	1.1	1.7
Río Negro	12	6,574	1.2	20.7	0.7	0.9	1.6
Salta	13	4,364	1.4	33.9	0.9	0.8	0.8
Corrientes	14	4,044	1.2	26.9	0.5	0.7	1.2

(Table continues on following page.)

Table 4.1. (Continued)

Provinces	Judicial index ranking 1997	Per capita GDP (dollars)	Provincial GDP (% total GDP)	Unsatisfied basic needs index (NBI)	Deposits (% total deposits)	Loans (% total loans)	Nonperforming loans (% total non-performing loans)
Tucumán	15	4,222	1.7	24.6	1.2	1.4	2.0
Misiones	16	5,105	1.5	30.0	0.5	0.6	0.5
Jujuy	17	3,094	0.6	33.6	0.6	0.3	0.7
La Pampa	18	9,068	0.9	12.0	0.8	0.9	1.3
San Juan	19	5,689	1.0	17.2	0.7	0.5	0.7
Santa Cruz	20	12,750	0.8	15.2	0.3	0.3	0.5
San Luis	21	15,722	1.7	18.7	0.7	0.3	1.2
La Rioja	22	9,533	0.8	23.6	0.2	0.3	0.7
Santiago del Estero	23	2,516	0.6	33.6	0.7	0.3	0.6
Catamarca	24	6,326	0.6	11.7	0.2	0.3	0.8
Total	—	8,626	100.0	17.3	100.0	100.0	100.0

Source: FIEL based on INDEC and BCRA.

The Argentine Financial System

The financial system was reformed in the early 1990s. The reforms put in place a new monetary regime that included a currency board and gave the Central Bank greater autonomy. Further reforms overhauled capital and provisioning standards and improved supervision. The result was improved economic growth and increased capital flows.

The Financial System under the Convertibility Plan

A central feature of the 1991 Argentine reforms was the adoption of a new monetary regime based on a currency board (the Convertibility Law). Under this regime the exchange rate was fixed to the U.S. dollar, and the Central Bank fully backed the monetary base with foreign reserve assets. This simple rule was aimed at eradicating inflationary expectations, gaining credibility, and reversing the strong dollarization of the preceding years. As a second main step, a new Central Bank charter was enacted in September 1992 that established the bank's independence from the executive branch and made preserving the value of the currency its main objective. The Central Bank would also maintain financial stability by regulating and supervising the banking system. The Convertibility Law and the new charter restricted the extent to which the bank could intervene as a lender of last resort to the financial system.

The Argentine economy grew strongly throughout the 1990s, although disruptions in international capital markets had strong effects, provoking recession in 1995 and again in 1999 (Table 4.2). In spite of international financial crises, the degree of monetization of the economy increased consistently, and capital did not flee.[2] Moreover, after 1995 the banking system underwent significant modernization, including consolidation and the entry of many foreign banks.

Despite the country's economic achievements and the strengthening of the banking system in 1991-94 (including capital and provisioning requirements that exceeded international standards), the December 1994 devaluation of the Mexican peso had serious repercussions for Argentina. The

---

[2] The sequence of the crises was the following: December 1994, Tequila effect; October 1997, Asian crisis, August 1998, Russian crisis; January 1999, Brazilian crisis.

Table 4.2. Argentina: Main Economic and Financial Indicators, 1990-98

Indicator	1990	1991	1992	1993	1994	1995	1996	1997	1998
GDP real growth (%)[a]	-1.9	10.6	9.6	5.7	5.8	-2.8	5.5	8.1	3.9
M2 (% GDP)[b]	—	10.8	11.7	17.4	20.7	19.8	22.3	25.3	29.2
Interest rates[c]									
Libor (international)	8.3	6.1	3.9	3.4	5.1	6.1	5.6	5.9	5.6
Country risk[d]	—	—	12.0	7.4	6.5	12.2	7.2	3.7	6.2
Documents discount (90 day term)[e]	—	42.6	26.8	21	17.8	18.5	12.9	10.7	11.2
Mortgage in dollars (0-5 years)	—	—	—	17.8	16.5	17.7	14	13.3	13.2
Argentine prime rate in dollars (30 day term)	—	—	—	7.8	8.2	14.0	6.9	6.7	8.7
Foreign capital inflow (in US$ millions)									
Foreign direct investment (in US$ millions)	—	—	4,013	2,515	3,432	5,279	6,513	8,094	6,455
Total foreign financing plus international reserves change (in US$ millions)	—	—	12,064	16,633	13,133	6,416	15,881	19,863	21,386
International reserves in the Central Bank (in US$ millions)[f, g]	—	4,367	11,056	15,084	16,049	15,980	17,651	17,938	19,404
Deposits (total in US$ millions)[f]	—	14,679	25,198	39,708	45,757	43,561	53,418	68,500	76,673
Deposits in pesos / deposits in dollars[f]	—	1.2	1.2	1.0	1.1	1.0	1.0	1.0	0.9

— Not available.
a. GDP rate of growth at constant prices of 1993.
b. M2 composition: Current accounts In pesos and dollars; saving accounts In pesos and dollars; time deposits In pesos and dollars; bills and coins.
c. Annual average of monthly Interest rates.
d. Spread of FRB Brady bond over US Treasury bonds of the same maturity — BBV Banco Francés.
e. From 1991 to 1993, source: Cronista Comercial.
f. End of year.
g. Gold and Foreign Currency held at the Central Bank.
Source: Ministry of Economy and Public Works and Central Bank.

sharp fall of Argentine asset prices created doubts about the solvency of certain, mostly small institutions, some of which experienced runs and had no deposit insurance. In 1995 the country's worsening fiscal position and increasing uncertainty about the outcome of the May 14 presidential election caused a more systemic run on the system. The run was halted only by a new agreement with the International Monetary Fund (IMF), together with additional multilateral funds, in mid-March. Deposits recovered strongly after the election. Loans also grew but lagged behind deposits owing to the caution of both banks and potential debtors. Still, by the end of the year the financial system had resumed its rapid growth rate and embarked on an even more rapid period of modernization.

The 1994 Tequila crisis had several significant effects on the Argentine banking sector. First, the crisis led to a considerable refinement of banking regulations. Second, it accelerated the consolidation process that was already under way. Third, the successful resolution of the crisis accelerated foreign investment. Although the banking sector had been liberalized in the early 1990s, the post-Tequila period saw the largest increase in foreign capital inflows.

Through these distinct processes (consolidation and foreign investment), the concentration of lending in the banking sector continued to increase after the Tequila crisis. In 1997 just 20 banks accounted for 80 percent of loans extended through advances and document discounts and 100 percent of mortgages. The concentration of deposits also increased to nearly the same levels. Moreover, some 40 percent of deposits were held in banks with a foreign controlling interest—a figure that rises to 69 percent if only the private banking sector is considered. These structural changes also affected bank performance. Administrative costs fell, albeit from a very high level by international standards, and efficiency ratios improved significantly. Yet profits remained relatively low as high spreads fell in line with high costs. These high spreads and costs reflected both the small scale of the banking sector and legal and other administrative fees. In addition, as a result of economic stability and improved credit risk management (and despite tighter reporting rules), ratios of nonperforming loans declined. Since these ratios remain high compared with international levels, provisioning costs are also a significant factor in explaining the relatively high spreads.

Prudential Regulations in Argentina

Prudential regulations in Argentina have been substantially overhauled since the inception of the 1991 and 1992 Central Bank charter. In 1992-94 Argentina adopted capital and provisioning standards that were well above international norms and began improving supervision. Basic minimum capital requirements, for example, had reached 11.5 percent of assets at risk by the end of 1994. At the time Argentina also had a very high level of reserve requirements on sight deposits, which were considered liquidity reserves.

These improvements notwithstanding, the Tequila crisis brought out several weaknesses in the banking system, and after the crisis the government introduced several additional reforms. Capital requirements were tightened, and a set of explicit liquidity requirements replaced traditional reserve requirements. The new liquidity requirements applied to virtually all liabilities with rates that depend on residual maturities rather than on the type of liability. These new requirements were remunerated, thereby lifting a substantial tax from the system. Under the new system liquidity requirements amounted to an average of 20 percent of the deposit base. The reforms have won praise from independent assessors: Moody's (1998) cites the strength of the financial system as the main factor underlying the upgrade of Argentina's bond rating.

Capital and Provisioning Requirements

The minimum capital ratio was increased to 11.5 percent of risk-weighted assets. But counterparty capital requirements also depend on the interest rate on each loan and the Superintendency of Banking's CAMELS risk rating.[3] On top of minimum capital requirements, the Central Bank imposed market risk and interest rate capital requirements for total minimum requirements that average over 14 percent for the financial system. But banks' actual capital amounts to about 20 percent of assets at risk (measured according to a Basle methodology). Provisioning requirements depend on the category of the loan. The Central Bank uses five categories ranked from 1

---

[3] The CAMELS system rates five crucial aspects of banking on a scale of 1 to 5, with 1 as the top rating. The ratings are based on capital adequacy, asset quality, management capacity, earnings stability, and liquidity sufficiency.

for "normal" to 5 for "nonrecoverable" and applies a compulsory provision of 1 percent (on all new loans in category 1) to 100 percent (on loans in category 5). Loans are additionally categorized according to their status as commercial or retail. For commercial loans the category is similar to a forward-looking rating, while for retail loans only arrears are taken into account. Commercial loans of less than $200,000 may be treated as retail in this respect.

Disclosure Rules on Borrowers

The Central Bank collects and disseminates information on virtually all retail and corporate borrowers through a database of some six million entries that is available at the Central Bank's website.[4] The website gives the general public as well as banks access to the credit status of private citizens and firms. Data on larger corporate loans (debts of over $200,000) and on nonperforming loans of more than $50 (loans to individuals and small firms) are available on a modestly priced compact disk that contains the entire database.[5]

The Credit Market

As discussed above, the structure of the Argentine credit market changed markedly in the 1990s. In the early 1980s the financial system comprised 402 financial institutions and 5,043 branches distributed throughout the country. By the end of 1994 it included just over 200 institutions. In early 1996, in the aftermath of the Tequila crisis, some 50 of those institutions were closed, most of them small and midsize private institutions (private domestic banks, cooperatives, and credit unions). BCRA (1997) distinguishes three stages in this restructuring process. The first stage consisted of small bank mergers at the regional level. The second involved a smaller number of

---

[4] The Central Bank's website is http://www.bcra.gov.ar.

[5] A number of private companies (Veraz, Fidelitas, and Serinco, for instance) also provide credit information on potential clients. They take the Central Bank's basic data and construct full client histories that include complementary data from judicial and other sources. These companies may also provide basic scoring services.

mergers between midsize and large entities. In the third stage foreign banks began to enter the Argentine market by purchasing leading domestic banks.[6] In late 1998 the number of banks fell to 127 (Table 4.3).

Despite the relatively low profitability of Argentina's banks, the financial system attracted a significant amount of foreign capital. These foreign entrants undoubtedly placed a high value on the banking system's growth potential, since levels of bank penetration were low compared with those of other countries with similar per capita incomes. The existence of this potential market sparked a significant expansion of branches throughout the country. In 1997 some 269 branches were opened in a single year (a total of 4,060 were functioning in December 1996). In the same year the financial system's deposits grew by approximately 30 percent.

In 1997 the service sector continued to receive the greatest proportion of credit (some 40 percent of total loans), although loans to households (23.9 percent) and the manufacturing industry (18.1 percent) were also significant. In 1993 the housing mortgage market had begun to grow after a long period of economic instability that depressed home buying. Mortgages constituted one of the fastest-growing markets in the years after the Tequila shock, although this market started from a very low base. Loans to the manufacturing sector were granted mainly to large companies. A breakdown of loans by amount indicates that 50 percent were for amounts of more than $1,000,000. Within the consolidated banking system, 50 borrowers accounted for almost 10 percent of credit.

---

[6] Among these foreign banks the most important are: Banco Bilbao Vizcaya (Spain), Banco Santander (Spain), Scotia International Ltd. (Canada), O'Higgins-Central Hispanoamericano S.A. (Chile), Abinsa S.A. (Chile), and HSBC Latin America BV (Holland). BCRA (October 1997) points out the advantage of foreign banks operating as liquidity providers to the domestic market under systemic crises. This role is possible due to the existence of central banks in the source country operating as "extended" lenders of last resort. A similar opinion can be found in Gavin and Hausmann (1997). According to Cañonero (1997), while the concentration process may have improved the efficiency of domestic financial intermediation, it may also have contributed to the contraction in bank lending observed during 1995, due to the presence of information asymmetries. He identifies a loss of information due to the contracting of small (well-informed) institutions and the expansion of large institutions during the concentration process.

Table 4.3. Argentina: Financial System Structure, December 1998

Type of institution	Number of institutions	Share in deposits
All financial institutions	127	100.0
All banking institutions	104	99.5
Public banks	17	35.0
Nationwide	3	15.2
Provinces/local governments	14	19.8
Private banks	87	64.5
Commercial banks	66	46.6
Cooperatives	4	2.0
Foreign branch banks	17	15.9
All nonbanking institutions	23	0.5
Financial companies	15	0.4
Credit unions	8	0.1

Source: Central Bank data.

Types of Contracts and Collateral

Although the available information on loan contracts and other bank services in Argentina is fairly good, information on the use of credit and the precise nature of credit relations is at times sketchy. A 1995 survey of the manufacturing industry gives an overall picture of firms' use of credit in the 1990s. The survey classifies companies' size both by number of employees and by total sales (FIEL 1996a). According to survey data, an average of 25 percent of all firms did not use bank loans.[7] (The actual proportions ranged from 36 percent for small firms to zero for large firms.) On average each firm was associated with three banks (one bank for most small firms but 14

---

[7] This figure is impressive considering that the information was collected among formal enterprises before the Tequila crisis. In many cases the interest rate was considered too high relative to what the business would earn, or the entrepreneur did not ask for a loan for fear of being rejected. Bankers indicated that many formal firms presented deficient balance sheets or unsuitable projects. Bankers' fears were in part based on poor repayment rates among small and medium-size firms.

for large businesses). This feature is consistent with the prevalent pattern among small businesses and is confirmed by Central Bank figures showing that some 15 percent of commercial borrowers operated exclusively with one bank.

In conjunction with the changes in the banking structure in the 1990s, banks altered their business strategies. Several banks focused on lending to top companies, a very competitive segment, while other banks moved down the corporate chain seeking higher margins by establishing strong customer relationships with medium-size companies. Powell, Broda and Burdisso (1997) develop a simple theoretical model of customer relations in which companies may face a search cost when moving to another bank, giving banks a degree of local monopoly power. The authors argue that this scenario may account for relatively high interest rates (especially on overdrafts) and heterogeneous interest rates (which reflect search costs), even though competitive entry drives profits to low levels.

Banks also developed special departments for different types of collateral, or pledges (such as automobiles, manufacturing machinery, and agricultural machinery) and for housing mortgages. Several institutions began developing warrants for agricultural producers and made leasing a distinct product line.

Interest Rates

Despite a marked decline after the Tequila crisis, the average lending rate in Argentina remained high by international standards throughout the late 1990s, reflecting rates on personal loans and overdraft facilities (Table 4.4). Vicens (1998) concludes that excessive administrative costs (including legal expenses) and heavy charges for default risk explained the high average rates. He finds that administrative costs fell in 1996 due to bank restructuring. According to Buera and Nicolini (1997), the risk implicit in these lending contracts could explain the high spreads, though only approximately. Rates on loans secured by collateral, mortgages, and loans advanced on documents (bill discounted) were all substantially below the average. Mortgage lending and loans backed by collateral were associated with lower rates owing to the presence of guarantees and in spite of the shortcomings of the Argentine judicial system.

Table 4.4. Argentina: Interest Rates and Lending by Type of Contract, 1997
(percent)

Type	Proportion of total lending	Interest rates[a] Argentine pesos	Dollars
Overdraft	17.0	26.0	13.5
Bill discount	29.7	10.7	10.5
Mortgages	17.7	14.6	13.1
Pledges	5.7	16.4	14.1
Personal loans	10.5	35.4	20.1
Others	19.4	—	—
Total/average	100.0	18.4	13.2

— Not available.

a. Annual average of monthly interest rates. The spread between lending rates in pesos and dollars reflects the devaluation risk on loans and collateral.

Source: Central Bank data.

Nonperforming Loans and Legal Loan Recovery

In December 1994 nonperforming loans net of provision accounted for 25.9 percent of banks' net worth. This proportion grew to 38 percent after the Tequila crisis but diminished to 23.6 percent by mid-1997. Public banks continued to have significantly higher proportions of nonperforming loans than private banks, reflecting the allocation decisions of public institutions, which do not necessarily aim to maximize profits. But the number of nonperforming loans held by private banks is also high by international standards.

The Central Bank categorizes all borrowers in one of six risk categories (Table 4.5). Toward the end of 1997, some 11 percent of commercial debtors and 21 percent of household borrowers were faced with repayment difficulties or more serious credit risks (categories 2-6). For loans secured by some guarantee or collateral (around 38 percent of all loans), only 2 percent presented repayment problems, suggesting that the existence of guarantees clearly and positively affects loan performance. The value of the guarantees covered 39 percent of all secured loans and 12 percent of total loans.

Table 4.5. Distribution of Credit, December 1997
(percent)

Loan classification	Type of borrower		Loans with collateral
	Commercial	Household	
1- Normal	89.5	79.2	97.8
2- With arrears	2.5	6.2	0.4
3- Potential default	2.1	3.4	1.0
4- High risk of default	3.0	5.2	0.7
5- Unrecoverable	2.6	5.7	0.1
6- Technically unrecoverable[a]	0.3	0.1	—
Total	100.0	100.0	100.0

— Not available.
a. Borrowers holding loans with bankrupt banks.
Source: Central Bank data.

The existence of guarantees also has a strong impact on banks' loan recovery strategies. Because no published evidence is available on this issue for Argentina, a survey was carried out specifically for this analysis (Table 4.6). The survey showed that the vast majority of court cases (almost 80 percent) involved unsecured loans. Banks confirmed that when a loan reached category 3, they frequently threatened and then took legal action. However the percentage of such legal actions that ended up as actual lawsuits was relatively low and was even lower for loans with collateral, because these borrowers were clearly more willing to repay than unsecured borrowers. Among the lawsuits involving secured loans, pledges were the most significant (11 percent of total lawsuits). Most of these loans financed car purchases, and recovery rates for these loans were probably the highest for any type of secured lending.

The distribution of loans in litigation differed across banks and in areas with different credit structures. Banks reported considerable differences in loan-recovery strategies. Some were willing to use legal action as a sign of toughness, while others were more reluctant to bring legal action without first exhausting all other possibilities for negotiation and refinancing. Be-

Table 4.6. Distribution of Lawsuits for Selected Banks, 1997

(percent of total loans in litigation)

Type of loan	Percent
Unsecured loans	78.2
Personal loans	21.4
Current accounts	24.4
Credit cards	26.4
Others	6.0
Pledges	11.0
Mortgage for housing	6.9
Other mortgage loans	3.9
Total debt claims in court	100.0

Note: Banks provided the number of cases, broken down by type. Total loans by bank and type were used as weights for aggregation.

Source: Foundation for Latin American Economic Research.

cause of the problems banks reportedly faced in taking legal action, many opted for strategies other than litigation.[8]

Characteristics of Provincial Credit Markets

Argentina is a large and extremely diverse country. In terms of total land area, it is larger than Western Europe, with many climatic variations and divergent income levels. The GDP of Argentine provinces differs markedly as well, as does the composition of provincial GDP in terms of sectors and the size of productive enterprises. Not surprisingly, credit markets also differ substantially.

Between 1992 and 1997 deposits as a percentage of GDP grew in all provinces, with some provinces experiencing increases of over 20 percent of

---

[8] Catão (1997) notes that legal limitations on seizing collateral and the costs and lengthiness of judicial procedures have hindered efforts to bring debtors into compliance. The result is higher potential costs to borrowers and incentives to reduce lending. Even if there is excess demand for loans, then, high interest rates will not clear the market, resulting in some type of credit rationing.

GDP. Loans rose sharply in 15 jurisdictions and fell in nine, in some cases substantially. The nonperforming loan portfolio also declined nationwide, although a group of 17 provinces recorded an increase in the ratio of nonperforming loans. Commercial loans predominated in the overall portfolio, accounting for the largest proportion of the decrease in nonperforming debt. An analysis of loans to households showed a worsening in nonperformance in all provinces.[9]

In mid-1998, however, some aspects of regional credit markets remained much as they had been in the past. Bank branches, deposits, and loans were heavily concentrated geographically in the capital city of Buenos Aires and the surrounding area, largely because of income and demographics. The city of Buenos Aires alone accounts for 25 percent of GDP and 8.5 percent of total population, and it is the headquarters of most large companies doing business in Argentina.

As has been noted, the economic reforms taking place at the time prompted important changes in the banking structure of half the provinces as a result of the privatization of public banks. Between 1993 and 1996 some 15 banks were privatized, including one national bank, 13 provincial banks, and a municipal bank. These banks had worked as provincial government financial agencies, administering public funds as well as granting loans to the private sector. In general this allocation of lending was highly inefficient, and many of the projects the banks had financed were risky or simply economically unfeasible. In essence, this lending mechanism had allowed local governments to subsidize certain economic activities.

The number of head offices and branches of banks per inhabitant varied widely across provinces. Some provinces had as few as 0.4 branch per 10,000 inhabitants, while the province with the largest number had almost 10 times as many (3.7 per 10,000 inhabitants). In some provinces the leading lenders were regional institutions.[10] The importance of these regional lenders is reflected in the fact that in 1997 their participation in total financing in 10 provinces exceeded 40 percent, and in five provinces it was over 50 percent.

---

[9] This increase probably reflects tighter regulatory standards rather than an actual deterioration in loan quality.

[10] Whether a bank is a regional entity depends largely on two interrelated criteria. The first is that the entity's loan portfolio is concentrated in a given province (50 percent or more). The second is that it should not have branches in more than four jurisdictions.

What is the significance of the strong presence of these regional private banks? First, these banks operate primarily within one province, in some cases extending into others but remaining strongest in their home province. Second, the monetary authority did not issue explicit regulations governing the establishment of these banks or protecting them. Some of these banks originally belonged to provincial governments but were privatized between 1992 and 1996.

Third, regional banks (both public and private) have a number of unique features. They grant more of their loans in local currency than other banks do, particularly personal loans. They further depend heavily on current account deposits and borrow less from abroad. They concentrate on consumer lending and thus ask for fewer guarantees; their nonperforming portfolios are consequently larger. Public regional banks have nonperforming portfolios on the order of 35 percent of total loans, while private regional banks record rates higher than those of their nonregional peers. Regional banks are also less efficient than other financial institutions, with higher-than-average administrative expenses in relation to their assets. Such institutions are also smaller on average than their peers (measured in assets per branch), and cater to those seeking smaller loans, but they pay higher returns on deposits. As part of the banking structure, these banks are significant for at least two reasons: they tend to develop closer relationships with their clients than other banks, and to a certain extent their presence suggests a segmentation of the provincial financial market.

In addition, the size of the credit market (loans as a percentage of GDP) differs significantly across provinces. Loans granted in the city of Buenos Aires in 1997 represented 60 percent of provincial GDP, the highest percentage for the country, while in the province with the smallest ratio of loans to GDP that figure was only 4.4 percent. The proportion of lending to households also differed widely among jurisdictions, ranging from a minimum of 17.3 percent to a maximum of 55 percent. The variations are slightly smaller for bank deposits, ranging from 6.5 to 46 percent of GDP.

The proportion of nonperforming loans was also significantly higher in some jurisdictions than in others. Nationwide nonperforming loans accounted for 13.8 percent of total loans in 1997, but in 15 of the 24 provinces loans in arrears exceeded 20 percent of total lending, rising to a maximum of more than 35 percent. Significantly, the nonperforming portfolio showed far greater variation for commercial loans than for loans to households. Five provinces had a nonperforming portfolio of commercial loans in excess of 40 percent, while the nonperforming loan ratio for household credit was between 31.5 and 12.4 percent of total loans.

Clearly, Argentina's provincial credit markets display a marked heterogeneity. Some provinces have relatively high levels of deposits as a percentage of GDP and relatively high credit penetration, while others have very low levels of both deposits and credit. From 1992 to 1997 credit increased in some jurisdictions, but in others credit intermediation actually declined, even though deposits rose in all provinces.

Creditor Rights: Legal Protection and Judicial Enforcement

Legal regulations defining the credit contract and the rights and obligations of debtors and creditors influence credit market operations (volumes and costs). In Argentina this contractual relationship has a solid grounding in law. Many of these contracts, such as sureties, pledge loans, mortgages, warrants, and letters of credit have been covered by legislation since the end of the nineteenth century. In some cases the laws have been modified to reflect new market developments. Other laws, such as those regulating trusts and leasing, have emerged in the context of recent economic reforms.

Argentine legislation specifically protects the rights of creditors. Such rights, however, are not absolute. The Civil Code and corresponding legislation restrict the proportion of debtors' assets that can be seized or sold, including wages (established by the Employment Contract Law) and items that are considered family property. In addition the legislation specifies the legal actions creditors can take to preserve their rights in the event of default and special procedures for executing instruments in support of their rights.

FIEL (1996a) developed a comparative analysis of regulations on mortgage lending and consumer loan recovery in the United States and Argentina. Comparing the body of legislation restricting loan agreements and creditor remedies in the case of debtor default in the two countries, it concludes that restrictions on remedies for default are less severe in Argentina.[11]

---

[11] In only one instance (the maximum percentage of workers' salaries that can be garnished) are the restrictions on the remedies more severe in Argentina. The rate is 5 percentage points lower in Argentina (20 instead of 25 percent). This difference is significant, as this remedy is one of the most effective for the recovery of unpaid debt.

This result is encouraging, implying reduced costs for borrowers (lower explicit interest rates and lower potential for quantitative restrictions on loans) and creditors.[12] Thus the financial sector's collection problems must have other causes. Possible explanations include high credit risk stemming from macroeconomic volatility, incentives for banks to take on excessive risk, and lack of judicial enforcement.

Judicial Enforcement of Loan Contracts at the Provincial Level

In Argentina national codes and laws define and regulate bank loan contracts. As discussed above, the country's federal structure places responsibility for enforcing these regulations in the hands of independent judiciaries. Local courts take a variety of approaches to enforcement, leading to regional differences in access to credit. Costs may also vary if the parties anticipate difficulties in resolving the conflicts arising out of the loan contracts. Such difficulties may take the form of excessive costs for legal procedures, slow or partial debt recovery, a general increase in uncertainty regarding the results of the lawsuit, or any combination of the above.

Several types of regulations establish legal costs for each province. These are:

- Basic national law, which contains procedural regulations. The law is applicable in all jurisdictions and covers matters such as the general principles of creditor protection, bankruptcy, and pledges (seizure or enforcement). The laws may be applied differently across provinces, however, because of the criteria judges use to interpret the regulations.

- Codes of procedure issued by the various provinces. Provincial codes of procedure do not differ substantially from those for federal courts.

---

[12] Coinciding with these results, La Porta *et al.* (1996) examine legal rules covering protection for corporate shareholders and creditors in 49 countries. According to these researchers Argentina's shareholder and creditor rights are similar to those in the United States. Even though Argentina's legal system is based on the civil law tradition, which typically provides less protection for investors, regulations governing public companies and bankruptcy were substantially reformed in 1971 and 1995, respectively. The new legislation introduced modern features that were in line with international experience.

- Laws on professional fees, which regulate the costs of lawyers, procurators, notaries, courts, witnesses, auctioneers, and others. These laws differ across jurisdictions. Judges award fees as a percentage of the total lawsuit, taking into account not only the amount of the suit but such factors as the outcome, work involved, and social impact. In calculating fees some jurisdictions emphasize the amount claimed and others the amount awarded. As a result several provinces have high maximum limits relative to the fees set in the capital and other provinces (Table 4.7). Mandatory contributions to lawyers' professional associations represent an additional cost for plaintiffs. Certain court procedures (such as lifting injunctions or recovering deposits) cannot be undertaken unless these contributions have been paid.

- Court tax regulations, which are also local, with wide disparity among provinces.

Court costs vary not only across jurisdictions but also in terms of how they are calculated—that is, whether they are based on the amount of the claim, the nominal principal, or the restated principal. Some jurisdictions (seven out of 24) impose no costs for seizing pledges, and in three provinces the maximum in such cases is $90 for court and filing costs together. Contributions to the lawyers' associations vary according to jurisdiction from nothing to a fixed amount that ranges between $4 and $17.50. Other jurisdictions impose a surcharge on the court tax that in some cases is significant (up to 2 percent of the principal). Property registry costs are also significant in some jurisdictions, and delays in processing registrations can run to several months. Publishing an edict in the official gazette or newspaper of a jurisdiction can

Table 4.7. Mandatory Legal Costs Compared by Province

Level of costs	Provinces
Relatively less expensive	Federal Capital, Chubut, Neuquén, La Rioja, Tierra del Fuego, Santa Cruz, Tucumán, Chaco, Catamarca, Jujuy, Corrientes
Intermediate	Formosa, Buenos Aries, San Luis, Río Negro, Santiago del Estero, Entre Ríos, Salta, La Pampa, Misiones, San Juan
High	Córdoba, Mendoza, Santa Fé

cost between $120 and $600. Finally, professional fees also differ considerably. In some provinces awards can total up to 30 percent of the amount claimed, while in others fees are capped at 16 percent.

As an example, Table 4.8 considers two types of transactions: mortgage loans and pledge seizures. The court costs are calculated from the three categories in Table 4.7.[13]

If auction costs are added to the above costs, total expenses as a percentage of the amount of the claim range between 8 and 13 percent for mortgages and 16 and 21 percent for pledge seizures.[14]

Obstacles to Effective Judicial Recovery

A survey of leading local banks (FIEL 1996b) summarizes the obstacles financial entities face in their role as creditor plaintiffs.[15] The major points are highlighted here.

Delays in Recovery

In most cases lawsuits are excessively drawn out, so that banks often accept settlement proposals involving high discounts rather than pursue a lengthy legal procedure and run certain risks—for instance, that the debtor will dis-

---

[13] A more detailed discussion can be found in FIEL (1996b).

[14] The law states that the purchaser of the asset bears this cost. However, from an economic point of view these costs can be defined as transaction costs for the banks. In an extreme case in which the bank decides to purchase the property or the item being sold off to protect its price, the total cost of intermediation falls fully on the bank.

[15] This survey included a questionnaire and an interview with each entity and was performed in the third quarter of 1997. The information has been updated for this study. Banks were selected for interview on the basis of the size of their loan portfolios, the variety of instruments they used, and the distribution of their business over different jurisdictions. The data represent almost 40 percent of the commercial loan portfolio of the financial system, 30 percent of the consumer and housing loan portfolio, and more than 20 percent of all bank branches nationwide. It should be noted, though, that in the case of Banco de la Nación, the possibility this bank has of bringing action in the Federal Courts (which it does in 73 percent of cases) means that the relevance of its experience is limited for the purposes of this discussion. The banks surveyed show better-than-average performance for nonperforming loans in categories three to five (6.6 percent of the total amount financed as opposed to 11.1 percent for the system as a whole). The banks also record a lower percentage of guaranteed loans compared with the system total, partly because of the lower volume of housing loans in the cases analyzed.

Table 4.8. Court Costs for Loan Enforcement
(percent of total claim)

Jurisdiction	Costs	
	Mortgage ($200,000)[a]	Pledge seizure ($20,000)[b]
Capital Federal	4.11	4.10
Buenos Aries (province)	5.27	7.80
Córdoba	5.93	8.83
Mendoza	5.91	4.11

a. The lower amount for bank disclosure set by the Central Bank in the case of company debt.

b. The average value banks assign to pledges of vehicles and machinery.

Note: Does not include cost of transfers, professional fees, judicial delays or interest rate caps administered by courts.

Source: Foundation for Latin American Economic Research (FIEL).

appear. In addition, guarantees become obsolete in many cases, such as for loans guaranteed by motor vehicles. In several jurisdictions courts admit actions by debtors that delay trials, in spite of the existence of strict procedural rules. Delays in the Property Registry also have a direct impact on the security and collection of loans. Finally, vacancies in some courts because of leaves, lack of appointments, and resignations further impede speedy resolution.

Risks Arising from Unfavorable Rulings

These risks include being required to pay the opposite parties' fees for attorneys and expert witnesses. Proceedings may also be declared null and void, or the judge may award total or partial payment exemptions.

Legal Caps on Interest Rates

In certain jurisdictions magistrates set a cap on interest rates (a percentage not exceeding compensatory and punitive interest together) that affects the agreement between the parties.

Lack of Legislation or Jurisprudence for New Credit Systems

Credit cards are a good example. In some jurisdictions legal proceedings to recover credit card debt involve a lengthy and uncertain process.

Technical Difficulties in Treating Matters of Commercial Banking Law

Banks often indicate that judges are overcautious owing to the complexity of the financial problems involved. In some provinces, for example, admission of the procedure for automatically seizing pledges is relatively new. Other new regulations on matters such as the reform of the mortgage foreclosure regime or the changes to the regime for creditor protection and bankruptcy have encountered resistance in provincial courts (particularly mortgage foreclosure reforms).

Political Risk

In addition to the technical difficulties, banks mentioned problems deriving from the political influence that is exerted on courts in certain jurisdictions.

Table 4.9 shows the frequency of replies that describe excessive costs and judicial obstacles in each province. The percentages reflect the share of each item in total replies for the 24 jurisdictions. Thus "fees and contributions to professional colleges" (excessive costs), which is mentioned 8.7 percent of the time, heads the ranking. It is followed in importance by "suspension of auction because the debtor files for creditor protection or bankruptcy" and "court costs."

Table 4.10 compares the provinces declared by the banks to have the worst performance with those considered to have the best performance. The criteria include the length of procedures and the number of claims recovered in full (net of court costs and fees).

Enforcement actions and commercial mortgages in the slowest jurisdictions take three times as long as they do in the fastest—almost one year. Other forms of legal action can take almost twice as long in some jurisdictions they do in others. Measuring the length of proceedings from start to auction generally doubles the time involved in both high and low-performing provinces. In the slowest jurisdictions, then, proceedings take on average more than two years, compared with less than one year in high-

Table 4.9. Excessive Legal Costs and Obstacles to Judicial Effectiveness by Province

Cost or obstacle	Total (%)	Ranking
1– Court tax		
1.1– Ordinary	7.5	3
1.2– Enforcement	7.5	4
1.3– Pledge seizures and applications for bankruptcy	7.2	5
2– Other procedural costs	6.0	6
3– Fees and contributions to professional colleges and councils	8.7	1
4– Professional fees		
4.1– Lawyers	3.9	11
4.2– Procurators	3.6	12
4.3– Auctioneers	3.3	13
4.4– Expert witnesses	3.3	13
4.5– Notaries public	3.6	12
5– Registry expenses		
5.1– Property	4.5	10
5.2– Pledges on vehicles	2.4	15
5.3– Pledges on other movable property	2.1	16
6– Edicts	5.7	8
7– Notary public fees for deed registration	1.2	17
8– Jurisdiction favoring trial proceedings for enforcement	6.9	7
9– Impossibility of enforcement on basis of third-party guarantees	3.0	14
10– Delays from court vacancy	4.5	10
11– Suspension of auction because debtor files for creditor protection or bankruptcy	8.4	2
12– Possibility of enforcing loans under Law 24,441	5.4	9
13– Others	1.2	17
Total replies	100	

Source: Foundation for Economic Research in Latin America.

Table 4.10. Judicial Performance by Province
(average months)

Province	Worst performance			Best performance		
	Start to ruling	Start to auction	Recovery (%)[a]	Start to ruling	Start to auction	Recovery (%)[a]
Enforcement action for items such as checks, and discount bills	10.8	21.8	20	4.0	11.8	42
Pledge seizures	2.3	8.6	55	15	4.7	67
Foreclosures	9.5	18.4	67	4.0	9.8	75
Enforcement of other loans	12.5	24.0	56	3.5	11.5	63
Other actions	36.0	48.0	10	18.0	24.0	40

a. Claims recovered in full, net of court costs and fees.

Source: Foundation for Economic Research in Latin America.

performing provinces. Net recovery levels are lower in provinces that record the worst performance, as costs are higher and there are more obstacles to full recognition of creditor rights. But these differences are not as great as they are for the length of time involved, except in the case of enforcement actions.

Developing a Judicial Performance Indicator

A judicial performance indicator was constructed based on the information presented in Table 4.9. This index allows for the testing of hypotheses on the importance of judicial effectiveness to the operation of the credit market. The indicator was constructed in two stages. First, the estimated legal costs based on provincial regulations and laws were reconciled with the banks' opinion (as reflected in the survey). Second, the frequency with which each province was mentioned in terms of total costs and obstacles was taken as an approximate indicator of the costs and obstacles in that province.

The analysis of mandatory legal costs had already allowed for the classification of provinces in the broad groups (high, intermediate, and low cost) shown in Table 4.7. The information from the survey of banks was used to check the classifications and widen the scope of the analysis to include other judicial obstacles such as court delays, suspended auctions because of debtor bankruptcy, and a preference for trial proceedings.

In order to compare the overall judicial efficiency of the various provinces, it was necessary to produce a ranking based on all costs and obstacles banks face. The judicial indicator shown in Figure 4.1 was based directly on the frequency of the banks' assessment of obstacles by province. No weights were applied to reflect the importance of each bank in the jurisdiction or the relative importance of each type of obstacle and legal cost. This simple method was preferred to attaching weights to the various items owing to the lack of exact information about legal costs and obstacles.[16] Finally, a bias toward the overrepresentation of provinces with the most financial activity

---

[16] A rational basis for weighting each item would be the costs banks incur as a percentage of any legal claim. Although this approach may sound simple, it is in fact complex. During 1998 a legal team put together by the Central Bank under the direction of the authors revised 2,500 claims on loan recovery filed in the provincial courts and sentenced in 1997. Analysis of these data has generally confirmed the ranking presented here and will allow a more rigorous construction of the judicial index in future research.

Figure 4.1 Judicial Performance Index

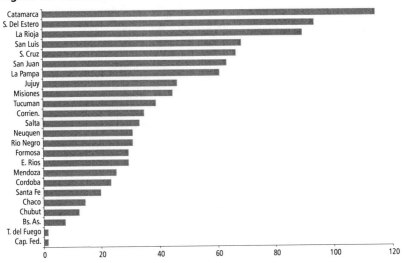

Note: The provinces have been ordered according to their degree of judicial effectiveness. Higher values represent poor judicial performance. Because of the lack of data for Tierra del Fuego, it has been considered similar to the capital.
Source: Foundation for Economic Research in Latin America.

was corrected by adjusting the ranking using alternative measures of credit market size (total loans and number of banks for each province).

The Banking System in the Provinces: A Study of Judicial Enforcement in the Loan Market

The previous sections have discussed the two primary developments in the Argentine banking system. First, economic liberalization, stability, and growth prompted a significant restructuring process in the banking system, significant increases in the levels of on-shore credit intermediation, and decreases in the lending rates. Second, although levels of nonperforming loans declined, they remain high by international standards, and the issue of willingness to repay clearly remains important. However, such problems are not necessarily connected to the design of legal instruments themselves but rather to their effective judicial enforcement. This section presents a more rigorous analysis using econometric techniques, specifically indices of judicial effectiveness by province. Data from the indices for the provinces and over time are used in the creation of panel data models to test hypotheses concerning the implications of judicial effectiveness for credit market performance.

The Hypotheses

The evidence on banking regulations, loan contracts, and the operating methods of financial institutions detailed in the previous sections provides a basis for the construction of the following hypotheses:

- A negative relationship is anticipated between the development of the credit market (loans outstanding/provincial GDP) and judicial costs, since these may discourage the supply of credit. Interviews with executives of banks nationwide confirm that costly and ineffective judicial enforcement discourages lending. Some banks report setting targets for loans in various provinces based on judicial experience. These targets are lower in provinces where courts have proved unreliable in providing redress once the normal recovery and negotiation process for loan repayment is exhausted.

- A positive relationship is expected between legal transaction costs and the stock of nonperforming loans. Judicial effectiveness impacts the portfolio of nonperforming loans in two distinct ways. First, low judicial costs provide borrowers with incentives to repay, because debtors know that nonperformance is likely to meet with legal action. Second, effective courts deal with arrears swiftly, reducing the steady-state stock of nonperforming loans on bank balance sheets.

- Additional hypotheses relate to the structure of the local financial system. In particular, the models test whether the presence of a public provincial bank increases the stock of loans outstanding and the level of nonperforming loans. Many public provincial banks essentially acted as treasuries that channeled loans for development, in some cases to politically favored groups. For this reason provincial public banks were often weak financially compared with private banks and had a larger proportion of nonperforming loans. The privatization of provincial banks changed their market environment drastically and prompted them to screen customers more carefully. In addition their nonperforming loan portfolios were cleared out before privatization. Therefore the existence of public provincial banks should be linked to relatively large stocks of nonperforming portfolios, and privatization should result in relatively low levels of arrears. In turn the increase in borrowing requirements that comes with privatization should result in a reduced volume of financing to the private sector.

- Lastly, the models test whether the presence of private regional banks increases the availability of credit. This hypothesis is related to the notion that in Argentina banks have increasingly sought to deepen customer relations. According to this view, local banks should know local clients best, and provinces with more local (private) banks should have more loans outstanding. In contrast, provinces where only national banks operate, supposedly on the basis of poor information, should exhibit more rationing and thus less credit. Local banks may use their close client relationships to substitute for ineffective legal systems, thus increasing willingness to repay.

Econometric Results

Two equations are estimated using a panel of provincial data for 1992-97. The first equation explains the behavior of the stock of credit to the private sector. The second equation illustrates the behavior of the nonperforming portfolio.

Definition of Variables

The variables used in the econometric analysis are defined in Box 4.1. Unfortunately, no data on interest rates by province are available.[17]

---

[17] Bankers pointed out that the differences in interest rates by type of loan clearly dominated the differentials by locality and in some cases even declared that there were no differentials based purely on province.

Box 4.1. Definitions of Variables

CRP/GDP (credit to the private sector as a percentage of GDP): Total credit to the private sector, including loans in arrears, for the 23 jurisdictions and the capital for 1992-97. GDP for the period 1996-97 is estimated on the basis of the electricity consumption of each province.
Source: For credit to the private sector, Central Bank, *Statistical Bulletin*, various issues; for GDP, Ministry of Domestic Affairs estimates.

CRPA/CRP (loans in arrears as a percentage of total credit to the private sector): Available for the whole period (1992-97) for the 24 provinces (including the capital).
Source: Central Bank, *Statistical Bulletin*, various issues.

PUB (public provincial banks): Binary variable that equals 1 at the moment the provincial bank is privatized and 0 otherwise. It is available for all 24 provinces (including the capital) for the whole period under analysis.
Source: Estimate based on Central Bank information.

DES (unemployment rate): Number of unemployed as a percentage of the total active population (employed and unemployed). It is available for all 24 provinces (including the capital) for the period analyzed (1992-97).
Source: Institute of Statistics and Census.

CALL (interest rate on interbank loans): Interest rate charged for bank-to-bank loans in national currency for nominal monthly periods nationwide (no variance among jurisdictions).
Source: Central Bank, *Statistical Bulletin*, various issues.

RP95 (participation of regional banks in the respective jurisdictions): Share of loans by regional banks in each province's total loans for all 24 provinces (including the capital), but only for 1995.
Source: Central Bank.

JUSMR, JUS1, or JUS2 (index of effectiveness of provincial judicial systems): Constructed on the basis of a survey of banks nationwide.[a] Both the index and ranking do not vary over time but only among provinces. JUSMR is the ranking of the JUS1 variable, 1 being the province with the best performance and 24 being the province with the poorest performance.
Source: FIEL.

---

a. The replies were divided by the total amount of loans in each province (JUS1) or the number of bank branches, including headquarters (JUS2). The indices JUS1 and JUS2 assume continuous values from 0 (the province with the highest judicial effectiveness) to 1 (the least judicial effectiveness).

Structural Differences among Argentina's Provinces

A number of factors are responsible for the large differences in levels of credit among provinces. This analysis relates provincial credit levels to judicial performance indicators, controlling for macroeconomic shocks and the structural characteristics of the provincial banking market. The results are strong, in that the judicial performance indicators (which are constants for each province) are all highly significant.

However, like any econometric analysis, this one does not provide a full explanation of all variations—in this case, regional variations in the size of provincial credit markets. The analysis does not control for other factors that affect the dependent variable. For example it does not include variables that capture differences in the structure of production (such as whether an activity is credit intensive) or population differences (including such factors as age).[18]

The Effect of Judicial Performance on Lending

The following reduced-form equation was used to test for the influence of judicial transaction costs on the size of the loan market in each province:

$$(CRP/GDP)_{it} = \alpha + \beta_1 PUB_{it} + \beta_2 DES_{it} + \beta_3 RP95 + \beta_4 CALL_t + \beta_5 JUS_i + \varepsilon_{it},$$

where $JUS_i = JUS1$ or $JUS2$ or $JUSMR$.

Table 4.11 shows the results of estimations of three separate specifications that use different variables to measure judicial performance in Argentine provinces. In equation 1 credit behavior (as a percentage of provincial GDP) is related to the $JUSMR$ ranking of the judicial system and a series of variables that control for other significant effects. Equation 2 differs from the previous one only by the $JUS1$ variable (the index of judicial performance divided by the share of each province's loans in total countrywide loans). The index varies between 0 and 1, with the highest value corresponding to the poorest judicial performance. Equation 3 relates the dependent variable with the alternative $JUS2$ judicial system index (the index of judicial performance divided by the share of branches).

---

[18] These differences could be captured by a fixed-effects specification, but that exercise would prevent the inclusion of the JUS variable because of collinearity problems.

Table 4.11. Credit Equations

Variable	Equation 1	Equation 2	Equation 3
C	0.3250	0.3060	0.2698
	(7.5088)	(7.5514)	(7.1643)
PUB	−0.0267	−0.0320	−0.0342
	(−2.6283)	(−3.0806)	(−2.9941)
DES	−0.0048	−0.0044	−0.0033
	(−2.5893)	(−2.4495)	(−1.7866)
CALL	−0.0500	−0.0509	−0.0463
	(−1.8179)	(−1.8228)	(−1.6234)
RP95	−0.0366	−0.0413	−0.0289
	(−1.1481)	(−1.2463)	(−0.8555)
D95	0.0211	0.0198	0.0161
	(1.0919)	(1.0084)	(0.8149)
JUSMR	−0.0049		
	(−3.8713)		
JUS1		−0.1190	
		(−3.7355)	
JUS2			−0.0661
			(−2.5840)
R^2	0.2127	0.1870	0.1175
Adjusted R^2	0.1783	0.1514	0.0788
F–statistic	6.1704	5.2514	3.0387
Prob(F–statistic)	0.0000	0.0001	0.0080

Note: The dependent variable is CRP/PBG. See Box 4.1 for variable definitions. The sample is for 1992-97 for 24 provinces in Argentina. The variance-covariance matrix is estimated by White's method to correct for heteroskedastic errors. *t*-statistics are in parentheses.

Source: Authors' calculations.

The results are consistent with the hypothesis that poor judicial performance has a negative effect on the credit market. When measured by the ranking of provinces (the variable *JUSMR* in equation 1), judicial efficiency accounts for a difference of nearly 11 points in the loan/GDP ratio between the provinces with the best and worst ratings. Judicial efficiency also accounts for a difference of 5.6 points between the average province and that with the worst rating. Regression 2 is based on the *JUS1* indicator, which takes into account not only the ranking but also the level of judicial performance. The results are consistent with those of regression 1. If the worst province were to move to the position of the best in terms of legal performance, the resulting increase in credit market size would be virtually the same as that estimated by regression 1. If it were to increase to the average value of judicial performance, its loans outstanding would rise by an estimated 7.7 percentage points of GDP—a somewhat larger value than what was obtained from regression 1.

With the *JUS2* variable the effect of judicial performance is slightly lower, as shown by the estimated coefficients of regression 3, but still highly significant. If all Argentine provinces had the judicial performance of the top province, the increase in the level of credit in terms of national GDP would be close to 2 percent. If below-average provinces converged to the average level, total loans would increase by 0.3 of a percentage point of GDP.[19,20] The conclusion is clear: judicial performance is a highly significant variable affecting credit growth in Argentina and in fact constrains it.

Moreover, the signs of the control variables suggest the following interpretations. A province that has privatized its provincial bank has a lower volume of private-sector credit. In terms of GDP the effect is a decrease of between 2.7 and 3.5 percent (see the variable *PUB*). Taking into account that in 1992-97 average private sector credit in Argentine provinces was 16.5

---

[19] These figures are influenced by the concentration of credit in Buenos Aires, which is considered the jurisdiction with the best judicial performance.

[20] The construction of JUS1 includes the inverse of total loans by province, allowing for an intuitive interpretation of this index as a proxy of provincial transaction costs owing to judicial ineffectiveness per dollar of loan in each province. However, the fact that loans to the private sector by province are the numerator of the dependent variable and that total loans by province appear as a denominator in the index in the right-hand side of the equation may affect the results. In particular it may bias the sign of the coefficient of the judicial ineffectiveness variable. However, the results obtained with the JUS1 variable are consistent with those obtained with the JUS2 variable, in which the scaling variable is the number of provincial branches rather than total provincial loans. (The inverse of the number of branches is not significantly correlated with the regression's dependent variable.) Together with the natural interpretation of the coefficient of the JUS1 variable, this point made it advisable to keep this result. The authors wish to thank Marco Pagano for raising this point.

percent of GDP, the privatization of provincial banks during this period can be considered an important explanation for the change in total credit to the private sector. The coefficient of the unemployment rate variable (*DES*), which is used as a proxy for the level of local economic activity, indicates that an increase of one percentage point in the unemployment rate causes a reduction in private-sector credit of approximately 0.45 percent in terms of GDP.

The coefficient of the interest rate for interbank loans, *CALL*, captures the impact of the cost of credit on credit volumes. This coefficient shows that an increase of one percentage point in interest rates reduces credit to the private sector by 0.5 percent of GDP. Contrary to expectations, the share of loans granted by regional banks (*RP95*) has a negative if imprecisely estimated coefficient. Finally, 1995 (the year of the Tequila crisis) was not particularly different relative to other years, in that the coefficient of the corresponding dummy variable (*D95*) does not differ significantly from 0. The effects of that critical year may be captured by other variables, such as the interest and unemployment rates.

Judicial Performance and the Quality of the Loan Portfolio

The analysis next tests the hypothesis that legal performance affects the stock of nonperforming loans through factors affecting willingness to pay (the second hypothesis). The estimate is expressed in the following reduced form equation, which relates the proportion of credit in arrears with the performance of the judicial system, again controlling for macroeconomic fluctuations and structural changes within the banking system. To capture changes in the regulations that affect how nonperforming loans are calculated, the equation includes a dummy variable for 1992.[21]

$$(CRPA/CRP)_{it} = \alpha + \beta_1 PUB_{it} + \beta_2 DES_{it} + \beta_3 RP95_i + \beta_4 CALL_t + \beta_5 D92 + \beta_6 JUS_i + \varepsilon_{it},$$

where $JUS_i = JUS1$ or $JUS2$ or $JUSMR$.

---

[21] Other changes in the relevant regulations at other dates did not appear significant to the analysis.

The results are shown in Table 4.12. As in the previous table, they are very robust. The judicial performance indicator is statistically significant and has the expected sign.

Regression 1, which includes the ranking *JUSMR* as an indicator of judicial performance, shows that the province with the worst performance

Table 4.12. Nonperforming Loans Equations

Variable	Equation 1	Equation 2	Equation 3
C	−0.3771	−0.3595	−0.3213
	(−3.5174)	(−3.2935)	(−2.7366)
PUB	−0.0448	−0.0385	−0.0338
	(−1.7236)	(−1.4911)	(−1.2181)
DES	0.0016	0.0014	−0.0006
	(0.5358)	(0.4752)	(−0.1790)
CALL	0.9495	0.9550	0.9918
	(5.3889)	(5.3145)	(5.0467)
RP95	0.0315	0.0410	0.0196
	(0.8356)	(1.0654)	(0.4468)
D92	−0.7038	−0.7063	−0.7356
	(−6.1238)	(−6.0176)	(−5.7390)
JUSMR	0.0070		
	(3.8001)		
JUS1		0.1835	
		(3.4706)	
JUS2			0.0881
			(2.2546)
R^2	0.2967	0.2921	0.2335
Adjusted R^2	0.2659	0.2611	0.2000
F-statistic	9.6351	9.4250	6.9592
Prob(F-statistic)	0.0000	0.0000	0.0000

Note: The dependent variable is CRPA/CRP. See Box 4.1 for variable definitions. The sample is for 1992-97 for 24 provinces in Argentina. The variance-covariance matrix is estimated by White's method to correct for heteroskedastic errors. *t*-statistics are in parentheses.

Source: Authors' calculations.

has arrears averaging 16 percent more than the top-performing province and 8 percent more than the average. The corresponding estimates in regression 2, which relates arrears to the variable $JUS1$, are 18 and 12 percent, respectively. In contrast to the results shown in the credit equation, the results of the judicial performance ranking ($JUSMR$) differ significantly from those obtained with the indices $JUS1$ and $JUS2$. This finding indicates that the absolute differences in judicial performance and not just the ranking of provinces affect the amount of arrears. For the allocation of credit among provinces, only the relative position is important.

The response of arrears to the control variables is also interesting, although not directly relevant to the judicial system. The existence of a public provincial bank increases the proportion of the portfolio that is in arrears. The PUB variable indicates that privatizing a bank implies a 4 percent reduction in arrears (as a fraction of the total private loan portfolio).[22] At the same time, and contrary to what might be expected, the more important regional banks are in a province, the greater the provincial arrears. The participation of regional banks in the local credit market ($RP95$) indicates that a province where regional banks have a share of local credit that is 10 percent higher than it is in other provinces has a higher incidence of arrears (approximately 0.3 percent). However, the statistical significance of the relevant coefficient is low.

With cyclical variables the nonperforming loan ratio is positively related to the unemployment rate (DES) and to the interbank interest rate ($CALL$). While the coefficient of unemployment is imprecisely estimated, that of the interest rate is highly significant and indicates that an increase of one percentage point in the interest rate increases private sector arrears by almost 10 percent. This coefficient captures the increased difficulty debtors confront in repaying their debts when the interest rate increases unexpectedly, because the rate of interest on bank loans is correlated with that on interbank loans. This coefficient may also capture an adverse selection effect induced by the increase in the interest rate, even though this effect cannot be separately identified in the estimates.

The statistically significant effects can be described as follows:

- The credit/GDP regressions suggest that loans outstanding are lower in provinces where judicial enforcement is less effective.

---

[22] This result is explained in part by the privatization process and clean-up of the portfolio in arrears, which was retained by the state.

Table 4.13. Elasticities

Equation	JUS variable	CRP/PBG Coeff.	Elasticity	CRPA/CRP Coeff.	Elasticity	Mean of JUS variable
1	JUSMR	−0.0049	−0.3703	0.0069	0.3174	12.5000
2	JUS1	−0.1190	−0.2518	0.1835	0.2327	0.3494
3	JUS2	−0.0661	−0.1401	0.0880	0.1119	0.3502

- The arrears regressions show that judicial ineffectiveness and interest rate hikes increase the proportion of nonperforming loans.

- Privatizing a provincial bank increases the availability of credit and reduces the amount of nonperforming loans.

Table 4.13 summarizes the results in terms of the elasticities of credit and the ratio of the nonperforming portfolio to judicial performance.

According to these elasticities, the average province would benefit substantially from even relatively small improvements in judicial institutions.[23] A 10-percent improvement in judicial efficiency is associated with an expansion of the credit-to-GDP ratio of between 1.4 and 3.7 percent and with a decrease in nonperforming loans of between 1.1 and 3.2 percent.

Concluding Remarks

The efficacy of contractual regulations depends not only on the norms they contain but also on how courts interpret and apply them. In Argentina both legal costs and judicial effectiveness vary greatly among provinces. The data used here cover a number of provinces and time periods in order to test the implications of variations in the performance of the legal system that could affect the credit market.

---

[23] A 10-percent decrease in each judicial indicator may be interpreted as moving up to the next position in the ranking.

Overall, it is clear that improving the effectiveness of the legal system would yield significant economic benefits for Argentina. Judicial effectiveness plays an important role in increasing the total amount of credit available and in reducing the stock of nonperforming loans. For example, if the effectiveness of legal enforcement nationwide reached the level of the province with the best judicial enforcement (the city of Buenos Aires), credit would grow by some 2 percent of GDP at the national level. For the provinces with the worst judicial performance, the improvement could be as much as 11 percent of provincial GDP. Implementing the needed reforms remains an important challenge that needs to be addressed if Argentina is to enjoy the benefits of fully developed financial markets.

CHAPTER 5

Credit Markets in Brazil: The Role of Judicial Enforcement and Other Institutions

Armando Castelar Pinheiro and Célia Cabral

Sound financial markets have long been recognized as essential to economic development. Not only do they help mobilize savings to finance investment and production, but they also contribute to economic efficiency through their role in selecting and monitoring investment projects. In many low and middle-income countries, however, financial markets have found little room to flourish. Poor economic policies and market failures are usually blamed for the absence of well-developed financial markets. Macroeconomic instability increases credit risk, and low, unevenly distributed income reduces market size and increases unit costs. High risk and costs keep interest rates high as well, limiting the pool of viable projects and increasing default rates. Furthermore, the shortage of well-trained labor and the high cost of information make it difficult for banks to assess borrowers' ability to repay their loans. As a result, very little credit flows to the private sector.

Recent studies have suggested another explanation for the underdevelopment of financial markets in developing countries: institutional failure. The role of institutions in fostering economic development has long been recognized, but the link to financial markets has been made only recently. The theory is grounded in the concept of contract rights.

Armando Castelar Pinheiro heads the Economics Department of the National Economic and Social Development Bank (BNDES). He is also a researcher at the Center for the Study of Reforming the State and Professor of Economics at the Federal University of Rio de Janeiro. Célia Cabral is Professor of Economics at the New University of Lisbon. This study was carried out at the Institute of Pure and Applied Mathematics and the Center for Studies on State Reform. Extended versions of the sections on credit markets and loan recovery appear in Castelar Pinheiro and Cabral (1998).

Secure contract rights are essential if financial institutions are to function as the "brain" of the economy. Shleifer and Vishny (1996) discuss how weak contract enforcement reduces debtors' willingness to pay and thus creditors' willingness to lend. La Porta *et al.* (1998) assemble a data set on legal mechanisms for protecting investors' rights and on the enforcement of such rights in 49 countries. The researchers found that legal rules, judicial enforcement, and accounting standards differ greatly and systematically across countries. In another study, La Porta *et al.* (1997) show empirically that markets in countries with sound legal environments are broader and more highly valued than markets in countries with weak legal frameworks.

Although much progress has been made in understanding the importance of institutional failure in explaining creditors' unwillingness to finance firms and individuals, the empirical literature still has one important shortcoming: it does not distinguish among the effects of legal protection, accounting standards, and judicial enforcement. This chapter tries to close that gap by analyzing the discrete effect of judicial enforcement on the performance of credit markets.

The literature has emphasized the importance of efficient judicial systems to the development of complex intertemporal transactions, such as those taking place in credit markets (Castelar Pinheiro 1996; Williamson 1995). Williamson in fact suggests that one indirect measure of the quality of a judicial system is the complexity of the economic transactions the system is able to support. Castelar Pinheiro (1998) shows that judicial inefficiency reduces output growth in Brazil and presents anecdotal evidence that the inefficient enforcement of loan contracts reduces loan volume and increases the price of credit.

This chapter begins with a description of Brazil's credit markets, the legal and judicial institutions protecting creditors, and the alternative institutions that substitute for good judicial enforcement of credit contracts. The analysis uses judicial performance as a measure to assess differences among credit markets in various states. The findings suggest that governments need to foster the sound judicial institutions credit markets require. Because developing such institutions takes time, however, governments should also support private sector institutions that act as effective substitutes.

Brazil's Credit Markets

Since the launching of the *Plano Real* in 1994, credit to households (other than for home purchases) has posted very high growth rates. Meanwhile, however, the overall volume of performing credit as a percentage of gross domestic product (GDP) has fallen (Table 5.1).[1] Two factors contributing to this decrease are the decline in loans to the public sector owing to privatization, and the substitution of other forms of credit for bank loans, including credit cards, securities, and direct retail credit.

Banks, particularly private banks, concentrate their credit operations on working capital loans, export finance, credit for the acquisition of goods by firms and households, and personal loans and overdraft facilities. Together, the 10 most common types of short-term credit to firms amounted to 6.0 percent of GDP at the end of 1996 and 5.7 percent at the end of 1997, or roughly half the total credit to private industry, commerce, and other services. The equivalent totals for households were 1.7 and 2.0 percent of GDP, or about two-thirds of the total nonhousing credit extended by the financial system. Most of this credit is short term.

The banking sector includes a relatively large number of public institutions created to enable credit activities that would not flourish naturally in a highly inflationary environment. State banks account for about 60 percent of all deposits and assets and virtually all long-term credit, including almost all credit for business investment and housing. They also account for almost all lending to the public sector. Their loans to the private sector have traditionally been concentrated in the industrial, housing, and rural sectors and are the primary type of lending in the latter two areas. In 1997 public banks accounted for 52.1 percent of all performing loans, private national banks for 36.2 percent, and foreign banks for the remaining 11.7 percent.

One reason for the low volume of bank credit in Brazil is the very high real interest rate firms and households face as a result of banks' high borrowing rates and large spreads. The high passive rate (the rate at which banks borrow) is mainly a consequence of overreliance on tight monetary policy,

---

[1] This is unlike the overall stock of credit, which went up quite substantially as a result of a large increase in the volume of overdue and defaulted loans. This contrast was particularly marked for loans to the private sector.

Table 5.1. **Financial System Lending: Performing Loans in Brazil, 1988-97**
(percentage of GDP)

Sector, type of loan	1988	1989	1990	1991	1992	1993	1994	1995	1996	1997
Public sector										
Federal government	3.9	2.0	1.7	1.4	1.3	1.6	1.1	0.8	0.6	0.4
States and municipalities	5.7	4.4	4.3	3.1	4.3	4.1	3.6	3.9	4.7	2.2
Total[a]	9.6	6.4	6.0	4.6	5.6	5.7	4.7	4.8	5.3	2.5
Private sector										
Industry	5.7	3.6	4.5	4.1	5.8	11.1	6.8	6.7	6.2	6.1
Housing	9.3	10.4	7.9	5.4	7.8	7.4	7.9	7.2	6.2	5.8
Rural	2.5	1.2	1.7	2	2.4	2.3	2.9	3.1	2.2	2.4
Commerce	3.8	0.8	1.1	1.2	1.7	2.5	3.3	2.9	2.6	2.2
Household credit[b]	0.8	0.5	0.3	0.5	0.8	1.1	2.7	1.8	2.4	3.2
Other services[c]	1.9	1.2	1.6	1.4	2.5	3.7	3.6	3.0	2.6	2.5
Total	23.9	17.7	17.2	14.6	20.9	28.2	27.2	24.6	22.3	22.4
Financial system total	33.5	24	23.2	19.1	26.5	33.9	32	29.4	27.6	24.9

a. Includes state enterprises.

b. Includes all credit to individuals other than for housing.

c. Includes foundations, institutes, and other institutions maintained with public sector budgetary funds.

Note: Values do not include the special compulsory social security fund (*Fundo de Garantia de Tempo de Servico*, or FGTS), which earns the reference rate (TR) plus 3 percent per year and from which workers can withdraw money only if they are laid off, retire, or marry. All ratios are calculated with the stock of loans and IGP-DI as of December 31 and GDP measured at end-of-year prices. The IGP-DI is a general price index made up of the consumer price index (30 percent), wholesale prices (60 percent) and construction prices (10 percent).

Source: Central Bank.

which has substituted for a more effective fiscal policy since 1994. In 1994-97 the real interest rate on federal government securities averaged 21.5 percent per year—close to the rate banks pay on their certificates of deposit. The large spreads have several causes: taxes levied on loans, the high compulsory levels for current account and time deposit balances, and banks' low productivity, particularly in credit-granting activities. Although the problem is widespread throughout the banking sector, it is particularly significant for public banks, which are responsible for a large proportion of the banking sector's activities and are much more inefficient than their private counterparts (McKinsey Corporation 1998).

Firms pay lower interest rates than households. Still, annual interest rates on working capital loans averaged 74 percent in 1995-97, against a mean annual inflation rate of 12 percent. Typical loans to households (other than for house purchases) include overdraft accounts and loans for consumption and personal credit. Annual interest rates for these loans in 1995-97 averaged 124.7 percent, 144.2 percent, and 198.0 percent, respectively. Real interest rates for loans indexed to the exchange rate are much lower than those for loans in reais because of the cost of hedging against a devaluation. In 1995-97 the two most popular types of loans indexed to the dollar had average annual interest rates of 20.3 percent and 31.8 percent, respectively, including the exchange rate devaluation.[2]

Interest rates on development bank credit and home purchase loans are much lower. Development banks finance a large share of nonhousing investment, charging rates that vary from the standard long-term interest rate (TJLP) to the TJLP plus 6 percent annually. In 1995-97 the TJLP averaged 16.4 percent annually. Mortgages, however, are governed by two systems. The *Sistema Financeiro da Habitação* (financial system for housing,

---

[2] The loans were Advancement of Foreign Exchange Contracts (loans to exporters guaranteed by an export contract, abbreviated as ACC in Portuguese) and Resolution 63 loans (bank loans indexed to the foreign exchange rate and funded with resources borrowed in foreign markets). ACC interest rates are lower than those for Resolution 63 because the credit risk is lower. While Resolution 63 debtors are national firms or banks, ACC debtors are importers buying the goods to be exported. ACC loans are also secured by the exportable goods, which have already left the country when the loan is granted. Therefore, ACC creditors do not incur the risk associated with Brazil as a country from either a macroeconomic or judicial point of view. Any application to the judiciary to recover a loan takes place in the importing country.

SFH) is strictly regulated by the government, which sets caps on the value of eligible houses and loans. The *Carteira Hipotecária* (mortgage portfolio) allows banks to set contract conditions. Loans are financed primarily by savings accounts, which pay an interest rate (fixed by the government) equal to the reference rate (TR) plus 6 percent annually and carry a government guarantee. With the SFH system borrowers pay a fixed rate of TR plus 12 percent annually (in 1995-97, this rate amounted to 32.5 percent). In the *Carteira Hipotecária* system, the rate ranges from TR plus 14 percent to TR plus 16 percent.

Another reason for Brazil's high interest rates is the relatively high default rate: the ratios of overdue and default loans to performing loans averaged 3.3 and 29.2 percent, respectively, in 1997-98.[3] Public banks have the highest default rate, followed by national private and foreign banks. Private sector borrowers, however, are largely responsible for these high averages. The stock of nonperforming debts at the end of 1997 had approximately the same value as the stock of performing loans, largely because of the high interest rates and penalties levied on the former. A survey by the National Association of Finance, Administration and Accounting Executives showed that banks charge monthly penalties ranging from 9.8 to 16.0 percent on overdue personal loans and overdrafts of accounts that exceed their credit limit.[4] Table 5.2 attempts to net out these two components from the stock of nonperforming loans. At the end of 1997, the original stock of loans overdue and in default accounted for just 8 percent of the total stock of nonperforming loans. The default rate, measured as the ratio of loans overdue and in default to the total stock of extended loans, net of income to appropriate, equaled 7.2 percent.[5]

---

[3] The Central Bank considers a debt overdue if it has been due for over 60 days. Loans are considered in default when they have been overdue for more than 180 days and have guarantees that are not considered sufficient. Even with satisfactory guarantees, loans are in default when they are more than 360 days past due. The reported values include interest and penalties, calculated on an accrual basis.

[4] Reported in *O Globo*, August 23, 1998, p. 37.

[5] *Income to appropriate* means the interest and penalties that should have accrued to the creditor on the loan, or the difference between the nominal value of the debt and the original principal.

Table 5.2. Total Loans of the Financial System by Payment Status, 1995-97
(millions of R$)

Item	Description	1995	1996	1997
(a)	Performing loans	209,309	245,846	255,137
(b)	Overdue loans	7,529	5,351	5,430
(c)	Defaulted loans	64,514	107,815	247,634
(d)	Overdue plus defaulted loans	72,343	113,166	253,064
(e) = (a) + (d)	Total	281,652	359,012	508,201
(f)	Income to appropriate	43,766	95,607	233,137
(g) = (e) − (f)	Total net of income to appropriate	237,886	263,405	275,064
(h) = (d) − (f)	Overdue and defaulted loans net of income to appropriate	28,577	17,559	19,927
(i) = (h)/(g)	Default rate (percent)	12.01	6.67	7.24

Note: These figures include the social security fund (*Fundo de Garantia de Tempo de Servico,* or FGTS) and for this reason differ from those reported in Table 5.1.
Source: Central Bank.

Recovering a Loan: What Are a Creditor's Alternatives?

When a debtor defaults, the branch that extended the loan initiates recovery. If necessary, the credit recovery department of the bank takes over the process, at which point extrajudicial collection formally starts. Nonperforming debtors face heavy penalties, which, combined with the high rates of interest, cause the debt to mushroom. As a consequence, banks usually renegotiate debts with large discounts, at times recovering a mere 40 percent of the outstanding value (an amount that may nevertheless exceed the loan's original value).

If extrajudicial collection fails, creditors may choose to take their case to court. The legal action used least, because it takes so long, is the *ordinary action*. It starts with a *cognizance action*, in which the plaintiff tries to establish that a debt of a given value exists and is due. The defendant has 15 days to respond before the debt is considered executable, or liquid, certain, and due.[6] However, if the judge is not convinced of the existence, value, or maturity of the debt, a judicial process begins. In this case a creditor may proceed to the *execution action* only after a favorable court ruling. The execution action requires the defendant to pay the debt or name assets that can be held as a guarantee of payment (*penhora* of the assets) within 24 hours. If the debtor does not comply, a court officer lists the assets for the *penhora*. The execution action is suspended until either the court officer or the creditor locates such assets. Only after the *penhora* is complete can the case be judged. Although from a legal point of view the process is no different for secured and unsecured loans (in both cases the creditor must go through the motions described here), the existence of a real guarantee insures that there will be assets for the *penhora*.

Debtors who want to defend themselves do so through another judicial action called an *embargo to the execution action*. Typical embargoes argue that interest rates are too high, that an asset may not be used in the *penhora* because it is essential if the firm is to continue operating and eventually pay back the debt, or that loss of an asset will also result in job loss (an argument to which many judges are sensitive). The embargo may also contest the use of compound interest, which many judges see as illegal. In some cases the debtor argues that the person who signed the contract was not authorized to do so. If after the *penhora* the debtor has still not paid and has failed to get the judge to accept his embargo, the assets are publicly auctioned (or transferred to the creditor, if there are no interested buyers).

Some credit securities are ruled by specific legislation guaranteeing that they satisfy liquidity and certainty requirements. If a loan based on such securities is not paid when due, the creditor first notifies the public registry. This step is known as the protest of the security, or *protesto*. The creditor can then proceed directly to an execution action. For this reason, these securities are considered self-executable. Banks usually structure loans using these securities, because judicial collection in case of default is much faster than it would be otherwise. Banks only initiate a cognizance action if, owing to an error or to legal impediments, the loan contract is not an extrajudicial title.

Under certain conditions, a creditor may try to collect a debt by requesting that the debtor be declared bankrupt. Banks rarely follow this route,

---

[6] A debt is *liquid* when there is no doubt about the amount the debtor must pay. It is *certain* if it has been structured according to the law.

however, in part because bankruptcy legislation gives priority to debts involving workers and the tax authorities. In practice, however, these groups also do not initiate bankruptcy actions, since workers want to protect their jobs and the tax authorities, overwhelmed by a large number of tax evasion cases, suffer from inertia. Usually only after a firm stops paying suppliers and banks (generally the last to suffer in a default) does it run the risk of a bankruptcy request. In any case, the incentives to initiate bankruptcy actions are not strong, since the little that is left over after paying for lawyers and for court fees is generally barely enough to pay workers and the tax authorities, let alone any other debts.

Insolvent debtors may ask a judge to let the firm go into reorganization. A reorganization does not affect the debts the firm has with its employees and the tax authorities, credits secured by real guarantees, or privileged credits. It basically suspends payments only to unsecured creditors (usually, those that provide the firm's working capital, such as banks and suppliers). Although the law technically allows creditors to participate in the firm's reorganization process, it is practically impossible to interfere unless the owner consents. Because the reorganization dries up all sources of credit, firms that depend on supplier credit (such as retailers) tend to consent, and creditors often manage the whole reorganization process.

Overall, the legal procedures ruling judicial execution are perceived to be excessively cumbersome, with too many ways to postpone a decision. A cognizance action lasts, on average, five years. Once a decision is reached and the execution action begins, the debtor has five days after the *penhora* to present an embargo. In general, a judge takes about six months to rule on the merits of an embargo, but the decision may take much longer if the judge requests an expert opinion. Once the judge reaches a decision, the debtor can initiate another embargo action. The process of requesting embargoes may continue indefinitely. The debtor may also request negotiations at any time during the process, and the creditor is then asked to participate in good faith. And even after a judge has ruled on all embargoes and reached a decision, the debtor may still appeal to a higher court. In São Paulo, Brazil's financial center, the Appeals Court may take two years just to assign the case to a judge. An additional two years may pass until a decision is reached, and the debtor is again allowed to present embargoes. The entire process can take up to 10 years, depending on the creditor's case and the skill of the debtor's lawyers.

The cost of an action is yet another problem. Lawyers charge between 10 and 20 percent of the value of the debt. In Rio de Janeiro judicial costs include a fixed fee of R$42.83 plus a judicial tax of 2 percent of the value of the debt, with a floor of R$23.29 and a cap of R$10,000.00. Creditors also have to pay for such things as registering documents and having the court officer notify the debtor or list the assets for the *penhora*. The costs are so high that in general court action is worthwhile only when creditors have their own in-house lawyers and the loan exceeds a certain amount.

The Impact of Judicial Performance on Credit Markets: A Cross-State Analysis

In Brazil creditors perceive courts as providing weak protection against opportunistic behavior by borrowers. Even when the law clearly guarantees creditor rights, the judiciary often does not provide adequate enforcement. This analysis looks at the link between the quality of judicial enforcement and the credit market and attempts to determine whether the market's size depends on the quality of the judiciary. It takes advantage of Brazil's federal political system, under which laws protecting creditors apply nationwide but are enforced by state courts, to separate out the discrete impact of judicial inefficiency on credit markets. It also looks at differences across states in the size of credit markets and tests whether judicial performance explains these differences.

Data for 1997-98 show substantial differences in the volume of rural and nonrural credits across Brazil's regions and states. Most credit activity is concentrated in the southeast—around one-fourth of overall rural credit and two-thirds of the much larger total of other credits. In this region São Paulo is by far the state with the largest credit volume. Among other regions, the south accounts for a third of overall rural credit, the center-west region accounts for around a fourth, and the northeast accounts for 13 percent. Shares of other credits are relatively small in all regions outside the southeast. The north is the region with the least credit activity (around 2.4 percent of rural credit and 1.5 percent of other credits).

One important reason for the different regional and state shares in total credit is the size of the regional economies. There are, however, significant differences in the ratio of credit to GDP among regions and states that remained more or less stable in 1990-96. This fact suggests that the size of the economy is not the single (linear) explanation for the uneven distribution of credit among states. Judicial performance is a likely complementary explanation. According to Aith (1998, p. 94), judicial inefficiency is one factor that limits "the expansion of the [credit] sector's activities and, more importantly, considerably increases banks' spreads—by up to 30 percent, depending on the situation."

The quality of judicial enforcement is not uniform across Brazil's 27 states, for different reasons. First, in some states courts are less independent of the government and politically influential groups than in others. Second, some state courts (especially those on the lower level) are very "politicized"— that is, the interpretation of the law may change to accommodate judges' political views, especially in areas such as privatization and the legality of charging compound interest. Judges may also place more or less importance on the article of the Constitution stating that property has a "social role" to play (although this role is not defined). Some judges interpret this article as license to overrule contract clauses they see as opposing "social justice." Such judges feel it is their duty to redistribute income (or property) in what they perceive to be a fair way. Third, corruption is a bigger problem in some states than in others. Fourth, both court and lawyers' fees in credit recovery cases vary from one state to the other. And finally, training for judges is not uniform across the country. Judges in the more developed regions are perceived as better prepared.[7]

To gauge judicial performance, data are drawn from two surveys conducted by the Institute for Economic, Social, and Political Studies (IDESP) of São Paulo that asked businessmen in different states to rate the judiciary with respect to slowness, fairness, and costs (Castelar Pinheiro 1998). The first survey, with 602 responses, was carried out in the first semester of 1996; the second, answered by 279 businessmen, took place a year later. The two surveys included state enterprises, private national firms, and medium- to large-scale foreign companies. In both surveys the question concerning the respondent's view on the quality of judicial enforcement was exactly the same and was placed at the beginning of the questionnaire. The remainder

---

[7] Several lawyers raised this point in interviews. Some judges reportedly do not understand how leasing, factoring, and other less traditional credit operations work. One lawyer mentioned that a judge he was arguing before still used the old Civil Code, which has been revoked.

of the questionnaire differed. Respondents rated slowness as the worst of the three problems, followed by high costs and then unfairness. These results are used to build an index of judicial inefficiency for both years by calculating a simple average of the performance of the judiciary in each area in all states. Courts in the south and the southeast are ranked first and second, those in the center-west third, and those in the north and northeast are ranked fourth and last. However, the ratings varied widely across states in the same region and for the three judicial characteristics within states.

Regressions are run for the ratios of total, rural, and nonrural credit to GDP against per capita income and judicial inefficiency (Table 5.3). The regressions for total and rural credit also include the share of agricultural activities in GDP. The regressions are run using a panel of the 22 states covered by the IDESP surveys, using annual data from 1990-96 for the ratio of credit to GDP, per capita GDP, and the proportion of agricultural activities in state GDP.[8] The measure of judicial inefficiency is fixed for all years, and time effects are captured using year dummy variables. For each type of credit, six regressions were run for each specification of the dependent variable, all with per capita GDP as an explanatory variable. The first regression includes all observations (including the five states absent from the IDESP surveys) and excludes the variable for judicial inefficiency. The second repeats the same functional specification but considers only the states for which complete information is available. The third regression introduces the judicial inefficiency index as an explanatory variable. The other three equations use the same model, substituting the index of judicial inefficiency with separate indices for cost, slowness, and unfairness.

Overall, the regressions show a reasonable fit, statistically significant independent variables, and coefficients robust to model specification. The regressions provide persuasive empirical evidence that judicial inefficiency has a distinctly negative impact on the volume of credit extended by financial institutions. The regressions also provide several other noteworthy results.[9]

---

[8] The data used in the regressions are presented in Castelar Pinheiro and Cabral (1998). Because of the lack of information on judicial inefficiency, five states were left out of most of the regressions: Acre, Amapá, Rondônia, Roraima, and Tocantins. All five are in the northern region and are among the smallest states in Brazil, both demographically and economically.

[9] Both linear and log-linear specifications are estimated for each dependent variable, and although only the latter are reported in Table 5.3, the conclusions are essentially the same for

First, per capita GDP has a positive, statistically significant impact on the ratio of total and nonrural credits to GDP (it is not statistically significant for rural credit).[10] These coefficients remain essentially unchanged when estimating regression 1 in each block with fixed and random effects rather than with the judicial inefficiency index. But the significance of this coefficient is highly dependent on the inclusion of the Federal District (DF) in the panel of states. When the regressions are estimated without the DF, the coefficient of per capita GDP is no longer statistically significant. However, the coefficient of judicial inefficiency and its statistical significance are not sensitive to the exclusion of the DF from the panel.

Second, the single most significant variable for rural credit is the share of agricultural activities in GDP. Interpreting this variable is also statistically significant in the regressions for total credit. Interpreting this positive coefficient requires some thought, since initial expectations were that states with a relatively large proportion of agricultural activities would show proportionately less total credit activity (as opposed to the positive effect of rural activities on credit). A possible explanation is state intervention—that is, states with strong agricultural sectors are able to secure a disproportionate amount of rural credit, which is provided mainly by public banks. This result is consistent with anecdotal evidence showing that congressmen linked to agricultural interests are usually very successful at extracting government favors in the form of a large supply of credit.

Third, all measures of the quality of judicial enforcement, except for slowness, show a statistically significant impact on the ratio of total, rural,

both. Log-linear specifications are preferred because, in most cases, the Jarque-Bera test on the linear form rejects the null hypothesis that the residuals are normally distributed. For some regressions the hypothesis of homoskedasticity is rejected and t-statistics are derived using White's asymptotic covariance matrix. The regression residuals also display time-series autocorrelation, but reestimation with a Prais-Winsten correction reveals little change in coefficient estimates and their statistical significance. A comparison of equations 1 and 2 shows that the results are not sensitive to the exclusion of the five states for which no information is available. The coefficient of per capita GDP remains virtually unchanged, while that of the share of agricultural activities in GDP is only slightly reduced.

[10] The analysis does not deal with the possibility that per capita GDP could be endogenous, primarily because of the lack of adequate instrumental variables to test this hypothesis. However, per capita income at the state level is not much influenced by the volume of credit activity in the same or near periods, for two reasons. First, many other variables (such as education) are more important in determining per capita income. Second, economic agents in one state may easily access credit from banks in other states and incur only minor additional costs.

Table 5.3. Results of Cross-State Regressions

Variable	Log(total credit/GDP)							
	1	2	3	4	5	6	1	2
Constant	−2.9669	−2.5901	−0.7486	−1.7267	−2.5521	−1.7589	−4.8803	−4.7861
	(−16.47)	(−14.05)	(−1.87)	(−6.62)	(−4.56)	(−7.42)	(−22.05)	(−19.68)
Per capita	0.2235	0.2046	0.1350	0.1656	0.2038	0.1542	0.0058	0.0254
GDP	(6.11)	(5.87)	(3.85)	(4.87)	(5.33)	(4.56)	(0.158)	(0.72)
Share of	2.9262	1.4299	1.5078	0.9335	1.4462	0.7379	7.0117	6.4621
agricultural	(4.97)	(2.19)	(1.90)	(1.50)	(2.26)	(1.19)	(7.74)	(5.22)
Activity in								
GDP								
Index of			−2.8667					
judicial			(−5.08)					
Inefficiency								
Cost				−1.4306				
				(−4.44)				
Slowness					−0.0415			
					(−0.07)			
Unfairness						−2.0401		
						(−5.06)		
Dummy 1992							0.3346	
							(1.75)	
Dummy 1995	0.3041	0.3433	0.3574	0.3571	0.3432	0.3620		
	(1.92)	(2.17)	(2.44)	(2.40)	(1.96)	(2.47)		
Dummy 1996	0.3793	0.3425	0.3661	0.3565	0.3428	0.3608		
	(2.40)	(2.17)	(2.50)	(2.40)	(2.33)	(2.47)		
Adjusted R^2	0.231	0.236	0.3492	0.3256	0.2357	0.3483	0.3272	0.2389

Note: For total credit, normality is rejected in regression 1; in regression 5, t-statistics were calculated using White's consistent covariance estimates. For rural credit, White's consistent covariance estimates were used in all regressions; normality was rejected in all regressions but 4. For nonrural credit, no heteroskedasticity problems were encountered, but normality was rejected in regressions 1, 2, and 5.

log(rural credit/GDP)				log(nonrural credit/GDP)					
3	4	5	6	1	2	3	4	5	6
−3.0246	−3.7766	−5.4787	−3.9768	−2.8228	−2.6092	−0.7193	−1.7785	−2.5333	−1.9670
(−4.84)	(−10.81)	(−5.95)	(−11.56)	(−20.34)	(−20.24)	(−1.87)	(−8.38)	(−4.58)	(−10.60)
−0.0407	−0.0198	0.0411	−0.0231	0.1959	0.1937	0.1269	0.1638	0.1914	0.1619
(−1.00)	(−0.57)	(0.96)	(−0.66)	(5.28)	(5.91)	(3.85)	(5.23)	(5.22)	(5.12)
6.2025	5.8901	6.1647	5.7984						
(5.14)	(5.05)	(4.88)	(4.66)						
−2.7382						−3.0390			
(−3.34)						(−5.17)			
	−1.6690						−1.5664		
	(−3.88)						(−4.75)		
		0.7558						−0.0758	
		(0.80)						(−0.14)	
			−1.9802						−1.9117
			(−3.96)						(−4.57)
				0.4843	0.4284	0.4373	0.4324	0.4287	0.4327
				(2.66)	(2.60)	(2.87)	(2.80)	(2.59)	(2.79)
				0.6144	0.4885	0.5105	0.4983	0.4893	0.4990
				(3.37)	(2.95)	(3.34)	(3.22)	(2.95)	(3.21)
0.2783	0.2863	0.238	0.2793	0.1895	0.2390	0.3503	0.3347	0.2340	0.3280

and other credits to GDP, with relatively large t-statistics. Only for rural credit does one indicator of judicial inefficiency—slowness—show a sign opposite to what was expected, but without statistical significance. The problem with this variable is that the judiciary is perceived as very slow in all states, so that there is not enough variance to allow for a good estimation. Fourth, the index of judicial inefficiency generally results in a better fit than the other individual measures of judicial performance, as the higher values of adjusted R^2 indicate.

To assess the economic impact of the different variables on credit activity, the analysis looks at how the dependent variables changed with a one-standard-deviation increase in each explanatory variable (Table 5.4). Results for the linear equations indicate the increases in percentage points, and for the log regressions show the percentage increase in these ratios. It can be seen that the ratio of total credit to GDP goes up by 11.9 percentage points, or 25.8 percent, as a result of a one-standard-deviation increase in per capita GDP. That is, raising per capita income from R\$3,200 (1996 prices) to R\$4,900 increases the volume of credit by 12 percent of GDP. The corresponding results for nonrural and rural credit are 10.5 and 0.4 percentage points, respectively. The increase in the volume of nonrural credit is 24.1 percent,

Table 5.4. Sensitivity of the Credit-to-GDP Ratio to a One-Standard-Deviation Increase in Independent Variables

Variable	Standard deviation	Linear equations (increase in percentage points)			Log equations (percentage change)		
		Total credit	Rural credit	Other credit	Total credit	Rural credit	Other credit
Per capita GDP	1.6999	0.1187	0.0044	0.1045	25.80		24.08
Share of agricultural activities in GDP	0.1055	0.0537	0.0296		17.24	92.39	
Index of judicial inefficiency	0.0975	−0.0846	−0.0103	−0.0762	−24.38	−23.43	−25.64
Cost	0.1654	−0.0739	−0.0096	−0.0669	−21.07	−24.12	−22.82
Unfairness	0.1315	−0.0703	−0.0129	−0.0602	−23.53	−22.93	−22.23

while for rural credit the increase is roughly equal to a tenth of the simple average of the ratio of rural credit to GDP across the 27 states.

Table 5.4 confirms the high sensitivity of the ratio of rural credit to GDP to the share of agricultural activities in GDP. A one-standard-deviation increase in this variable causes the ratio to expand by almost 3 percentage points, an increase of roughly 92 percent. For total credit the corresponding figures are 5.4 percentage points and 17.2 percent, respectively. These results are less significant than they may seem. The share of agriculture in GDP would have to go up by 10.6 percentage points (a 77 percent increase, on average) for the volume of total credit to rise by 15 percent (an elasticity of roughly 0.19).

The most important result is the high sensitivity of the ratios of total, rural, and nonrural credit to GDP to the quality of judicial enforcement. This result is robust to the measure of judicial performance used. A one-standard-deviation increase in the index of judicial inefficiency (a deterioration of the quality of judicial enforcement) reduces the ratio of rural credit to GDP by 1.0 percentage point. For nonrural and total credit, the reductions are 7.6 and 8.5 percentage points, respectively. In all three cases the credit contraction is in the range of 21-25 percent. The impact of the judicial inefficiency index is thus of the same order of magnitude as that of per capita GDP, suggesting that differences in the quality of judicial enforcement are as important as per capita income differentials in explaining cross-state differences in the ratio of credit to GDP. The results indicate that increasing the volume of credit by 8.5 percent of GDP requires improving the average grade of judicial enforcement by 17.8 percent—the equivalent of lowering the proportions of "bad" and "very bad" assessments from 54.8 to 45.1 percent.

Ensuring Willingness to Pay

The Brazilian legal and judicial systems offer creditors relatively weak protection and inefficient judicial enforcement is a significant obstacle to the expansion of credit activities. The volume of lending in Brazil would be even lower, however, were it not for contracting arrangements and institutions that attempt to circumvent the ineffectiveness of the courts. In Brazil these contractual relationships, which differ from those implicit in classical contract law, enable certain types of credit transactions that would otherwise be unfeasible in an environment of weak creditor protection. These forms of governance rely mainly on the private ordering of contracts, as opposed to judicial enforcement. Three such institutions are discussed here in the context of specific credit activities: the informational infrastructure (such as credit histories and related records), public banks, and mechanisms that rely on peer pressure to ensure repayment.

A Theoretical Model

Institutions that provide information on potential borrowers reduce the risk of default and have a positive impact on the volume of credit. But such institutions have an added benefit: they increase the likelihood that debtors will repay loans, using mechanisms such as reputation. In Chapter 2 of this volume, Jappelli and Pagano provide evidence (based on international credit databases) that is consistent with this hypothesis. In particular, lending activity appears to be positively correlated with the presence of such databanks. They argue that these information effects may explain why central banks forcibly create public credit registries, particularly when creditor protection is poor and alternative private arrangements for sharing information are lacking.

Reliable and readily available information on borrowers is an important feature of the Brazilian credit market. The interviews show that creditors perceive ex ante screening mechanisms as their best protection against bad debtors. A simple theoretical model helps demonstrate the importance of informational factors in determining the cost and availability of credit.[11] Two types of borrowers are posited. Type-1 borrowers pay back their loans in full. Type-2 borrowers always default, but renegotiation allows the bank to recover the principal plus a return of $r(1 - \alpha)$ (r is the loan interest rate). Proportion π of borrowers belongs to this group. It is then assumed that r is set to equal the expected return to the risk-free interest rate i plus a risk premium:

(5.1) $$r(1 - \alpha\pi) = 1 + a\sigma_{return}$$

where:

(5.2) $$\sigma^2_{return} = r^2\alpha^2\pi(1 - \pi).$$

---

[11] See Castelar Pinheiro (1996) for the full model.

From this equation it is possible to derive:

(5.3)
$$r = \frac{i}{1 - \alpha\pi\left(1 + a\sqrt{\dfrac{1-\pi}{\pi}}\right)}.$$

Clearly, the larger the values of α, π and a, the higher r/i will be. While a reflects risk aversion, α and π depend directly on the protection the law and the courts award creditors against type-2 borrowers. With laws and courts that protect creditors, type-2 borrowers would settle for a low α. The value of α and the possibility of being penalized by the courts then determine the value of π.

This simple model may capture the way creditors in Brazil have reacted to the unexpected rise in default rates that followed the explosion in consumer credit after price stabilization. Because households had no access to credit during the high-inflation period, they did not have credit histories and were not aware of the consequences of defaulting on loans. In turn, creditors had little information that might have allowed them to discriminate among borrowers (and little practice in making such distinctions). As the model predicts, creditors reacted by charging very high interest rates so the expected returns would remain positive despite the high values of π and α. In practice, however, if π and α are too large, r is much larger than i, and even type-1 borrowers become a bad credit risk. This situation generates a low-level equilibrium with low credit volumes, high default rates, and very high interest rates.

A simple extension of this model helps to clarify the role of information sharing in protecting lenders and increasing borrowers' willingness to pay. The assumption is that an institution collects credit-rating information and makes it available for the fee f. With this information the probability of lending to a type-2 borrower falls from π to ρ ($\rho<\pi$). In this case both the expected value and the variance of the bank's return on the loan change, so that:

(5.4)
$$E(return)\,|_{with\ info} = r(1 - \alpha\rho) - f,$$

and

(5.5)
$$\sigma_r^2\,|_{with\ info} = r^2\alpha^2\rho(1-\rho).$$

The interest rate is then determined by:

$$(5.6) \qquad r = \frac{i+f}{1 - \alpha\rho\left(1 + a\sqrt{\dfrac{1-\rho}{\rho}}\right)}.$$

The model demonstrates that the two key determinants of the cost of credit are the cost of obtaining information on borrowers and creditors' ability to use the information (and thus reduce the probability of lending to a type-2 borrower). Moreover, information-sharing and good legal and judicial systems reduce interest rates through different channels. Information-sharing operates by reducing the proportion of bad debtors who manage to obtain credit. Legal and judicial systems operate by directly lowering the actual proportion of bad debtors and the losses they impose on banks.[12]

Credit Bureaus

Several information-sharing institutions that collect data on potential debtors are available in Brazil. On request they will run credit checks on individuals and companies, as well as on the owners and top managers of a firm. In general, just being listed as a bad credit risk is enough to exclude a person or a firm from the credit market, and creditors negotiating with debtors are able to use the threat of reporting them as bad risks to win concessions.

The Returned Check Register

The main public databank creditors use is the Returned Check Register, which lists all the people in Brazil who have issued checks with insufficient funds. This register is managed by the Central Bank and is particularly useful for credit analysis, since checks are widely used in Brazil (a practice inherited from the high-inflation period). Banks are required to supply information on returned checks. Once an individual's name is included in this register, it remains there for five years, a period during which that person is not al-

---

[12] But information-sharing mechanisms also help reduce the actual probability of default π, since type-2 borrowers know that the probability of borrowing again once they default on a loan will be much lower.

lowed to have a bank account. Another but less important public databank is the Register of Defaulters, which was originally intended only for public financial institutions. Currently, however, all public institutions may submit information to the register, whether or not the information is related to credit activities. This register is not available to private creditors.

Credit Protection Service

The Credit Protection Service (SPC) comprises around 1,200 established, nonprofit municipal institutions overseen by local Associations of Retailers (CDLs). The SPC includes information only about individuals, and only on commercial or trade-related debts, not on noncommercial debts such as those to schools or landlords. While much of this information is specific to the city or locale, the institutions exchange information among themselves, in effect forming a national network. The SPC's databank contains information collected from retailers, banks, credit card administrators, financial firms, and other sources. The national Association of Retailers manages another databank that collects similar information about firms. This databank also provides information on *protestos* and on debtors against whom judicial actions have been initiated. The CDL also tells members whether restrictions have been placed on customers' checks.

Private Credit Bureaus

The two main private credit bureaus in Brazil that collect and sell information on borrowers are SERASA (Centralized Bank Services, which has been acquired by Equifax) and SCI (Secure Credit and Information). Both operate nationwide. Other similar but smaller firms, such as Seta and Asteca, service only the main markets, especially São Paulo, where the largest banks are located. SERASA was created in 1968 by three of Brazil's main banks, but currently all medium and large Brazilian banks are shareholders. It has 1,400 employees and offices in all state capitals and main cities. It maintains large databases on firms and individuals (including addresses, personal and professional information, financial commitments, negative records, and financial and economic analyses). SERASA relies primarily on information from other databanks (including the Central Bank's) and on information banks supply directly. SERASA offers creditors a menu of

products, from simple checks on "black lists" to more sophisticated information on credit limits and risk of default. Access to some of these products is conditional on reciprocity.

SCI offers products similar to SERASA's. However, SCI's services are
not based on reciprocity, so a client may obtain information without providing any in return. However, SCI does try to enforce reciprocity with an
incentive system that offers discounts for sharing information. In recent years,
demand for SCI's services has expanded substantially, but the company remains much less important than SERASA.

Postdated Checks

Information-sharing institutions have been an essential part of the recent
expansion of financing for nondurable goods, a phenomenon that is largely
ignored in Central Bank statistics. Since 1994, retailers have been financing
sales of clothes, footwear, toys, foodstuffs, and similar goods by installments.
Even services are often paid for in this way. The instrument that has made
this form of financing possible is the postdated check. In São Paulo about 36
percent of all sales are paid for using postdated checks, against 37 percent in
cash and 21 by credit card (Table 5.5). A survey by Banco Fenícia and the
Economic Research Institute Foundation (FIPE) in São Paulo in mid-1997
showed that 49.5 percent of respondents used postdated checks. Such checks
have become the most important source of consumer financing, followed
by retailer credit (40.8 percent), credit cards (24.5 percent), and store-
specific credit cards (11.9 percent). Another indication of the importance of
this instrument is the fact that in May 1998, 60 percent of all checks issued
in Brazil were postdated.

It is virtually impossible to measure the volume of credit extended
through postdated checks. A crude lower bound may be derived from the
activity of factoring companies, which recycle these funds.[13] In 1997, factoring activity involved 726 firms and operations amounting to R$14.75 bil-
lion (up from R$11.4 billion in 1996). These figures are comparable to the
stock of household credit at the end of 1996 and 1997, which totaled R$19.6
and R$28.9 billion, respectively.

---

[13] Factoring companies purchase a firm's credit from sales and thus assume the credit risk.

Table 5.5. Forms of Payment in São Paulo, 1996-97

(percent of total sales)

Form of payment	November 1996	April 1997	August 1997	November 1997
Cash	33.0	33.2	38.7	44.4
Credit card	25.0	20.6	18.4	18.3
Postdated check	36.0	41.9	35.1	32.2
Bank loan	3.0	1.1	4.1	4.8
Other	2.0	3.2	2.1	0.4

Source: Commerce Federation of the State of São Paulo.

What makes credit through postdated checks interesting to the analysis is that it operates largely outside the formal framework described earlier. It is not supported by collateral or personal guarantees. Its low unitary value precludes recourse to the judiciary in case of default.[14] Moreover, unlike other Latin American countries, Brazil has no punitive mechanisms for issuers of checks without funds: they do not go to prison or pay a fine. Issuers may also suspend payment on a check before it is presented without suffering any legal sanction. In fact, postdated checks are not even legally recognized, since legally creditors may cash them at any time.

Thus this entire market segment is essentially supported by information-sharing institutions and retailers willing to wait to cash checks. Easy, low-cost access to information on the person writing the check and the high cost to the consumer of being placed on a "black list" for writing a check without funds have made postdated checks the most widely used form of consumption financing. The efficacy of informal sanctions is reflected in the interest charged by factoring firms: 4.9 percent (monthly rate in April 1998), much lower than the rates charged by credit card companies. Default rates are also lower than they are for financial institutions' credit portfolios (2.9 percent in São Paulo in 1998). This rate also compares favorably with the proportion of retail credit payments that are late: 10 percent, according to the Banco Fenícia/FIPE survey.

---

[14] In the Banco Fenícia/FIPE survey, more than half of the loans were for less than R$500.

Public Banks

In Brazil, as in other developing countries, state intervention through public banks is policymakers' usual response to both market and institutional failures in financial markets, for several reasons. First, public banks have access to comparatively low-cost funds with long maturity terms. Second, being state-owned and virtual monopolists in their market segments, these banks are able to mitigate the negative effects of weak creditor protection. And in some cases, policymakers create governance structures that also grant debtors protection from government expropriation, fostering economic activities that would be impossible in private hands. One such case is analyzed here: the financing of private investment in infrastructure.

While some infrastructure projects are financed through traditional corporate finance instruments, others are not. Among those that are not are projects in industries such as oil drilling and electricity generation. The volume of lending for these projects is so large that it would quickly exhaust the investment capacity—and compromise the credit rating—of most private investors. The traditional solution is *project finance*. Overall, an estimated one-half of all loans for infrastructure projects in recent years have been channeled through project finance operations. Most of these operations have a similar structure: about 30 percent of the projects are financed with equity and 70 percent with loans, which are extended almost exclusively through the National Economic and Social Development Bank (BNDES), Inter-American Development Bank (IDB), and International Finance Corporation (IFC). Foreign banks participate through the IDB and IFC, and capital markets and domestic financial institutions play minor roles. Creditors proportionately share the same guarantees, and no creditor has seniority. The project itself is the main guarantee for all loans—both revenues and assets, including all the project company's available assets (such as shares and mortgages of fixed assets).

The two instruments lenders use most often in Brazil to encourage debt repayment—collateral and credit rating—are inefficient in the case of project finance. The project company is poor collateral, since its assets are highly specific and have low resale value (especially before the project is complete). Mortgaging the fixed assets prevents the investor from using them to request other loans, and the project is committed entirely to the lenders.

It is, however, unlikely that the bank will foreclose on such mortgages, as their market value is too low. Emphasizing this point, one bank officer asked what the bank was expected to do with a money-losing power plant. In addition, the project company does not have a credit history, and the sponsors' credit history provides only imperfect guidance, since creditors have no recourse to the sponsors' assets.

How do lenders view the protection the law and judiciary afford project finance operations? These loans are based on carefully written contracts, which follow the law strictly (Brazil's or New York's, depending on the contract) and foresee recourse to the judiciary if necessary. Nonetheless lenders argue that in cases of default in this kind of project, the solution is to find a new group of investors to manage the project or, if that effort fails, to renegotiate the loan. Another bank officer noted that appealing to the judiciary was the worst possible option. For this reason, credit contracts for project finance contain clauses giving lenders the right to step in if necessary. The riskier the project, the stricter are the covenants allowing creditors to step in.

The most important role for the legal and judiciary systems in the financing of infrastructure is to protect investors (and creditors, indirectly) against the political risk of administrative expropriation, rather than against default. So far, with the privatization process still underway and the federal government in control, judicial action has not been necessary. But an independent and strong judiciary is still essential, if only to assure creditors that regulatory agencies will respect contracts, even in the long term.

Meanwhile, financing by public and multinational banks provides for governance structures that restrain opportunism on the part of both the government and borrowers. On the one hand, borrowers are more willing to pay when they know that they may have future dealings with the same lenders. Because a public bank like BNDES often has a monopoly in its market segment, borrowers know they are likely to resort to the same bank in the future. Thus the monopolistic position of public banks in long-term credit markets is essential in reducing the benefits of opportunistic default. On the other hand, government opportunism is discouraged by the fact that the government shares in any losses (through public banks) and the knowledge that any problems could compromise the country's ability to obtain financing through multilateral institutions.

Peer Pressure

Mechanisms based on peer pressure combine the advantages of formal and informal lending. As with informal lending, lenders tend to know the borrowers well and have access to a better monitoring and enforcement technology than they might in other formal lending schemes. However, these mechanisms minimize the negative aspects of informal lending, such as increased market segmentation, lack of sufficient risk diversification, and small-scale operations. Peer pressure schemes include credit cooperatives and group lending. The latter provides particularly strong incentives, in the sense that all members of a group are liable for repayment and will be sanctioned if any member defaults. As a consequence, individuals in the group provide information and help enforce contracts.

Most of the examples of group lending found in Brazil are in the field of microcredit. One such initiative is BNDES Solidarity, which lends very small amounts (from 150 to a few thousand reais) to small, often informal businesses that in general have no bank accounts. Credit cooperatives are also active in microcredit, but mostly to individuals. Neither type of financing is intended to subsidize borrowers. The interest rates charged are close to market levels, and the programs are expected to be self-sustaining. These initiatives rely on a complex governance structure based on peer pressure, information-sharing, and public credit that is very different from the structures of classical contract law. In any event, the loans are too small to be formally registered, let alone enforced in the costly Brazilian judicial system.

BNDES Solidarity is a program created to provide funds to nongovernmental organizations (NGOs) engaged in microlending. To be eligible, NGOs must meet three criteria. First, they must have at least six months of successful experience in microcredit. Second, a public or multilateral institution or another reputable NGO must have financed at least a quarter of the NGO's earlier loans. And third, if the NGO was created by a municipality, this municipality must have at least 250,000 inhabitants. BNDES provides funds equal to 100 percent of the total value of the NGO's stable resources, up to a maximum of R\$3.0 million per contract. It does not interfere, however, with the way the NGO operates.

The high cost and difficulty of obtaining bank credit have driven individuals to form credit cooperatives that provide general-purpose microcredits. Relatively low interest rates (2 to 5 percent monthly) and the certainty of obtaining a loan when needed have fueled the growth of these institutions. In 1989 some 300 such organizations had been formed in Brazil. By 1998 their number had risen to 1,100, with about 1 million associates and R$1.4 billion in resources. Cooperative equity is drawn from members' paychecks every month. In some cases, the amount is a percentage (about 1 percent), while in other cases it is a fixed fee (for example, one cooperative charges members whose salaries are considered low R$12 and those with higher salaries R$17). To facilitate cooperatives' credit operations, in 1997 the Central Bank authorized the upgrading of two cooperatives to cooperative private banks, Bancoob and Banficred. Together, these banks have a net worth of over R$700 million, and Bancoob is among the 20 largest private banks in Brazil.

NGOs engaged in microlending often charge high interest rates and apply stiff penalties in case of default (Table 5.6). As high as these interest rates might seem, however, they are still well below the rates charged for other forms of credit available to these borrowers.[15] Penalties are also much lower than those that banks charge on similar operations. Although default rates vary considerably, they are not high by market standards. Peer pressure, foreclosure on real and personal guarantees, and the threat of a bad credit report tend to ensure willingness to pay. Judicial enforcement is not perceived as an alternative in most cases because it is too costly. In fact, for most loans the cost of taking judicial action—and even of reporting the default to the relevant public register—is higher than the value of the loan. Only for the larger loans are these procedures justifiable.

The Findings and Their Implications

This analysis of the Brazilian credit market reveals a set of stylized facts and produces two important results. The findings confirm the link between judicial inefficiency and credit market size and suggest that private arrangements may be an effective substitute for a well-performing judiciary. What follows presents the stylized facts, the results, and comments on policy implications.

---

[15] In August 1988, moneylenders (*agiotas*) were charging an average monthly interest rate of 20.53 percent (or 940.03 percent per year). In some cases, borrowers were paying interest rates as high as 33.64 percent per month (*O Globo*, August 23, 1998, p. 37).

Table 5.6. Basic Practices and Results of NGOs Engaged in Microlending, 1998

NGO	Monthly interest rate (percent)	Guarantees[a]	Default rate (%)[b] June 1998	Default rate (%)[b] July 1998	Procedures in case of default
Portosol	3.5	Individual *aval*, mutual *aval*, or real guarantees	5.00	4.45	One day after the loan is due, a credit officer visits the client to try to arrange an immediate new date for payment. At the same time both debtor and guarantor receive a collection letter. If no payment is made on the new date, the credit officer visits the client and the guarantor again to try to negotiate a final payment date. At this time the debtor must give the reasons for the delay, either personally or in writing, or the loan is considered in default and an additional 1 percent of the monthly interest rate is assessed (2 percent on loans over 30 days past due). If the loan is not paid in full on the final due date, the case is passed to a lawyer, and the name of the debtors and the guarantor are sent to the Credit Protection Service (SPC). The lawyer then tries to arrange collection. If these efforts fail, the lawyer initiates the judicial collection process.
Blusol	4.8	Individual *aval*, mutual *aval*, or real guarantees	0.0	0.2	The credit officer visits the debtor to learn the reasons for the delay, notify the client that payment is overdue, and explain the penalties and additional interest (*juros de mora*) that will be charged. If the borrower is part of a group, all members are informed of the penalties. If no payment is made within 15 days of the original payment date, the loan guarantor is notified. After 25 days, both debtor and the guarantor receive a final warning explaining that in five days the creditor will initiate a judicial collection process and that collection fees will be added to the debt. The name of the debtor is also sent to the SPC.

		Guarantees[a]			
FAEP[c]	3.9	Individual *aval*, mutual *aval*, or real guarantees	0.76	0.32	If any part of the debt is not paid on time, the debtor must give the reasons for the delay personally or in writing 24 hours before the debt is due. Otherwise, the loan is considered nonperforming, and the debtor pays an additional 2 percent in interest and a 1 percent penalty for delays over 30 days. After that period the loan is considered due in its full amount.
CEAPE-PE[d]	5.3	Individual *aval* and real guarantees	3.2	3.1	A penalty and an additional interest rate are charged on overdue loans. Since October 1996 CEAPE-PE has required that borrowers open a savings account linked to their loan. Each time borrowers receive a credit, they make a deposit. The savings accounts thus provide a partial guarantee in case of default.
Viva Cred	3.9	Individual *aval* and promissory note issued by the borrower	2.0	2.6	In case of delay, a credit officer visits the client. If the delay seems justified, the credit officer works out a solution that is taken to the credit committee, which makes a decision on the matter.

a. The guarantees that are demanded depend on the purpose and type of the loan. *Aval* is a form of personal guarantee, though not the only one.
b. The proportion of loans overdue for 30 days or more.
c. Fund for the Support of Popular Initiatives.
d. Center for the Support of Small Businesses.
Source: BNDES.

Macroeconomic instability has long curtailed the development of credit markets in Brazil. Only since the *Plano Real* of 1994 has the sharp reduction in inflation allowed the volume of credit to households to increase substantially. Despite this positive development, the ratio of performing loans to GDP has also decreased since 1994. Private domestic credit is concentrated primarily in short-term operations, with public banks providing most long-term loans. Further, interest rates in Brazil are among the highest in the world. These rates are the result of two factors: tight monetary policy, which keeps banks' borrowing rates high, and large loan spreads generated by low productivity, high taxes, and high default rates, among other factors. The existence of good collateral (with, for example, mortgage loans or fiduciary alienation) and of "protection" to creditors from judicial slowness (with ACC loans, for instance) helps reduce the interest rates charged by banks.

Brazil's legal and judicial systems provide creditors with only weak protection. Slowness is a major problem, and the laws offer debtors several ways to postpone a court decision. Cost is also an issue, particularly for low-value credits. Further, the preference bankruptcy law gives to liabilities with workers and tax authorities in practice eliminates protection for other creditors. A set of legal institutions tries to compensate for the underperformance of the judiciary—a situation common to other French civil law countries. These institutions include self-executable securities and special forms of collateral, such as fiduciary alienation.

This analysis has attempted to assess the impact of Brazil's poor judicial enforcement on the development of the credit market, in part by testing whether differences in judicial performance explain cross-state differences in credit market size. Although the legislation protecting creditor rights is the same throughout the country, the quality of judicial enforcement is not uniform across the states. To measure judicial performance, an index of judicial inefficiency was created that builds on a survey of businessmen in different states regarding the speed, fairness, and cost of the judiciary in protecting creditors.

First, the analysis shows that *the lack of proper judicial enforcement significantly reduces the ratio of credit to GDP in Brazil,* even after controlling for the level of per capita income. Regression results show that judicial inefficiency has a distinctly negative impact on the volume of both rural and nonrural credits and that the ratio of credit to GDP increases with per capita income. These results may explain, at least in part, why credit markets in

Latin American countries are smaller than in industrial economies. They also suggest that differences in the quality of judicial enforcement are as important as per capita income differentials in explaining cross-state differences in the ratio of credit to GDP.

Second, the analysis suggests that *governance structures in the financial market itself support important credit activities in the absence of strong legal and judicial protection for creditors.* Three main institutions allow these forms of governance to flourish: a well-developed information infrastructure, public banks, and mechanisms that rely on peer pressure to ensure repayment.

A sound information infrastructure allows for the widespread use of postdated checks, for example. Easy, low-cost access to reliable information on those writing such checks and the high cost to consumers of being "black-listed" in the credit market have made postdated checks a widely used, low-cost credit instrument for financing nondurable consumer goods and basic services.

Public banks not only have access to comparatively low-cost funding with longer-than-average maturity but are also virtual monopolists in their market segments. These advantages permit them to structure their credit operations in ways that mitigate the negative effects of weak creditor protection. In some cases they provide for governance structures that also protect debtors from government expropriation, creating a situation that supports economic activities in a way private markets do not—for example, private investment in infrastructure, which is largely supported by public funding sources.

Peer pressure schemes constitute the third institution. They include credit cooperatives and group lending. These initiatives rely on a complex governance structure based on peer pressure, information-sharing, and public credit.

The results suggest three policy implications:

- Improving the quality of judicial enforcement is important to the development of credit markets—and indirectly to economic development and growth.

- Because judicial reform is a slow process, governments should support institutions that serve as substitutes for good judicial enforcement in encouraging debtors to repay (information sharing and group lending, for example).

- Finally, more detailed assessments are needed of the comparative advantages and disadvantages of the governance structures discussed here relative to judicial enforcement. For instance, the low productivity and high default rates of public retail banks suggest that, although they may be effective in allowing certain credit activities to take place, they might not be the most efficient solution if creditor rights were properly enforced. But even if creditor rights were efficiently enforced, information-sharing would still be warranted because of its low cost and strong disciplinary effects.

CHAPTER 6

Why Borrowers Repay: Understanding High Performance in Chile's Financial Market

J. Rodrigo Fuentes and Carlos P. Maquieira

La Porta *et al.* (1997, 1998) classify Chile as one of the group of French civil law countries that, according to these researchers, offer relatively poor protection for creditors and consequently have narrow financial markets.[1] Yet Chile turned in an outstanding performance in terms of bad debt compared with other countries in the same class. International evidence shows that the ratio between nonperforming loans and total loans was lower in Chile than in other economies at a similar stage of development (see Table 1.3 in Chapter 1 of this volume).

This chapter seeks to identify the reasons Chile's financial markets have performed so well, especially since increasing competition spurred Chilean banks to move into riskier segments. As Fuentes and Basch (1998) show, banks faced increasing competition from institutional investors (mainly private pension funds) in the 1980s and from leasing companies, public debt issues, and the expansion of department store credit in the 1990s. This situation led to lower bank margins and forced banks to turn to riskier customers, including households and small businesses. But it did not generate a concomitant rise in defaulted loans.

Why is repayment so high? And more generally what are the determinants of loan repayment in Chile? The results of La Porta *et al.* (1998) suggest that to reach a relatively high level of protection for creditors—and consequently to develop a capital market—a country needs to move from a

J. Rodrigo Fuentes is Assistant Professor of Economics at the Universidad de Chile, Santiago, Chile. Carlos P. Maquieira is Associate Professor at the Universidad de Chile.
[1] The main characteristic of this legal structure is that laws rather than judicial precedent determine the rules that apply to economic transactions.

French civil law to a common law system. But this chapter shows that although Chile's legal system is based on French civil law, its institutional arrangements protect creditors and provide strong incentives to repay debt. The analysis examines these institutional arrangements in detail while controlling for macroeconomic variables that may also affect the default rate.

Willingness to repay in the financial market is key to the existence of a healthy financial system. Institutional arrangements that ensure repayment should be one of the main concerns of policymakers overseeing the operation of the banking system, since credit market failures are usually the result of imperfect information, limited enforcement, or both (Besley 1995). Situations in which creditors' rights are hard to enforce may exacerbate problems of moral hazard and adverse selection, since such situations increase the probability that debtors will default even when they can repay their debts.

Debtors may be unable (rather than unwilling) to repay their debts because of exogenous shocks such as macroeconomic crises. In Latin America many external crises in the 1980s and 1990s were associated with difficulties in the financial sector—Chile in 1982, Mexico during the so-called Tequila crisis and Argentina in 1995. Sometimes these external crises led to local currency devaluations (Chile and Mexico) that unleashed an internal crisis and demonstrated the weakness of the financial system. In these situations debtors were often unable to meet their obligations. This scenario suggests that controlling for current macroeconomic conditions is a key prerequisite to isolating the structural determinants of local debtors' default rate, especially for Latin America.

The three key variables considered here as potential determinants of loan repayment and credit market development are the macroeconomic environment, financial market regulation, and information sharing. Calculations using monthly data for 1986-97 show that good macroeconomic performance and the introduction of "white" information sharing are negatively correlated with past-due loans.[2] A broader analysis of the determinants of credit market development, based on yearly data, indicates that good macroeconomic performance, major financial market reforms, and information sharing are all associated with the development of the credit market.

---

[2] White information (i.e., data other than defaults) is shared only among banks. Black information (i.e., data about defaults) is given to the public.

A number of other qualitative determinants of the level of arrears are incorporated into the analysis, including access to the credit market, the legal framework, and relevant private sector arrangements. Of particular importance is the degree of efficiency of the judicial system and the characteristics of the bankruptcy code, as well as private arrangements, including information sharing, prescreening techniques, collection technology, and contracts. All these factors contributed to the low default rate during the rapid expansion of the Chilean credit market.

International Comparisons

French civil law countries are generally characterized by poor creditor rights protection and underdeveloped capital markets (La Porta *et al.* 1997, 1998). But the Chilean capital market is relatively developed compared with the rest of the countries in the French civil law group (Table 6.1).

The enforcement variables (panel A) do not differ appreciably from the average of the French civil law countries, except for the rule of law variable, for which Chile scores higher than other countries in its group. Otherwise, Chile's scores are lower than those for countries where the legal system is of English origin. For all four enforcement variables, Chile scores far lower than countries with legal systems of German and Scandinavian origin. Accordingly, the development of the Chilean capital market should be comparable to the development of similar markets in other French civil law countries.

Panel B shows, however, that Chile's indicators for capital market development are consistently above the average of the French civil law counries. They more closely resemble the average of countries with legal systems that originated in English, German, or Scandinavian law. The same can be said with respect to the number of bad loans. This variable is hard to compare across countries, which have different rules determining when loans become nonperforming or past due. In Chile banks rate a loan as past due when it has been overdue for 90 days, but in Brazil a loan is past due after 60 days. International comparability is equally problematic if loan loss reserves are taken as a proxy of nonperforming loans. But if they are also taken with a good dose of caution, these data may produce useful information (Table 6.2).

Table 6.1. Law Enforcement and Financial Development by Type of Legal System

Indicator	Type of legal system					
	Chile	French	English	German	Scandi-navian	Sample average
Panel A. Rule of law						
Efficiency of judicial system	7.25	6.56	8.15	8.54	10.00	7.67
Rule of law	7.02	6.05	6.46	8.68	10.00	6.85
Corruption	5.30	5.84	7.06	8.03	10.00	6.90
Risk of contract repudiation	6.80	6.84	7.41	9.47	9.44	7.58
Panel B. External capital markets						
External capital/GNP	0.80	0.21	0.60	0.46	0.30	0.40
Number of domestic firms/ population	19.92	10.00	35.45	16.79	27.76	21.59
Initial public offerings/ population	0.35	0.19	2.23	0.12	2.14	1.02
Debt/GNP	0.63	0.45	0.68	0.97	0.57	0.59

Note: Figures for groups of countries are averages. All indices are measured on a scale of 0 to 10. A relatively high value indicates a relatively efficient judicial system, a tradition of law and order, low levels of corruption, and a reduced risk that the government will repudiate contracts. A relatively low value indicates the opposite.
Source: La Porta et al. (1997, 1998).

Chile features levels of defaulted loans that are closer to those of industrial countries than to those of other Latin American countries. In the late 1990s nonperforming loans in Chile were on the order of 1 percent—a value closer to Canada's and the United States' than to Brazil's or Peru's.

Major Determinants of Loan Repayment and Credit Market Development

Institutional arrangements per se do not always adequately protect creditor rights. They can fail for many reasons, such as an inefficient judicial system,

Table 6.2. International Comparisons of Nonperforming Loans

Country	Nonperforming loans/total loans (percent)	Number of banks used in estimate	Loan loss reserves/total loans (percent)	Number of banks used in estimate
Argentina	—	—	3.79	97
Brazil	6.31	94	3.63	95
Chile	0.93	29	0.34	31
Colombia	7.34	24	1.74	27
Mexico	7.09	22	2.88	22
Peru	8.93	23	3.45	18
Australia	3.70	12	0.34	34
Canada	2.34	7	0.79	17
Germany	—	—	0.60	1,596
Italy	5.21	235	1.74	250
Spain	4.74	19	0.98	163
Sweden	7.02	15	1.12	16
United Kingdom	—	—	0.16	59
United States	1.65	495	0.56	497

— Not available.
Source: Chapter 2.

insufficient third-party collateral or guarantees, and a lack of publicly disseminated default data. At least three groups of factors potentially affect loan repayment. The first includes macroeconomic determinants. Macroeconomic stability can result in low default rates, but credit rationing caused by macroeconomic factors can also explain them, since when credit is tight banks lend only to creditworthy borrowers (Stiglitz and Weiss 1981).

The second group of determinants relates to regulation and enforcement. Changes in the regulations governing Chile's financial markets may be key to the development of the credit market and the low level of arrears. If a country has a clear set of rules that protect creditor rights and enforcement is efficient, the incentive to repay will be high.

The third set of explanatory variables involves private solutions to unwillingness to repay. This group includes information-sharing systems, prescreening techniques, collection technology, and private contracts. Without information on borrowers' debt and credit histories, financial intermediaries often cannot control their clients' total indebtedness. This problem is intensified by the lack of effective supervision within the financial sector (Edwards 1995).

Macroeconomic Stability

A key issue in this study is determining how to separate willingness to repay from ability to repay. After the 1982 crisis Chile experienced a high rate of gross domestic product (GDP) growth (7.7 percent annually from 1986 until 1997, Figure 6.1). At the same time the country enjoyed rapid decreases in the inflation rate (Table 6.3).

Not only did inflation reach its lowest level in the 1990s, but it also steadily declined throughout the decade. This phenomenon explains why the standard deviation of the inflation rate in the 1990s was higher than in the 1980s, when inflation fluctuated less but around a higher average.

In the 1990s Chile demonstrated a relatively stable macroeconomic pattern. This stability coincided with the development of the financial market. Part of the explanation for the low level of nonperforming loans and the

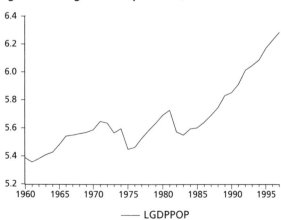

Figure 6.1. Log of Per Capita GDP, 1960-97

Table 6.3. Inflation Rate

Years	Average	Standard deviation	Variation coefficient
1960-69	24.85	12.11	0.4873
1970-79	175.21	174.42	0.9955
1980-89	20.69	6.28	0.3037
1990-98	11.68	7.28	0.6234

successful development of the credit market is likely to reside in this stability, which facilitated loan repayment.

Financial Market Regulation and the Banking Sector

In the early 1980s Latin American economies underwent a deep financial and macroeconomic crisis. Chile was no exception. At the time of the Chilean financial crisis (which started in mid-1981), the economy was open to international trade and foreign financial markets. This openness was the result of the reforms implemented during the first years of the military government that seized power in 1973. The main features of the reforms were the drastic trade liberalization carried out in 1974-79, the opening of the capital account starting in 1978, the reduction in the size of government in order to control inflation, the privatization of state-owned firms and commercial banks (many of which had been nationalized by the former government), and the elimination of price and interest rate controls.

After several decades of financial repression characterized by credit ceilings and interest rate controls that generated a negative real interest rate, the Chilean financial sector was not ready for the sudden reforms. According to De la Cuadra and Valdés (1992), banks were not equipped with the technology, human capital, or managerial skills necessary to operate in a free financial market. They ended up with very risky portfolios on which they charged high interest rates that in turn resulted in high spreads.

The same was true for the Superintendency of Banks and Financial Institutions. Prior to liberalization this regulatory agency had focused on enforcing credit recovery and controlling interest rates. The agency lacked the know-how required to monitor and control risk, primarily because of the absence of prudential regulation (De la Cuadra and Valdés 1992). Implicit deposit insurance generated the problem of moral hazard in bank lending, and the lack of prudential supervision allowed banks to channel funds to affiliated companies. Large groups of companies owned banks and other firms that went bankrupt when external financial resources became scarce. These groups, with the exception of export-oriented groups and those with a low leverage in dollars, were especially affected by the devaluation of the peso during the second semester of 1982 (Maquieira and Sierralta 1990).

Until 1982 the external debt crisis was a private sector crisis, but in 1983 foreign banks forced the government to guarantee private external debt. Given the dimension of the crisis, the economic authorities decided to bail out the banking system. In 1982 the Chilean Central Bank began to buy delinquent loans at their face value in order to alleviate bank losses. The banks were obliged to repurchase those loans over time. But this approach—which in truth was a makeshift solution designed to improve bank balance sheets—did not improve the solvency of most banks.

Why did the banks fail to require collateral for loans before the crisis worsened? Among the main reasons, according to De la Cuadra and Valdés (1992), were the lack of monitoring by the banks themselves, the sluggish and inefficient judicial system, and the conflict of interest between banks and the corporate groups to which they belonged. Bank owners were not about to liquidate collateral that also belonged to them.

In 1980 the Superintendency of Banks and Financial Institutions ascertained that independent auditing firms were not doing their job properly in rating bank loans. In particular the agency found severe problems in the ratings of self-granted loans (that is, loans to firms associated with the lending banks). To address the problem it instituted a transparent, efficient credit system. As a first step loans were rated in four categories.[3] In August 1981 the government increased the superintendency's power to control banks through an amendment to the prevailing law that was designed to end self-

---

[3] Category A: Normal loans with no problems in terms of recoverability (principal and interest).
Category B: Loans of substandard quality because of weakness in the conditions under which they were granted or because of poor performance. These loans do not necessarily become bad debts.
Category C: Loans that may be unrecoverable, including all loans granted under conditions that depart significantly from normal conditions.
Category D: Loans in default.

granted lending. This change empowered the regulatory agency to obtain information from each bank on the 300 most important debtors (for both paid and unpaid loans). The amendment also required banks to classify the loans by type (such as consumer and mortgage) and set up a rating system that operated smoothly.

For the first time the regulator also spelled out the rules with respect to loan loss reserves and past-due loans. Loan loss reserves for overdue loans were set at the equivalent of 100 percent of all loans past due during the first six months and 50 percent of those past due during the second six months. The regulation included a general reserve requirement of 0.75 percent of the total amount of loans, but the large corporate groups found ways to bypass this regulation (De la Cuadra and Valdés 1992).

All these efforts came too late to prevent the banking crisis, however. In 1983, following the new risk rating, the government liquidated three banks and intervened in the administration of five others. These activities took place during the deepest recession Chile had experienced since the 1930s. In 1983-84 an intense debt rescheduling process took place that changed both interest rates and terms for debtors. The banks that were bailed out were reprivatized in 1985-86 through the so-called system of popular capitalism. Under this system the banks were sold to small stockholders who had access to governmental credit under special conditions.

A new institutional framework for banking in Chile was set up in 1986 with the enactment of a new banking law that contained measures similar to those the superintendency had introduced in 1981. The new legal framework aimed to prevent a new banking crisis and to increase the transparency of the banking business.[4] To this end the law mandated a more active role for the superintendency in rating bank risk according to the loan classification system, increased disclosure of information to the public, and placed strict restrictions on banks' ability to do business with affiliates. In addition the law established an active role for private risk-rating agencies; as a complement, the Security Market Law set limits to bank secrecy (Ramírez and Rosende 1992). The government also restricted deposit insurance in order to induce depositors to seek more information on bank risk.

---

[4] See Ramírez and Rosende (1992) for a summary of the changes in Chile's banking legislation.

The new banking law included two important changes designed to protect creditors' interests. First, banks could no longer give preferential treatment to parties directly or indirectly related to the owners of a bank or to bank officials (insider trading). The grace period of a loan, the interest rate, and guarantee requirements had to be the same as those offered to other borrowers. Second, banks were not allowed to grant loans either directly or indirectly to members of their own boards of directors or the directors' representatives.

These changes did indeed improve the efficiency of the banking system, as changes in total loans per capita indicate (Figure 6.2). The Chilean government had already liberalized the interest rate in 1975, setting in motion the liberalization of the financial market. The growth of per capita loans stalled after the 1981 crisis but resumed vigorously after 1991.

Information Sharing

Information sharing may be an important mechanism in mitigating both adverse selection and moral hazard. According to Pagano and Jappelli (1993), the financial market can use information-sharing techniques to prescreen loan applicants, partially solving problems of adverse selection. This arrange-

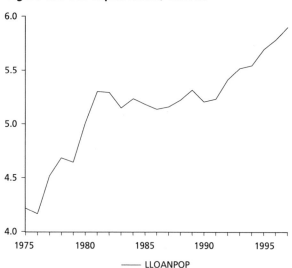

Figure 6.2. Per Capita Loans, 1975-97

ment is most useful when borrowers are heterogeneous, the credit market is large, and the cost of sharing information is low.

Similarly, information sharing reduces problems of moral hazard, since it increases willingness to repay. Information sharing provides an incentive for borrowers to repay on time by allowing banks to share information on defaulters. Debtors know that the entire credit market has access to information on their creditworthiness (or lack of it). This mechanism does more than simply ensure a lower default rate, however. It also allows banks to keep interest rates low.[5]

Evidence supports the positive relationship between information sharing and the ratio of total debt to gross national product (see Chapter 2). Weaker evidence suggests that information sharing is negatively associated with default rates. To a certain extent the positive correlation between information sharing and the ratio of debt to GDP can reflect reverse causation. Historical evidence for the United States suggests that credit bureaus tend to be created in the wake of consumer credit booms (Pagano and Jappelli 1993). The number of U.S. credit bureaus increased dramatically in the 1920s and 1950s—periods of buoyant growth in consumer credit.

Consistent with this historical pattern, Chile's main credit bureau (DICOM) began operating in 1979, toward the end of the credit boom that followed the 1975 liberalization. The Chilean Chamber of Commerce, which has a 50 percent stake in the bureau, and a group of entrepreneurs set up DICOM at the suggestion of international credit card companies that were introducing their cards in Chile. Although the Chamber of Commerce issued a list of bad checks and overdue bills of exchange (the Commercial Bulletin), these international companies required better and more up-to-date information to evaluate creditworthiness.

DICOM started with four products: information drawn from the Commercial Bulletin, address verification, job verification, and a consolidated system of default verification for credit issued by department stores (SICOM). DICOM also provided information on individuals interdicted from opening checking accounts and data available from the Official Bulletin.[6] At the beginning of the 1980s, the Chilean Association of Banks called a public

---

[5] See, for instance, Padilla and Pagano (2000).

[6] Information in the Official Bulletin includes company charters, names of partners, equity of companies, bankruptcy filings, and laws enacted and amended.

tender to contract out information services. DICOM won the contract, but it was not until a decade later that the bureau became an effective credit information system. In 1989 it began signing individual contracts with each bank to process white and black information about debtors. This information was available (and still is) only to the banking system—that is, DICOM processes the data supplied by the banks. In addition it receives black information from department stores and the so-called Real Estate Mutual Funds. DICOM provides black and white information to banks, but only black information to other financial intermediaries and the public.[7]

DICOM has a competitive advantage in processing information, mainly because of economies of scale and scope. Despite cost reductions in the data processing industry, banks still use its services.[8] This fact is consistent with theoretical arguments that increasing returns to scale make information-sharing activities a natural monopoly (Pagano and Jappelli 1993). Certainly this notion applies to DICOM.

Banks and financial institutions are also obliged to provide information on individual customers (both households and companies) to the Superintendency of Banks and Financial Institutions, which processes these data in order to compute the total debt and the unpaid debt of each customer.[9] The consolidated figures are returned to the banks, which then know the total outstanding bank debt of any customer or prospective customer (but not the names of creditors).

Empirical Analysis

An econometric analysis shows that several institutional changes affected the rapid growth of the banking system and the performance of bank loans. These changes included the reforms of the 1970s and 1980s and the advent of information sharing in the financial sector.

---

[7] See Fuentes and Maquieira (1999) for details on the type of information that DICOM provides.
[8] At present DICOM issues the equivalent of 1.4 million full credit reports per month to some 20,000 clients. The company grew between 15 percent and 20 percent annually over the 1990s (measured in terms of requests for reports). Its scope may explain the low price of a full report, which is only US$0.4, compared with the United States (US$1.5), Peru (US$2) and Argentina (US$3).
[9] Each individual or company is identified by an individual identification number (CUSIP), which is used to consolidate the information. These numbers correspond to individual identification card numbers, passport numbers, driver's license numbers, and Social Security numbers.

The Chilean Credit Market, 1993-97

Between 1993 and 1997 credit grew quickly in Chile compared with the economy as a whole (Table 6.4). This rapid growth confirms the trend shown in Figure 6.2. While GDP increased by 7.7 percent, the credit market grew by 12.5 percent. Bank loans were by far the most important type of contract in the credit market, but department store credit and credit cards had the highest growth rate. This evidence is consistent with Fuentes and Basch (1998).

The rapid growth of the credit card and department store credit markets reflects the general trend in consumer loans. As noted earlier, strong competition within the financial system prompted banks to move into new market segments such as household credit. The combined share of consumer and housing loans in total bank loans increased from 19 to 25.4 percent between 1993 and 1997—not as fast as credit cards and department store

Table 6.4. Size of the Chilean Credit Market, 1993-97

(US$ million)

Type of loan	1993	1994	1995	1996	1997
Net bank loans	31,002	33,123	38,764	43,622	49,340
	(13.0)	(6.8)	(17.0)	(12.5)	(13.1)
Leasing contracts	1,130	1,421	1,670	1,777	1,976
	(47.7)	(25.7)	(17.6)	(6.4)	(11.2)
Bonds	1,468	1,851	1,770	1,750	1,408
	(24.6)	(26.1)	(−4.4)	(−1.1)	(−19.6)
Credit cards	454	582	739	886	1,025
	(31.7)	(28.1)	(26.9)	(19.9)	(15.7)
Department store credit	204	427	664	880	1,165
	—	(109.1)	(55.4)	(32.6)	(32.4)
Total	34,259	37,404	43,608	48,915	54,913
Percent of GDP	62.4	64.5	68.0	71.0	74.5

— Not available.

Note: Figures in parentheses are growth rates (in percent).

Source: Superintendency of Banks and Financial Institutions, Superintendency of Securities and Insurance, and Chilean National Chamber of Commerce.

202   FUENTES AND MAQUIEIRA

credit, but still faster than corporate loans (Table 6.5). Past-due loans accounted for approximately 1 percent of total loans throughout the period.[10]

Some types of loans perform better than others (Table 6.6). The credit card segment has a higher default rate, but if "past due" is defined as at least 30 days overdue, then the fraction of such loans is also very small. Bank loans perform much better than other contracts. The reason for this strong performance may well be that banks offer customers several products and therefore have some leverage. If a loan is not repaid on time, the bank simply cancels all the customer's contracts. Banks may also have better screening, monitoring, and loan recovery technology than other financial institutions.

Econometric Analysis

The financial market liberalization of the 1970s positively affected the development of the banking system. An annual database of per capita banking loans (in real terms) made between 1960 and 1997 provides some insight into the nature of the impact. A natural variable to control for is per capita GDP, since in the long term the banking system should be developing along with the economy.

The reforms of the 1970s included financial liberalization and changes in reserve requirements. Reforms instituted in the 1980s established a new pension fund system, amended the banking law, and introduced information sharing, among other measures. A regression analysis helps to explain the effects of the most important institutional innovations.

The variables included in the regression analysis are:

- Log (per capita GDP): Log of per capita GDP expressed in 1986 pesos.

- Log (per capita loans): Log of per capita banking loans expressed in 1986 pesos.

---

[10] According to the regulations of the Superintendency of Banks and Financial Institutions, a loan that has not been paid within 90 days after its maturity is classified as a past-due loan. This rule differs from the measure for loan loss reserves banks use to classify their portfolios according to default risk.

Table 6.5. Distribution of Bank Loans, 1993-97
(percentage of total loans)

Balance	1993	1994	1995	1996	1997
Corporate loans	54.33	55.82	55.53	55.64	56.10
Consumer loans	7.05	7.87	8.66	10.35	10.74
Housing	11.92	12.81	12.95	14.16	14.67
Foreign trade	19.14	15.85	15.09	12.39	10.51
Past due	0.84	1.05	0.94	0.98	1.00
Credit line	3.13	3.36	3.53	3.59	3.58
Rescheduled	2.06	1.49	1.04	0.75	0.54
Other	1.53	1.74	2.25	2.14	2.86
Net loans (million US$)	31,002	33,123	38,764	43,622	49,340

Source: Superintendency of Banks and Financial Institutions.

Table 6.6. Nonperforming Loans, 1993-97
(percentage of total credit)

Type of loans	1993	1994	1995	1996	1997
Past due loans (over 90 days)	0.8	1.1	0.9	1.0	1.0
Leasing contracts (over 90 days)		6.0	4.0	3.4	2.9
Credit cards (1 to 90 days)	—	—	10.2	10.9	9.6
Credit cards (30 to 90 days)	—	—	2.3	2.6	2.9
Credit cards (60 to 90 days)	—	—	0.6	0.8	0.8
Department store credit	1.1	1.5	1.5	1.6	2.0

— Not available.

Source: Superintendency of Banks and Financial Institutions, Superintendency of Securities and Insurance, and Chilean National Chamber of Commerce.

- Log (loans/GDP): Log of ratio of banking loans in 1986 pesos to real GDP.

- D7597: Dummy variable that takes the value 1 for 1975-97 (the postreform period).

- D8697: Dummy variable that takes the value 1 for 1986-97 (the period of the new banking law).

- D8997: Dummy variable that takes the value 1 for 1989-97 (the period of information sharing among banks).

Other structural changes tested using dummy variables were not significant. For example, per capita loans were unaffected by the pension fund reform (1981-97) or the information-sharing network that operated before 1989, when private contracts between DICOM and individual banks were introduced.[11]

The results of the regression show that both per capita loans and the ratio of loans to GDP are strongly and positively correlated with per capita GDP (Table 6.7). The reforms of the 1970s had a positive impact on the development of the banking system, but Law 18,576 (enacted in 1986) had a negative impact on the growth of per capita loans and the ratio of loans to GDP. The structural changes of 1986 had an impact on the intercept or the slope coefficient. Each was separately significant, but dummies for the intercept and the slope simultaneously were not.

DICOM began gathering public information and providing it to the market in 1979, but private contracts became a feature of its relations with banks only in 1989. The search for structural changes occurring in 1979 was not found to be statistically significant. The structural changes of 1989, however, affected both the intercept and the slope coefficient in different directions. Per capita loans became less sensitive to the growth rate of the economy, and a one-time increase in the intercept in 1989 may be the effect of the improved information-sharing system.

The literature on growth and financial development suggests that per capita GDP is endogenous and jointly determined with the proxies for credit

---

[11] The limited information-sharing network begun in 1979 was based on public data pooled by DICOM and did not include indebtedness with the financial system.

Table 6.7. Development of the Banking Sector, Ordinary Least Squares Estimation

Variable	Log (per capita loans)	Log (per capita loans)	Log (loans/GDP)	Log (loans/GDP)
Constant	−6.650	−6.657	−5.301	−5.309
	(−3.615)	(−3.616)	(−2.837)	(−2.838)
Log (per capita GDP)	1.372	1.373	0.888	0.889
	(3.899)	(3.899)	(2.674)	(2.675)
Log (per capita loans)_1	0.745	0.744		
	(14.331)	(14.330)		
Log (loans/GDP)_1			0.786	0.786
			(14.697)	(14.689)
D7597	0.307	0.307	0.271	0.271
	(3.554)	(3.557)	(3.198)	(3.200)
D8697	−0.135		−0.159	
	(−3.563)		(−3.653)	
D8697*Log (per capita GDP)		−0.024		−0.028
		(−3.565)		(−3.657)
D8997	4.484	4.355	3.248	3.097
	(2.386)	(2.354)	(1.715)	(1.660)
D8997*Log (per capita GDP)	−0.800	−0.778	−0.583	−0.557
	(−2.429)	(−2.398)	(−1.754)	(−1.700)
R^2	0.987	0.987	0.980	0.980
S.E. of regression	0.124	0.124	0.130	0.130
Log likelihood	28.482	28.486	26.967	26.969
Durbin-Watson	2.201	2.200	2.178	2.177

Note: t-ratios are in parentheses. The estimation procedures used ordinary least squares to correct the variance-covariance matrix by the Newey-West HAC procedure.

market development. Therefore estimations can be made with instrumental variables that use one lag of per capita GDP. The results, however, do not change much (Table 6.8).

The long-term elasticity of capital market development to per capita GDP decreased dramatically after 1989 (Table 6.9). One possible reason for this decline is the beginning of "white" information sharing among banks after 1989.

**Table 6.8. Development of the Banking Sector,
Instrumental Variables Estimation**

Variable	Log (per capita loans)	Log (per capita loans)	Log (loans/GDP)	Log (loans/GDP)
Constant	−6.692	−6.701	−8.427	−8.439
	(−2.458)	(−2.460)	(−2.549)	(−2.550)
Log (per capita GDP)	1.380	1.382	1.427	1.429
	(2.650)	(2.652)	(2.444)	(2.445)
Log (per capita loans)_1	0.744	0.743		
	(13.459)	(13.462)		
Log (loans/GDP)_1			0.721	0.721
			(9.887)	(9.881)
D7597	0.308	0.308	0.334	0.334
	(4.695)	(4.702)	(3.571)	(3.572)
D8697	−0.135		−0.197	
	(−2.833)		(−2.793)	
D8697*Log (per capita GDP)		−0.024		−0.035
		(−2.828)		(−2.794)
D8997	4.523	4.396	6.227	6.042
	(1.641)	(1.619)	(1.899)	(1.874)
D8997*Log (per capita GDP)	−0.807	−0.784	−1.109	−1.076
	(−1.667)	(−1.645)	(−1.921)	(−1.897)
R^2	0.987	0.987	0.978	0.978
S.E. of regression	0.124	0.124	0.135	0.135
Durbin-Watson	2.198	2.200	1.943	1.941

Note: t-ratios are in parentheses. The estimation procedures used TSLS to correct the variance-covariance matrix according to the Newey-West HAC procedure.

What Were the Determinants of Overdue Loans as a Share of Total Loans?

A yearly series could not be constructed, but a monthly series of overdue loans (from January 1986 to December 1997) was built (Figure 6.3). Bank loan losses offer an alternative measure of unpaid debt, but overdue loans are generally a better proxy. Both measures decreased over time, however. Regulatory improvements and strong economic growth may explain this trend for the years after the financial crisis of the early 1980s.

Table 6.9. Capital Market Development and Per Capita GDP:
Long-Term Elasticities

Dependent variable	1960-85	1986-88	1989-97
Log per capita loan	5.3774	5.2840	2.2335
Log (loan/GDP)	5.1219	4.9964	1.1398

Figure 6.3. Unpaid Debt, 1986-97
(percent)

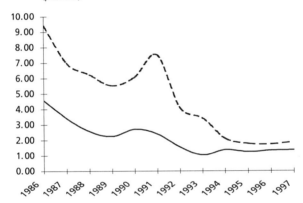

——— Past-due loans (% effective loans)   − − − Loan losses (% effective loans)
Source: Superintendency of Banks and Financial Institutions.

The ratio of overdue loans to total loans is regressed on macroeconomic variables and seasonal dummies. Because banks have 90 days to register an unpaid loan as past due in their balance sheets, the calculations include macroeconomic variables that capture the cycle with a lag of four months. The four candidates to explain the short-term economic situation are the loan interest rate, an index of economic activity constructed monthly by the Central Bank, the inflation rate, and the standard deviation of the inflation rate.[12]

---

[12] The Central Bank index is the Monthly Index of Economic Activity (IMACEC), which is available starting in January 1986.

Also included are structural changes that can be explained by the effects of information sharing. Some information-sharing activities were already in place even before August 1986, when the new law went into effect. Therefore no major changes occurred during the sample period, except for the private arrangements between DICOM and the banks, which began sometime in 1989 (the exact date is unclear). For this reason the structural changes were verified backward month by month beginning in January 1990. A structural change seems to have occurred in October 1989.[13]

The actual variables used for the analysis are as follows:

- LPDUEPR: Ratio of past-due loans to total loans for the private banking system.

- Interest: Loan interest rate.

- Yearly %ΔIMACEC: Percentage change in economic activity measured by the IMACEC.[14]

- DINFO: Dummy variable that takes the value 1 from October 1989 to December 1997.

Table 6.10 shows the regression results for this exercise. The first column gives the regression of past-due loans (as a proportion of total private bank loans) on a number of variables. Coefficients of seasonal dummy variables are not reported, but all of them are statistically significant. The interest rate positively affects past-due loans—that is, an increase in this variable is associated with an increase in overdue loans. A drop in economic activity also increases overdue loans, but this coefficient is not significantly different from zero.

The last column of Table 6.10 shows the results when the dummy variable DINFO is introduced. In October 1989 both the intercept and the slope coefficient undergo a change: past-due loans decline after that date, all other things remaining equal. However, the sensitivity of past-due loans with respect to per capita loans also decreases. A comparison of the estimates before and after October 1989 shows that the coefficient of the interest rate

<hr/>

[13] The Chow test for this month has the lowest p-value and is thus consistent with the inclusion of the dummy variable (DINFO).
[14] IMACEC (Indicador Mensual de Actividad Económica) is the Monthly Indicator of Economic Activity computed by the Central Bank of Chile.

Table 6.10. Past-Due Loans, Macroeconomic Variables, and Information Sharing

Variable	LPDUEPR	LPDUEPR
Constant	0.0003	0.0002
	(0.0816)	(0.0696)
Interest$_{-4}$	0.0125	0.0950
	(2.2241)	(3.8538)
Yearly %ΔIMACEC$_{-4}$	−0.0025	−0.0072
	(−0.8960)	(−2.1505)
DINFO		−0.0019
		(−3.6947)
DINFO* Interest$_{-4}$		−0.0685
		(−2.7533)
DINFO* Yearly %ΔIMACEC$_{-4}$		0.0056
		(2.6067)
LPDUEPR$_{-1}$	1.2172	1.1229
	(14.2244)	(13.2340)
LPDUEPR$_{-2}$	−0.2945	−0.2575
	(−2.4338)	(−2.5314)
LPDUEPR$_{-4}$	−0.1987	−0.2554
	(−1.7588)	(−2.3140)
LPDUEPR$_{-5}$	0.2481	0.3259
	(2.9615)	(3.4503)
R^2	0.9926	0.9939
S.E. of regression	0.0008	0.0007
Log likelihood	739.2267	751.8486
Durbin-Watson statistic	1.8781	1.9392
Number of observations	128	128

Note: t-ratios are in parentheses. The estimation procedures used OLS to correct the variance-covariance matrix according to the Newey-West HAC procedure.

diminishes from 0.095 to 0.027. At the same time the impact of economic activity decreases (in absolute value) from 0.0072 to 0.0016. Neither the average nor the standard deviation of the inflation rate is statistically significant in any of the regressions.

Table 6.11 shows the long-term coefficients. The information-sharing feature substantially decreases the sensitivity of the level of arrears to the busi-

Table 6.11. Long-Term Coefficients

Variable	January 1986 to September 1989	October 1989 to December 1997
Interest$_{-4}$	1.4808	0.4131
Yearly %ΔIMACEC$_{-4}$	−0.1119	−0.0253

ness cycle. In fact, comparing both time periods, the sensitivity drops more than 70 percent with respect to both the interest rate and economic activity.

Other Determinants of Loan Repayment: Stylized Facts

Some determinants of loan repayments cannot be included in the regression analysis. These include access to credit, the legal framework, and private solutions. Private solutions encompass prescreening techniques, collection technology, and private contracts.

Access to Credit

The fact that small firms and households have limited access to credit arguably affects a credit market's performance. But this constraint does not seem to affect the Chilean market, where consumer loans constitute one of the fastest-growing segments. To a certain extent the development of the household credit market relies on two factors. First, banks tend to require collateral for loans to households more often than for loans to firms. Second, collateralized consumer loans generally carry a lower default risk than loans to firms, as survey data collected from banks in 1998 show. Nine of 28 Chilean banks operating in 1997 provided information on several variables. Both large and small banks and foreign and domestic institutions responded, making the sample generally representative of the structure of the Chilean banking system.

Figure 6.4 shows the percentage of loans to households and firms that were covered by collateral and other guarantees. The data indicate that a higher proportion of loans to households were secured (with collateral and

Figure 6.4. Secured and Unsecured Loans in the Banking Sector
(percent)

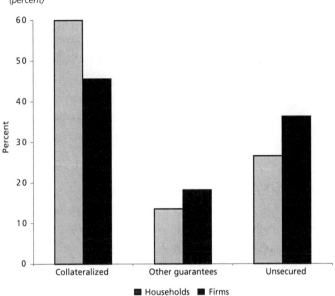

■ Households   ■ Firms

other guarantees). The rationale for requiring some form of security for household loans more often than for business loans lies in the uses to which the funds are put. Households are more likely to use loans for consumption, and therefore these loans do not generate cash flows (Townsend 1995). Instead, most loans to firms are used for investment, producing a cash flow that can be used for repayment.

Fuentes and Maquieira (1999) show that collateralized loans to households are far less risky than unsecured loans and are even safer than collateralized loans to firms. In fact the default rate is lower for uncollateralized loans to firms than it is for collateralized company loans—the reverse of the situation for household loans. This situation may simply be the result of the fact that banks ask for collateral from the companies with the highest risk, so that ex post the highest proportion of defaults is for collateralized loans.

The Legal Framework and Willingness to Pay

As discussed earlier, Chile has a French civil law framework. Laws exist to regulate creditor rights—for instance, Law 18,010 of 1981 governs credit transactions, including the terms and conditions of loans, interest payments, and type of currency. Additionally the Code of Commerce in the Civil Code contains general rules regulating business transactions.

As noted earlier, civil law systems provide weaker support for creditor rights than common law systems (La Porta *et al.* 1997, 1998). For this reason civil law countries tend to have less developed financial markets. But that tendency does not apply to Chile. What sets Chile apart is the fact that major changes in the financial market beginning in the early 1980s progressed hand in hand with the modernization of the legal framework and the passing of new laws.

The law is not the only significant issue, though. Enforcement matters as well, and in Chile enforcement lags behind the law. The Chilean judicial system is inefficient in resolving disputes, costly, and generally unlikely to produce an effective result. Similarly, punishment can be a significant determinant of willingness to pay, and the Chilean system tends to discriminate among debtors. For example bad checks are treated differently in Chile than overdue bills of exchange. (Bills of exchange are a type of promissory note in which an agent recognizes a debt to somebody else—for instance, firms sign this type of note with suppliers.) But such bills are harder to collect than checks, since delinquent debtors can go to prison, while companies that do not pay bills of exchange are under no such threat. This fact explains why bad checks account for less than 1 percent of total checks, while overdue bills of exchange make up between 7 and 10 percent of total bills of exchange.[15]

Changes to the bankruptcy code in 1982 (Law 18,175) were intended to improve the efficiency of the judicial system. In part they were intended to protect both debtors and creditors and to resolve the problem of preferential treatment for some creditors.

The Judicial System

In Chile the judicial system is more efficient than in other French civil law countries—that is, its efficiency is higher than the average for the group.

---

[15] A new credit instrument, the postdated check, is widely accepted by department stores. Customers with checking accounts can pay for their purchases with three postdated checks. This type of credit is not included in the statistics on the size of the financial market.

However the efficiency of the judicial system is below the average for the whole sample and is even worse compared with the average of the other groups (Table 6.1). The information provided by La Porta et al. (1997, 1998) is based on the assessment of foreign investors who have done business in the country. The analysis in this chapter instead includes statistics on the efficiency of the judicial system. Table 6.12, for example, shows statistics on lawsuits resolved in 1993-96. Executory lawsuits include all types of lawsuits that include a payment agreement—for example, lawsuits involving unpaid loans or car accidents. Distinguishing among the different types of cases is impossible, so the figures provide an overall idea of how well the judicial system operates.

The number of lawsuits ruled on in any given year is smaller than the number of lawsuits filed during the same year, except for bankruptcy cases. To compute the length of the average lawsuit the stock of lawsuits at the end of year t is divided by the lawsuits resolved during the period $t+1$. The number of lawsuits that can be classified as debt litigation was available for 1995, and the average share of this item is then applied to total lawsuits filed in 1990-96. Table 6.13 shows that the estimated length of a lawsuit varies from 1.5 to 2 years.[16]

In addition to being lengthy, judicial proceedings are costly. Attorneys charge 10 percent of the amount recovered. Considering the time required to settle a lawsuit in the courts and the costs involved, banks have every incentive not to take legal action. As a result, only 20 percent of unpaid loans are taken to court. Most of them are settled through private arrangements, because banks prefer to negotiate private agreements with debtors rather than file a lawsuit. Thus the operation of the judicial system cannot explain the low level of arrears in the banking system.

The Bankruptcy Code

The current bankruptcy code, which was enacted in 1982, replaced a law dating back to 1925. The new law made two important changes designed to accelerate bankruptcy proceedings. First, bankruptcy receivers would be private agents designated by creditors and supervised by the National Bank-

---

[16] This result confirms the information obtained during interviews with banking sector executives.

Table 6.12. Percentage of Lawsuits Resolved in 1993-96

Type of litigation	1993 Filed	1993 Ruled	1994 Filed	1994 Ruled	1995 Filed	1995 Ruled	1996 Filed	1996 Ruled
Bad check	32.5	38.0	30.7	34.4	28.0	35.8	25.8	33.5
Overdue bill of exchange	9.9	11.6	5.9	7.6	5.4	7.4	4.2	5.9
Bankruptcy	0.1	0.2	0.1	0.2	0.1	0.1	0.1	0.1
Executory lawsuits	57.5	50.2	63.3	57.8	66.5	56.7	69.9	60.5
Total number	175,679	126,816	236,909	154,747	233,104	187,749	259,069	216,366

Source: National Institute of Statistics and Department of Statistics, Court of Appeals. Data on stock and length of lawsuits developed by authors.

Table 6.13. Estimated Length of Lawsuits, 1990-96

Year	Lawsuits filed	Lawsuits ruled	Stock of lawsuits at the end of the year	Length of a lawsuit (years)
1990	128,494	117,831	205,656	1.95
1991	127,380	105,625	227,411	2.10
1992	123,026	108,233	242,204	1.91
1993	175,679	126,816	291,067	1.88
1994	236,909	154,747	373,229	1.99
1995	233,104	187,749	418,584	1.93
1996	259,069	216,366	461,287	

Source: National Institute of Statistics and Department of Statistics, Court of Appeals. Data on stock and length of lawsuits developed by authors.

ruptcy Receivership. Second, the law mandated a deposit of U.F. 100 (approximately US$3,117) for each bankruptcy petition against another party.[17] Under the previous code petitioners incurred no costs, and many bankrupt companies and individuals had no assets. Bankruptcy proceedings for those with assets are much shorter under the new code (Table 6.14).

The means are different at the 1-percent level of significance. According to this measure, then, the new bankruptcy code did improve the efficiency of bankruptcy proceedings. Moreover, the variance in duration decreased considerably, making the length of the procedure more predictable.

An important economic implication of a bankruptcy code is how well the law protects debtors' as opposed to creditors' interests. The National Bankruptcy Receivership groups bankruptcies into three categories according to cause—fortuitous, guilty, and fraudulent. Fortuitous bankruptcies are spurred by an unexpected event such as a natural disaster. The guilty category includes bankruptcies that result from negligent management. Fraudulent bankruptcies are those in which the debtor has acted illegally.

---

[17] Unidad de Fomento (denomination unit).

Table 6.14. Length of Bankruptcy Proceedings

Code	Number of bankruptcies	Years	Mean duration of proceedings	Standard deviation
4,558 (from 1925)	1,218	1929-83	4 years and 10 months	4 years and 11 months
18,175 (1982)	887	1983-96	3 years and 1 month	2 years and 5 months

Source: National Bankruptcy Receivership, Bulletin 54.

Debtors must file their bankruptcy petition within 15 days after failing to pay a liability. They must also submit the required financial statements identifying creditors, the amount of all liabilities and assets, and a statement explaining the company's poor financial performance (if applicable). The creditors' committee designates the bankruptcy receiver, whose first action is to collect all the debtor's accounting books and other relevant material in order to compile a list of the assets (normally within seven days).[18] The receiver is responsible for the management of the firm while the assets are sold, including collecting any outstanding accounts. The receiver then sells the assets and settles with the creditors. First-class debts that have not been challenged during the judicial process have priority.[19] Second-class debts include those guaranteed with assets. Mortgages follow, and then unsecured debt. Debts are paid in proportion to the original amount.

By law, anyone acknowledged as a creditor by the bankruptcy receiver has voting rights on the creditors' committee and thus helps determine the future of the bankrupt firm.[20] In this sense Chilean standing law does not assign any special role to secured creditors, as do the codes in the United

[18] These actions were completed within seven days in 86 percent of bankruptcy cases, according to the National Bankruptcy Receivership.

[19] First-class debts are as follows: judicial expenses, expenses related to managing the bankruptcy, expenses incurred due to the illness or death of debtor, employees' salaries, Social Security contributions owing, legal compensation for workers, taxes, and withholding tax claims. In general, the priorities in descending order are as follows: direct costs associated with the bankruptcy, expenses associated with the debtor's illness or death, debts to workers, and tax debts.

[20] The law requires that at least two of the creditors attend meetings of the creditors' committee and that they represent no less than 25 percent of the creditors entitled to vote.

Kingdom and United States.[21] Under the current Chilean code, creditors can agree either to continue operating the company or to liquidate its assets.[22] The law requires that a majority of creditors (at least 67 percent) agree in order for a firm to continue operating and that a 50 percent majority authorizes liquidation. These practices compare well with those of industrial countries. In the United Kingdom secured creditors can liquidate a firm even if it is worth more as a going concern to all creditors; in Germany all creditors vote. In the United Kingdom the bankruptcy receiver has complete control of the firm for purposes of liquidation and does not need the approval of the creditors to sell the company's assets. In Germany the firm's assets can be sold over time (the average time is 27.5 months).

Under the revised law bankruptcy procedures in Chile progress faster than similar procedures in industrial countries because of the time limit on liquidating assets. In addition, permitting all creditors to vote prevents a possible redistribution of wealth from unsecured to secured creditors—an improvement over the situation in the United Kingdom and the United States. The new German code (effective in 1999) gives the same voting rights to all creditors but allows a much longer period of time for liquidating assets.

The debtor, like anyone else, can file a petition for bankruptcy. Between 1982 and 1994 financial institutions were the most frequent petitioners for bankruptcy in Chile (38.9 percent), followed by debtors themselves (34.9 percent).[23] These figures make sense: financial institutions are in a position to provide resources to companies to continue in business, and debtors must avoid being classified as guilty or fraudulent in bankruptcy.

The efficiency of bankruptcy proceedings also depends on their direct and indirect costs.[24] Altman (1984) is one of the first authors to attempt to measure the indirect costs for a sample of 19 firms in different industries in the United States. He finds that these costs are between 8.1 and 10.5 percent

---

[21] For a more detailed discussion see Franks, Nyborg and Thorous (1996).

[22] The firm can continue partial or full operations for at the most two more years. If assets are liquidated they must be sold within six months (nine months for real property such as land and buildings).

[23] Data from the National Bankruptcy Receivership.

[24] The direct costs of bankruptcy include the time managers spend dealing with creditors, legal expenses, court costs, and advisory fees. The indirect costs are the unexpected losses generated by the high probability of winding up in bankruptcy. For example in the three years prior to bankruptcy companies often experience unexplained reductions in sales and increases in operating, administrative, and financial costs.

of the market value of the firm prior to bankruptcy and may run as high as 17.5 percent of the market value of the firm one year prior to the bankruptcy. Direct bankruptcy costs vary from 2 to 4 percent of the market value of the firm before bankruptcy.

Maquieira (1993) tries to estimate direct and indirect bankruptcy costs in Chile. He finds that these costs represent, on average, 16.2 percent of the market value of the firm a year before the bankruptcy. This result suggests that total bankruptcy costs in Chile are on average higher than in the United States. It further suggests that, though relatively fast, the procedure is expensive enough to seriously reduce the probability that creditors will succeed in collecting by petitioning for bankruptcy.

Private Solutions

Given the time and expense involved in petitioning for bankruptcy, banks have developed a number of private solutions to prevent default or deal with its consequences. These include improved prescreening techniques and collection technology. By avoiding a judicial process, banks can significantly increase their chances of recovering a portion of unpaid loans.

Prescreening Techniques

Banks apply different prescreening procedures to companies and households. Corporate loans are judged on a case-by-case basis. Among the most important variables that banks analyze in order to allocate commercial credit are:

- the company's track record with the bank and the financial system (confirmed through DICOM)

- the company's capacity to generate the cash flows needed to meet financial costs

- the ownership structure, because banks will loan to firms with some cash-flow problems if the owners have good business references[25]

---

[25] As Avery, Bostic and Samolyk (1998) show, for small U.S. businesses personal assets serve as a substitute for business collateral for credit purposes. But personal guarantees do not appear to be substitutes for personal collateral.

- any bad checks or bills of exchange under litigation

- the company's leverage and liquidity.

The functional level at which banks decide whether to grant credit depends on the amount requested and the type of collateral available. A bank executive generally makes small credit decisions, while boards of directors decide on credit applications involving large amounts. In either case, the better the collateral is, the more likely the borrower will repay the loan.

Consumers can obtain loans from banks, department stores, and finance companies.[26] Banks are mainly concentrated in the household segment with the highest income level. Finance companies deal with more moderate-income households, and department stores on average cater to those households with the lowest incomes. Given that each group has a different level of risk and that the interest rates reflect these risks, the consumer credit market is segmented.

Since consumption credit is a type of retail credit, finance companies and retail banks use a statistical technique called credit scoring to discriminate between high and low-quality borrowers. Among the variables included in the statistical analysis are past and current indebtedness with the financial system, number of arrears, commercial track record (checks and bills of exchange under litigation), past performance with the finance company, past performance with credit cards, job situation (economic activity, net income, and job tenure, for instance), plus demographic variables. Banks do not generally use credit scoring because most of their customers are businesses.[27]

Fuentes and Maquieira (1999) provide a data set of 38,281 consumer loans granted between June and August 1997 to which credit scoring was applied. Of these some 14,507 (37.9 percent) should have been rejected under the scoring system, but applicants nevertheless received credit. This data set provides a good opportunity to examine the efficiency of consumer lending in Chile, as the same credits were observed one year later. Some of them were still outstanding and others were past due. The researchers find that

---

[26] Finance companies are those institutions that by law are not allowed to provide current accounts. The companies receive money from banks as deposits and lend to individuals for consumption purposes.

[27] DICOM also calculates a credit score banks can either use directly or apply to their own models. DICOM's score may not consider some characteristics appropriate to bank customers.

the cutoff policy established under the scoring system appears to be too restrictive. Only 8.9 percent of the loans that would have been rejected using the scoring system were 90 days overdue.

Collection Technology

The technology used to collect past-due loans depends on the type of contract, the issuer, and the debtor. Banks may outsource collection to a collection agency (mainly for consumer and large household loans) or use an internal office called the Department of Normalization (mainly for firms). By law banks cannot profit from collection activities, but they are allowed to charge interest on past-due loans.

Chile's financial sector began developing collection technologies when banks started concentrating on the consumer loan market (an outcome of the disintermediation process). Both the volume of loans in this market and the fact that banks cannot profit from collection activities contributed to the development of a collection industry. Banks charge interest on overdue loans, and collection agencies charge a collection fee. The banks' owners control some collection agencies, but others are independent.

Collection is an important aspect of the household credit market. Collection usually starts five days after the due date for credit cards, 15 days after the due date for consumer loans, and 45 days after the due date for mortgages. Banks, finance companies, and department stores work with collection agencies before taking a case to court. A positive correlation exists between the existence of collateral and the time a financial institution allows to elapse before it initiates collection activities.

Technical developments in telecommunications have improved the financial sector's ability to collect unpaid loans. The liberalization of the telecommunications industry at the end of the 1980s triggered a change in collection technology simply by decreasing telephone costs dramatically. The cost of computer-based activities also fell as computer technology improved.

Creditors begin their collection activities by sending lists of past-due loans to collection agencies on a regular basis. The most advanced type of collection technology is an electronic device that consolidates, integrates, and evaluates all the information on a debtor in a single database. This device ranks the likelihood of recovery through payment on the basis of the information available.

Department stores use another kind of credit technology. When they want to collect an unpaid loan, they simultaneously send the information to a collection agency and to DICOM. Notifying DICOM is one of the most effective mechanisms for recovering a loan, since department stores' clients do not have access to other sources of credit and therefore must resolve the situation with the creditor as soon as possible.

When a corporate loan is past due, banks initially try to negotiate an agreement with the debtor. They resort to different methods to collect the loan, often by changing the conditions. They may be willing to reschedule the terms of the loan, accept new collateral, reduce the interest rate, refinance the debt based on a partial cash payment at the time of rescheduling, liquidate guarantees, or finance a new project.[28] When all negotiations fail or the debtor is dishonest, the case is sent to the bank's legal department for action. The success of these activities depends on the existence of collateral and the type of guarantees. When no collateral exists, the bank's ability to collect will simply depend on the debtor's willingness to repay.[29]

Concluding Remarks

Several features of the Chilean financial market make this economy a unique case study of debt repayment issues. First, although the Chilean legal framework is based on French civil law, the economy performs better than other economies in the same group in terms of nonperforming loans and capital market development. Additionally, in the 1990s the Chilean financial market featured increasing competition and the gradual disintermediation of banks. The result of these developments was a reduction in margins that led banks to seek new, relatively high-risk market niches such as households and small business. However, this shift in focus did not increase the number of arrears in the banking system.

The plausible explanations for this performance fall into three groups: the macroeconomic environment, the legal framework, and private solu-

---

[28] Assets must be liquidated within a year, as a bank cannot hold an asset longer.

[29] If collateral exists loan recovery depends on the type of guarantee. Collateral could be a mortgage in the case of real estate or a pledge in the case of equipment. To liquidate the collateral the bank first needs to take the debtor to court. When the court rules and the debtor is notified, the bank can auction the assets.

tions. Monthly data for 1986-97 indicate that good macroeconomic performance and the introduction of positive (or white) information sharing are negatively correlated with overdue loans. Moreover information sharing reduces the sensitivity of defaults to the business cycle. In addition, yearly data show that good macroeconomic performance, major financial market reform, and positive information sharing are positively related to credit market development. Information sharing reduces the impact of the economy's growth rate on credit market development.

Considering the high increase in loans per capita in the last 20 years, limited access to credit can hardly be an explanation for the low level of arrears in the financial system. The amount of collateral banks require on household loans may be perceived as excessive because it exceeds what banks require from companies. These large collateral requirements could be a symptom of households' limited access to credit. However, banks are not the only intermediaries that serve households: finance companies and department stores are also very active in this segment. Finance companies are slightly more selective than department stores and apply a stricter prescreening process. Department stores provide small amounts of credit guaranteed by purchased goods. Clients of department stores have limited access to the financial system. Because they depend on department stores alone for credit, these borrowers tend to repay their loans on time.

Countries with a legal framework based on French civil law have poorer law enforcement than other countries. Chile is no exception. Banks are reluctant to take unpaid loans to court, preferring instead to reschedule them (except at the time of a generalized crisis). Such a stance signals an inefficient judicial system. Lawsuits can drag on for up to two years, attorneys cost around 10 percent of any amount recovered, and banks recover part of their losses only when they hold some collateral. Considering the time and costs involved in a judicial procedure and the fact that more efficient alternatives are available, banks have almost no incentive to go to court to recover loans.

The new bankruptcy code accelerates the proceedings relative to the former law and also relative to industrial countries, since it sets a one-year limit for liquidating assets. The new code also allows unsecured creditors to sit on the creditors' committee and to vote during the bankruptcy process—in short creditors are allowed to protect their rights. The creditors' committee designates the bankruptcy receiver, who is a private agent that manages the firm during the proceedings, identifies debtors, liquidates assets, and pays creditors.

Banks have several private solutions to the problem of unwillingness to pay. The first is information sharing, which in Chile started as a private initiative in 1979. Only in 1989 did the system begin to handle both black and white information on debtors. This information is available only to banks and positively impacted both the development of the banking system and the proportion of nonperforming loans. Banks use credit bureau data to "score" households applying for credit. This technique reduces arrears but could end up shutting out too many solvent debtors if it is not checked. Department stores are reluctant to share information and consequently do not have any information about their clients' total debt to the banking system. However these stores do not display high levels of arrears, probably because their borrowers have limited access to the credit market and thus are careful about paying back their loans.

Chile has relatively well-developed collection technologies due to the reductions in telecommunications fees and the development of relatively sophisticated techniques. Banks tend to outsource overdue household loans to specialized collection agencies, improving recovery of these loans. In the case of firms, banks rely on an internal normalization department that seeks to negotiate an agreement with the firm. Only if these negotiations fail or the debtor turns out to be dishonest is the case taken to court.

All these factors—the macroeconomic environment, financial market regulations, reform of the bankruptcy code, information sharing, and collection technology—help to explain the low default rate Chile's financial system enjoys. The judicial system does not contribute to the economy's performance in this regard. Reforming the judicial system, however, could only contribute further to this impressive performance and to the further development of the country's financial markets.

CHAPTER 7

Enforcement, Contract Design and Default: Exploring the Financial Markets of Costa Rica

Alexander Monge-Naranjo, Javier Cascante and Luis J. Hall

This chapter examines the institutional determinants of incentives to repay in Costa Rica and their effects on defaults and the design of financial contracts. Enforcement mechanisms help to determine how much is paid back to creditors and how much shareholders receive as dividends. Theoretically, however, the most important effects will be on the observable characteristics of contracts, as rational agents foresee the incentives of other parties. As courts enforce contracts and punish defaulters, they determine the form contracts take and the magnitude and direction of investments.

Recent work by La Porta *et al.* (1997) reports significant differences in the financial markets of countries that have different types of legal systems. The most notable difference is between countries with a French civil law system and those with British common law traditions. Costa Rica is much closer to the civil law tradition.[1] While this international comparison is by itself highly suggestive, a closer look at actual enforcement, contracting design, and creditors' outcomes in Costa Rica can provide a better understanding of the effectiveness of the legal framework, alternative enforcement mechanisms, and lenders' responses in allocating credit.

This chapter contains findings on the practices of financial intermediaries that are discussed in the context of contract theory, with a focus on the

---

Alexander Monge-Naranjo is an Assistant Professor in the Department of Economics at Northwestern University. Javier Cascante and Luis J. Hall are researchers at the Institute for Research in Economic Sciences and Professors of Economics at the University of Costa Rica.
[1] Costa Rica is not included in their study. The corresponding values are derived from the authors' own readings of the Civil and Commercial Codes. The values are reported in Monge-Naranjo, Cascante and Hall (2001).

formal financial intermediaries that are scattered throughout the country.[2] Much of the information comes from primary sources, including a sample of almost 1,700 civil trials and a detailed survey on the credit policies of 31 intermediaries.[3] The data cover a large variety of intermediaries, permitting an investigation of the ways outcomes vary with creditor practices.

This chapter reviews the creditor-borrower relationship at all stages— ex ante, interim, and ex post. The evidence supports the importance of collateral and other ex post repayment incentives. Collateral is a critical variable in granting a loan, as well as in determining how closely the bank follows it, how much is recovered in case of default, and how efficiently the courts function as an enforcement mechanism. The evidence also suggests that, contrary to the common view, banks are not passive lenders. They remain alert to how well projects perform and rely on previous experience and a rather sophisticated informational network in granting credit.

Financial Intermediation in Costa Rica

Despite Costa Rica's small economy, a diverse group of financial intermediaries operates in the country.[4] While demographic heterogeneity could explain the variety of intermediaries, government intervention has also had a remarkable effect. After the civil war in 1948, the new government nationalized the three largest commercial banks. Together with the already public National Bank, these banks have since allocated most of the credit in Costa Rica. The new government regarded nationalization as one of its major achievements, and later attempts to liberalize these banks faced fierce opposition from specific interest groups as well as widespread skepticism and general unpopularity. Important political sectors still oppose efforts to complete the privatization of the remaining public financial intermediaries. Nationalization prevented private entities from accepting deposits, but gov-

---

[2] Thus important sectors such as housing credit, trade and retail credit, and informal credit are omitted.

[3] Box 7.1 below identifies the banks interviewed.

[4] As of September 1998, the Superintendency of Financial Institutions (SUGEF) was regulating three commercial public banks, 23 private banks, 35 savings and loan cooperatives, 17 private nonbanking financial companies, nine mutual funds for housing, and three other intermediaries created under special laws.

ernment intervention was not confined to the creation of this "deposit monopsony." The Central Bank was given direct control over interest rates (both lending and borrowing) and over the allocation of credit through quantitative restrictions on lending for different activities.

The events of the second half of the twentieth century in Costa Rica can be succinctly summarized as a very slow but persistent reversal of earlier nationalization policies. In 1972 nonbanking institutions were allowed to obtain funds from the public in the form of investment certificates. While restrictions were placed on the maturity of these certificates, the simple fact of their existence resulted in a remarkable growth in private intermediaries, both in number and in shares of total bank credit (Figures 7.1 and 7.2). In 1984 private banks began intermediating resources from foreign loans, national institutions, and multilateral cooperation agencies. In the second half of the 1980s, the authorities lifted credit quotas and ended direct regulation of interest rates. Moreover, after the liquidity crisis of 1987, the General Auditor of Banks extended its authority to include nonbanking institutions,

Figure 7.1. Share of Bank Credit by Type of Intermediary, 1974-97

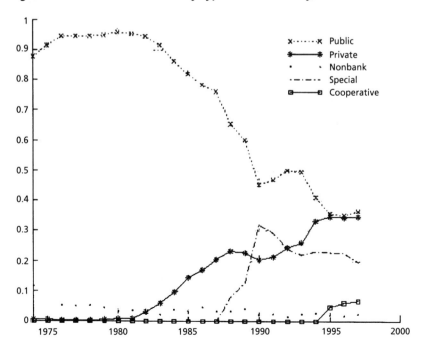

Figure 7.2. Number of Financial Intermediaries, 1974-97

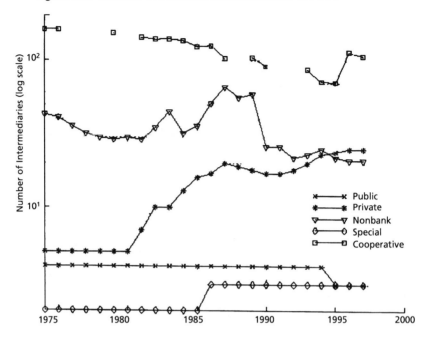

becoming the General Auditor of Financial Institutions (AGEF). But the reform maintained important asymmetries among intermediaries. First, private banks could not receive deposits with a maturity of less than 180 days. Second, they did not have access to the Central Bank discount window. Third, the AGEF did not regulate cooperatives and other intermediaries created by special laws. Fourth, the Central Bank implicitly backed only those deposits issued by public institutions.

Liberalization generated a trend of decreasing concentration in the banking industry, as illustrated by the most common concentration indices, here applied to the assets of regulated intermediaries (Figures 7.3 and 7.4).[5]

---

[5] The following explanation applies: N is the number of firms in an industry and $j=1,2,3...,N$ indexes each of them. In addition p_j is the share of firm j in the industry. The Hirschman-Herfindhal index is defined as $HH \equiv \sum_{j}^{N} = p_j^2$. HH is always between 0 and 1, and the higher it is, the more concentrated is the industry. Entropy is defined as $E = -\sum_{j=1}^{N} = p_j \log_2(p_j)$. It ranges between 0 and $\log_2(N)$, and the lower E is, the higher the concentration. Relative entropy is defined as $E/\log_2(N)$, so its values range between 0 and 1, independently of N. Overall

Figure 7.3. Banking Industry Concentration, 1970-2000

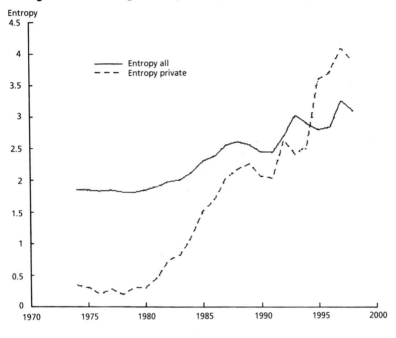

The figures show that the decrease in concentration is the result of the greater presence of private banks and also the lower concentration *within* the group of private intermediaries.

The 1990s ushered in a new wave of liberalization. Restrictions on operations in foreign currency that had long been in place were, for all practical purposes, relaxed for all types of banks. Asymmetries in the regulation of financial intermediaries were eliminated. Private banks were given access to the discount window of the Central Bank and allowed to accept deposits with any maturity, including demand deposits.[6] In 1998 the government instituted a further reform, creating three superintendencies to regulate financial markets under the control of the National Council of Financial Su-

---

assets rather than just credit are used here, because government debt and other bonds are an important component of banks' portfolios. The calculations exclude institutions like Banco Popular, the Fund of the National Teachers Association (ANDE), and the cooperatives, which until recently were not regulated.

[6] Banking intermediaries can create checking accounts, provided they open agencies in rural areas or deposit part of these accounts in the public banks.

Figure 7.4. Banking Industry Concentration by Alternative Indices, 1970-2000

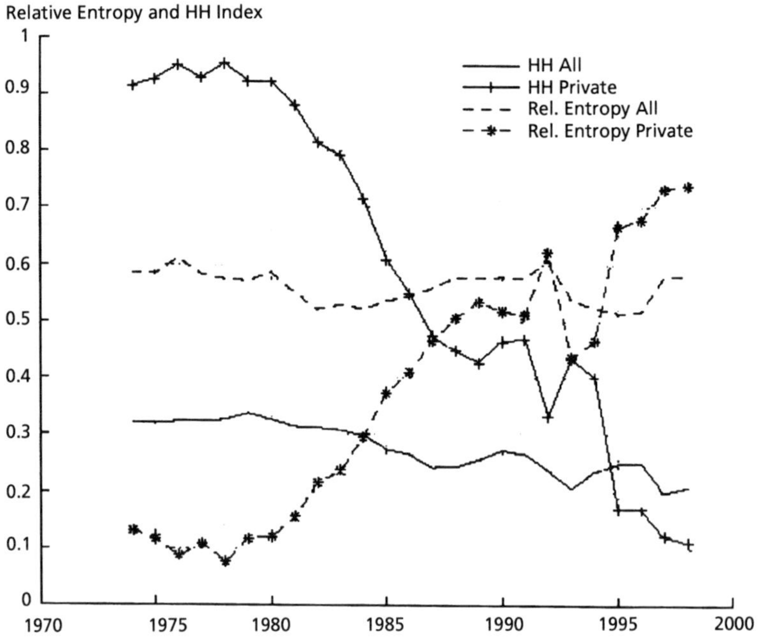

Relative Entropy and HH Index

pervision (CONASIF). The AGEF became the General Superintendency of Financial Entities; two other agencies, the General Superintendency of Stock Markets (SUGEVAL) and the General Superintendency of Pension Funds (SUPEN) regulate the securities markets and pension funds, respectively. The new Superintendency of Financial Entities extended its supervisory powers to the savings and loan cooperatives and other special banks like Banco Popular, which is financed with compulsory savings from workers and employers. The superintendency follows the guidelines set out in the Basle Accords. While regulation in terms of capital, liquidity, and management varies across types of intermediary, credit is regulated and graded uniformly. Despite these changes, the Central Bank still insures only the deposits of public banks.[7]

---

[7] This fact is not explicitly stated. But the Central Bank backed the deposits of the liquidated Banco Anglo, although it has not covered the deposits of liquidated private banks such as Banco Germano.

Figure 7.5. Percentage Shares of Activities Financed by Intermediaries in Costa Rica

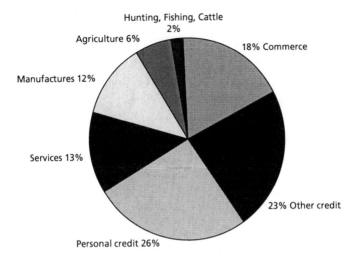

Intermediaries finance a wide variety of activities (Figure 7.5).[8] The largest share is personal credit, which encompasses any financing used for household consumption, including credit cards (housing, however, is included under "other"). Services include tourism, the country's fastest-growing industry since the late 1990s. Agriculture and other primary sectors represent a very small fraction of bank credit. While bank credit is not necessarily representative of total credit, this breakdown of activities financed by banks shows the variety of uses for credit.[9]

---

[8] Cooperatives are not included because, as of 1998, they had not been added to the database.

[9] Several biases exist, however. First, a large fraction of credit for agricultural uses is generated in nonbanking institutions, as in the coffee sector. Second, as confirmed by interviews with bankers conducted as part of this study, many loans to other productive sectors are classified as personal credit because borrowers want to speed up the approval process. Third, a large share of personal credit is allocated by cooperatives, retail stores, and other traders. Fourth, housing is largely financed by the *mutuales*, financial companies that specialize in housing credit. Some casual evidence also suggests that the credit extended by street vendors, informally called *polacos*, is important for urban low-income households.

Figure 7.6. Credit by Type of Intermediary

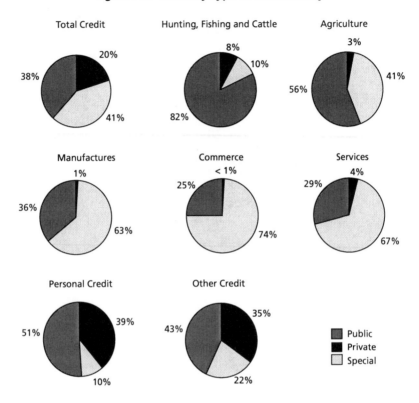

Since 1995 public and private banks have shared the credit market almost equally (Figure 7.1).[10] Yet the activities they finance differ (Figure 7.6). Public banks are markedly more dominant in agriculture, reflecting their extensive network of agencies and branches in rural areas and their institutional expertise. But credit to the fastest growing productive sectors—manufacturing, commerce, and services—is largely in the hands of private banks, reflecting the greater flexibility these banks show in responding to new activities. In some sectors special banks have acquired a market share, including the Fund of the National Association of Teachers (ANDE) and Banco Popular (personal credit) and the National Bank of Mortgages and Housing (BANVHI), which provides housing credit.

---

[10] The balance has been changing, however. In February 1998 private banks had a larger share in total credit.

Overall default rates are not very high, especially for public and private banks, and reflect mostly arrears. Moreover banks experience the highest default rates in those sectors where their participation is lowest (Figure 7.7). On average private banks have lower default rates than public banks. Except for the small number of loans in legal collection, however, the difference in the default rates of private and public banks is not great. For special banks, instead, the default rates can be significant. The largest number of defaulted loans are in the manufacturing sector (55 percent of loans are late or in legal collection). This pattern suggests that the intermediary's expertise in the sector reduces the default rate.

Contract Design and Bank-Borrower Relationships

Since the legal framework is common to all intermediaries, any differences in the number of defaults across banks must result from differences among the banks themselves—and their clients. Matching borrowers and intermediaries, a process probably complicated by adverse selection, can account for some of the differences. But ultimately these differences are determined by the intermediaries' credit policies, which affect repayment incentives. These policies set screening procedures, collateral requirements, methods of monitoring active loans, and actions taken on nonperforming loans.

The information presented here on credit policies is based on responses from a sample of 31 intermediaries to a 1998 questionnaire.[11] The sample consists of 15 branches of the three public banks, eight private banks, five savings and credit cooperatives and three other banks (Banco Popular and two private banks) owned and managed by groups such as cooperatives and labor unions (Box 7.1).[12] The sample provides geographic and demographic variety. It contains 13 intermediaries in the San José metropolitan area (all with headquarters in San José) and 18 intermediaries scattered in various rural areas, including the southern and northern regions and the Pacific and Atlantic watersheds.

---

[11] No public record or comprehensive study on the credit policies of intermediaries is available. The questionnaire was answered by the intermediaries' credit manager with the help of credit and collection personnel.

[12] The two cooperative banks were liquidated in 1999.

234

Figure 7.7. Status of Debt by Activity and Intermediary (share)

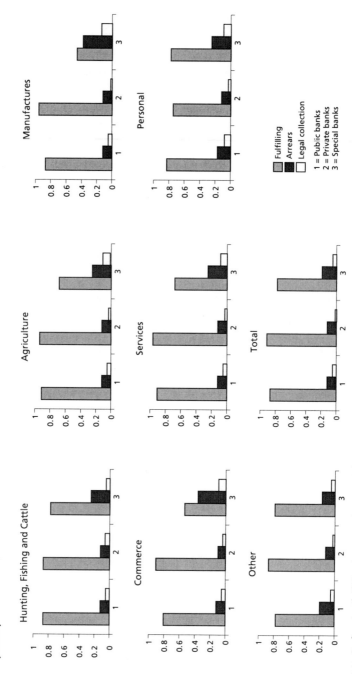

Note: Performing/fulfilling loans are those repaid on time. Arrears are those that have not been repaid on time but that have not gone into judicial procedure. Legal collection indicates loans for which the bank has started a judicial process.

Box 7.1. Intermediaries in the Sample

Intermediary	Rural/metropolitan	Phone calls	Visits	Questionnaire
Private bank				
Banco CQ	R	30	3	Complete
Banco de San José	M	33	3	Complete
Banco del Comercio	M	40	4	Complete
Banco ELCA	M	35	4	Complete
Banco Improsa	M	24	2	Complete
BANEX	M	36	4	Complete
BFA	M	35	3	Complete
Interfin	M	70	3	Complete
Bancrecen	M	21	2	Unanswered
Public bank				
Banco Crédito				
Agrícola de Cartago	M	16	3	Complete
Banco de Costa Rica				Complete
San José	M	50	3	Complete
Guápiles	R	30	1	Complete
Liberia	R	32	1	Complete
Limón	R	12	1	Complete
Puntarenas	R	38	1	Complete
San Carlos	R	27	1	Complete
Turrialba	R	15	1	Complete
Banco Nacional de Costa Rica				Complete
San José	M	30	6	Complete
Guápiles	R	10	1	Complete
Limón	R	20	1	Complete
Puntarenas	R	10	1	Complete
San Carlos	R	28	1	Complete
Turrialba	R	38	1	Complete
Cooperative				
COOCIQUE	R	25	3	Complete
COOPEALIANZA	R	15	3	Complete
COOPESANRAMON	R	10	2	Complete
COOPESPARTA	R	17	1	Complete
COOTILARAN	R	10	1	Complete
COOPESANMARCOS	R	15	1	Unanswered
Special bank				
Banco Federado	M	25	2	Complete
Bancoop	M	20	3	Complete
BPDC	M	29	3	Complete
Total	33	845	69	

The intermediaries are classified according to demographic type (metropolitan or rural) and institutional type (public, private, cooperative, and other). The questionnaire used three types of multiple-choice questions designed to measure how often intermediaries take certain actions and whether certain items are relevant to credit procedures. The first involves the frequency of a given action by the intermediary; the alternatives are never, rarely, occasionally, frequently, very frequently, always. The second type asks the relevance of a given item; the alternatives are irrelevant, little importance, some importance, important, very important, crucial. The third type is a yes-or-no question. For tractability the answers are grouped as "frequently to always" and "important to crucial."[13]

Screening Projects and Borrowers

In general, entrepreneurs know more about themselves and their projects than creditors do. Most theoretical models take one of two extreme views: that the characteristics of the project are common knowledge or that only the entrepreneur knows them. The latter view leads to models of adverse selection in which intermediaries' contracts must consider the incentives to entrepreneurs of revealing such information. In practice, however, banks can try to acquire information on projects and entrepreneurs. This type of information gathering is costly, but it can help banks decide whether to grant loans and what terms to apply.

The questionnaire asked banks about the process used to investigate credit applications. The questions covered every practice that could conceivably yield useful information about the prospects of a project and the characteristics of the borrower and the collateral. The results show that banks (especially private institutions located in the San José metropolitan area) actively screen potential borrowers (Table 7.1). For example, 85 percent of metropolitan banks and 75 percent of private banks visit firms that apply for credit, especially new clients. In general, intermediaries check the applicant's reputation, although metropolitan and rural banks use different mechanisms.

---

[13] The choices for frequency are never, rarely, occasionally, frequently, very frequently, and always. The options for relevance are irrelevant, little importance, some importance, important, very important, and crucial. The results are grouped as "frequently to always" and "important to crucial," and these categories are used in the analysis.

Table 7.1. Screening Mechanisms Used Frequently or Always
(percent)

| | Total | Demographic type | | Type of institution | | | |
| | | | | | | Cooper- | |
Item	Sample (31)	Metro. (13)	Rural (18)	Public (15)	Private (8)	ative (5)	Other (3)
Visit the firm	64.5	84.6	50.0	60.0	75.0	60.0	66.6
Study the project evaluation	87.0	92.3	83.3	93.3	87.5	60.0	100.0
Study financial statements	93.5	100.0	88.8	93.3	100.0	66.6	100.0
Analyze project risk	87.0	76.9	94.4	93.3	75.0	66.6	100.0
Analyze sectoral risk	61.2	61.5	61.1	60.0	62.5	60.0	66.6
Analyze international risk	19.3	30.7	11.1	13.3	37.5	20.0	0.0
Assess liquidity of collateral	93.5	92.3	94.4	93.3	100.0	66.6	100.0
Assess market value of collateral	96.7	100.0	94.4	100.0	100.0	66.6	100.0
Check reputation of applicant	90.3	100.0	83.3	93.3	100.0	60.0	100.0
Physically audit collateral	80.6	92.3	72.2	66.6	100.0	100.0	66.6
Suggest modifications to project	54.8	61.5	50.0	60.0	50.0	60.0	33.3

The most common screening activity is careful scrutiny of both the collateral and the borrower's overall assets, including a review of relevant financial statements. Regulation indeed provides an incentive to demand collateral, because banks are required to maintain reserves on loans (depending on performance); for large loans, reserve requirements depend on collateral. While banks take project risk into account, they assign only moderate importance to sectoral and international risk. Finally, intermediaries sometimes suggest modifications to the intended use of funds, but this practice is not particularly pervasive.

The questionnaire allowed respondents to prioritize various criteria for granting a loan. Because different combinations of these items could produce the same result for an application, respondents were asked to note how much a positive assessment of each item would increase the chances of approval.[14] All the items included in the questionnaire are rated as very im-

---

[14] As opposed to a negative assessment—that is, how much a negative report on an item would affect the chance of approval.

Table 7.2. Criteria for Granting Loans Considered Important to Crucial
(percentage of sample)

Item	Total Sample (31)	Demographic type Metro. (13)	Rural (18)	Public (15)	Private (8)	Cooper- ative (5)	Other (3)
Solvency of applicant	100.0	100.0	100.0	100.0	100.0	100.0	100.0
Existence of project evaluation	90.3	84.6	94.4	100.0	75.0	66.6	100.0
Profitability of project	96.7	92.3	100.0	100.0	87.5	100.0	100.0
Credit references	100.0	100.0	100.0	100.0	100.0	100.0	100.0
Existence of collateral	100.0	100.0	100.0	100.0	100.0	100.0	100.0
Type of collateral	100.0	100.0	100.0	100.0	100.0	100.0	100.0
Value of collateral	100.0	100.0	100.0	100.0	100.0	100.0	100.0
Liquidity of collateral	96.7	92.3	100.0	100.0	87.5	100.0	100.0
Previous experience with borrower	96.7	100.0	94.4	100.0	87.5	100.0	100.0
Information from visit	96.7	92.3	100.0	100.0	87.5	100.0	100.0
Risk of project	93.5	84.6	100.0	93.3	87.5	100.0	100.0
Economic sector of project	87.0	84.6	88.8	100.0	87.5	60.0	66.6

portant (Table 7.2). But borrowers' characteristics—including solvency, credit references, previous experience, and collateral—are considered more relevant than project characteristics.

Determining the Interest Rate and Other Terms

According to economic theory, banks and entrepreneurs consider each other's incentives when designing contractual agreements. These incentives appear at different times—before and during the period covered by the contract and after the contract is concluded. Contractual arrangements may stipulate action plans and payment schedules, but one key variable is the interest rate. Respondents were asked to rate the importance of various loan characteristics in setting the interest rate (Table 7.3).

Surprisingly, the most important consideration in setting interest rates is the sector (economic activity of the project). This finding seems to be the inertial heritage of the interventionist epoch. However, items such as collat-

Table 7.3. Criteria for Setting Interest Rates Considered Important to Crucial
(percentage of sample)

Item	Total Sample (31)	Metro. (13)	Rural (18)	Public (15)	Private (8)	Cooper-ative (5)	Other (3)
Loan term	45.1	46.1	44.4	40.0	75.0	20.0	33.3
Type of economic activity	83.8	84.6	83.3	93.3	75.0	60.0	100.0
Amount requested	38.7	46.1	33.3	33.3	87.5	0.0	0.0
Collateral	45.1	53.8	38.8	40.0	87.55	0.0	33.3
Credit references	29.0	38.4	22.2	26.6	62.5	0.0	0.0
Previous experience	35.4	46.1	27.7	26.6	62.5	20.0	33.3

(Demographic type: Metro., Rural; Type of institution: Public, Private, Cooperative, Other)

eral, credit references, and previous experience—which are very important in the approval process—still retain some importance in setting interest rates, especially for private banks.

Interest rates are only one element in the contracts, which usually include a section on terms of reference that sets out certain procedures for both parties. The contents of this section are unlimited, and in principle it can be used to introduce responses to contingencies as well as communication and monitoring procedures. Banks make active use of this section. For instance, covenants can make provisions for contingencies—useful for dividing risks between entrepreneurs and intermediaries (Table 7.4). Table 7.5 shows the number of banks using covenants to cover shocks (called "unforeseen problems" in the questionnaire). Contrary to the predictions of models of risk sharing using private information, intermediaries set forth covenants more frequently for idiosyncratic shocks than aggregate shocks, even though the latter are more easily observable. Of the groups examined, public banks in rural areas set forth the greatest number of covenants for aggregate shocks. No private bank uses covenants for regional shocks, and only one metropolitan branch of a public bank does so. Covenants for shocks from projects and entrepreneurs are much more common among private banks. For the most part, cooperatives do not use covenants.

Table 7.4. Banks Using Covenants Frequently to Always
(percentage of sample)

Item	Total Sample (31)	Demographic type		Type of institution			
		Metro. (13)	Rural (18)	Public (15)	Private (8)	Cooperative (5)	Other (3)
Reports of the project results	83.8	92.3	77.7	93.3	87.5	40.0	100.0
Evolution of the investment plan	93.5	92.3	94.4	100.0	87.5	80.0	100.0
Visit of bank executives to the firm	87.0	92.3	83.3	86.6	87.5	80.0	100.0
Suspension clauses	93.5	92.3	94.4	100.0	87.5	80.0	100.0

The responses suggest that, if anything, covenants are used to monitor the projects that are financed. Intermediaries were asked how frequently they use covenants to specify alternative monitoring mechanisms (Table 7.6). The responses to this question differ radically from the responses to the previous one. Banks use covenants primarily to oblige entrepreneurs to report on the results of the investment, to call back a loan or enact other suspension measures, and to mandate visits from bank officials. All but one of the private banks and cooperatives reported using the clauses for these purposes. It is safe to say, then, that covenants are used for monitoring purposes and not to offer insurance to entrepreneurs.

Table 7.5. Banks Using Covenants to Cover Contingencies
(percentage of sample)

Item	Total Sample (31)	Demographic type		Type of institution			
		Metro. (13)	Rural (18)	Public (15)	Private (8)	Cooperative (5)	Other (3)
Regional shocks affecting project	22.5	7.6	33.3	40.0	0.0	20.0	0.0
Sectoral shocks to project	38.7	38.4	38.8	46.6	12.5	40.0	66.6
Idiosyncratic shocks to project	54.8	76.9	38.8	60.0	62.5	20.0	66.6
Other shocks to borrower	54.8	69.2	44.4	66.6	50.0	20.0	66.6

Table 7.6. Banks That Monitor Ongoing Loans Frequently to Always
(percentage of sample)

Item	Total Sample (31)	Demographic type		Type of institution			
		Metro. (13)	Rural (18)	Public (15)	Private (8)	Cooper-ative (5)	Other (3)
Visit of bank representatives	58.0	76.9	44.4	66.6	62.5	20.0	66.6
Phone calls	58.0	76.9	44.4	60.0	87.5	0.0	66.6
Service or technical support	22.5	30.7	16.6	20.0	37.5	20.0	0.0
Bank-firm meetings to evaluate course project	32.2	53.8	16.6	33.3	50.0	0.0	33.3
Monitor investment plan project	90.3	92.3	88.8	100.0	87.5	60.0	100.0
Check and audit financial statements	74.1	92.3	61.1	73.3	87.5	40.0	66.6
Check general solvency of the firm	77.4	84.6	72.2	86.6	87.5	40.0	66.6
Keep informed of other client debts	45.1	53.8	38.8	60.0	50.0	0.0	33.3
Check the behavior of input prices	19.3	23.0	16.6	20.0	37.5	0.0	0.0

Monitoring

The questionnaire asked intermediaries about monitoring practices on out-standing loans. Again, most theoretical models make one of two extreme assumptions: that entrepreneurial effort (or physical investment) is unverifiable or that it can be verified at no cost. Both parties are better off if effort is verifiable, since the absence of moral hazard enhances possibilities for risk sharing and allows for relatively large projects (among other things). Contrasting these stylized models suggests that any mechanism banks can use to verify borrowers' actions can benefit both parties, the only counterweight being the cost of the mechanism. For instance, intermediaries would like to commit to monitoring borrowers, even in a random fashion, unless monitoring costs are prohibitive.

Table 7.6 reports the frequency of different actions across banks in the sample. As before, each entry indicates the number of banks within each category. Banks were asked how frequently they take each action before problems such as delays in payment develop. The findings show that banks actively follow projects' development and that they actively monitor, especially whether the loan is effectively used for the investment plan agreed upon. They require copies of invoices or other documents showing how resources were used, send bank officials to visit firms, and keep abreast of firms' overall solvency by reviewing financial statements.

Previous Experience

In the presence of constraints on incentives, the repeated interaction of parties can radically change the nature of the optimal contract and effectively increase expected welfare. The intuition is simple: future payments and actions can be set as functions of current outcomes and actions, and since repeated replication of static contracts is always feasible, repeated interactions must necessarily increase the set of attainable allocations that is compatible with incentives.

Intermediaries were asked how they use the information acquired during previous experience with the borrower (Table 7.7). Nearly all the intermediaries keep a record of their experiences with the borrower and maintain an automated grading system. Borrowers are not always aware of this practice, however. Given the potential role of incentives in loan repayment, it is surprising that intermediaries are not more inclined to tell their clients about

Table 7.7. Use of Information on Previous Experience
(percentage of sample)

Item	Total Sample (31)	Demographic type		Type of institution			
		Metro. (13)	Rural (18)	Public (15)	Private (8)	Cooper- ative (5)	Other (3)
Keep record of previous clients	96.7	92.3	100.0	100.0	100.0	100.0	66.6
Inform clients of this record	58.0	46.1	66.6	66.6	37.5	80.0	33.3
Maintain a client grading system	97.5	100.0	94.4	93.6	100.0	100.0	100.0

it. In fact, only three out of eight private banks tell their clients about this record.

How does such experience affect contracts between banks and borrowers? As already noted, previous experience is very important in deciding whether to grant loans. But it is also important in setting the terms of contracts (Table 7.8). It has a significant effect on most of the activities under consideration. Some 24 of 31 respondents regard it as important to the speed with which they process loan applications, the collateral requirements, the overall credit evaluation, the amount lent, and other renegotiation clauses. Previous performance can be described as relationship collateral, since it plays a role similar to physical collateral. Only its effect on the repayment terms of the loan is surprisingly small. Fewer than two-thirds of lenders (19 respondents) regard previous experience as important in setting the maturity, interest rate, repayment schedule, and grace period. Thus long-term relationships with banks are important in facilitating Costa Rican companies' access to credit, even though the relationships have few effects on interest rates and other terms of loan contracts.

Table 7.8. Effects of Previous Experience on Loan Contracts
(percentage of sample)

	Total Sample (31)	Demographic type		Type of institution			
		Metro. (13)	Rural (18)	Public (15)	Private (8)	Cooper- ative (5)	Other (3)
Item							
Time for processing applications	80.6	84.6	77.7	86.6	87.5	60.0	66.6
Type of collateral required	83.8	84.6	83.3	80.0	87.5	100.0	66.6
Value or liquidity of collateral	80.6	76.9	83.3	73.3	75.0	100.0	100.0
Evaluation required of credit	77.4	69.2	83.3	93.3	75.0	60.0	33.3
Maturity of loan	58.0	46.1	66.6	73.3	50.0	40.0	33.3
Interest rate charged	54.8	46.1	44.4	84.0	87.5	40.0	66.6
Repayment schedule	61.2	53.8	66.6	60.0	62.5	60.0	66.6
Grace period	51.6	53.8	50.0	53.3	62.5	40.0	33.3
Amount lent	77.4	61.5	88.8	73.3	87.5	100.0	33.3
Other renegotiation clauses	77.4	61.5	88.8	80.0	75.0	80.0	66.6

Implicit Contingencies, Default, and Renegotiation

Projects financed by banks and other intermediaries usually entail risks that are beyond the control of both the entrepreneur and the creditor. A financial contract defines how the returns of the project will be divided. The repayment schedule, a function of how well the project is realized, defines how risk is allocated. In the absence of agency problems, both parties' attitude toward risk and the agents' hedging ability determine the optimal repayment schedule. One assumption that is commonly made—and that has intuitive appeal—is that financial intermediaries have greater risk tolerance, because they finance many projects with (partly) uncorrelated returns. The optimal contract under these circumstances allocates most of the risk to the creditor.

This result contrasts sharply with actual financial contracts, most of which are debt contracts that in principle assign all risk to the borrower. Theoretical models can explain this fact with the presence of agency problems. For example if the efforts of entrepreneurs are not observable or simply not contractible, entrepreneurs must face risks that stimulate effort. Alternatively, if only the entrepreneurs observe the outcome but intermediaries can audit at a cost, the optimal contract takes the form of debt with the possibility of default. But incentive problems only limit the scope for risk sharing. Generally, theory predicts that repayment depends on how well projects are realized.

As has been noted, explicit contingency clauses are a common feature of loan contracts. But what about implicit contingency clauses? Table 7.9 shows the response of banks to four different types of shocks. A significant number of intermediaries are willing to consider renegotiating their contracts when shocks occur. Metropolitan banks are more inclined to do so than rural banks, and intermediaries are more likely to renegotiate because of idiosyncratic shocks than they are because of aggregate shocks.

The questionnaire also asked also about the terms banks are most willing to renegotiate when a borrower has difficulty making payments (Table 7.10). Banks appear to be most flexible in extending the term of the loan; many are even willing to grant grace periods. Metropolitan banks are more inclined to renegotiate than rural banks on all points. Private and public banks tend to be willing to renegotiate different items but in general renegotiate more frequently than cooperatives and other types of banks. Contrary

Table 7.9. Shocks That Frequently to Always Justify Renegotiation
(percentage of sample)

Item	Total Sample (31)	Demographic type		Type of institution			
		Metro. (13)	Rural (18)	Public (15)	Private (8)	Cooper- ative (5)	Other (3)
Regional problems	35.4	38.4	33.3	40.0	37.5	40.0	0.0
Sectoral problems	45.1	69.2	27.7	33.3	75.0	40.0	33.3
Problems linked directly to the project	54.8	2	44.4	53.3	62.5	40.0	66.6
Borrower problems not directly linked to the project	45.1	46.1	44.4	33.3	50.0	80.0	33.3

to widespread belief, cooperatives do not offer more flexibility than other banks.

Finally, the questionnaire asked how the characteristics of both borrower and project affect the bank's willingness to renegotiate rather than take the case to court. In general, banks in the sample replied that they are willing to renegotiate as long as they are confident that the client is willing to repay. Accordingly previous experience with the borrower and reputation

Table 7.10. Banks That Frequently or Always Reset Contracts Because of Shocks
(percentage of sample)

Item	Total Sample (31)	Demographic type		Type of institution			
		Metro. (13)	Rural (18)	Public (15)	Private (8)	Cooper- ative (5)	Other (3)
Extend period of loans	64.5	84.6	50.0	53.3	100.0	60.0	33.3
Grant grace periods	51.6	61.5	44.4	66.6	62.5	20.0	0.0
Realign interest or principal	51.6	69.2	38.8	40.0	62.5	60.0	66.6
Offer additional loans	12.9	0.0	22.2	20.0	0.0	20.0	0.0
Rearrange terms of liquidation	38.7	53.8	27.7	20.0	100.0	20.0	0.0

Table 7.11. What Banks Consider Important or Crucial in Renegotiations or Legal Collection
(percentage of sample)

Item	Total Sample (31)	Demographic type Metro. (13)	Rural (18)	Public (15)	Type of institution Private (8)	Cooper-ative (5)	Other (3)
Experience with client	87.0	92.3	83.3	80.0	100.0	100.0	66.6
Experience with client activity	74.2	84.6	66.6	86.6	100.0	0.0	66.6
Value of collateral	96.7	100.0	94.4	93.3	100.0	100.0	100.0
Net assets of borrower	83.8	92.3	77.7	80.0	100.0	80.0	66.6
Other client debts	77.4	84.6	72.2	86.6	87.5	40.0	66.6
Primary information about administration of the project	74.1	92.3	61.1	73.3	100.0	40.0	66.6
Entrepreneurial problems not related to the project	93.5	92.3	94.4	93.3	100.0	100.0	66.6
Client's reputation in the community	93.5	92.3	94.4	93.3	100.0	100.0	66.6
Political or sectoral pressures	32.2	53.8	16.6	6.6	62.5	40.0	66.6

in the community are key variables in the decision (Table 7.11). Repayment capacity and information about the effort and care put into the project are also considered important.

Collateral and Default

The survey breaks loans down into six categories:

- unsecured loans
- loans secured by real estate
- loans backed by other real assets, such as cars or other durable goods
- loans backed by fiduciary collateral, allowing the borrower's income to be seized in case of default

Table 7.12. Estimated Composition of the Credit Portfolio
(percent)

Client and type of collateral	All	Public	Private	Cooperative	Other
Individuals					
Number	31	15	8	5	3
Unsecured credit	1.4	n.a.	n.a.	n.a.	n.a.
Real estate	41.4	49.2	34.9	35.9	28.7
Other real assets	10.0	8.9	12.7	3.9	18.4
Fiduciary	37.9	36.4	27.2	52.4	49.8
Securities and others	5.5	1.7	5.4	3.1	3.0
Guarantor and other	3.9	4.0	5.2	4.4	0.0
Firms					
Number					
Intermediaries	26	15	8	0	3
Unsecured credit	0.8	n.a.	2.6	n.a.	n.a.
Real estate	55.4	62.7	44.1	n.a.	49.6
Other real assets	16.1	18.1	13.9	n.a.	13.3
Fiduciary	17.2	12.0	23.0	n.a.	26.7
Securities and others	4.2	3.5	4.9	n.a.	7.3
Guarantor and other	5.6	4.5	9.3	n.a.	3.0

n.a. Not applicable.

Note: By law cooperatives may not lend to firms.

- loans secured by stocks or other securities

- loans in which a third party guarantees repayment.

As Table 7.12 shows, loans backed by real estate and fiduciary collateral are the most common type of credit. Only two private banks grant unsecured credit, and then only to well-known entrepreneurs with whom the banks or their owners have had a long relationship. The fraction of loans backed by real estate is significantly higher for firms, as is the number of loans backed by other real assets (except for other banks). The proportion of loans backed by real estate is also higher for public banks than for other types of intermediaries for loans to firms and households. Cooperatives and other banks account for the largest proportion of household loans backed by fiduciary collateral.

Table 7.13. Average Ratio of Loans to Guarantees

Client and type of collateral	All	Public	Private	Cooperative	Other
Individuals					
Number	31	15	8	5	3
Unsecured credit	n.a.	n.a.	n.a.	n.a.	n.a.
Real estate	78.5	81.0	72.1	80.0	81.7
Other real assets	69.9	71.8	66.5	66.3	77.3
Fiduciary	34.9	30.7	39.9	38.8	39.2
Securities and others	90.4	90.6	86.9	92.5	100.0
Guarantor and other	93.8	100.0	93.3	90.0	100.0
Firms					
Number	26	15	8	0	3
Unsecured credit	n.a.	n.a.	n.a.	n.a.	n.a.
Real estate	78.3	81.0	73.3	n.a.	81.7
Other real assets	71.1	71.8	67.0	n.a.	77.3
Fiduciary	34.0	30.7	39.9	n.a.	39.2
Securities and others	90.5	90.6	88.6	n.a.	100.0
Guarantor and other	93.6	100.0	88.3	n.a.	100.0

n.a. Not applicable.

Note: By law cooperatives may not lend to firms.

A more direct measure of each institution's lending policy is the ratio between the total amount of the loan and the value of the collateral. If liquidity and the value of collateral have any effect on loan contracts, intermediaries should be adjusting the terms and amounts of loans to the characteristics of the collateral. In Table 7.13, the figures show, except for fiduciary guarantees, the ratio of the principal to the estimated value of the asset backing the loan. For fiduciary guarantees, the figures show the fraction of the borrower's monthly income that is necessary to make the loan payments. The salient feature is the considerable variation among types of guarantees and intermediaries. Loans backed by fiduciary guarantees are far less collateralized than all the others. Other banks seem to be the most liberal, since they lend the largest amounts against almost all types of collateral. Private banks appear to be the most conservative, except when it comes to fiduciary guarantees. Moreover while public and other banks do not differentiate their policies across firms or individuals, private banks are more liberal in granting credit to firms than to households, except when a guarantor is available.

What is the default rate within each type of credit? One problem with answering this question is the lack of a standard definition of default. When asked, intermediaries gave several definitions of nonperforming loans. These definitions fall into three categories: payments that are more than one day late, payments that are more than 10 days late, and payments that are more than 15 days late. The boundary between performing and nonperforming loans varies with the type of bank. In general, cooperatives and other banks are the most lenient, private banks are the most rigorous, and public banks are somewhere in the middle. What is surprising is how sharp these differences are. Six of eight private banks use the first criterion, while all the cooperatives and two of the three other banks use the third criterion. All but one of the public banks define default according to the second criterion. But despite these differences there is a pattern to the default rates for the various intermediaries and kinds of collateral.

First, even though private banks use the first and strictest criterion, their default rates are lower than those of public banks, except for loans to individuals backed by real assets other than real estate (Table 7.14). Private banks also have lower default rates than cooperatives, but the two types of intermediaries are not really comparable because they use different criteria. Similarly, the two other banks have the highest default rates in loans backed by real estate, other assets, and fiduciary collateral, although they use the third and weakest criterion.

Second, bankers report that default rates differ according to the type of collateral. These differences are independent of the characteristics of the institution and borrower and of the criteria used to measure the default rate. The default rate on loans backed by securities and other assets or guarantors is usually negligible, and the default rate on loans backed by real estate tends to be lower than the rate for loans guaranteed by other real assets or fiduciary collateral. This evidence supports the hypothesis that the type of collateral has a significant effect on the allocation and performance of loans—a phenomenon consistent with the variations in loan-to-collateral ratio as a function of the collateral type. Given this fact, it is appropriate to ask whether collateral affects the mode of resolution for defaulted loans, and whether it affects the amount recovered by the lender.

Most defaulted loans never reach the courts (Table 7.15). Civil trials carry serious costs that represent a net loss for both borrower and lender. For this reason both parties are willing to bargain rather than turn to the

Table 7.14. Nonperforming Loans
(percentage of total loans)

Client, criterion, and type of collateral	All (31)	Public (15)	Private (8)	Cooperative (5)	Other (3)
Individuals, more than one day					
Number of intermediaries	7	1	6	0	0
Unsecured credit	5.0	—	5.0	—	—
Real estate	9.1	12.5	8.4	—	—
Other real assets	14.7	14.5	14.8	—	—
Fiduciary	11.8	17.0	10.8	—	—
Securities and others	5.4	—	5.4	—	—
Guarantor and other	5.4	—	5.4	—	—
Individuals, more than 10 days					
Number of intermediaries	14	13	0	0	1
Unsecured credit	—	—	—	—	—
Real estate	14.5	15.3	—	—	5.0
Other real assets	11.8	11.2	—	—	20.0
Fiduciary	27.3	28.7	—	—	10.0
Securities and others	—	—	—	—	—
Guarantor and other	—	—	—	—	—
Individuals, more than 15 days					
Number of intermediaries	10	1	2	5	2
Unsecured credit	—	—	—	—	—
Real estate	16.5	6.0	3.0	15.3	31.5
Other real assets	14.9	5.0	6.5	9	34.0
Fiduciary	22.2	30.0	16.0	19.2	29.0
Securities and others	4.6	—	—	11.5	—
Guarantor and other	0.3	—	—	0.4	—
Firms, more than one day					
Number of intermediaries	6	1	6	—	—
Unsecured credit	—	—	—	—	—
Real estate	8.1	12.0	7.3	—	—
Other real assets	8.9	—	8.9	—	—
Fiduciary	8.5	—	8.5	—	—
Securities and others	1.3	—	1.3	—	—
Guarantor and other	—	—	—	—	—
Firms, more than 10 days					
Number of intermediaries	14	13	0	0	1
Unsecured credit	—	—	—	—	—
Real estate	12.8	13.0	—	—	8.8
Other real assets	11.5	12.0	—	—	8.9
Fiduciary	14.9	15.9	—	—	17.1
Securities and others	—	—	—	—	—
Guarantor and other	—	—	—	—	—
Firms, more than 15 days					
Number of intermediaries	5	1	2	0	2
Unsecured credit	—	—	—	—	—
Real estate	14.2	—	4.0	—	31.5
Other real assets	18.8	—	7.0	—	34.0
Fiduciary	21.3	15.0	12.0	—	29.0
Securities and others	0.8	—	1.5	—	—
Guarantor and other	1.0	—	15	—	—

— Not available.

Table 7.15. Nonperforming Loans Resolved by Renegotiation and Court Procedures
(percentage of total loans)

Client, type of collateral	Sample (31) Court	Renegotiation	Public (15) Court	Renegotiation	Private (8) Court	Renegotiation	Cooperative (5) Court	Renegotiation	Other (3) Court	Renegotiation
Individuals										
Unsecured credit	5.0	95.0	—	—	5.00	95.0	—	—	—	—
Real estate	13.0	87.0	15.6	84.4	7.9	91.4	13.9	86.1	13.7	86.3
Other real assets	13.1	86.9	14.4	85.6	11.5	87.9	0.4	99.6	18.7	81.3
Fiduciary	20.1	79.7	24.7	75.3	16.0	83.3	20.1	80.0	13.0	87.0
Securities and others	1.1	98.9	0.6	99.4	2.3	97.7	—	100.0	—	100.0
Guarantor and other	3.3	96.7	3.00	97.0	4.8	95.2	—	100.0	—	—
Firms										
Unsecured credit	3.0	97.0	—	—	3.00	97.0	—	—	—	—
Real estate	10.0	90.0	10.7	89.3	6.9	92.5	—	—	13.7	86.3
Other real assets	11.3	88.7	12.3	87.7	6.1	93.1	—	—	18.7	81.3
Fiduciary	13.0	86.8	13.0	87.0	12.9	86.4	—	—	13.0	87.0
Securities and others	1.6	98.4	0.83	99.2	2.8	97.2	—	—	—	100.0
Guarantor and other	5.0	95.0	3.00	97.0	6.02	93.3	—	—	—	—

— Not available.

courts. As Table 7.15 shows, private banks resolve a larger number of defaulting loans through renegotiation than public banks. In addition, both public and private banks are more likely to settle loans to firms through direct bargaining than loans to households. Finally, defaulted loans that are guaranteed with stocks or guarantors are enforced in court less frequently than loans backed by other types of collateral.

Table 7.16 reports only loans extended to firms and thus excludes cooperatives. As the table shows, recovery rates are uniformly much lower with court procedures than with direct renegotiation. The proportion of loans recovered through renegotiation is remarkably high.

Civil Law and Its Enforcement

Courts are commonly considered the ultimate enforcement mechanism, since the law explicitly defines contractual forms and procedures for resolving conflicts among agents. But procedures are only one part of the story. The key issue is how effectively the law is enforced. Costa Rica has two different types of procedures for collecting debts, one for individual debts and the other for the total liabilities of an individual or a firm. The procedures are similar to those used in other civil law countries (see Monge-Naranjo, Cascante and Hall 2001).

Procedures for Collecting Individual Debts

Depending on how well defined the debt is, the creditor needs to start either an ordinary or executive trial. Ordinary trials require the creditor to establish the existence and amount of the debt, while executive trials simply enforce the debt. The type of executive procedure used depends on the form of collateral and can be simple (no specified collateral), mortgage (real estate) or pledge (other assets). A different procedure applies when one of the parties belongs to the public sector (Table 7.17).

Simple trials set in motion procedures that allow the creditor to seize enough assets from the debtor to repay the debt plus 50 percent of the interest and costs of the proceeding. The procedure is faster with specified collateral, requiring little in the way of valuation procedures and research to

Table 7.16. Nonperforming Loans Recovered through Renegotiation and Legal Collection

Collateral	All (26)		Public (15)		Private (8)		Other (3)	
	Legal collection	Renegotiation	Legal collection	Renegotiation	Legal collection	Renegotiation	Legal collection	Renegotiation
Unsecured credit	30.0	67.1	—	—	30.0	100.0	—	—
Real estate	100	94.8	84.5	99.3	91.9	100.0	89.2	100.0
Other real assets	87.3	75.0	72.9	97.9	80.7	97.1	80.00	50.00
Fiduciary	99.6	100.0	72.3	95.8	50.0	95.0	76.7	90.0
Securities and others	76.0	80.0	0	100.0	100.0	100.0	—	100.0
Guarantor and other	91.7	100.0	80.0	100.0	—	—	100.0	—

— Not available.

Table 7.17. Procedures for Judicial Collection of Single Debts

Type of trial	Purpose
Ordinary	The court needs to establish the existence and amount of the debt.
Executive	The court only enforces the debt; executive documents determine the amount of the debt.
Simple	The debt is not backed by a specific good or asset.
Pledge	The debt is directly linked to a specific asset.
Mortgage	Collateral is in the form of real estate.
Monitory	One or more of the requirements for an executive trial are not fulfilled, or the debt is based on a document without executive force.

determine ownership of the asset(s).[15] With collateral other than real estate, it is automatically presumed that the debtor accedes to executive privilege, that is, that the document defines the existence and amount of the debt. With real estate the contract must explicitly specify whether the debtor accedes to executive privileges. If not, the only legal procedure required is a simple trial.

Procedures Governing Total Debt of Individuals and Firms

A number of procedures govern the total debt of firms and individuals: bankruptcies (firms), insolvencies (individuals), administration with reorganization by judicial intervention (a procedure very similar to Chapter 11 in the United States), and special proceedings for liquidating financial intermediaries and securities market traders (Table 7.18). All procedures begin by freezing payments on any debt to give the bankruptcy receiver time to examine the documents backing all claims. Debtors as well as creditors can initiate these proceedings, usually for one of the following reasons:

- A debtor defaults on one or several debts (proof is required).
- A business closes or a debtor disappears unexpectedly.
- A debtor transfers all or a large share of assets to third parties.

[15] Specifying collateral requires listing the loan in the Public Registry.

Table 7.18. Procedures for Collecting Multiple Debts

Procedure	Purpose	Effect on creditor
Bankruptcy	Applies to a firm that cannot repay its debts and seeks liquidation.	Initially freezes payments. Divides creditors into common and separate. Pools all assets for liquidation.
Insolvency	Identical to bankruptcy but applies to individuals.	Identical to bankruptcy.
Administration and reorganization with judicial Intervention	Helps firms in financial distress survive.	Stops the repayment of debts and interest buildup. Stops ongoing collection trials and initiation of new ones.
Assembly of creditors	Applies to debtors in financial distress. Coordinates creditors to attain a settlement with the debtor.	Depends entirely on bargaining between debtor and creditors.
Collective execution	Occurs when multiple trials are taking place and one or more creditors believe the debtor's assets are insufficient.	Like bankruptcy but takes place only when debts are backed by executive documents.
Liquidation of financial intermediaries	Used in place of the administration and reorganization with judicial intervention.	Depends on intervener, who decides whether interest accrues during the procedure.

The process defines two types of creditors: common and separate. Separate creditors are those with specified collateral (mortgages and pledges), those with claims arising from renting farms or real estate to the debtor, and the public sector. Debts to the government have priority over all others.[16]

---

[16] Even with specified collateral, separate creditors are adversely affected by a bankruptcy. First, the value of the collateral must be set by a specialist named by the court. Second, unless a date is set for the legal auction, the bankruptcy proceeding must include a court hearing—often a source of considerable delay. Creditors may also benefit: if the auction does not generate enough money to cover the debts, separate creditors can become a common creditor. This option can be valuable if ex post the creditor learns that the value of the collateral is lower than expected.

In 1989 a new procedure was introduced for firms in financial distress: administration with reorganization and judicial intervention (Table 7.18).[17] A debtor could initiate the procedure on very minor grounds. The debtor was required to show up-to-date accounts for the last year and to present a financial statement and details of liabilities; the debtor must not have declared bankruptcy, had bankruptcy procedures initiated against the firm, or been convicted of criminal damage to private or public property. When the court declared the procedure open, it named a receiver in charge of managing the firm and its assets. This legal protection could last up to three years. The debtor was required to turn over management of the firm to a receiver (by law a lawyer) and to stop distributing dividends.

The new procedure had profound effects on creditors. First, it eliminated all executive and ordinary trials against a debtor, as well as any other procedure that involved the debtor (even as a guarantor). Second, it impeded the initiation of new collection procedures against the debtor. Finally, interest on affected debts ceased to accrue. In a country like Costa Rica, where inflation has caused nominal interest rates to rise to more than 30 percent, stopping the accrual of interest can in itself significantly erode the real value of a debt. As expected, before the 1996 reform the law prompted many firms, even large ones, to request such legal protection.

Legal Enforcement

Three measures are important in appraising how well courts function: their accuracy in determining and enforcing commitments, their accessibility to the contracting parties, and their effectiveness in resolving conflicts promptly. The first is largely abstract, since no ideal benchmark exists for verdicts and no analysis has been undertaken. For this reason this analysis is confined to the two other measures.

Monetary Costs of Procedures

The cost of legal trials is an important dimension of the laws that protect the rights of creditors. Either party must take the costs of initiating a legal procedure into consideration when deciding to pursue a lawsuit. These net costs

---

[17] The law was amended in 1996.

arise because of legal fees, procedural costs, and most importantly, because of lawyers' honoraria, which are aimed at increasing the potential net payoff at the expense of the other side. Thus, regardless of the verdict, both parties could be better off resolving a conflict on their own, replicating the transfers a judge would dictate and saving all the resources that would be sunk into the legal process. The more resources the procedures require, the more likely it is that parties will find alternative methods of resolving disputes. More importantly, rational forward-looking agents will avoid the possibility of conflict or change the conditions they will confront if a conflict arises. They can even avoid contracting in the first place.

From the perspective of a creditor deciding whether to start a trial, lawyers' honoraria are the single most important monetary cost to consider. Other judicial costs that are not covered by general tax revenue (such as required certifications) are very minor. Lawyers' effective fees therefore give a good indication of the cost to the creditor of accessing the civil courts.

In Costa Rica the Colegio de Abogados y Notarios, the lawyers' association, is very powerful. Any practicing lawyer or notary (also a lawyer) must be a member of the Colegio. Lawyers' honoraria for each type of procedure are fixed by the *Tabla de Horarios*. This document is a government decree and is jealously watched over by the College.[18] Interviews with several lawyers specializing in civil law and with banking officials revealed that all lawyers charge the rates stipulated in the *Tabla*. Indeed, the only alternative is not to charge at all.[19] Table 7.19 shows the marginal rates stipulated for the relevant collection procedures, as determined by the 1996 decree. The amounts have been converted using the October 1998 exchange rate of 250 colones to the U.S. dollar.

The *Tabla* defines marginal rates. For example, the lawyer for a plaintiff claiming a debt of US\$5,000 backed by a document with executory force would be paid according to the formula $0.125 \times 4,000 + 0.09 \times 1,000$, or \$590 for the entire process. This example shows that the *Tabla* is regressive, as honoraria increase less than proportionately with the amount of debt. Arguably, the

---

[18] However, in 1998, after the first draft of this chapter was written, professional fees were liberalized.

[19] The competition among lawyers seems to be based on the quantity and characteristics of cases, and some anecdotal evidence (but no formal evidence) suggests that there is an excess supply of lawyers.

Table 7.19. Marginal Rates for Lawyers' Honoraria

	Amount of debt (in US$)			
Type	0-4,000	4,000-8,000	8,000-20,000	20,000 +
Ordinary (percent)	25	18	14	10
Executive (percent)	12.5	9	7	5
Bankruptcy (percentage of assets)	5	5	5	5
Judicial intervention (percentage of assets)				
Concourse of creditors (percentage of assets)				

scheme should be even more regressive, as the lawyer has to perform practically the same amount of work regardless of the amount involved in the trial. The reason for the positive link between the honoraria and the amounts in dispute is to provide lawyers with an incentive to serve clients well.

These rates apply to the lawyers for each party. In the case of a debt worth less than $4,000, then, conflicting parties would spend 50 percent just in lawyers' fees. In bankruptcies, judicial intervention, and concourse of creditors, the lawyer acting as receiver and overseeing the liquidation of assets receives the honoraria. Creditors wanting a lawyer's assistance to collect debts in any of these procedures must pay according to the rates displayed above for ordinary or executive trials.

The rates differ in two important ways. First, an ordinary trial costs twice as much as an executive trial, encouraging creditors to back their loans with documents that have executive force. Second, the same rate applies to executive trials regardless of the type or amount of collateral, even though the duration of a trial, the stages it goes through, and the outcome all depend on the collateral. If the collateral is substantial, for instance, the trial is settled in the first stage. Thus even if the cost of complete executive trials is in principle independent of the collateral, collateral determines the effective cost because it determines the length of the trial. In fact, the collateral may determine whether the case goes to court at all, depending on how the creditor perceives the debtor's intention to repay. For this reason lawyers are not paid the full honorarium up front; instead, they are paid at each stage of the trial.

As a measure of the effectiveness of legal enforcement, this analysis uses the time involved in executive procedures, which involve enforcing repayments without having to establish the existence and amount of a debt. Different variables—type and amount of collateral, amount of the loan, and type of plaintiff—clearly affect the duration of trials (Table 7.20). In addition, disputes are resolved differently (a critical distinction). Some trials are abandoned, for instance, when the plaintiff agrees to settle.

The analysis is based on two samples from courts in San José, the *Juzgado Sexto Civil* (Sixth Civil Court) of trials ending in the period 1995-97 (945), and the *Alcaldía Tercera Civil* (Third Civil Court of Small Claims) of trials ending in the period 1996-97 (734). The courts were chosen on the basis of their willingness to provide information. The following information was recorded for each trial:

- the duration of each trial in calendar days

- the type of guarantee (simple, pledge, and mortgage)

- the amount of debt, deflated using the consumer price index for that month

- the type of plaintiff (financial and non financial)

- the reason for terminating the case.

Clerks recorded some of this information themselves, but each file was examined thoroughly in order to verify information. The summary statistics in Table 7.20 reveal a pattern of right skewness: for most cases the duration falls in the left tail of the distribution. In some cases, the trials are extremely long. For example, in the *Juzgado* one case that went to trial lasted 4,941 days and another lasted 4,842 days.[20]

Duration of Trials by Type of Collateral

The summary statistics show that trials involving debts backed by specified assets are much shorter than trials involving loans not backed by specific assets (simple trials). This effect can arise from different procedural rules, but it can also reflect differences in the optimal strategies of the creditor and

---

[20] Approximately 13.54 and 13.27 years, respectively.

Table 7.20. Duration of Trials in San José, 1990s
(Days)

Statistic	All	Trials settled out of court						Sentenced trials					
		All	Simple	Pledge	Mortgage	Inter-mediary	Other	All	Simple	Pledge	Mortgage	Inter-mediary	Other
Juzgado Sexto Civil: Executive trials, 1995-97													
Mean	222.8	213.7	272.6	181.5	146.1	172.1	250.0	301.9	342.5	215.0	246.3	271.1	316.3
Standard deviation	106.0	347.2	452.7	262.7	155.2	354.2	337.3	660.8	798.1	202.5	181.1	756.7	616.0
Median	397.7	102.0	119.5	98.0	88.5	77.0	134.0	141.5	105.0	155.0	187.0	43.0	155.0
Maximum	4,941.0	4,842.0	4,842.0	181.5	146.1	4,842.0	2,460.0	4,941.0	4,941.0	864.0	525.0	4,508.0	4,941.0
Cases	945	835	342	373	120	389	446	110	73	29	8	35	75
Alcaldía Tercera Civil: Executive trials, 1996-97													
Mean	340.1	295.1	308.0	149.8	45.8	287.7	306.5	588.7	593.0	98.0	n.a.	529.7	660.1
Standard deviation	391.4	362.4	369.2	228.0	44.4	352.3	378.1	449.6	449.2	n.a.	n.a.	425.0	471.9
Median	200.5	158.0	174.5	68.0	32.5	172.0	147.0	489.0	494.0	98.0	n.a.	398.0	540.0
Maximum	2,396.0	2,396.0	2,396.0	1,202.0	107.0	2,396.0	2,297.0	2,072.0	2,072.0	98.0	n.a.	2,072.0	1,788.0
Cases	750	635	586	45	4	384	251	115	114	1	0	63	52

n.a. Not applicable.

debtor. The difference is present in both cases brought to trial and cases settled out of court. It is also present in simple cases and pledges in the *Alcaldía*. Differences also exist in the cases of pledges and of mortgages, but these variations are not as strong and unambiguous. At the contracting date, or even prior to the decision to access courts, rational creditors and debtors are likely to foresee these effects, helping to explain why loans guaranteed by specified collateral perform much better than other loans.

Duration of Trials by Type of Plaintiff

The actions of the parties affect the duration of trials. A creditor's experience can influence both the outcome and duration of the proceedings. Experienced agents are likely to be more successful in collecting debts, both in and outside the courts, for several reasons. Their experience teaches them how best to pursue repayment for each type of debt and when to take a case to court. Similarly (and independent of their ability to collect loans), financial intermediaries are likely to have better judgment about granting a loan than other types of lenders. Trials in which a financial intermediary is the plaintiff should therefore be shorter than other trials. The information in Table 7.20 supports this prediction. In all four cases the mean and the median for nonintermediaries are much higher than they are for intermediaries.

Separating the Effect of Collateral and Plaintiff

Is it possible to disentangle the effects of the different variables on the time required to resolve a case? As plaintiffs, for instance, banks may have negative effects on the duration of cases simply because banks require specific types of collateral. But as long as no perfect deterministic relationship (multicollinearity) exists between the characteristics of the plaintiff and those of the collateral, simple regression techniques are enough to consistently estimate the effect of each of the variables.

There is a more interesting econometric problem, however. The same variables that determine whether a trial is resolved by sentencing or settled out of court may also explain the time required to reach either type of resolution. Estimating the effect of each variable on the duration of trials using separate regressions for sentenced and settled cases would provide results that are biased because of sample selection. The two pools of cases are not random, and the estimated effects of the characteristics of plaintiff and collateral on duration would be biased because these effects are capturing in part the probability of observing the case in either pool. The authors designed an econometric model (a double Tobit) for this analysis that resolves this econometric problem by explicitly taking sample selection into account. The model estimates the effect of observables on the probability of a trial proceeding to sentencing or being settled and on the duration of the proceedings for both types of plaintiff (Monge-Naranjo, Cascante and Hall 2001).

The findings are summarized here. First, the coefficient of the amount disputed is insignificant in the probit regression that separates the cases terminated in settlement from those terminated in court. Second, collateral in the form of a pledge is the only variable whose coefficient is not insignificant in the probit. In simple cases pledges increase the probability of a settlement. The effects of different types of collateral are, however, significant in regressions for duration, in which the point estimates are much higher than for sentences. The type of plaintiff is significant in both but is negative only in the equation for settlements. The positive effect on sentencing could reflect the existence of very old debts in public banks, which seem to have been common before the 1980 reforms.

Recent Changes

The second part of the 1990s saw some important changes in the Civil Law. Table 7.21 offers a synopsis of the major changes.

Prior to the reforms the process of notification created an avenue of escape for debtors. The law required that defendants be notified in person (or by validated communication at their domicile) before a trial was initiated. Debtors could avoid being notified by changing their address or simply hiding. The new law on notifications introduced a variety of modifications intended to make notification easier. First, parties to a contract can specify their domicile in case of default. If any of the parties wishes to initiate a trial, the notification must be directed to the specified address. If the address is invalid, the court can legitimately notify the defendant by publishing an edict in the *Judicial Bulletin* and in a newspaper with national circulation.

The most important reform (in October 1998) altered the law governing administration with reorganization and judicial intervention. The re-

Table 7.21. Recent Changes in the Administration of Civil Law

Item	Main reform
Notifications	If prearranged contractually, initial notification can be made using newspaper announcements.
Deposit of costs	Parties can no longer require other parties to deposit the total legal costs at the inception of the trial.
Auction of collateral	The procedure is faster, and restrictions designed to reduce the use of fake bidders have been increased.
Lawyers' honoraria	Honoraria are no longer necessarily set according to the *Tabla* but can be set by bargaining with clients.
Judicial intervention	The debtors' prerequisites for qualifying for this procedure are more stringent, and the benefits of using this procedure have been reduced (for instance interest accrues to creditors during the intervention).

form was initiated in response to a sharp increase in the number of cases during the first half of the decade. The new law tightened the eligibility requirements for this procedure and reduced the benefits to debtors. Under the new law the judge must be convinced that the debtor's business is able to survive the financial hardship of reorganization and intervention. The law allows the judge to directly initiate bankruptcy if the business is not viable. In addition, the procedure can be used only if a firm's bankruptcy entails substantial social costs. While the judge has considerable discretion, the law suggests the number of employees and business partners necessary to qualify for the procedure. Further, a procedure can include all the individuals and firms belonging to what is termed the "same economic interest group," whether inside or outside the country. Finally, the debtor is required to present a plan for the restructuring and repayment of all debts.

For debtors the law now excludes certain types of debts (such as those already in legal liquidation, those with guarantees not directly linked to a firm, and payroll debts). Most importantly, the new law mandates the accrual of interest on defaulted debts. The rate, however, is set at a level that is likely to be below the rate specified in the contract.[21]

---

[21] Specifically, for debts in colones, the rate is the *Tasa Básica Pasiva*, a bank-borrowing rate reported by the Central Bank, and for debts in U.S. dollars the rate is the prime rate. However the creditor does not lose the difference between these and contracted rates, as they accrue to the principal but do not compound.

Other changes have been introduced to expedite notification prior to the auctioning of an asset and to increase the effectiveness of the auctions. In addition the provision that allowed any party to a civil dispute to require the other party to deposit the full amount of legal costs (including lawyers' honoraria) during the proceedings has been eliminated. Under this provision the courts typically denied the right to appeal a verdict if such a deposit was on record prior to sentencing, significantly increasing the cost of the proceedings.

Finally, in September 1998 the lawyers' fees set in the *Tabla* were abolished. In a recent interpretation of the antitrust law, the Office of the State Attorney (*Procuraduría*) made the practice of fee setting by professional associations illegal. Thus these associations can no longer mandate the fees their members charge. This change will have important effects in the services and labor markets, but the most important overall effect is likely to be a decrease in the cost of accessing civil courts. Lawyers and their clients can freely negotiate fees for their services, payments, and any other contingency (for instance, they can stipulate different honoraria for different verdicts). Time is needed for these changes to have measurable effects. Some professional associations are even discussing a legal challenge, but the reform is likely to survive.

An Additional Device: Communication among Intermediaries

In addition to the courts, other social institutions such as peer pressure, family and social collateral, and informal networks can help sustain intertemporal trade in the economy. Theoretical, empirical, and policy research emphasizes the importance of these institutions (Besley and Coate 1991; Coate and Ravallion 1993; Rashid and Townsend 1994; Stiglitz 1990). Anecdotal evidence also suggests that they are important in many transactions in Costa Rica; in fact, unsecured credit is the best-performing category of credit.[22]

In large economies, a mechanism such as a credit bureau that records and makes publicly available borrowers' earlier transactions can enhance

---

[22] In one particularly picturesque practice, owners and managers of bars and cantinas in some rural areas display the nicknames and the arrears of clients who leave without paying.

Table 7.22. Banks Using Credit Bureaus

	Use public bureaus		
Use private bureaus	Yes	No	Total
Yes	8 (4)	3 (3)	11 (7)
No	10 (5)	10 (1)	20 (6)
Total	18 (9)	13 (4)	31 (13)

Note: Numbers in parentheses are for banks operating in the San José metropolitan area.

contracting possibilities, as borrowers are more predisposed to repay if their future access to credit depends on their references.[23] Credit bureaus can be private or public; they can be managed directly by a coalition of creditors, or they can operate as independent firms.

All these variations are present in Costa Rica. A sampling of banks shows that these institutions are widely used (Table 7.22). About 60 percent of all the banks use at least one type of bureau, and private and public bureaus are used almost equally. The response of intermediaries in the metropolitan area differs dramatically from the response in the countryside, however. Almost all of the intermediaries in the metropolitan area make use of some type of bureau, while 10 out of 17 banks in rural areas do not use any, as they are more likely to have first-hand information on the borrowers.

Two bureaus are operated by coalitions of intermediaries, and several are independent private firms. The coalitions are the Information Center of the Costa Rican Association of Banks (*Central de Información de la Asociación Bancaria Costarricense,* or CI-ABC), a private entity, and the Debtors' Information Center (*Central de Deudores de la SUGEF,* or CD-SUGEF), a publicly administered entity. Among the second group are companies such as Protectora de Crédito, Credicomer, Teletec/Telesoft, Sincom Inversiones Rolani, Protecsa, and others.

Interviews were conducted with the managers of CI-ABC, CD-SUGEF, and two of the independent bureaus. The managers of the private bureaus were reluctant to answer some of the questions, as they have faced threats

---

[23] For a discussion of these issues, see Melumad and Reichelstein (1986).

and even legal action in the course of doing business. Competition in the credit information area is also fierce. Both bureaus requested anonymity, so they have become Bureau A and Bureau B in Table 7.23.

All the bureaus said that they require their members to commit to providing their own information.[24,25] CI-ABC and CD-SUGEF serve only banks, while independent bureaus service creditors such as department stores and car dealers. All four bureaus differ in several important ways. For example CI-ABC and CD-SUGEF report only credit histories; bureaus A and B also provide information on assets and civil trials. CD-SUGEF's services are free; CI-ABC charges a fixed fee per month. The cost of consultations with Bureau B is much lower than with Bureau A (Bureau A argues that it provides higher-quality information than Bureau B). Bureau B's services, which are standardized, are surprisingly cheap: an individual credit report costs only 100 colones (US$0.4). It includes personal data and information on bounced checks and involvement in civil trials as well as a credit record. It also reports which of the bureau's clients have requested data for this individual previously. For the same cost, Bureau B will examine property and assets and provide information on mortgages and obligations. A complete study that includes all of the above as well as a record of previous transactions and involvement in firms costs 400 colones (US$1.6). Finally a corporate business record costs 600 colones (US$2.4) and includes the name and personal data of the legal representatives and the executive board; information on capital, outstanding credits, and civil trials; and credit references.

Table 7.23 shows that the bureaus differ in size, number of years in operation, services provided, and information technology used. For example, Bureau A has been in business 41 years, and Bureau B for only one year. While Bureau A takes full responsibility for the accuracy of its reports, the other bureaus do not, as their data are updated directly by the clients. Bureaus A and B estimate the number of debtors for whom they have data at around 700,000 and 600,000, respectively. However, Bureau B had 1,219 businesses and organizations as members at the time of the interview in 1998. Since the entire population of Costa Rica is around 3.5 million, exist-

---

[24] For instance, Bureau B expelled one of the public commercial banks because it was not providing information.

[25] After this chapter was written, however, the authors learned that one of the bureaus had sold information to a public bank without requiring reciprocity.

Table 7.23. Four Credit Bureaus in Costa Rica

Item	Managed by coalitions		Independent firms	
	SUGEF	ABC	Bureau A	Bureau B
Years in operation	2	1	41	5
Number of clients	103 intermediaries	8 banks	Not revealed	1,219
Individuals in database	424,342	Unknown	700,000[a]	600,000[a]
Employees	4	2	60	15
Processing of debtors' information	Banks	Banks	Employees	Clients/ Employees
Clients committed to providing own information	Yes	Yes	Yes	Yes
Type of information	Positive and negative	Negative	Positive and negative	Negative
Grading of debtors	Yes	No	Yes	No
Other information	No	Not yet	Yes	Yes
Consultations per day	200[a]	Not revealed	Not revealed	7,500
Transfer of information	Messengers	Modem	Phone-modem	Modem-fax
Waiting time for information	24 hours	Instant	Instant; 24 hours for updates	Instant
Memory	Infinite	10 years	Infinite	3,000 days
Other services	No	No	Yes	Yes
Charges	Free	Monthly fee	Per consult	Per consult
International services	No	No	Yes	Yes

a. Figures are approximate.

ing bureaus have information on the majority of debtors and serve a significant and growing share of creditors.

Besides formal credit bureaus, creditors use other mechanisms to gather and share information. The CI-ABC itself evolved from an informal communication network among a group of bankers that operated under a "gentlemen's agreement." The intermediaries in the northern region (San Carlos) have a similar agreement, and advertise it by displaying posters and giving away stickers with the logo of all the intermediaries, encouraging the prompt repayment of loans.[26] Such communication is absent in other communities. In the Valley of El General and the region of Los Santos, intermediaries have no communication and seem to be rivals. Even the branches of the same national commercial bank behave differently, depending on the region.

Finally, many agents, informally known as hawks (*gavilanes*), specialize in obtaining information from the Public Registry and other judicial institutions. They work independently for one or several large creditors, including financial intermediaries and commercial retailers, or for lawyers who specialize in collection trials. They gather information on assets, pending trials, and other transactions effected by debtors.

Concluding Remarks

This chapter has examined the institutional features and practices of creditors that help determine repayment incentives in Costa Rica. The diversity of intermediaries' behavior and the dispersion in the default rates make clear that the efficiency of the laws protecting creditor rights cannot be understood without reference to the strategies creditors adopt in their relationships with borrowers. Although serious weaknesses exist in the effectiveness of courts, the relatively low average default rate indicates that banks are taking corrective actions to protect themselves, both by requiring collateral and by relying on their knowledge of specific borrowers (relationship lending). The evidence seems to support the view that the ineffectiveness and high cost of judicial protection are reflected not in default rates but in the efficiency of the credit market, the volume of lending, and the types of loan contracts. Further, other institutional constraints are relevant to the behavior of different types of banks. For instance, private banks have lower default rates than other financial institutions, possibly because their incentives are dictated by profit maximization rather than by political considerations.

---

[26] Both posters and stickers have the logo of Banco de Costa Rica, Banco C.Q., BanCrecen, Banco del Comercio, Banco Federado, Banco Nacional, Banco Popular, Coocique R.L., and Mutual Alajuela. Freely translated into English, the sticker reads "I pay my bills on time: To be punctual in the payment of your bills is to open for yourself the doors of the northern zone's financial system." (The original Spanish reads "Yo mantengo mis cuentas al día: Ser puntual en el pago de sus cuentas es abrirse las puertas en el sistema financiero de la zona norte.")

The analysis here has emphasized the design of credit contracts and the relationship between banks and borrowers. Intermediaries are actively coping with the incentive problems of borrowers, but some of the findings are puzzling in the light of theoretical models. A salient conclusion is that repeated interaction and borrowers' reputation play a crucial role. But while ex ante screening and interim control are important considerations, the evidence also shows that ex post repayment incentives also play a critical role, as emphasized by recent literature on incomplete contracts and contracting under limited commitment (Besley and Coate 1991; Coate and Ravallion 1993; Hart and Moore 1988; Monge-Naranjo 1999). The value and type of guarantees influence the decisions of banks and the outcomes of the relationship at all its stages, including the decision to grant credit, the performance of loans, the resolution in case of default, and the amount recovered from nonperforming loans.

The analysis has also looked at the judicial enforcement system. The evidence strongly supports the notion that collateral has a significant effect on the effectiveness of courts in protecting creditors. This conclusion further underlines the importance of collateral to lending relationships. Finally, the chapter has argued that a rather sophisticated information network among creditors (used mainly by intermediaries in the metropolitan area) helps to protect creditors from default. These networks seem less important for intermediaries in rural areas, possibly because rural institutions have more accurate informal knowledge of borrowers' characteristics. Overall, however, information-sharing systems play—and will continue to play—an important role in preventing defaults and enforcing willingness to pay.

CHAPTER 8

Ensuring Willingness to Repay in Paraguay

Stéphane Straub and Horacio Sosa

As in many other Latin American countries discussed in recent studies, the legal system in Paraguay performs badly when it comes to protecting and enforcing creditor rights (La Porta *et al.* 1997, 1998). A lack of willingness to repay loans is one consequence of the inefficient legal framework that has had profound effects on the financial industry. This chapter examines the methods developed by various segments of the financial market to work around the lack of legal avenues for enforcing debt repayment. It looks at the influence of these alternative procedures on the functioning of the Paraguayan financial market, its evolution during the 1990s, and the levels of key variables (interest rates, default rates, and types and volumes of loans).

Analyzing the characteristics of financial markets in a country like Paraguay is not an easy task. Owing to the magnitude of the informal sector and the importance of informal activities throughout the economy, much essential data are lacking, and the data that do exist are often unreliable. This chapter is an attempt to fill this gap. The analysis relies on a variety of official sources as well as direct interviews and replies to a questionnaire prepared by the authors.[1]

Stéphane Straub was a research economist at the Centro Paraguayo para la Promoción de la Libertad Económica y de la Justicia Social (CEPPRO) and is currently pursuing graduate studies at the Université de Toulouse; Horacio Sosa is a research economist at CEPPRO.
[1] Official sources included units of the Central Bank (the Banking Superintendency, Clearing House, and Technical Unit for the Execution of Microlending Programs). Interviews were conducted with officials from banks as well as public officials. Unfortunately, very few replies to the questionnaire were collected.

Macroeconomic and Financial Characteristics
of the Paraguayan Economy, 1989-98

In 1989, when Paraguay emerged from 35 years of dictatorship under Alfredo Stroessner, its economy was sluggish. Individuals and interest groups related to those in power were engaged in rent-seeking activities. The regulatory and institutional economic framework suffered from the effects of entrenched and excessive state interference. Corruption was the general rule in both the real and the financial sectors. This period saw an important development that was to shape the way the financial system functioned: the emergence of an informal commercial center for smuggling and reexportation in the southern cone. Activity in this zone helped compensate for the growth slowdown after the completion of the Itaipú Dam in 1981 and the progressive exhaustion of the agricultural frontier toward the end of the 1980s.[2] The zone's activities also generated uncontrolled financial flows to the local banking sector.

In the 1970s and the first part of the 1980s, this unregistered trade involved primarily smuggling from Brazil. In the mid-1980s the so-called reexportation business appeared. Several factors explain these activities: high tariffs without an import-substitution strategy; multiple exchange rates; the complacency of those in power and related groups; and, in the case of reexportation, protectionism in Brazil and Argentina that prohibited imports of products like alcohol, cigarettes, perfumes, electronic devices, and sport shoes. Owing to high internal taxes, products were also introduced from Brazil and reexported to the same country. After 1989 the government decided to validate the reexport business by lowering tariffs on so-called tourism goods (reexports), and in 1991 the value-added tax (VAT) on these goods was set at 2 percent, far below the overall level of 10 percent.[3] The size of the reexporting business is certainly considerable. According to statistics from the International Monetary Fund (IMF) and Paraguay's own Department of

---

[2] The Paraguayan economy had a period of major growth (about 8 percent a year) in the 1970s during the construction of the Itaipú Dam. This project, involving the biggest dam in the world (owned half by Paraguay and half by Brazil), boosted the construction sector and gave an important push to the commercial and financial sectors.

[3] In 1995 several of these goods were included in the MERCOSUR exception list, which contains 399 low-tariff products that are due to converge with the Common External Tariff in 5-10 years.

Transportation, in 1994 unregistered exports equaled 179 percent of registered exports. Unregistered imports were equivalent to 66 percent of registered imports.[4]

The Paraguayan economy is characterized by fiscal evasion, unregistered trade, a big informal sector of small productive and commercial enterprises, and large firms operating at different levels of formality. Recent estimates by the IMF (1998) show a 30-40 percent tax evasion rate and gross domestic product (GDP) levels that are underestimated by half. Paraguay's informal tendencies, however, have legitimate roots. The World Bank (1996b) notes that informality persists because going formal involves high costs and offers few benefits. Traditional businesses in Paraguay generally maintain multiple sets of books in order to avoid taxes and regulations, and a large part of their profits goes undeclared. In a recent statement, the president of the National Value Commission (the regulatory body of the Stock Exchange) observed that 70 percent of firms engage in "underground movements" and maintain two, three, and four sets of books.[5] The tax system suffers from distortions that affect the way businesses function. The high corporate income tax rate (30 percent) and the absence of a personal income tax result in the reporting of corporate profits as personal income, worsening the already low transparency of the overall economic structure.

Arguably, this informality is a major obstacle to the efficient functioning of the credit market. In fact the financial sector mirrors the duality of the real economy. Until 1995 banks accepted deposits at different levels of informality (or "colors") on a large scale: white (officially registered), gray (official bank receipts, but no registration in the official books), and black (only personal receipts).[6] The official credit market coexists with a large informal credit market that is based on a variety of instruments, among which the postdated check has been dominant. Mafia-style enforcement techniques,

---

[4] The emphasis on taking advantage of neighboring countries' "comparative disadvantages" continues at the expense of Paraguay's own comparative advantages, hindering the development of national productive units. Nevertheless, the tariff convergence process and the probability of tax harmonization later on will require the country to define a new export-oriented development strategy.

[5] "The 1991 fiscal reform did not have the expected effect and left half of the firms living in marginality . . . More than half of them. We are talking about 70 percent if we include underground movements" (*Diario El Día de Asunción*, August 11, 1998).

[6] World Bank (1996b).

including the threat of physical harm, are among the most common enforcement procedures.

The Paraguayan financial sector is also suspected of being a key center for money laundering. According to the U.S. State Department, during six months of 1995 transfers to U.S. banks amounted to US$357 million from Argentina, $342 million from Brazil, and $1 billion from Paraguay (CEPPRO 1996). These figures become more striking in light of the fact that Paraguay's GDP is a fraction of Argentina's (1/37th) and Brazil's (1/76th). Recently the Brazilian Ambassador to Paraguay declared to a Paraguayan newspaper that in Ciudad del Este (on the border of Brazil and Argentina), $8 billion is laundered each year, an amount equivalent to 80 percent of Paraguay's GDP.[7] Understanding this general framework is useful to any analysis of the macroeconomic and financial evolution of the country.

Macroeconomic Trends

Between 1989 and 1997 Paraguay experienced some stabilization (Table 8.1). The inflation rate was in the single digits by 1996, and the fiscal balance remained satisfactory throughout the period.[8] International reserves soared to $1.1 billion in 1995, and the external debt decreased to around $1.44 billion in 1997 (approximately 14 percent of GDP), the lowest relative level in Latin America.[9]

During this time the government instituted measures to revitalize the economy (Box 8.1). Among the first of these were the freeing of the foreign exchange market and the capital account and the liberalization of the financial market. Monetary policy progressively eliminated rediscount operations and shifted to open market operations, although support to some specific sectors like cotton did not disappear altogether.[10] Monetary financing of the public sector was also ruled out. In practice, Paraguay's monetary policy can be characterized as "bi-anchor:" in a variation of the *tablita* scheme, the Central Bank regulates the growth of monetary aggregates through open

---

[7] *ABC Color*, June 3, 1998.

[8] Unlike its neighbors Argentina and Brazil, Paraguay has not experienced hyperinflation or high fiscal deficits in recent decades.

[9] See Straub (1998) for a detailed analysis of the macroeconomic evolution.

[10] Until 1994, for example, the central government supported an indirect rediscount scheme, allowing financial institutions that supported cotton planting to reduce their reserves.

Table 8.1. Macroeconomic Indicators, 1989-97

Indicator	1989	1990	1991	1992	1993	1994	1995	1996	1997
GDP per capita (1982 US$)	1,618	1,616	1,612	1,597	1,619	1,625	1,656	1,634	1,634
GDP growth rate (percent)	5.8	3.1	2.5	1.8	4.1	3.1	4.7	1.3	2.6
Central government fiscal balance (% GDP)	2.4	3.0	−0.3	−0.3	−0.7	1.0	−0.3	−0.8	−0.8
Nonfinancial public sector surplus (% GDP)	1.9	5.2	1.6	0.9	1.2	2.4	2.5	1.7	—
External debt/exports of goods and services (percent)	148	89	81	66	44	36	30	32	37
Inflation rate (percent)	28.5	44.1	11.8	17.8	20.4	18.3	10.5	8.2	6.2

— Not available.

Source: Central Bank and Finance Ministry (preliminary data for 1997).

market operations, while a "dirty float" policy in the exchange rate market reduces pressure from imported goods.[11] Given the difficulty of controlling the quantities of money in an extremely informal economy where unregistered financial operations cannot be limited and the fact that almost half the money supply is denominated in U.S. dollars (Table 8.2), the exchange rate component has assumed increasing importance.

The antiexport bias of the economy and an erratic growth rate have had a profound effect on the industrial sector.[12] The industrial sector barely maintains its share of total production, and activity in illegal speculative, real estate, and financial operations has soared.

Evolution of the Financial Market, 1989-95

Despite some positive aspects, the reforms were essentially incomplete. While they liberalized interest rates, reduced reserve requirements, and permitted

---

[11] The *tablita*, or crawling peg, was applied in Argentina at the end of 1980. The *tablita* scheme involved periodically devaluing the exchange rate in order to slow inflation.
[12] Reflected in the real exchange rate appreciation, as well as in the fiscal and legal dispositions that favor the reexport of foreign imports over local production.

Box 8.1. Major Legal, Economic and Institutional Reforms, 1989-97

General reforms . . .

1989 *Exchange rate reform.* Introduces a free-floating exchange rate (Dec. 216/89).

1991 *New tax law.* Introduces the VAT, simplifies the tax structure (from about 80 to only nine taxes). Does not introduce personal income tax.

1991 *Asunción Treaty.* Funds the MERCOSUR common market.

1992 *New Constitution.* Introduces important changes in the political and administrative field, allowing judicial reform, among other things, but lays no groundwork for economic reforms. Contains major flaws, including the regulation of privatization and the failure to grant independence to the Central Bank.

1995 *Initiation of MERCOSUR.* Marks the official start of the MERCOSUR common market on January 1.

. . . and financial reforms

1989–96 *Reduction of reserve requirements.* Reduces local currency deposits from 42 percent in 1989 to 25 percent in 1994. In 1996 introduces a differentiated system ranging from 15 percent for current account deposits to 0 percent for time deposits longer than 18 months. Holds foreign currency deposits at 30 percent until 1996, then decreases them from 27 percent for current account deposits to 0 percent for deposits longer than 36 months. Since 1996, remunerates legal reserves above 7 percent in local currency and 10 percent in foreign currency.

1990 *Interest rate liberalization.* Eliminates ceilings on interest rates (active and passive).

1991 *Creation of the National Value Commission* (CNV, Comisión Nacional de Valores) and the *legal framework for the development of the capital market.* Permits firms to join the stock exchange (about 60 as of 1997), though operations are concentrated in the money market.

1993 *Liberation of public funds.* Allows these funds to be deposited in the private financial sector.

1994 *Law on foreign currency contracts (Law 34/94).* Allows contracts in foreign currencies.

1995 *New Central Bank Organic Law (Law 489/95).* Fails to give independence to the Central Bank.

1996 *New Banking Law (Law 861/96).* Introduces, among other things, Basle Standards, but passed only after the 1995 financial crisis.

1996 *New Check Law (Law 805/96).* Makes the postdated check legal.

Table 8.2. Coefficient of Dollarization of the Economy, 1989-97
(percent)

1988	1989	1990	1991	1992	1993	1994	1995	1996	1997
4	23	27	30	36	43	38	33	37	40

Note: Deposits are in U.S. dollars as a percentage of the total monetary aggregate. Since the peak in 1993, public sector deposits have tended to reduce the role of dollar deposits.

Source: Central Bank.

contracts to be denominated in foreign currency, they did virtually nothing to eliminate major sources of inefficiency, such as those arising from public intervention in the financial sector. Directed credit was still permitted, public banks were not privatized (as of the end of 1997 they still represented 16 percent of total deposits, 22 percent of total lending, and 20 percent of the total assets of the banking sector), and only functional changes were introduced. The liberalization took place before the supervisory body was strengthened or the regulatory framework improved, however, and this incorrect sequencing has been deemed responsible for the failure of the reforms (IDB 1996).[13]

Controls during this period were weak, and capital requirements remained low.[14] As a result, the number of financial institutions increased rapidly, and 13 new banks and 38 finance companies opened between 1989 and 1994. As of 1994 (before the financial crisis) the Paraguayan financial market was composed of 34 banks and 65 financial companies (apart from savings and credit companies, cooperatives, and housing loan companies), as shown in Table 8.3).[15] Soon Paraguay had one financial entity for every 47,000 inhabitants, compared, for example, with a ratio of 1 to 200,000 in neighboring Argentina (in 1994 before Mexico's Tequila crisis).

In general, these banks were managed in one of two ways. Most foreign banks and some well-managed national banks followed prudent strat-

---

[13] As of 1998 the Banking Superintendency still needed to be dramatically reformed.

[14] Until the banking law was changed in 1996, a bank could open with no more than $3 million and a finance company with $1 million.

[15] Finance companies are regulated financial institutions and are permitted to offer all types of banking services except checking accounts and international transactions.

Table 8.3. Paraguay's Banks, 1989-98

Type	1989	1990	1991	1992	1993	1994	1995	1996	1997	1998
Total banking sector	26	26	27	29	29	34	35	32	30	23
Majority foreign capital	14	14	13	13	13	13	13	14	15	15
Majority national capital	10	10	12	14	14	19	20	16	13	7
Public banks	2	2	2	2	2	2	2	2	2	1
Finance companies	29	37	40	50	52	65	68	60	50	44

Source: Banking Superintendency.

egies and focused their financial activities on first-class local clients. But other institutions, often poorly managed national banks and finance companies, extended loans to firms linked to them through common ownership or sought high gains through consumer loans and credit card operations. These institutions rapidly accumulated risky assets, and their off-book portfolios grew very quickly. A significant portion of their resources went to finance informal and illegal activities. Because these financial institutions needed to attract deposits in order to finance their risky operations (or to cover growing losses), interest rates remained high.

The dichotomy in the system led to credit rationing in some sectors—for example, among small and medium-size enterprises (SMEs) that were not related to a financial group—and the rapid growth of credit portfolios in other activities like real estate and informal business. Between 1989 and 1995 the ratio of bank loans to GDP rose from 10.8 to 19.5 percent. In other words, in this period the growth of credit in real terms, as captured by the ratio of real credit growth to GDP growth, was 6.2. This ratio was similar to that of countries with a comparable financial penetration level, like Argentina and Colombia (*Economist* 1997b; Straub 1998). Among national banks this ratio rose to a clearly unsustainable 10.4.

The combination of these circumstances, weak supervision, and a lack of political will to enforce existing rules pushed the Paraguayan financial market into crisis in 1995. The crisis affected four banks that together accounted for 11 percent of the banking system's assets and 10 nonbank financial institutions. Despite the passage of a new banking act and the tightening of prudential regulations, several institutions remained extremely weak (IMF 1998). In 1997 a new financial crisis occurred, and the Central

Bank intervened in two more banks (including the largest national bank) and a savings company. Depositors turned from national to foreign banks, and banking in Paraguay became increasingly concentrated in foreign branches. As of December 1997, the five major foreign entities accounted for more than 38 percent of the total credit market. As of December 1998, 12 more national financial institutions had either dissolved or been closed by the Central Bank.

The Financial Crisis and the Functioning of Credit Markets

The literature documents the issues leading to the financial crisis—the faulty sequencing of reforms, poor prudential regulation and enforcement, weak supervision, poor bank management, and the underlying consumption and lending boom—as well as the vicious recessionary circle that followed (Goldstein and Turner 1996). In many ways the Paraguayan financial crisis is a textbook case. For instance, the seven main causes of banking crises in developing countries characterized in Goldstein and Turner were all present in Paraguay. But in another way the Paraguayan crisis was unique, in that the economy's financial fragility was a result of high-risk, illegal, and un-controlled activities. Straub (1998), using the framework presented by Gavin and Hausmann (1996), argues that the banking crisis after 1995 was the result of internal and external shocks that occurred in a context of vulner-ability caused by adverse macroeconomic evolution. In this particular case, the consumption boom, fueled by excessive credit growth, was closely linked to the growth of the informal sector, illegal financial activities, and unregis-tered capital flows.

An examination of the mechanisms through which creditors assured borrowers' willingness to repay is key to understanding how the formal and informal markets developed. As the following sections show, the weak insti-tutional framework, the inefficient Paraguayan judicial system, and the seri-ous enforcement problem negatively affected credit markets. These factors, existing as they did in a highly informal economy, led to the growth of cer-tain types of instruments and contracts, altered the cost of credit, and skewed the growth of various credit portfolios. Each segment of the market (formal and informal) developed its own legal remedies and mechanisms to work around the existing difficulties. These features in turn contributed to the banking crisis and its effects on the real sector.

Enforcement Mechanisms

In Paraguay, the Code of Civil Procedure (CPC) outlines the judicial enforcement of economic claims. There are two types of procedures: ordinary and executive.

Ordinary Procedures

Judicial disputes that do not fall under any special procedure are categorized as ordinary procedures. Ordinary procedures, for many reasons, are not useful tools for enforcing the repayment of loans. First, the procedure is long and tedious. Normally it takes three to five years, if not longer, to obtain judgment. Second, debtors have many defenses against creditors. For example, it is unlikely that creditors will be allowed to attach any assets at the beginning of the procedure. To complicate matters, a judge's decision can be appealed at any stage of the procedure. Finally, the process is very expensive.

Executive Procedures

Creditors can enforce their rights through executive procedure if they hold an executable document (a mortgage, promissory note, pledge, or check) on which they need to collect. The CPC stipulates that during the execution procedure, a judge's decisions cannot be appealed, except for sales and the liquidation of costs. The executive procedure is faster than the ordinary procedure, but it is restricted to suits against debtors defaulting on loan payments. The process has several steps. Initially, the judge carefully examines the creditor's document and, if it is executable, issues a writ of attachment for the debt, interests, and costs. The writ of attachment is given to an officer of the court, who within three days notifies the debtor that the debt must be paid. If the debtor does not pay, the court officer attaches the debtor's properties up to a value equal to the debt plus interest and costs. Once the properties are attached, the creditor asks for a motion. The debtor is served with the request and has five days from the time of service to present his defense. If the debtor does not present a defense, or if it is rejected, the judge orders a public auction of the attached property.

De Facto Enforcement Issues

The executive procedure is clearly more effective for creditors, simply because it is shorter, restricts appeals, and allows for only a very limited defense. Because it is shorter it is also less expensive. Despite its advantages, however, several problems remain in using it. These problems are common to all judicial processes in Paraguay. For instance, the whole procedure takes place in writing. Judges' orders, testimonies, reports, and requests for evidence must all be in writing. Petitions for obtaining evidence require a written order of the judge before they can be served. Electronic mail and facsimile communications to the parties or to the judge are not allowed. In exceptional cases the judge orders service by telegram or certified letter. (The cost of these options is not included in the liquidation of costs, however.) Further, in cases requiring expert testimony—for example, to advise the judge on the authenticity of a debtor's signature—the court appoints experts. If one expert declines or if one of the parties objects to an expert, the judge must call a second expert. Such time-consuming details seriously hamper the efficiency of the courts.

The infrastructure of the Paraguayan court system is in the process of being modernized, but very slowly. Word processing equipment is used in some courts, although others still use ordinary typewriters. Officers of the court still must search through stacks of files for the correct case, as there is no effective information retrieval system. The 1997 annual report on the judiciary shows low institutional capacity that further hinders efficiency. Paraguay has only one judge per 50,000-60,000 inhabitants, and each judge processes an average of 3,000 proceedings a year. As a result judicial processes are far slower than they should be.

Legal Problems

The Paraguayan court system is beset with problems that make the process of collecting debts far more difficult than it should be. Among these problems are the competency of judges hearing the cases, problems locating debtors, and the bankruptcy law, which can allow debtors to escape their obligations.

The Problem of Competency

The type of judge hearing a suit depends on the amount of the claim. Controversies involving relatively small amounts of money (up to the sum represented by 60 days' minimum salary or $530) are handled by a justice of the peace, who does not necessarily hold a law degree. Cases involving large amounts (from $530 to $2,650, or 300 days' minimum salary) are handled by a judge holding a law degree. Court officers, often including the judge, cannot ensure a speedy settlement and are vulnerable to corruption because of their small salaries.

Creditors that lend from $530 to $2,650 can require collateral only in the form of small assets such as appliances or a salary, and the law forbids the collection of these guarantees for more than 25 percent of their value. In any case these goods can be traded during the term of the loan without the lender's knowledge, since they are not recorded in the public registry. If the judge orders an attachment at the beginning of the procedure and the collateral disappears, the creditor must seek other assets to attach. If there are none the creditor can petition the judge for an order prohibiting the debtor from selling registered property such as vehicles or real estate. In this case the creditor does not collect the debt even though any assets the debtor acquires in the following five years can be attached. The creditor must be persistent, continuing the attachment procedure until the judge orders a sale.

The Address Issue

Another problem with enforcement is related to the debtor's address. For private instruments such as the promissory note, parties to a loan can agree on a special address. Once the debtor has defaulted on a payment and the creditor has decided to judicially enforce the debt, the creditor must notify the debtor at the actual and current address. According to the prevailing interpretation of the Paraguayan courts, the debtor must acknowledge the note in court in order to assure that the document is authentic and enforceable. If the debtor has moved, the creditor is not allowed to use the address indicated in the note but must locate the debtor's current address. If the search is unsuccessful, the creditor can ask the judge to serve the debtor through the newspapers, as the law allows. However, the creditor must prove due diligence in looking for the debtor. Service through a newspaper is costly.

Publishing a notice in one newspaper for five days costs about $300. The total cost for the first publication is estimated at $600—a sum that sometimes makes recovering small loans not very cost-effective.

The Bankruptcy Law

The bankruptcy law is another barrier to effective enforcement, and creditors perceive it as a sure way for debtors to avoid repaying most, if not all, of their debts. Debtors engaged in commercial activities who become insolvent are obliged by law to file for bankruptcy or request a meeting with their creditor. The court decides whether to accept a petition for bankruptcy. When the court decides for bankruptcy, the decision is published in a newspaper and the judge nominates a trustee to review the documentation submitted by creditors.

A reorganization procedure protects insolvent debtors, who can continue administering their assets. Creditors cannot continue or start legal actions against debtors whose petition for a creditors' meeting has been accepted by the court, with two exceptions: loans guaranteed by mortgages or pledges and loans taken out by salaried employees. In these cases debtors must present a payment proposal in a meeting with creditors. If the payment term is less than two years, the debtor can propose a rebate of up to 50 percent, but if the term exceeds two years (the maximum authorized is four), the rebate cannot exceed 30 percent of the credit. If the creditors or the court turn down a proposal, the debtor must declare bankruptcy. Creditors then have the option of collecting a substantially reduced sum, usually without interest, or voting for bankruptcy. If they vote for bankruptcy, creditors must hope for payment after liquidation, when assets are sold and the proceeds distributed. However, when the funds are distributed, unsecured creditors are paid after labor claims, the trustee in bankruptcy, and any secured creditors.

The Costs of Judicial Enforcement

The cost of enforcing an economic claim in the courts varies according to the type of process. By law, legal fees in an execution procedure can never be lower than 8 percent of the value of the claim, so lawyers can be costly. Judges may set lawyers' fees at up to 20 percent of the value of the claim, and additional expenses must be considered. In addition, the government charges a tax of 0.40 percent of the value of the claim, and legal notifications cost

$2.50 if the debtor lives in Asunción. Restrictive measures (attachment of assets) cost from 1 to 5 percent of the value of the claim. In a public auction creditors must pay for announcements in newspapers and fees to judicial auctioneers. Thus, the total cost of collecting a debt runs from 9.4 to 25.4 percent, plus the cost of notifications in newspapers.

The Formal Credit Market

In order to explain the structural deficiencies of the Paraguayan financial system and the disruptive financial crisis that began in 1995, this analysis stresses a number of issues. First, banks are poorly managed, and the overall regulation and incentive structure is inadequate. Although there has been some improvement in recent years, these problems still exist. Further, Paraguay's interest rate spreads are some of the highest in the world. Additional difficulties include short-maturity loans, excessive reliance on credits backed by some kind of guarantee, credit rationing and excessively high interest rates for perceived high-risk markets, poor credit evaluation capabilities, and a very high overall default rate, especially in recent years.

The financial sector does not function independently of the rest of the economy. Banks cannot develop an adequate credit management process because of the high level of informality of the market. The lack of transparency of many firms (in particular those using multiple balance sheets) and the absence of information make it almost impossible to evaluate the real creditworthiness of the potential debtors. As a result, even well-managed banks with adequate credit evaluation capacity extend loans only with some kind of guarantee, or only to selected sectors. To compensate for high perceived risk, banks charge high interest rates, shorten the loan's maturity, or both. The informality of the real sector leads banks to ration credit to clients lacking a formal guarantee, leaving them without access to formal loans. The informal credit market usually caters to these economic units.

High Interest Rates and Spreads

Despite the total liberalization of the financial market in 1990, a falling inflation rate, and substantial reductions in reserve requirements, interest rates in national currency have not declined significantly. As a result real lending rates have actually risen, real deposit rates are low, and the financial spread has remained above 20 percent (Table 8.4).[16] During a visit to Paraguay in 1994, Michel Camdessus, former head of the IMF, declared, "The country's financial cost record should be recorded in the Guinness Book of Records. ... [as] one of the highest in the world." As Camdessus noted, high financial spreads are "an unequivocal symptom of financial underdevelopment."

An array of factors contributes to the persistence of high interest rates and the large spread between deposit and lending rates. Powell, Broda and Burdisso (1997) offer three explanations for the high rates and spreads. These explanations, which the authors describe as "traditional," are certainly relevant to the situation in Paraguay:

- First, the heavy concentration of unregistered commercial activities such as smuggling and "connected" lending have resulted in excessive risk-taking behavior by the country's banks. This behavior has created a spiral of rising interest rates, riskier lending, and accumulations of poor assets. The ratio of credit growth to GDP growth and the level of nonperforming loans are indicators of the extent of the problem and the speed with which it has developed.

- Second, financial and administrative indicators show low levels of managerial efficiency. As of December 1997 the gap between foreign and domestic institutions in terms of administrative and managerial efficiency was considerable (Table 8.5). This discrepancy is even more striking given that several inefficient national banks had already left the market and that inefficient public banks are not included in the comparison.

- Finally, market power in the financial sector is oligopolistic, largely because of the extreme profitability of banking in Paraguay. Foreign banks have earned a high return on their capital in recent years, at least by international standards, and the system itself is quite profitable (Table 8.6).[17] The behavior of foreign banks, which demon-

---

[16] Interest rates in foreign currency fluctuate in much the same way as international rates. Nevertheless during the period, the premium on domestic lending rates was between 4 and 8 percent, compared with the U.S. prime rate.

[17] According to Powell, Broda, and Burdisso (1997) and others, banking profitability normally ranges between 10 and 15 percent on capital in developed countries.

Table 8.4. Interest Rates, 1991-97
(national currency)

Type	1991	1992	1993	1994	1995	1996	1997
Lending (annual nominal rate)							
Development loans	27.5	31.8	30.5	29.4	32.6	28.9	24.9
Commercial loans	30.8	33.8	36.8	34.3	32.6	30.0	26.8
Personal loans	39.6	39.4	44.0	39.1	40.6	41.4	31.9
Credit card[a]	49.0	44.1	46.1	47.5	56.5	53.4	48.9
Overdraft	49.0	49.6	52.7	54.6	60.1	56.6	53.4
Average (weighted)	34.5	39.5	40.8	38.3	42.8	40.0	36.0
Deposit (annual nominal rate)							
Savings accounts	14.1	11.3	11.2	12.2	10.7	9.7	5.9
Term deposits	11.4	16.6	17.9	16.0	14.0	14.8	11.3
Savings deposit certificates	21.0	22.5	24.7	23.2	22.2	17.1	14.4
Average (weighted)	14.8	15.4	14.7	18.3	14.7	13.0	7.6
Spread	19.7	24.1	26.1	20.0	28.1	27.0	28.3
Inflation	11.8	17.8	20.4	18.3	10.5	8.1	6.2
Lending (annual real rate)							
Development loans	14.0	11.9	8.4	9.4	20.0	19.3	17.6
Commercial loans	17.0	13.6	13.6	13.6	20.0	20.3	19.4
Personal loans	24.9	18.4	19.6	17.6	27.2	30.8	24.2
Credit card	33.2	22.3	21.4	24.7	41.6	41.9	40.2
Overdraft	33.2	27.0	26.9	30.7	44.9	44.8	44.4
Average (weighted)	20.3	18.4	16.9	16.9	29.2	29.5	28.0
Deposit (annual real rate)							
Savings accounts	2.0	−5.5	−7.6	−5.2	0.2	1.5	−0.3
Term deposits	−0.4	−1.0	−2.1	−2.0	3.1	6.2	4.8
Savings deposit certificates	8.3	3.9	3.6	4.1	10.6	8.3	7.8
Average (weighted)	2.7	−2.1	−4.8	0.0	3.8	4.6	1.4

a. No differentiation is made between 1991 credit card and overdraft rates.

Note: Values are for December each year.

Source: Central Bank.

Table 8.5. Financial and Administrative Indicators, December 1997
(percent)

Indicator	Branches of foreign banks	Banks with a majority of foreign capital	Banks with a majority of national capital	Public banks
Personnel costs/deposits	2.8	4.7	4.4	8.7
Administrative costs/deposits	6.7	8.5	9.8	11.6

Source: Banking Superintendency.

strate best administrative practices, follows the framework set out by Stiglitz and Weiss (1981). According to this framework, the optimal strategy in a market with imperfect information is to ration credit, excluding riskier clients from the borrowing pool. Using this strategy, foreign banks are able to increase their profits in two ways. They can set their lending rates just below those of the more inefficient banks, and they can offer lower-than-average deposit interest rates (they generally pay negative real rates on deposits), because of the flight to quality among depositors.

Along with these three factors, two other issues must be considered: the problems of information and imperfect enforcement, both of which increase the risk of default. Banks tend to charge higher interest rates to com-

Table 8.6. Banking Profitability: Earnings and Equity, 1991-97
(percent)

Type	1991	1992[a]	1993[a]	1994[a]	1995	1996	1997
Foreign banks	10.3	16.8	16.1	10.4	19.7	33.4[b]	28.2[b]
Banks with majority national capital	11.3	13.1	6.8	5.4	8.5	11.9	9.4
Public banks	7.3	15.1	14.5	3.8	5.0	4.7	−4.0
System average	9.8	15.4	13.1	7.5	13.5	21.0	23.2

a. As of September.
b. The figures would have been even higher had they excluded the two banks that started up in 1996 and have shown no profit.

Source: Banking Superintendency.

pensate for the perceived higher risk. A proxy of this risk might be the difference between interest rates for credit with and without collateral.

The evidence on this issue is mixed. First, of commercial and personal loans, personal loans are generally smaller and less likely to be backed by collateral. The interest rate gap between these loans varied from 5 to 13 percent during the 1990s. Another piece of evidence provided by two banks responding to the questionnaire shows a difference of 1-4 percent annually between rates for loans made with and without collateral, depending on the currency and the type of guarantee. In some cases loans with third-party personal guarantees have lower interest rates than collateralized loans.

In some cases the gap exists because of the size of a firm or a loan. The difference in interest rates on credits to small firms and on those to big firms may be as high as 8 percent. The difference in rates on loans of less than $10,000 and loans of more than $1,000,000 is around 5 percent (here, however, the fixed cost component may be a factor). Banks seem to have different policies, since some institutions do not apply different rates according to firm or loan size. A generic explanation may be that banks charge an interest rate premium to certain sectors or for certain types of loans they perceive as riskier. The perception of risk varies widely across banks according to the market segments in which they operate.

Short-Term Credit

The Paraguayan financial system has a very short-term orientation. As of April 1995 (no relevant data are available for later years), 87 percent of total credit to the nonfinancial sector had a maturity of less than one year, and 49 percent had a maturity of less than 60 days. The figures for corporate loans were only slightly lower, although still high in absolute terms.

Even though most loans are written as short-term contracts, they are generally rolled over into de facto long-term loans (Gavin and Hausmann 1996). Rolling over loans allows banks to transfer the risk to the borrower and also to exercise oligopolistic power. However, short-term loans generally do not involve the same type of evaluation as long-term industrial credits. Short-term lending reinforces the tendency of Paraguayan banks to concentrate their lending portfolio on a certain type of credit and client that do not require a thorough risk evaluation. Thus, banks favor credit backed by pledges or collateral and prefer lending to consumers with salaries, some kind of personal guarantee, or both.

Credit Rationing

Credit is concentrated largely in nonproductive sectors, mainly commercial and consumer loans (Table 8.7). Only 25.2 percent of the portfolio of private banks is devoted to productive sectors (e.g., agriculture, cattle, industry, and construction). More than 56 percent goes to commercial and consumer loans. This imbalance is a consequence of the incentive structure that benefits commercial triangulation and other illegal activities.

Banks have valid reasons for requiring collateral when extending a loan. These reasons include some of the issues already discussed, such as the legal complications that can affect small loans, enforcement problems and inadequate bankruptcy and reorganization procedures. In all cases collateral is the best protection because it makes collection faster and easier (six months to one year through an executive procedure, with a 75 percent or more chance of collection; see Box 8.2).

Under the new banking law, the effective equity-to-asset ratio must be at least 12 percent. Collateralized credits are considered low-risk assets and have a 0.50 coefficient, while noncollateralized credits carry a normal risk and have a 1.00 coefficient. Banks thus have an incentive to ask for collateral

Table 8.7. Credit by Sector, December 1997
(percent)

Type	Agri-culture	Cattle	Industry	Con-struction	Export	Con-sumer	Com-merce	Other
Foreign banks	4.9	4.9	9.3	2.5	3.2	12.5	47.4	15.3
National banks	6.3	5.5	14.2	1.3	4.3	12.3	42.0	14.1
Total private banks	5.8	5.3	12.3	1.8	3.9	12.3	44.0	14.6
Public banks	34.4	3.8	19.2	0.0	1.6	17.3	20.2	3.6
System average	12.7	4.9	14.0	1.3	3.3	13.5	38.3	11.9

Source: Central Bank.

Box 8.2. Collateralized Loans

Loans secured with mortgages or pledges are easier to recover than any other instrument of credit. First, the creditor can obtain an attachment for the collateral (real estate or movable property) listed in the public instrument. As mortgages and pledges are registered in the public registry, the officer of the court does not need to seek out the debtor's assets but instead can go directly to the registry. Attachments can be made for a value equal to the debt, interest, and costs. The debtor is unlikely to sell or trade the collateral, as potential buyers of the property are informed of the property's legal status through the public registry. Collateral can be sold to a third party only if that party knows about the debt and is willing to pay it.

Second, the debtor does not need to acknowledge in court loans that are notarized or related notes listed in the Public Registry, allowing the creditor to speed up the process (and save money). Third, with a notarized loan the parties can agree on a special address where the debtor can be notified of any court orders. Fourth, creditors holding loans guaranteed by mortgages or pledges do not need to get in line with creditors holding unsecured loans in the event of a reorganization procedure. Secured loans take priority, and creditors can collect capital, interest, and costs before other creditors are paid. Finally, in execution procedures a debt backed with collateral is more likely to be renegotiated than an unsecured debt (50-60 percent compared with 30 percent).

in order to increase their leverage. More practically, the highly informal nature of the Paraguayan economy makes screening potential borrowers difficult. One way to compensate for this information problem is to rely on some kind of guarantee.

Data from the Banking Superintendency show that 86.7 percent of the banking system's portfolio is backed by guarantees of some type: 49.3 percent by collateral (real estate and pledges) and 37.4 percent by a third-party personal guarantee. Furthermore, responses to the questionnaire show that 41-90 percent of all loans to individuals are backed by some kind of guarantee, as are 62-70 percent of corporate credits. Typical loan-to-value ratios are also quite high, ranging from 50-100 percent, but ratios at the low end of the range are the most common. This fact may indicate the need for a relatively large amount of collateral to compensate for a potential loss. The low loan-to-value ratio may also be the result of the general perception that the real estate market has been overvalued and that collateral may have to be sold at low prices.

Inadequate Credit Evaluation

The strong reliance on collateral in the Paraguayan market is the direct result of (and also an explanation for) the lack of adequate credit evaluation capabilities, since to some extent collateral is a substitute for such evaluations. Manove, Padilla and Pagano (1998) offer a relevant model of "lazy" banks that perform socially inefficient low-level screening. Other reasons for Paraguay's weak evaluation capabilities include the lack of transparency in most businesses, which complicates efforts at formal evaluation, and administrative inefficiency resulting from poor managerial practices. Paraguayan financial institutions organize the credit process as a series of steps, with a different person in charge of each successive step. This process has proven to be problematic, especially in terms of informational efficiency.

Some sources connect the lack of evaluation capabilities with the lending practices that were common in the Paraguayan financial market until 1997.[18] Banks with ties to industrial groups assigned credit based on these relationships without considering profitability or the borrower's administrative abilities.

The results of the questionnaire show that lenders rely heavily on data provided by Paraguay's sole private information agency (Box 8.3). All the institutions surveyed consider reports from this agency at least as important as their own data when it comes to deciding whether to extend credit, and some banks rely exclusively on the agency's information. A listing in the agency's registers virtually eliminates the possibility of obtaining formal credit, showing just how important this mechanism is as a means of disciplining borrowers (Padilla and Pagano 1996).[19] Banks also use the agency to

---

[18] See, for example, the interview with A. Caballero, Director of the Central Bank, *Diario ABC, Suplemento Económico*, June 22, 1997.
[19] Big borrowers reportedly can sometimes buy their way out of the registers.

Box 8.3. Information-Sharing Mechanisms in Paraguay

The Paraguayan market for credit information is a virtual monopoly in the hands of the private information agency, Informconf, which was created in 1963. Informconf provides many of the same services as private credit bureaus in industrial countries.

Type of data provided
Informconf provides a menu of data (both "white" and "black") on both persons and firms through the Internet. Among other items a personal report may contain the following:

- General data: name, date of birth, gender, documents, civil status, nationality, profession, and references.
- Current and past addresses.
- Current and past jobs (with dates).
- Lost documents reported to the police.
- References investigated by the agency at the request of some affiliate (and the reason for the request).
- Legal claims against the individual.
- Any bankruptcies and reorganization procedures involving the individual.
- Any judicial liquidations of property.
- Past-due operations.

The information varies slightly for firms and includes data about location, associates, and organizational structure. On request verifications are provided on properties, divorces, vehicles, and third-party powers of attorney. The agency may also make visits to firms in order to check the accuracy of information. Finally, general information can be retrieved, including judicial diaries and lists of closed accounts.

Sources of information
The agency gives no precise information about the sources of its information, but most of the data are gathered by the agency itself from the relevant institutions (mainly the judiciary and police). However anyone making an inquiry must state the reason for wanting the information (for instance, a loan or credit card applicant, to check on a guarantee, or to check on a potential renter). The nature of these inquiries is included with the information provided in response to subsequent requests. Moreover some files also

contain information on past-due operations reported by affiliates, although this type of information does not seem to be gathered systematically. Past-due operations are generally not included in the database unless they become judicial claims.

Costs

The cost of using the system is between $90 and $100. A monthly subscription costs around $35 and includes 40 free reports. Each additional report is billed separately, and the price depends on the type of report requested. A standard report costs about $2.50.

Volume of activity

Informconf is widely used in Paraguay. Affiliates include all banks and financial companies, as well as supermarkets, retail stores, cable TV firms, car dealers, import-export firms, and other businesses. Most affiliates resort to Informconf before authorizing any financial operation with their clients.

solve enforcement problems, since it allows creditors to monitor their clients in case of default before taking any action. In particular, if creditors discover that a client is involved in a judicial process, they rush to court. Most of the bankers interviewed, however, would like to see a more efficient credit-scoring organization that provides detailed information on prospective borrowers' histories and characteristics as well as on defaults. The Risk Central, implemented at the Central Bank in 1997 to fulfill precisely this function, may fill this gap.

High Default Rates

The structural deficiencies of the Paraguayan financial sector have negatively affected the default rates of domestic and particularly public banks in Paraguay (Table 8.8). Consistent with what has happened in other Latin American countries, the level of nonperforming loans in the Paraguayan system began deteriorating only *after* the 1995 financial crisis began (Gavin and Hausmann 1996).

Table 8.8. Level of Past-Due Loans, 1991-97
(percentage of total loans)

Type	1991	1992	1993	1994	1995	1996	1997
Banks with majority foreign capital	3.1	3.1	4.1	4.9	3.8	5.6	4.5
Banks with majority national capital	2.3	5.7	6.2	8.5	8.5	14.3	16.8
Public banks	9.6	21.6	10.7	16.4	11.7	17.9	35.6
System average	4.4	7.6	6.1	8.6	7.0	11.3	13.1

Note: Figures for 1992, 1993, and 1994 are as of September.

Source: Banking Superintendency.

The Informal Credit Market

The informal credit market attracts clients who typically lack the kind of guarantees that formal institutions require, such as collateral or reputation.[20] Informal creditors rely on alternative mechanisms to ensure repayment and compensate for potentially higher risk.

These lenders traditionally service microenterprises and SMEs. For practical purposes, such enterprises are most commonly defined by their size: microenterprises have 1-5 employees, small enterprises have 6-20 employees, and medium-size enterprises have 21-100 employees. Moreover, there are no accurate data on the number of such enterprises in Paraguay. The available figures from the Ministry of Industry's 1997 industrial census on a total of 9,002 firms indicate that 76 percent are microenterprises, 16 percent are small enterprises, and 6 percent are medium-size enterprises. The remaining 2 percent have more than 100 employees.

Estimates from the Paraguayan Industrial Union reveal the importance of small, mostly informal enterprises to the Paraguayan economy. These firms represent 97 percent of all businesses, account for 36 percent of industrial employment, and are responsible for 21 percent of industrial value added. Other estimates of commercial and service enterprises show that in 1994 Paraguay had 27,926 commercial firms and 8,624 service firms. Together,

---

[20] Informal credit institutions are those whose activities escape official notice—that is, they are not registered.

Table 8.9. Source of Financing by Firm Size, 1996
(percent)

Firm size	Internal financing	Commercial banks	Finance companies	Suppliers	External financing
Small	52	16	6	21	4
Medium	61	20	4	13	2
Large	55	23	3	14	5

Source: World Bank 1996a.

the number of urban microenterprises engaged in industrial, service, and commercial activities totaled approximately 400,000. More than half were independent workers.

This sector has fairly low access to the formal credit market (Table 8.9). Total financing from the formal financial sector (banks and finance companies) is only 22 percent for small firms and 24 percent for medium-size firms. Even for large firms such financing is low (26 percent).

Rural economic units, too, are frequent clients of the informal credit market. Around 75 percent of Paraguay's agricultural enterprises do not have access to formal credit, either commercial or public. This percentage rises to 88 percent when farmers with fewer than 5 hectares are taken into account (Hirsch 1994).

Like their counterparts in the formal credit market, lenders in the informal credit market prefer short-term loans, with maturities ranging from a few days or weeks to a maximum of six months. These loans usually finance short-term operations like the acquisition of raw materials or intermediate goods and more general production and commercial processes. When they are designed to finance medium-term operations, short-term loans are simply rolled over. Interest rates are usually well above the already high rates of the formal system (Table 8.10).

Credit operations in the informal market can be implemented through simple oral contracts, promissory notes, and an instrument found in few places other than the Paraguayan financial environment: the postdated check.[21] Oral arrangements and promissory notes are commonly used in

---

[21] It is also used in Bolivia and Brazil (see Chapter 5).

Table 8.10. Annual Interest Rates for Different Types of Credit, 1997
(percent)

Informal commercial credit by usurers[a]	Postdated checks (discount rate)[b]	Credit to micro-enter-prises[c]	Commercial credit by finance companies[d]	Commercial credit by banks[d]	Devel-opment credit by banks[d]	Corporate credit by banks, prime rate[b]	Cost of funds[d]	Inflation rate 1997[d]
120-180	43-150	70-80	38	26	22	18	15	6.2

a. Borda 1997.

b. Interviews (see footnote 2).

c. Technical Unit for the Execution of Programs (UTEP).

d. Average rates, Central Bank.

very short-term operations, such as urgent loans made by usurers to microenterprises. Clients needing such loans usually do not have bank accounts and cannot rely on overdraft facilities or the postdated check system. Postdated checks finance regular operations with suppliers or medium-term commercial credit (from 30 days to a few months).

Enforcement in the informal market tends toward Mafia-style tactics, with informal creditors relying on physical threats or the prospect of prison. The following story, told by the president of the Paraguayan association of finance companies, describes the kind of enforcement usurers favor:

> One of our clients was heavily indebted with several creditors, including us and a usurer. As a way to remind him of his obligation, the usurer sent him a bullet in an envelope. The client paid the usurer first and then filed a reorganization procedure. We recovered only a small fraction of the formal loans.

The Postdated Check before 1996

Before 1996 the law defined checks written against accounts without funds as "swindling" and therefore subject to criminal prosecution. Debtors who signed checks with a future date and did not have sufficient funds in the bank by the date on the check could go to jail. Creditors initiated a criminal procedure that allowed them, with an order of arrest issued by a judge, to demand payment in full. If the debtor did not pay, the creditor used the order of arrest to put the debtor in jail. This tactic invariably ensured that the loans would be repaid in full in a very short time, since most borrowers would do anything to avoid prison.

Similarly, postdated checks were used as a substitute for collateral in business transactions. The borrower wrote a postdated check to the lender for the amount of the loan. If the borrower did not pay the loan at the expiration date, the lender could deposit the check, causing it to bounce. The bank returned the check to the lender, who could then initiate the criminal procedure described above.[22] So the postdated check, which was initially used in genuine commercial operations somewhat like a credit bill, soon took on a life of its own, becoming a mechanism to ensure the borrower's willingness to repay in the informal credit market. This instrument had the added advantage of being a liquid one, since a broad (illegal) rediscount market for postdated checks soon developed.

These facts suggest that the postdated check is a very efficient instrument in terms of enforcement and help explain why it has been so widely accepted. The postdated check is in fact a relatively successful adaptation to the Paraguayan situation. Economic agents have developed it to suit their needs in the absence of other legal security (CEPPRO 1996).

The judicial statistics for the 1990s show exactly how widely the postdated check is used. The statistics reveal a large number of cases related to both postdated and regular checks.[23] Procedures involving checks without funds represented between 10 and 20 percent of the criminal proceedings initiated in the 1990s. Since a large number of the cases labeled as swindling are related to checks without funds, this figure could easily rise to between 30 and 40 percent of all criminal proceedings. Moreover, during the 1990s around 10 percent of the population of the National Penitentiary were incarcerated for issuing checks without funds.[24]

---

[22] World Bank (1994) describes a similar procedure in Bolivia.

[23] Knowing the potential prison penalty involved, people are less likely to issue a check against an account without funds if they believe the receiver will deposit it at once. They are more likely to issue a check dated several weeks or months ahead with the hope of covering it—and then to default when the time to pay arrives.

[24] All data are from judicial branch sources.

These data show that despite the protection postdated checks offer creditors, many people were jailed during the 1990s for passing checks without funds. In most cases of default, then, the problem may well have been inability to pay.[25] Separating defaults that result from an inability to pay from defaults arising from an unwillingness to repay is difficult. But the enforcement procedures in the informal market may make willingness to pay a relevant issue when debtors with multiple obligations give priority to creditors with the most threatening penalty.

The Postdated Check after 1996

In the aftermath of the 1995 crisis, the Paraguayan economy experienced a severe recessionary slump. However, the official banking statistics (which do not include statistics on credit provided by postdated checks) show neither a significant credit crunch nor a large drop in bank deposits after the crisis. Arguably the main impact came from the collapse of the credit market for postdated checks. Finance companies attached to banks had developed rediscount departments for postdated checks. The most active of these banks failed, resulting in a deep public mistrust of the instrument itself. Ultimately the situation was felt as a strong crunch in the informal credit market and was a major factor in the subsequent economic slowdown.[26]

As this fact became more evident, Paraguay's policymakers and other economic agents became preoccupied with restoring this credit channel. Postdated checks had served social as well as economic purposes, insofar as they were often used by productive units lacking access to the formal financial sector. This concern led to an important modification of the legal framework surrounding postdated checks. Hypothetically this change, and more importantly the shift in the enforcement level postdated checks provide, led to a modification and cleansing of market practices and a decline in the use of this instrument. The sequence of events was as follows:

---

[25] Here again it is worthwhile mentioning that the lack of effective mechanisms for evaluating credit is one consequence of the excessive reliance on guarantees.

[26] Obviously a banking crisis that severely affected the economy through other channels as well. But the crunch in the market for postdated checks was the first and strongest factor.

- First, a sharp drop occurred in the check-based credit market because people lost confidence in the banking sector, with strong and immediate recessionary effects on the economy.

- Second, the legislation governing postdated checks was modified in an effort to revive this market.

- Third, and unexpectedly (at least for policymakers), there was a further fall in the credit market for postdated checks because the new legal framework lowered the enforcement level. In this sense the judicial reform helped to amplify the recession.

In essence, the reform stipulated that writing checks without funds was no longer a criminal offense. Furthermore as of January 1, 1997 this law also established the postdated check as an instrument separate from the standard check. Banks, financial institutions, and customers (using a special checkbook) could operate with two types of checks. The rediscounting of postdated checks also became legal, and a normal check issued with a future date could also be paid at any time before that date.

The enforcement procedure for defaulting on postdated checks is no longer so severe. Banks can fine a person who writes checks without sufficient funds and does not pay the amount within three days of a request for payment. A person who is fined or has three checks returned for insufficient funds cannot operate a checking account in any bank in the country for one year. Banks must notify the regulatory institution, the Banking Superintendency, when accounts are closed, and other banks are informed within 48 hours. When accounts are closed and fines levied, the information must be published in two newspapers for two days. When the one-year period of suspension has expired, the individual can open a checking account, provided that the returned checks or the fine are paid in full. A person who writes a check against a closed account is barred from having an account for 10 years.[27]

The quantity of checks processed by the Central Bank Clearinghouse declined markedly after May 1995, the month that marked the date of the first banking problems (Figure 8.1). The total number of checks written (as

---

[27] But prison is still a possibility in this case, since issuing a check against a closed account is considered swindling.

Figure 8.1. Number of Checks Cleared in Main Cities, 1994-96

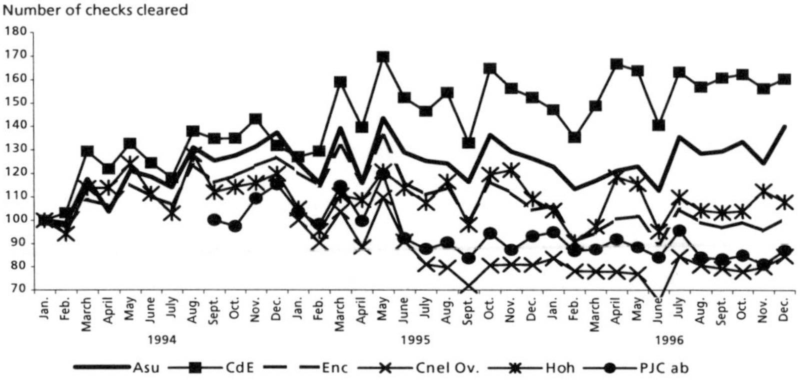

Number of checks cleared

Note: Index = 100 at the beginning of the period.
ASU = Asuncion, CdE = Ciudad del Este, Enc = Encarnacion, CNEL Ov = Ciel Oviedo, Hoh = Hohenau, PJCab = P.J. Caballero.
Source: Central Bank Clearinghouse.

well as the number of checks cleared) also fell. Controlling for the various factors embodied in this statistic is difficult. First, four banks ceased operations in the spring and summer of 1995, so a large number of current accounts disappeared. Second, the slowdown in economic activity translated into fewer transactions and thus fewer checks. Finally, these data include standard as well as postdated checks that came to maturity. Distinguishing between the percentage of the decrease attributable to the decline in the overall number of checks and the percentage corresponding to fewer postdated checks is not possible.

The closure of several banks had a clear impact on the credit market for postdated checks. The banks that closed were active in the market, both because they had a large number of small depositors holding current accounts and because they had rediscount operations for this instrument. The first two banks to fail in 1995 accounted for 8 percent of the banking system's total deposits and had very low requirements for opening an account.[28] A clear correlation exists between the closure of these institutions and the crunch in the postdated check market.

---

[28] Many well-functioning banks have fairly high requirements for opening an account, including minimum deposits, average balances, and references. Such requirements tend to shut out the kind of clients who operate with postdated checks.

Because no monthly or quarterly GDP data are available for this period, the best indicator of the economic slowdown is the level of tax collection, particularly of the VAT, which is directly related to sales levels. Tax collection levels began falling after July 1995. However, the magnitude of the decrease was quite small, since total tax collections for 1995 surpassed 1994 levels and even the goals set for 1995 (CEPPRO 1996). Aggregate GDP figures show economic growth of 4.7 percent for 1995, with the real recessionary impact appearing only during 1996, when growth fell to 1.3 percent and growth in the industrial and commercial sectors turned negative (−2.2 and −1 percent, respectively).

Opinion polls show that of all the economic sectors in Paraguay, the informal sector was probably the most badly hit. Thus it appears that the large decrease in checks in circulation in the second semester of 1995 was much greater than the slowdown in economic activity (Table 8.11).[29] This notion supports the idea that the declines in the quantity of checks cleared were in part the result of a drop in the use of postdated checks. Most deposits in the failed banks were covered by the Central Bank and then redeposited elsewhere in the banking system, and the total level of deposits did not fall.[30] There should have been a rapid recuperation in the level of checks processed, but this did not in fact occur.

The decline in small towns such as Ciel Oviedo or P.J. Caballero, which typically have few banks, was steeper and lasted longer than in the capital, Asunción, or the frontier town of Ciudad del Este (which conducts most of its financial operations with banks in neighboring Brazil). Since the credit market in these small towns is very poorly developed, many businesses rely on postdated checks, especially for commercial credit. The decline in postdated checks would have had a profound effect on the overall number of checks written in these towns. Though no regional data on the level of activity are available for comparison, field observation and interviews corroborate this point (see footnote 1).

---

[29] This analysis considers variations in three-month periods to reduce the distortion caused by the erratic behavior that was common around the time of bank failures. At that time depositors fleeing banks in trouble often wrote checks against those banks. In fact, the average amount of checks picked up in April and May 1995.

[30] As incredible as it might seem, in 1996 the Congress passed a law requiring the Central Bank to cover "black" unregistered deposits.

Table 8.11. Checks in Circulation, 1995
(percentage change)

City	Number of checks	Value
Asunción	−5.1	−20.5
Ciudad del Este	−3.2	−17.7
Encarnación	−11.2	−7.9
Ciel Oviedo	−16.6	−17.5
Hohenau	−0.8	−7.1
P.J.Caballero	−19.0	−30.3
Country total	−5.1	−19.9

Note: Figures are based on variations in March-May and June-August activity.

Source: Central Bank Clearinghouse.

Clearly some evidence exists to support the hypothesis that a crunch did occur in the postdated check credit market. Why did it occur? First, confidence in national banks fell dramatically in the second half of 1995, with everyone waiting to see which bank would fail next. As banks failed, other banks and finance companies became increasingly unwilling to accept postdated checks, fearing (not illogically) that the bank on which the check was written might collapse before the payment date. Second, and equally important, were the closings of various banks that had formerly been very active in this market. However, it is a challenge to determine what happened after the enactment of the new legal framework—especially whether the new legal mechanisms, which clearly imply a different enforcement process for check-based transactions, had any consequences on the volume, costs, and default rate in this market.

After the initial decrease in the total volume of checks traded, a slight but incomplete recovery occurred in 1997, but only in Asunción. As discussed above, the decrease was related to a decline in the use of postdated checks. Another contributing factor was the drop in current accounts in the banking system. As of 1997 the banking system had around 90,000 current accounts. Although no exact data exist on the number of current accounts before 1995, the closing of 10 banks, stricter requirements for opening ac-

Table 8.12. Current Account Requirements and Penalties, 1997
(U.S. dollars)

Bank type	Opening amount		Average required		Penalty[a]	
	National currency	Foreign currency	National currency	Foreign currency	National currency	Foreign currency
Foreign	500-1,800	4,000-10,000	300-700	1,000-5,000	10-50	20-50
	(1,100)	(5,000)	(500)	(3,000)	(25)	(30)
National	350-700	5,000[b]	270-350	1,000-3,000	20-28	30-50
	(350)		(350)	(3,000)	(25)	(30)

a. Monthly penalty for maintaining an average below the required minimum.
b. These are the only data available.
Note: Figures in parentheses are median figures.
Source: Newspaper *El Día de Asunción*.

counts, and higher minimum balances in the remaining institutions certainly restricted access to the banking system (Table 8.12).

Between January 1997, when the new legal framework was applied, and July 1998, some 4,807 accounts were closed and their owners banned from having a new account for one year.[31] This figure amounts to 5.3 percent of the estimated total number of accounts. Requirements and penalties linked to the operation of a current account have risen considerably from a few years ago (see Table 8.12). In many cases would-be depositors are now required not only to deposit and maintain specified minimums but to provide personal and commercial references. In some cases depositors must be able to show that they own land. Banks often refuse to open accounts even when depositors fulfill the requirements, indicating that banks are screening potential clients carefully. Bank officials also say that many banks now encourage their clients to close down accounts after the first problems occur.

Banks have improved their screening mechanisms in part because prison is no longer a threat. With better information about debtors and their businesses, banks are able to make loans to those most likely to repay. To a

---

[31] Some 4,499 persons lost their banking privileges for 10 years for issuing checks against closed accounts.

certain extent this situation implies that primary users of check-based credit for commercial operations are producers genuinely in need of supplies. But poor accounting standards and lack of transparency among most users of this instrument continue to make solid credit evaluations difficult, hindering the formalization of the credit market for postdated checks.

Probably for the same reasons, a rediscount market has not developed. A telephone survey with a dozen financial institutions yields the following results:

- Postdated check operations are concentrated in a few national banks and finance companies, although most of these institutions do not encourage their clients to use this instrument. Most foreign banks do not enter the postdated check business. They do not issue the necessary checkbook or provide any rediscount operations.

- In all cases demand for the checkbooks used for postdated checks is not high. Most operators still use the common check for postdated operations, in spite of the fact that such a check can be paid at any time before its due date. In fact, ignorance of the new legal framework appears to be widespread.

- Most of the institutions with rediscount operations for postdated checks are actually running traditional credit operations. They provide short-term credit with a promissory note, keeping the corresponding check in their files.

- Interest rates for these operations are the same as for other short-term instruments such as credit cards and overdrafts and run from 3 to 4 percent monthly. Maturity does not exceed 180 days.

- All the institutions surveyed stated that the number of postdated checks has decreased since 1995 and that there has been a corresponding cleansing of the market.

In short, since the enactment of the new check law in December 1995, market practices have been modified, leading to a decrease in the use of postdated checks, a partial formalization and cleansing of the market by the financial institutions themselves, and a greater concentration on genuine operations. The new legal framework, which has made enforcement more difficult for postdated checks, has clearly been a relevant factor in these developments. The increasing formalization of many financial practices of banks and finance companies, as well as the disappearance of many institutions that were deeply involved in informal activities, also contributed to these changes. As a result, the links between the formal and informal market have to a certain extent been weakened.

Links between the Formal and Informal Markets

The formal and informal financial sectors do not function independently of each other. In fact the informal sector depends heavily on its relationship with the formal system. The sectors are linked in two important ways. First, the formal sector provides credit to people who channel it to the informal sector, thus hedging the interest rate difference. This operation is made easier by the fact that credit is often assigned on the basis of formal guarantees (collateral) and relationships with bank owners rather than on a careful evaluation of the purpose of the loan. Informal lenders act as intermediaries between formal financial institutions and clients lacking guarantees.

The second link is the current account that allows potential debtors to issue postdated checks. Prior to 1995 the existence of an active rediscount market for postdated checks strengthened this link. The resulting liquidity of these instruments contributed to the development of the market for postdated checks.

The theoretical literature usually considers that while the formal sector has a comparative advantage in its ability to intermediate funds over space and create scale economies, the informal sector has a comparative advantage in its ability to solve enforcement and information problems (Besley 1995). In Paraguay, however, the situation is somewhat different, in that the informal sector's only comparative advantage is enforcement. There are two reasons for this difference. First, most economic agents operate informally and lack transparency, so that screening per se is a difficult task. Second, the informal sector's strong enforcement level itself works against the dissemination of information on clients, since informal lenders for the most part rely on Mafia-style enforcement rather than on close monitoring of debtors. Overall the informal sector's advantage when it comes to enforcement means that debtors with multiple obligations are often more willing to repay informal than formal lenders, as illustrated by the anecdote regarding the mailed bullet. In a pool of credit, then, informal lenders benefit from the highest rate of repayment, mostly through enforcement.

The informal market's solution to the problem of willingness to pay, however effective, is clearly not optimal from either a social or an economic point of view. Aside from the physical danger inherent in some informal enforcement mechanisms, lenders offer credit without adequately screening projects, and the general conditions of the loans are not satisfactory. Currently an alternative lending program is being explored in Paraguay that aims to develop new solutions to the enforcement and information problems of lending to small borrowers lacking guarantees.

A Credit Program for Microenterprises

As has been discussed, microenterprises pay extremely high interest rates when borrowing from the formal sector. There are several reasons for these steep rates, including high costs and the oligopolistic behavior of some financial institutions. But another important component of the high interest rate premium is related to the poor quality of available information and a real or perceived lack of willingness to repay. The Microenterprise Global Credit Program, developed in 1994 with a loan from the Inter-American Development Bank (IDB), aims to provide credit sources for micro and small enterprises at a reasonable cost by modifying the credit relationship and procedures (Box 8.4). The program is intended as a model for the rest of the financial sector. By introducing best practices in the credit process, it strives to influence the credit procedures of other institutions.

The program works with existing for-profit financial institutions rather than through subsidies.[32] It relies mainly on screening and monitoring, improved internal administration, and long-term relationships with clients.[33]

---

[32] Since the credits are partly covered by an automatic rediscount scheme, the program stabilizes the liabilities of the financial institutions involved and therefore may reduce their risk.

[33] No special practices have been introduced to address ex post enforcement problems. This fact may indicate that in general financial institutions have already adapted their operating procedures to the existing legal and judicial framework.

Box 8.4. The Microenterprise Global Credit Program

This program has a number of objectives. It is designed to do the following:

Generate a competitive credit market segment dedicated to microentre- preneurs. Developing such a segment will induce financial institutions cur- rently operating in the credit market to undertake loans to microentrepreneurs.

Improve the credit technology and administrative efficiency of lending insti- tutions in order to reduce costs. The program aims to change the traditional "chain" organization of credit management and put one person (a credit official) in charge of the entire credit process, including client evaluation, credit negotiation, follow-up, and collection. Credit officials will be paid based on their performance.

Reduce the information asymmetry by improving and maintaining screen- ing and monitoring in order to create a relevant information flow from clients to financial institutions. Credit officials will need to acquire some direct knowledge of their clients through personal visits, phone contacts, evaluations, and the drawing up of balance sheets. (Currently most micro and small entrepreneurs do not have balance sheets and do not actually distinguish between their commercial and personal activities and assets.) In this way lenders can generate and maintain a better flow of information about the client.

Generate incentives to repay loans for borrowers who typically have a low willingness to repay. Creating a stable, long-term relationship between the financial institution and the borrower through close and direct contact is a gradual process. In this relationship financial institutions are likely to fi- nance short business cycles first, repeating the operation once the first loan is repaid. The lenders' perception of the client's performance will in- fluence the availability of credit in the future, generating an incentive to avoid default.

Features of the Program

The program functions as an intermediate institution that channels resources to intermediate financial institutions (IFIs), which in turn provide credit to small productive units. The first phase of the program, from January 1994 to July 1997, was supported by a $12.7 million IDB grant (including a non-refundable technical cooperation component). The second phase, which began in July 1997, is supported by a $20 million IDB grant. Funds are delivered through the Finance Ministry to the Central Bank, which is the executor of the program through the Technical Unit for the Execution of Programs. Funds are transferred to the IFIs through an automatic rediscount mechanism of 80 percent of the amount of the new credits, at an interest rate equivalent to the current market marginal cost of funds.[34] The IFIs assume the credit risk, and the Central Bank assumes the exchange rate risk.[35]

The program has conditions with respect to the characteristics of clients, IFIs, and loans. Microenterprises are defined as all economic units employing 1-10 persons, including the owner. Such enterprises employ 42 percent of Paraguay's workforce and include mechanical workshops, ice or juice factories, bakeries, and dressmaking establishments (Table 8.13). Microentrepreneurs may work as merchants, carpenters, shoemakers, tailors, or artisans. Interestingly, most of these economic units are very stable: 25 percent have been operating for 5-10 years, and 39 percent for more than 10 years.

Microenterprises wishing to participate in the program must have total assets of less than $10,000 and total annual sales of less than $45,000. Each IFI must meet certain conditions:

- It must be able to show positive real economic results.

- It must have a ratio of net equity to risk-classified assets of no less than 8 percent.

---

[34] This rate is equivalent to the average rate of 180-day time deposits plus the reserve requirement effect (see Box 8.1).

[35] The program has an important and successful education component, directed to credit officials. For this reason its impact on willingness to repay is likely to operate through the mechanisms analyzed here.

Table 8.13. Workers Employed in Microenterprises, 1995

Number of employees	Total in country (urban)	Men	Women
1	193,950	93,753	100,220
2-5	363,425	230,380	133,012
6-10	93,031	66,494	26,563
Total	650,406	390,627	259,795

Source: Central Bank.

- No more than 10 percent of its credit portfolio may be more than 90 days past due.

- Large loans more than 30 and 90 days past due must not represent more than 10 percent and 3 percent, respectively, of the total credit portfolio.

- The loans must be in local currency, with a maximum of $7,000 and an average of $2,500.

Four major finance companies, another finance company formed when two struggling companies merged in 1997, and a mixed private-public bank are participating in the first phase of the program. This analysis focuses on the four finance companies, as the two other companies exhibited atypical behavior during the relevant period, and the bank had a unique approach to the program.[36] After June 1997 seven new IFIs, including a regional bank, entered the program's second phase, and a well-known international bank (Lloyds) prepared to enter. At that time the 10 biggest Paraguayan finance companies were participants. As of December 1997 the current portfolio consisted of 23,264 loans amounting to the equivalent of $28.18 million. Table 8.14 shows the relative size of the portfolios of the four institutions under discussion.

[36] This bank relied on group lending, offering bigger amounts and lower rates. It was actually forced to leave the program during 1997 because it no longer met the criteria for participation. It was closed by the Central Bank in September 1998.

Table 8.14. Relative Size of Intermediate Financial Institutions in the Microcredit Program, December 1997

Institution	Number of loans	Program loans portfolio (thousands of dollars)	Total loan portfolio (thousands of dollars)	Ratio of program to portfolio loans
Company A[a]	3,980	4,120	29,287	14.07
Company B[a]	3,397	2,603	19,723	13.20
Company C	1,509	1,522	9,167	16.60
Company D	1,879	1,350	13,289	10.16
Total	10,765	9,595	71,466	13.43
Company A[b]	3,252	2,784	29,287	9.51
Company B[b]	6,134	12,706	19,723	64.42
Total	20,151	25,085	71,466	35.10

a. Part of the microlending program which is backed by the program's rediscount scheme.
b. Part of the microlending program which is backed by the company's own resources.

Source: Central Bank.

As of December 1977 the Paraguayan market had 50 finance companies. The loan portfolios of these four companies accounted for 26.3 percent and their program loan portfolios accounted for 3.5 percent of total market loan portfolios (9.2 percent if loans backed by the companies' own resources are included). Of the four companies only one had previously worked with the type of clients that participate in the program. The other three focused on corporate and consumer credit. This fact affects comparisons of the data and the evolution of some indicators (such as average interest and default rates).

Assessing the Program's Impact

As a result of the new credit technology, overall costs have declined significantly, mainly through a reduction in default rates. Moreover, the primary effect has been on the availability of credit; effects on interest rates have been limited.

Reductions in Administrative Costs

It is not clear to what extent administrative costs have been reduced within the institutions implementing the new credit technology. Consistent with what occurred within the banking system itself, traditional ratios (different types of costs relative to operating margins and deposits) do not show a marked improvement or deterioration over the last three years, for a number of reasons. First, the program portfolio is only a fraction of each institution's portfolio, and thus any effects are marginal. Second, most of the companies are entering this market segment for the first time and thus have higher relative fixed costs than they did previously. There is virtually no follow-up for personal loans, but loan administration represents a lower relative fixed cost for large corporate loans than for loans of small amounts. Delayed costs for expansion (such as the opening of new branches) will also affect global administrative costs for a few years. And third, since loans are backed by an automatic rediscount mechanism rather than by deposits, the leverage ratio between deposits and loans rises, negatively affecting cost-to-deposit ratios without a loss of efficiency.

However, authorities of the main finance companies have stated that efficiency has improved. The head of Company A notes that the new technology reduces administrative costs because credit officials are involved in all aspects of administering the portfolio. Representatives of Company B share this sentiment. The fact that most institutions involved in the program gradually apply the new credit technology to their other operations suggests that the technology must be cost efficient.

Impact on Default Rates

The significant decline in default rates is another indicator of efficiency. Data on default rates show that for each finance company, default rates in the relevant program portfolios are below the default rates of the total portfolio (Table 8.15).[37]

Further, these institutions have different lending profiles—that is, some of them are directing nonprogram resources to types of lending other than

[37] The difference may be even larger, since the comparisons are between data for loans that are 60 days overdue and data for program loans that are 30 days overdue.

Table 8.15. Default Rates for Selected Portfolios, December 1997
(percent)

Institution	Total loan portfolio default rate (60 days)	Program loan portfolio default rate (30 days)
Company A	9.0	8.2
Company B	5.6	4.4
Company C	7.9	7.5
Company D	5.4	4.8

Source: Central Bank.

microenterprise credit, so that default rates in the overall portfolio are not strictly comparable. Officials of Company C observed that default rates on consumer credit (directed to people earning a regular salary) and on large corporate loans are usually lower than default rates on microenterprise lending. Nevertheless, the default rate for program loans is lower than the default rate for corporate lending.

Company B was already working with microenterprises prior to the program. Data on defaults on program and nonprogram credits across 11 branches of the company show that the company's default rate for the program portfolio was already relatively low (Table 8.16). Lower default rates mean fewer costs, both for providing and for recovering loans.

Impact on Interest Rates

Table 8.17 shows the average monthly rates charged by the different finance companies in microenterprise credit and the evolution of these rates over time.

Table 8.16. Default Rates for Branches of Company B, November 1997
(percentage of total portfolio)

Type of portfolio	A	B	C	D	E	F	G	H	I	J	K
Nonprogram	14.53	7.7	29.97	5.49	0.22	8.65	5.72	10.31	10.23	17.2	7.16
Program	4.24	3.61	5.2	3.02	1.1	5.87	3.36	8.7	4.4	3.0	0.58

Note: t-statistic, 6.37 is significant at the 1 percent level.
Source: Finance Company B.

Table 8.17. Program Interest Rates 1994-98
(percent)

Institution	December 1994	December 1995	December 1996	December 1997	July 1998
Company A	7.9	7.5	6.8	4.5	4.5
Company B	n.i.	n.i.	4.8	4.5	4.5
Company C	7.6	7.2	6.5	5.0	5.0
Company D	n.i.	n.i.	6.1	4.5	4.5
Average market-lending rate[a]	3.3	3.2	3.0	2.8	2.7
Interest rate premium	4.3-4.6	4.0-4.3	1.8 -3.8	1.7-2.2	1.8-2.3

n.i. Not involved in the program.

a. Average lending rate of finance companies (does not include banks).

Note: Rates are monthly on the outstanding balance of the loan.

Source: Central Bank.

These rates remain very high in absolute terms. In an environment of falling inflation (Paraguay has experienced single-digit levels since 1996), monthly rates of between 4.5 and 5 percent correspond to annual rates of between 70 and 80 percent in nominal terms and between 60 and 70 percent in real terms. Moreover, these rates are high even in comparison with those of other institutions implementing cost-covering microfinance projects in Latin America (Schor 1997).

There has been a downward trend in interest rates during the three years of the program. The maximum interest rate premium paid by micro-entrepreneurs (compared with the average lending rate of financial companies) has fallen from 4.6 to 2.2 percent in monthly terms. Yet the premium remains high. The lower bound went down but then leveled off at around 1.7-1.8 percent, essentially equalizing rates across lending institutions.

Evidence on how borrowers perceive the reductions in interest rates is mixed. A Central Bank survey from August 1995 on 320 clients of the microenterprise lending program showed that 68 percent of the micro-entrepreneurs considered the interest rates adequate, 10 percent considered them low compared with other sources, and 22 percent considered them high. Another extensive evaluation made at the end of 1996 found that 33 percent of the entrepreneurs thought the interest rates were high, while 23

Table 8.18. Perceptions of Microenterprise Program Credit, 1995 and 1996
(percent)

Characteristic	1995 Survey	1996 Survey
Term (sufficient)	72.0	100.0
Guarantee (reasonable)	66.2	83.3
Speed (fast enough)	58.8	76.6
Amount (sufficient)	83.4	66.6

percent said they were low and 43 percent perceived them as adequate (Borda 1997). Most clients of the program had previously dealt with informal lenders and usurers charging monthly rates of 5-9 percent.

Thus, despite some evidence that the introduction of the program led to a reduction in the interest rates for microentrepreneurs, program loans still carry a premium of almost 2 percent in monthly terms compared with the average market rate of financial companies. However, since finance companies have very different lending profiles, this average rate is of little significance. Companies involved in the program now charge microenterprises the same rate they charge for other types of credit.

Availability of Credit

Because the analysis concentrates on agents that traditionally do not take formal credit, calculating increases in the average amounts of credit extended is virtually impossible (see, for example, Petersen and Rajan 1994). But the mere fact that these agents access credit in conditions they consider satisfactory is a sign of improvement in the availability of credit. The 1995 and 1996 surveys just discussed support this point (see Table 8.18).

First, the majority of microenterprises entering the program (63.3 percent, according to the 1996 survey) are receiving loans from a formal financial institution for the first time. The 1995 survey showed that microentrepreneurs entering the program had previously relied on informal lenders for 51 percent of their financing and on suppliers for 11.9 percent. Some 79.6 percent stated that they had come to depend on the program for 50 percent or more of their financing. Other indicators show a low level of formal debt. The average debt ratio (debt to net equity) of the enterprises surveyed is only 0.20, with two very atypical exceptions. The average monthly credit payment (again ruling out an atypical case) is only 7.3 percent of total sales.

The evidence is strong that the program has improved access to credit for the businesses involved. In the 1995 survey 80.3 percent indicate that their sales have increased as a result of the credit (for 54.6 percent these increases were more than 25 percent) and 92.4 percent directly relate this improvement to the access to credit. The 1996 survey shows a similar pattern, with 66 percent declaring that their sales have increased as a result of credit.

Modifying the Credit Relationship

The literature that considers the effects of close relationships between lenders and borrowers usually stresses that such relationships positively affect the cost and availability of funds, but more in terms of quantity than price (Petersen and Rajan 1994). There are several explanations for this phenomenon. One is that financial institutions do not pass all cost savings along to their clients in the form of lower interest rates. Moreover, clients who have experienced credit rationing may well prefer bigger loans over lower rates. Finally, loan pricing generally responds to relatively rigid guidelines, and loan officers are often better able to influence the amount of a loan and to get it approved than they are to lower interest rates.

The credit program for microenterprises, however, has clear cost-based technical reasons for reducing the interest rates charged to microentrepreneurs, including cost-saving new technology and low program default rates. But are there cost motives for keeping the interest rates higher than those finance companies normally charge? As noted earlier, microenterprise lending carries higher relative fixed costs than personal or large corporate lending, mainly because microenterprise loans are on average very small. (The program average has been fluctuating between $932 and $1,243.) Furthermore, because so many of the borrowers operate informally, maintaining a steady flow of information is costly, even with the most efficient management. Thus, part of the premium may be related to costs, although probably not the entire 2 percent margin.

Monopolistic behavior is a relevant explanation for the high costs during the first years of the program, when the biggest finance company involved held more than 50 percent of the outstanding volume of loans and charged the highest interest rates. But after 1997 this situation changed, and interest rates began to equalize across institutions. The beginning of the second phase (after July 1997) saw the incorporation of seven more IFIs and created competition among the 10 biggest companies in this market segment.

Considering the very nature of lending to microentrepreneurs, it is safe to assume that in spite of increased competitive pressure, lenders do not pass all of their cost savings on to borrowers. Close relationships between financial institutions and microentrepreneurs may create private information about borrowers (through, for instance, on-site follow-up and informal knowledge of the business) that is not easily verifiable or transferable to other lenders.[38] As a result, credit would in fact become more widely available but interest rates would not fall.

Company B, which had been working with microentrepreneurs prior to the program, has a policy of maintaining interest rates for these borrowers at their normal level. The other institutions have gradually equalized their rates to match this company's, but there have been no further rate reductions. The interviews suggest that there is little flexibility in the interest rates applied. Instead, the close relationship a firm develops with its clients and the knowledge it gains about borrowers often lead to renewals of a credit line with larger amounts over a longer term but not to interest rate reductions.

Do entrepreneurs prefer more rather than cheaper credit? This question is difficult to answer. Most of the program clients experienced credit rationing before entering the program—if they were able to receive formal credit at all. Moreover, the surveys show no clear evidence to support the contention, since respondents have less positive responses to interest rates than to conditions of loans (amount and term).

The previous discussion suggests that higher costs, monopolistic behavior, and informational asymmetry, although important, do not explain the monthly interest rate premium of 2 percent or more. We must consider, then, the enforcement problem. At the time the program was introduced, banks perceived traditional Paraguayan microenterprises as having a relatively low willingness to repay. This perception was in part responsible for

---

[38] A transfer of information could occur if the credit official shifted to another institution.

the credit shortage and high interest rates. After a few years, however, the program changed this perception drastically, mainly because of the sharp decline in default rates and improved information. The consequence was a marked increase in the availability of credit and a relative reduction in interest rates. Many financial institutions outside the program were also induced to enter, including well-known international banks.

In the end it is possible only to approximate the reasons finance companies maintain a premium on microlending operations that is around 2 percent over the average market rate. The available data and interviews show that credit costs are higher because of the type of borrower, the small lending scale, and monopolistic behavior concerning the transfer of information on borrowers. Further the institutions participating in the program apply the same interest rates to all their operations, so that a consumer loan carries the same rate as a microenterprise loan. At least in these cases, the cost premium related to a real or perceived lack of willingness to repay has become negligible. The entry of more efficient financial institutions (large international banks) into the program should help determine whether this motive can be completely eliminated. If it can, the cost of credit to the microenterprise segment of the market will fall further, until it is reasonably in line with average market corporate rates. Such a change may not be possible, however, before certain flaws in the legal framework (especially those applying to small loans) and the weaknesses of the judicial enforcement process are addressed.

Some Final Thoughts

In order to assess the effect of the legal and institutional framework on financial markets in Paraguay, this analysis has looked at the functioning of both the formal and informal sectors. Each sector has developed different mechanisms to compensate for the flaws in information and enforcement that characterize financial contracts. However, none of these solutions (reliance on collateral and postdated checks, among others) has succeeded unequivocally, as strong structural deficiencies still affect the financial business. Credit shortages, very high interest rates, and a short-term orientation still dominate financial markets in Paraguay. Besides the well-known macroeconomic, regulatory, and managerial problems, the willingness to repay issue has played a profound role in the evolution of the Paraguayan financial system in the 1990s and in the still-unresolved banking crisis.

To counteract this situation, the Micro-Credit Global Program has introduced alternative mechanisms to solve the problems of asymmetrical information and weak enforcement. These mechanisms are more efficient than those traditionally implemented in the formal and informal sectors. The program has created a competitive lending market for a sector that formal institutions had previously ignored. While interest rates in this market segment have not fallen to the level of average corporate rates, preliminary evidence on costs and availability of credit suggests that this experiment is an innovative solution. It addresses the traditional problems of lack of information and high perceived risk (because of low perceived willingness to repay) of microentrepreneurs. The strategies devised by the Microcredit Program to overcome some of the traditional structural deficiencies of Paraguay's financial sector make the program a valuable component of the ongoing financial reform process.

CHAPTER 9

Growing Indebtedness, Institutional Change and Credit Contracts in Peru

Carolina Trivelli, Javier Alvarado and Francisco Galarza

Peru's credit market expanded rapidly during the 1990s. Between 1993 and 1998 the amount of credit allocated through formal financial intermediaries increased by 17 percent, and between 1994 and 1997 the number of households with credit doubled. By the end of 1998, bank loans totaled around 25 percent of gross domestic product (GDP). This expansion in credit activity is the result of several economic and institutional features.

The Peruvian economy itself has changed dramatically since 1990, when the government initiated a structural adjustment program that included a number of reforms, including privatization, market liberalization, and public sector measures. Within this adjustment program the financial system was liberalized and opened to the global economy. The reforms had a number of positive consequences, including putting an end to a long period of high inflation and improving most macroeconomic indicators. The result was a period of economic stability and, after 1993, of economic growth.

As part of the structural adjustment program, the financial sector underwent several important changes. The Banking, Finance, and Insurance Act of 1991 (modified in 1993 and 1996) allowed new specialized intermediaries to enter the market and strengthened the banking system by encouraging improvements and innovations in the procedures banks use to select clients. In addition, the Organic Act, which governs the Superintendency of Banks (SBS), restructured prudential regulation and supervision in line with the Basle Accords in an effort to make the SBS more effective.

These changes created the conditions necessary to permit increased amounts of debt in the Peruvian economy without endangering the foun-

Carolina Trivelli is affiliated with the Instituto de Estudios Peruanos. Javier Alvarado and Francisco Galarza are affiliated with the Centro Peruano de Estudios Sociales.

dation of the recomposed financial system. Traditional clients would have access to additional credit, and lenders would be able to target new client groups. Providing additional credit required significantly increasing the resources managed by intermediaries. The needed capital came mainly from external sources, which lent to domestic intermediaries or became their partners. Ultimately the system would depend heavily on these external resources.

Targeting new client groups required lenders to adopt new credit technologies that would reach potential borrowers lacking access to formal financial intermediaries. Two groups of lenders were responsible for developing most of these techniques. The first is a group of newly designed intermediaries that includes:

- *Cajas Rurales de Ahorro y Crédito* (Rural Credit and Savings Banks), or CRACs, small formal intermediaries serving primarily rural clients.

- *Cajas Municipales de Ahorro y Crédito* (Municipal Credit and Savings Banks), or CMACs, small formal intermediaries that work mainly with small businesses and microenterprises in urban areas.

- *Entidades de Desarrollo para la Pequeña y Micro Empresa* (Entities for the Development of Small and Microenterprise), or EDPYMES, development organizations that support small businesses and microenterprises. EDPYMEs were created to facilitate the formalization of informal institutional lenders. They can place funds but do not receive deposits.

The second group of lenders comprises informal institutional lenders, such as nongovernmental organizations (NGOs). Informal lenders operate outside the purview of the SBS—that is, they are unsupervised and not legally recognized as lenders.

At all levels the new lending practices and technologies demanded improved information-sharing systems, which were developed in both the formal and informal sectors. Small and informal intermediaries began developing new credit technologies based on improvements in borrower selection and credit monitoring. In most cases, however, the enforcement procedures for recovering loans in default did not develop fully and remain inefficient. A review of the experiences of innovative intermediaries leads to the conclusion that there is room to improve client selection by improving the use of available information at all levels and tailoring credit technology closely to client needs.

Lenders have found several ways to improve the use of information and to introduce innovative credit allocation procedures to serve a segment of clients unable to access credit under market conditions. These are:

- A new information-sharing system for public and private institutions, which has been growing rapidly.

- The CMACs.

- NGOs that serve as informal institutional lenders for small clients and try to use the market to allocate their credit (although most receive some kind of subsidy).

- A system of coordination between the informal and formal sectors, which has been mostly unsuccessful.

This chapter shows that information-sharing systems develop differently in order to serve a variety of demands. In this sense most of the efforts to improve information flows complement existing information-sharing systems. The poor results of efforts to coordinate bank and NGO activities reveal that improving the flow of information about borrowers through this channel is neither easy nor cheap, does not improve borrower selection, and fails to provide specific client groups with sustained access to formal credit.

Overall, limitations to the expansion of financial activities persist in Peru. Some reforms did not succeed in meeting their aims, and in certain sectors political and economic factors constrained the adoption of new procedures or counteracted the initial changes. As a result transaction costs in financial markets increased. Judicial enforcement procedures are a case in point. They are still inefficient, increasing the cost of credit for borrowers and the risk of lending for intermediaries.

Recent Developments in the Credit Market: Increasing Indebtedness

The formal financial system in Peru comprises five subsystems: full-service banks, financial institutions, CMACs, CRACs, and EDPYMEs.

Banks

As of December 1998 the banking subsystem included 26 banks, six of which were fully backed with national capital. These 26 banks are responsible for 98.36 percent of the loans and 98.33 percent of the savings deposits in the formal financial system. Their market shares differ widely, with the four most important banks accounting for 60.85 percent of loans and 70 percent of deposits (Table 9.1). In spite of this high concentration, the share of banks has been falling since 1996. Banks have increased their productivity significantly: the ratio of deposits to the number of workers rose from 57.32 in 1990 to 436.32 in 1994 and to 524.33 in 1998.[1]

Between December 1994 and December 1998, bank loans increased from the equivalent of US$5.4 to US$13.3 billion, 81.45 percent of them in foreign currency. In 1998 this amount represented more than 25 percent of GDP, much higher than the 8 percent of GDP it represented in 1993 (Marthans 1997a).[2] In this same period deposits increased from the equivalent of US$5.8 billion to US$13.1 billion, with 72.46 percent in U.S. dollars. Loans increased more than deposits owing to the rising external debt of intermediaries. Loans and deposits remain concentrated in Lima, the country's capital (79.4 percent of the total subsystem loans).[3] Some 86.6 percent of the loans were commercial credit, 7.7 percent were personal credit, and 5.7 percent were mortgage credit.

Although intermediation grew at a faster rate than the economy as a whole in 1994-98, it is still at relatively low levels compared with other countries in the region.[4] An indicator of the importance of bank loans can be obtained by comparing the results of the Living Standards Measurement Surveys from 1994 and 1997.[5] In 1994 only 16.6 percent of households had

---

[1] This increase in productivity can be traced in part to growth in the volume of resources managed by intermediaries.

[2] The increase in lending varies across sectors. Lending to commerce exceeds 20 percent of output, while lending to farming is less than 5 percent of output.

[3] The main agencies of all the banks are located in Lima.

[4] According to Marthans (1997a) only one of every five persons in Lima who saves money deposits it with a bank.

[5] The Peruvian Living Standards Measurement Surveys are conducted periodically (although not on a regular basis) as a way to track the economic development of Peruvian households. The surveys, which are based on a methodology devised by the World Bank, include socioeconomic and demographic information for a representative sample of households at the national level. The first survey was conducted in 1985, the last in 1997; a new survey is currently under way.

Table 9.1. The Peruvian Financial System, 1995-98

Variable	1995	1996	1997	1998[a]
Full-service banks				
Real liquidity (August 1990) (million US$)	9,824.87	12,067.69	13,877.18	14,560.77
Total loans (million US$)	7,481.22	10,051.08	12,715.29	13,320.41
Total deposits (million US$)	9,316.85	11,538.68	13,511.16	13,059.55
Debt and other financial liabilities				
(million $US)	1,550.35	2,472.05	4,307.52	5,089.04
Net profits (million $US)	227.77	276.29	255.58	160.38
Default rate (%)	4.82	5.22	5.31	6.96
Reserves/loans in default (million $US)	91.05	86.03	90.61	92.06
Number of banks	23	23	25	26
Number of employees	17,718	20,123	26,069	24,907
Number of branches	806	833	930	960
Four principal banks (% of total)[b]				
Total bank loans	69.37	68.69	63.51	60.85
Deposits	73.24	72.89	70.40	69.99
Equity	66.87	64.50	62.77	60.33
All regions outside Lima (% of total)				
Loans outside Lima	22.07	21.78	18.95	20.57
Deposits outside Lima	17.53	17.23	16.39	18.06
Other subsystems				
CRAC				
Number	15	16	17	14
Default rate (%)	12.77	13.61	14.57	17.38
Total loans (million US$)	26.70	39.62	52.17	51.96
Total deposits (million US$)	7.12	9.47	18.75	20.34
CMAC				
Number	13	13	13	17
Default rate (%)	10.07	8.66	7.74	7.51
Total loans (million US$)	56.38	71.76	89.34	90.90
Total deposits (million US$)	41.56	48.71	67.31	68.97
EDPYME				
Number	0	1	1	7
Default rate (%)		7.33	9.06	6.63
Total loans (million US$)	0.00	2.75	2.83	12.32
Total deposits (million US$)	0.00	0.00	0.00	0.00

a. Includes information on the defunct Banco República.
b. Banco de Crédito del Perú, Banco Continental, Interbank, and Banco Wiese.
Source: SBS.

some credit, and scarcely 7.0 percent of these mentioned banks as their main source of credit (Table 9.2). By 1997 there had been a substantial increase: 32.0 percent of households had some credit, and of these households 26.7 percent borrowed from banks. Growth was most evident in urban areas.

Banks increased their own debt exposure, especially with foreign intermediaries, in line with their increase in lending. According to Marthans (1997b), in the mid-1990s five banks had short-term debts totaling more than 200 percent of capital. This growth can be explained by the high rate of dollarization of loans and deposits, the high levels of legal reserves relative to deposits (in foreign currency), and the absence of legal reserve requirements for externally sourced loans.[6] In the short term the rapid growth of debts and other liabilities caused banks to worry about making their loans in dollars because of the exchange rate risk. Rojas (1997) notes that with the high levels of dollarization, banks matched deposits and loans by type of currency to avoid the exchange rate risk. They also tended to match the maturity structure of their loans and liabilities, and many intermediaries increased their interest rate exposure by borrowing at variable rates and lending at fixed rates.

Over the period analyzed, the lending rates in domestic currency decreased slightly, but the dollar rate remained steady. In December 1998 the average annual interest rate on loans in domestic currency (TAMN) was 36.45 percent, close to its value at the beginning of 1995. Meanwhile, the average deposit rate in domestic currency (TIPMN) was 12.55 percent, the lending rate in dollars (TAMEX) was 16.95 percent, and the deposit rate (TIPMEX) was 5.39 percent, 0.45 higher than the average at the end of 1994.

Interest rates varied considerably across banks, especially full-service and so-called retail banks. Retail banks do not provide full services, specializing instead in consumer loans that may be short term or high risk and often have no guarantees. In 1998 the country's largest full-service bank charged an average rate of 36.2 percent for loans in domestic currency for up to 360 days, while retail banks charged between 113.4 and 138 percent for the same loans. These extremely high interest rates raise two important

---

[6] During the entire period under analysis, the Central Bank maintained a legal reserve requirement of 45 percent on deposits in foreign currency. On July 1, 1998 the legal reserve on foreign currency deposits was reduced from 45 to 35 percent. At the same time interest on the average legal reserve was raised from 4.3 to 4.7 percent in order to reduce incentives to obtain funding for on-lending outside the country.

Table 9.2. Households with Credit, 1994 and 1997
(percent)

Indicator	1994			1997		
	Urban	Rural	Total	Urban	Rural	Total
Households with credit	16.7	16.4	16.6	38.1	22.1	32.0
Households with banks as main source of credit	10.3	1.4	7.0	33.9	7.2	26.7

Note: The sample size is 3,623 for 1994 and 3,843 for 1997.
Source: Living Standards Measurement Survey.

issues. First, they suggest that many borrowers may not know how to deal with banks or how to shop around for the best rates. Second, these high rates indicate that retail banks are using interest rates to compensate for the absence of guarantees and of information about borrowers.

The "bad debt" indicator, which proxies as an indicator of the soundness of the financial system, evolved favorably in the last half of the 1990s. The bad debts of banks fell after the end of 1994, reaching 6.96 percent in December 1998. Around 54 percent of loans in default in the banking system were in the process of judicial collection, an unusually high percentage that reflects the time involved in procedures of this nature.

Other Formal Intermediaries

Banks are the most important intermediaries, but others are growing in significance. As of December 1998, Peru had seven financial institutions, 17 CMACs, and 14 CRACs. These 38 institutions accounted for less than 2 percent of all financial system loans. But even though they intermediate small volumes, they are important for their local impact and for the type of client they work with (mostly small clients not served by banks). Trivelli (1998) finds, for example, that banks lend only to agricultural producers with more than 10 hectares of land, while CRACs and CMACs consider as ideal clients agricultural producers owning between 3 and 10 hectares. These intermediaries—mainly CRACs, CMACs and EDPYMEs—tend to establish innovative credit contracts based on information they gather on potential clients.

The institutions comprising these four subsystems were created to supply credit to specific groups of clients. Financial institutions, many linked to large department stores, were designed to increase sales through credit operations—that is, they grant loans to cover the cost of their products. CMACs are dedicated to serving primarily small clients (in terms of both loans and deposits), especially small urban enterprises and dealers. They cater to nearly 200,000 clients, of which 37 percent are microentrepreneurs and 44 percent are individuals (Chong and Schroth 1998). CRACs serve primarily small farmers (those with fewer than 10 hectares).[7]

CMACs and CRACs are the only intermediaries with a local rather than a countrywide focus. This characteristic restricts their chances of development—they have little opportunity to diversify risks, for example. But their focus also gives them an advantage, as they are able to draw on local information about their clients. Both CRACs and CMACs are recent innovations and have developed differently. Many of them perform poorly, and default rates for both types of intermediaries are higher than for banks.

In part, their poor performance is a function of their dependence on foreign funds, something banks—which can rely on deposits—do not share. These funds come mainly from the Financial Development Corporation (Corporación Financiera de Desarrollo, or COFIDE), which acts as a "second tier" bank.[8] Many analysts agree that this dependence on COFIDE is one of the principal causes of the poor performance of many CRACs and CMACs (see, for example, Alvarado and Ugaz 1998; Lazarte 1996; Trivelli 1998). At the same time, gaining access to these resources is an important reason for informal intermediaries to enter the formal sector by converting to an EDPYME or a CRAC.

The default rate of CMACs has decreased over time, but the rate for CRACs has risen (see Table 9.1). Nevertheless CRACs have raised their reserve levels, and in 1998 reserves covered 62.7 percent of the institutions' past-due portfolio. Several factors explain these patterns: differences in management capacity, experience with credit and financing, and the speed with

---

[7] As of December 1998, 36.2 percent of CMAC loans were commercial, while 58.4 percent of CRAC loans were agricultural.

[8] COFIDE, a public institution, obtains financial resources from international sources, mainly the Andean Development Corporation (Corporación Andina de Fomento). It then on-lends these funds through the financial system at market rates to specific economic sectors such as agriculture (including agribusiness) and to small and medium-size enterprises.

which operations grow. Generally CMACs have proved more efficient because they have more experience and have received more technical assistance from international organizations than CRACs. CMACs have also been more successful than CRACs in obtaining deposits from the public and diversifying their loan portfolio.

A New Framework for Credit Markets

Since 1990 important changes in the economic and institutional framework have induced or at least favored the growth of the Peruvian credit market. Lower inflation, increased openness, privatization, liberalized product and factor markets (including capital markets), and the overall structural adjustment program have changed the way the economy works.[9] Along with the economic adjustment program, the virtual elimination in 1992 of the guerilla movement (with the capture of the Shining Path's leader) marked the end of a long period of violence that had hindered economic activity (Table 9.3).

The economic adjustment program included several institutional reforms. The General Banking, Financial, and Insurance Institutions Act of 1991 defined the new legal framework within which financial liberalization took place.[10] New measures liberalized interest rates, prohibited intermediation by unauthorized persons and entities, eliminated all legal differences between domestic and foreign banks, and freed foreign currency operations. National development banks were eliminated, reducing the government's participation in the financial system to two entities (other than the Central Bank): COFIDE and the Banco de la Nación.[11]

The new legislation also strengthened the financial system by expanding the operations of nonbank institutions. The most important changes included:

- permitting all financial institutions in the system, including CMACs, CRACs, and EDPYMEs, to perform operations and functions previously reserved for banking institutions.

[9] For details of the recent economic changes, see Gonzales de Olarte (1998).
[10] The New Act for Banking, Financial and Insurance Institutions was passed in October 1993. It was also replaced, this time by Act 26702 (December 1996), which is currently in force.
[11] For more details about the financial reform, see Rojas (1996), Romero (1996), and Velarde and Rodríguez (1996), among others.

Table 9.3. Macroeconomic Indicators, 1990-98

Year	GDP (var.%)	Inflation (var. %)	Devaluation (var. %)	Net international reserves (US$ bn)	Current account/ GDP (%)	Liquidity/ GDP (%)	Dollari- zation[a]
1990	−5.40	7,649.70	6,946.97	0.7	−3.40	16.77	46.80
1991	3.20	139.20	309.82	1.93	−3.10	12.76	57.98
1992	−1.80	56.70	62.40	2.43	−4.50	14.61	63.21
1993	6.40	39.50	59.20	2.91	−5.20	15.31	68.34
1994	13.10	15.40	10.55	6.02	−5.10	16.76	63.14
1995	7.20	10.20	2.27	6.77	−7.30	18.06	60.74
1996	2.60	11.80	8.89	8.85	−5.90	22.55	63.48
1997	7.40	6.50	8.57	1.02	−5.20	23.80	60.57
1998	0.70	6.00	10.15	9.18	−6.00	25.00	62.08

a. Percentage of financial system liquidity in U.S. dollars.

Source: National Institute of Statistics and Information; Central Bank.

- Expanding the definition of risk to include market as well as credit risk.[12]

- Changing the period for which bank reserves are computed and the minimum legal reserve rate to help reduce liquidity problems.

- Raising the legal reserve level and eliminating the discount on most guarantees to improve portfolio quality.

- Reducing the maximum risk of financial leverage to 11 times the effective capital of each financial institution.

- Allowing collateral to be considered only as a subsidiary criterion in client selection.

- Initiating prudential supervision that focuses on the consolidated balance sheets of financial intermediaries.[13]

---

[12] Risk related to external factors (that is, not controlled by financial entities), such as fluctuations in interest rates and prices.

[13] To complement these measures the Central Bank promulgated the Organic Act.

According to bankers, the new legislation is mostly adequate and need not be modified further (except for small adjustments) because of the high cost of adapting to new legislation. To bolster this argument, many bankers point out that the current legislation is tougher than similar legislation in other countries in the region and in some cases is stricter than the standards set forth in the Basle Accords (Morris 1997).

The push to evaluate portfolio risk and borrowers' repayment capacity rather than their guarantees has encouraged the modernization of banks' client selection process. The new legislation encourages lenders to evaluate clients not simply on the basis of assets but on the project that is to be financed and the possibility of recovering the debt. These measures should help segments of the market that have not had access to formal credit, especially small businesses and microentrepreneurs. In addition, the information provided by rating registers has been broadened to allow a more complete evaluation of current and potential debtors. The diminished importance of guarantees in classifying clients and the changes in reserve requirements have increased the importance of information as a key instrument in determining credit risk.

Improving Borrower Selection

The intertemporal nature of credit and information asymmetries make it difficult for lenders to assess borrowers' willingness to repay a loan. For instance, lenders have no control over actions by borrowers that can affect repayment capacity. Lenders also have only limited or partial knowledge of exogenous events that can further affect the repayment capacity of potential borrowers. To minimize the risks of default, lenders perform a series of evaluative actions, which in the formal sector utilize all available information about the borrower. As the quantity and quality of information increases, lenders can lower or eliminate their requirements for real guarantees. In unconventional borrower selection procedures, adequate information completely eliminates the requirement for real guarantees. Financial intermediaries can use several strategies to reduce their informational disadvantage in lending. The most important of these strategies are information sharing and innovative contracts (formal and informal), plus a special contract involving both formal and informal lenders.

Information-Sharing Systems

Data supplied by credit information systems can reduce asymmetries in information between lenders and clients, facilitating an accurate evaluation of potential borrowers. Improving risk-rating registers reduces the risk of future insolvency and strategic default. Currently all financial institutions must classify each client and post this classification in the risk-rating registers. In this way all other intermediaries know more than simply how many debts a potential borrower has—for instance, they also know how former lenders evaluated the client.

Currently Peru has five risk-rating registers. Two are public: the register managed by the SBS and another run by the Chamber of Commerce. Three are private credit bureaus (Infocorp, Certicom, and Riesgo Cero). The effect on default rates is not yet clear, as the registers have been operating only a short time. However, intermediaries agree that the information these registers provide is a powerful instrument that can be decisive in improving the quality of a loan portfolio.

The SBS register records financial, credit, commercial, and insurance information about debtors in the financial and insurance systems, which include all formal financial intermediaries and insurance companies under the SBS's supervision. The information, which is consolidated and classified, is available only to firms within the systems and to the Central Bank.[14] Currently the SBS processes information concerning all types of credit in the financial system in amounts of more than S/.558 (the equivalent of US$4,332 as of December 31, 1998). IBM of Peru processes credit information for smaller loans, which account for around 20 percent of total credit and 80 percent of all borrowers, but this information is not yet complete. The SBS provides a spectrum of information about potential borrowers, including personal information (such as addresses) and debt ratings (nor-

[14] Not all the information in the register is available to the general public because of confidentiality rules. The general public can obtain information about cancellations of credit cards and checking accounts, either from the SBS itself or from a free Internet web page. The information is free to firms (the costs are included in the contributions they make to support the SBS) but is sold to private risk-rating registries.

mal, potentially problematic, deficient, doubtful, and loss). Information about firms includes details such as size and level of operations.[15]

The public register run by the Lima Chamber of Commerce—the National Debtor Register—records all guarantees (vouchers, promissory notes, warrants, and exchange bills) reported as being in default by the country's notaries and justices of the peace. The Chamber of Commerce is entrusted with the task of correcting records for guarantees that are no longer in default.[16] The cost of this information, which has been available since 1990, is between US$7 and US$10 for a single inquiry. Annual memberships (for multiple inquiries) run around US$360 for members of the Chamber of Commerce to US$430 for nonmembers.

Accessing private credit bureaus is more expensive for institutional lenders than accessing public rating registers. The Chamber of Commerce and SBS do not charge these institutions for information on potential debtors. The relatively high costs of private bureaus are justified by the quantity of background information the bureaus provide on financial and commercial system debtors. These credit bureaus buy information from the SBS, the Chamber of Commerce, and the National Tax Administration Superintendency (Superintendencia Nacional de Administración Tributaria).[17] They also contact commercial firms, including factories and warehouses, and any other sources that can provide information on clients that default. In the case of Infocorp the cost of each request for information about a single person or an entity ranges from US$0.95 to US$1.90, although clients making a large number of requests receive discounts.[18]

---

[15] Debt is also classified as outstanding, due, or high risk and as direct or indirect (that is, obtained through guarantees, promissory notes, or exchange bills). Information about debtors' finances also includes details of loans, overdrafts, discounts on bills and notes, and leasing. It notes any amounts of credit that have been written off, any seized collateral, and the interest debtors owe to particular institutions. Financial institutions supply information about provisions that cover direct financing and relevant contingencies and guarantees.

[16] Changing the records is important, because only when the guarantee is no longer in default can the debtor once again be considered for credit.

[17] For tax debtors in the process of enforced collection.

[18] Because the communications infrastructure in the country has improved, Inofocorp recently began offering its services over the phone at a rate of $1.99 per request. The charge is listed on the caller's phone bill.

Responsibility for the accuracy of the information provided by private credit bureaus rests solely with those offering the information. This point is particularly important because no documents (unpaid bill or letter of exchange, for example) are presented to the bureaus as proof of default.

Innovative Contracts in the Formal Sector

CMACs have succeeded not only in reaching a sizable number of microentrepreneurs but also in reducing the volume of bad debt through the use of innovative credit contracts.[19] Sullana CMAC, which has operated in the northern coastal region since 1986, provides an example of the innovative credit techniques these intermediaries use to reach a segment of borrowers that has traditionally been underserved. A credit analyst is in charge of all stages of the lending process, except for certain collection procedures for personal loans and pledges (Alvarado and Ugaz 1998). This procedure gives the analyst a strong incentive to screen potential borrowers carefully, since if they do not repay their loans, he or she is in charge of collection for the first 30 days after the loan is due.

Sullana CMAC begins with a "preevaluation." A firm must have been in business for at least six months to be considered for credit, and individual borrowers must hold a steady job. The analyst visits the firm or home and draws up a statement of income and expenses based on the information the applicant offers.[20] The analyst then consults various risk-rating agencies in order to verify or simply complement this information. The organization has its own data on repeat clients. As a general rule, at this stage information is more important than guarantees for loans up to the equivalent of US$4,000.[21] Real guarantees are important for larger loans.

After collecting all the available information, the analyst prepares an evaluation and submits the evaluation to a credit committee, which decides whether to grant the loan. The composition of the credit committee varies

---

[19] With the support of the German Agency for Technical Cooperation (GTZ). Recently the CMACs launched a nationwide network, the Peruvian Federation of CMACs.

[20] The procedure differs for farm loans, for which the analyst builds a cash flow statement.

[21] The emphasis on information is common to all CMACs, because the clients they work with (basically small enterprises and microentrepreneurs) usually do not have self-liquidating guarantees. CMACs often use what are called slow collection guarantees (pledges and mortgages). As of December 1998 such guarantees backed 54 percent of their loans.

with the size of the loan but may include a specialist in the economic sector where the loan will be used, the manager of the CMAC, a marketing specialist, and an accountant. Once a loan is granted, the analyst supervises repayment. If a borrower does not repay the loan within 30 days of the due date, the administration takes charge of the loan. After 60 days the loan is turned over to management and sent for judiciary collection, even when the sum involved is less than the legal costs. A loan can be refinanced if the borrower shows a willingness to repay and if the reason for the default is a temporary rather than a permanent setback.

An important feature of the Sullana CMAC (and of other of these intermediaries, notably the Piura CMAC, also in the country's northern coastal region) is its long-term relationship with its clients. Some 70 percent of the clients are repeat borrowers, and 60 percent borrow from the CMAC exclusively. These figures indicate that some of these organizations are achieving one of their objectives—to grow with their clients.

Innovative Contracts in the Informal Sector

The informal credit sector encompasses a variety of intermediaries ranging from individuals to specialized institutions. Because informal lenders are not under the supervision of the SBS, they cannot legally intermediate funds from third parties. They are permitted to use only their own resources for lending, cannot receive deposits, and must pay sales tax on their financial incomes. However, they also do not need to cover any potential losses with reserves. These informal lenders use different procedures to select, supervise, and collect their loans, and in most cases their lending policies are based on information about clients rather than on collateral or legal documents. The number of informal lenders in Peru—and the number of clients they serve—remains unknown. However, these lenders serve an important segment of clients that in general have no access to formal lenders, for a number of reasons. Formal lenders may be unavailable in rural areas, or borrowers may simply be too small to be considered for formal credit. The successful performance of several of these informal lenders—notably NGOs—has attracted the attention of researchers and formal lenders interested in learning about their techniques.

Since 1980 the number of NGOs in Peru has grown rapidly, and many of those that are concerned primarily with the economic development of low-income populations offer credit programs. These programs have not been studied in depth.[22] But their importance is so widely accepted that the Banking Act includes specific procedures for transforming NGOs with credit programs into formal lenders.

Solidarity Groups

The most important feature of the NGO credit programs is the solidarity group, which these programs use (along with some grassroots organizations) to obtain information about potential clients. Solidarity groups are made up of borrowers and potential borrowers (usually no more than 10) who agree to assume responsibility for loans made to any member. Group members sign documents to this effect, so that they become legally liable for the loans of all group members.[23] Sometimes real property guarantees are requested, but such property usually consists of goods that cannot be mortgaged, registered in guaranty registers, or legally seized without great difficulty and expense. Loans are made to individuals, who receive the money and decide how to invest it. To facilitate oversight, group members are often required to live in the same geographic area and in some cases to be involved in similar production activities, especially for agricultural loans.

In Peru this innovative arrangement has been used primarily for loans in rural areas and is not yet widespread. The groups provide two important benefits. They provide lenders with trustworthy information about borrowers that facilitates lending decisions. In exchange for this information, the groups and grassroots organizations become favored clients of a credit program. The groups are also very efficient in providing small farmers and peasants with access to credit and have resulted in default rates lower than those in the formal financial system. However, this type of arrangement has also shown some weaknesses. Innovative arrangements with groups work efficiently for a limited number of relatively small loans, but when the amounts are large the incentives to collude and default increase, especially when the country's limited enforcement capacity is taken into account.[24]

---

[22] Studies like the ones by Kervyn and Rojas (1995), Kervyn (1985), Alvarado and Ugaz (1998), Trivelli (1998) and Chaparro (1995) present overviews of the topic, but most of them emphasize the need for further research.

[23] To reduce the risk of default, the number of members in a group must remain small.

[24] Authors such as Schmidt and Zeitinger (1994) show that the risk of collusion rises as the amount of credit involved increases.

A Sample of NGOs

To better understand the credit practices instituted by NGOs, 21 NGOs that operate credit programs were interviewed (Table 9.4).[25] The stratified random sample is based on three groups of NGOs: 79 in Lima, 27 on the coast outside Lima, and 98 in the Andean region. (Because so many NGOs are concentrated in Lima, the group is split into three areas.) Of the 21 interviewed, eight are located in metropolitan Lima, 10 in the Andean region and three on the coast.[26] The methodology was bolstered by the fact that procedures for granting credit differ among these three regions.

The interviews initially identified a number of heterogeneous credit programs that differ not only in their scope but also in their objectives and procedures. The NGOs were then separated into two groups: those with specialized credit programs and those with credit programs that are a component of a larger development program. In addition, some NGOs were identified that do not have credit programs per se but that report carrying out some credit activities in order to keep open the option of starting a formal credit program.

The first group is the most rewarding in terms of studying the development of financial intermediation. These are the most dynamic NGOs, those most interested in attaining the lending volume of other small formal intermediaries and becoming formal credit institutions themselves. Ten of the 21 NGOs interviewed belong to this category (Table 9.5). Of these 10 only two (E and O) devote themselves exclusively to granting credit. These specialized organizations center their development activities around credit programs but do not always grant the largest loans or offer the lowest interest rates. Not all the NGOs place the same emphasis on credit or devote significant resources to it, however. Less specialized NGOs have additional programs that usually involve productive, commercial and educational activities for poor communities. The credit programs provide loans of varying sizes and offer different interest rates.

---

[25] To define the universe of NGOs offering credit programs, two sources were consulted: the NGO directory from the Ministerio de la Presidencia (1996) and Noriega (1997). In the two sources, NGOs that grant credit were listed, from which 21 were randomly selected.

[26] To maintain confidentiality we have identified the NGOs with a letter. The first eight letters of the alphabet (A-H) correspond to the NGOs in Lima, the next three letters (I-K) correspond to those on the coast, and the next 10 (L-U) correspond to those in the Andean region.

336

Table 9.4. Characteristics of NGO Credit Programs (from Sample)[a]

Characteristic	Lima					Coast						Andean region				
	A	B[a]	C[a]	E[a]	H	I	J	K	L	N	O	P	R	S	T	U
Average amount granted (US$)	50	—	200	195	1,000[b]	2,500	400	2,000	1,400	900	400	250	1,750	200	500[c]	120
Interest rates[d] (%)	2.5	5.0	4.0	3.0	3.5	3.0	4.0	1.6[e]	3.7[f]	2.0	2.0[e]	—	4.0	2.0	5.0	2.5
Default rate (%)	10.0	—	2.0	10.6	7.0	—	1.0	—	15	1.0	4.5	2.0	8.0	—	9.0	2.0
Number of clients	70	—	420	4,820	—	1200	—	—	572	—	3,200	58	742	—	1,000[g]	250
Average term (months)	3	6-9	4	4	6	4-10	4	12	6	6	6	6	6	5	6	5
Total funds (thousand US$)	2	300	62	937	2,500	3,000	100	—	819	280	1,300	26	440	5	2,000	100
Funds origin[h]	P	P	P	P	P,C	P,C	P,C	P,C	P,C	P	P,C	P	P,C	P	P	P
Target group[i]	M	C	T	M	E,T	C,M,E	C	C,M,E	C,E,T	C,M	C,T	M	C,E,T	C	C,E,T	C,T

— Not available.

a. This NGO has credit a program.

b. This institution grants initial credits of $1,000, which can later be raised to $15,000.

c. Loans granted between US$300 and US$10,000. Mortgages are demanded for loans over $4,000.

d. Monthly rate in soles.

e. Monthly rate in dollars.

f. The main credit program charges this interest rate. However, they have two other programs coordinated with private banks where the interest rate charged is 18 percent a year in dollars.

g. Estimated.

h. P = own or donation; C = credit (generally from external source).

i. C = peasants or rural population; M = women; E = microentrepreneurs; T = merchants.

Note: Only NGOs that had credit programs in 1997 are included in the sample (16 out of the original 21).

Source: NGO interviews.

Table 9.5. Sample of NGOs Interviewed

	Lima							Coast					Andean region								
	A	B[a]	C[a]	D	E[a]	F	G	H	I	J	K	L	M	N	O	P	Q	R	S	T	U
Type of NGO																					
Specialized	•	•	•		•		•	•	•	•	•	•		•	•	•		•	•	•	
Nonspecialized																			•		•
Did not grant credit in 1997				•		•	•						•				•				
Guarantee requested																					
Real assets	•		•		•			•[b]	•		•	•		•	•	•		•		•	•
Solidarity groups	•	•			•			•	•		•	•		•	•	•					•
Endorsement of social organization		•						•	•	•				•	•					•	•
Document (letter, guaranty)		•					•			•[c]		•		•		•		•	•	•	•
Information/history	•	•						•	•	•				•	•	•		•	•	•	•
Supervises credits	•	•						•	•		•	•		•		•		•	•	•	•
Recovery																					
In charge of the group	•	•			•			•	•		•	•		•	•	•			•		•
Executes guarantees	•	•	•					•	•	•	•	•		•	•				•	•	
Others (off the program)	•	•	•		•			•	•	•	•	•		•		•			•	•	
Discriminates between insolvent and strategic debtors	•	•			•			•			•	•				•					
Degree of formalization																					
Has coordinated with formal intermediaries								•	•	•	•	•						•			
Wishes to be formal		•						•	•	•		•				•					
Formalization in process or formalized		•						•	•	•	•	•				•					•

a. This NGO has a credit program.
b. Real guarantees are only requested for loans over US$2,000.
c. Both husband and wife must sign the contract and documents.
Note: Information is from interviews conducted in January–June 1998 with 21 NGOs selected randomly from among 204 that reported having credit programs. Interviews were based on a common guide designed especially for this research. Each NGO is identified with a capital letter.

Table 9.6. Equality of Means, Specialized and Nonspecialized Credit Programs

| | Means | | T-test for equality of means | |
| | Specialized | Non-specialized | T- value[a] | Significance (two tailed) |
Variable				
Average loan size (US$)	1,104.50	164.00	2.636	0.022
Interest rate (percent)[b]	3.32	3.22	0.189	0.306
Default rate (percent)	7.01	4.00	1.078	0.085
Number of clients	1,922.33	199.50	1.969	0.024
Maturity of loans (months)	6.30	5.08	1.175	0.260
Total funds lent in credit program (US$)	1,220,000	82,500	2.559	0.021

a. The results assume equality of variances but do not change if inequality is assumed.
b. Monthly rate for loans in U.S. dollars.

Comparing the means of several characteristics of the specialized NGOs in the sample with the means of nonspecialized NGOs illustrates the heterogeneity of these credit programs (Table 9.6). The amount of funds the NGOs work with and the source of the funding are related to the degree of specialization in the type of loan granted. Only the most specialized NGOs work with local formal intermediaries and lend capital from foreign banks.[27] Nonspecialized NGOs work only with their own funds, which they generally obtain from international donors and foreign aid agencies. Similarly the amounts NGOs work with vary considerably. Specialized NGOs tend to work with the largest sums. The two groups do not differ in the interest rates they charge or in loan maturity, but specialized NGOs have more clients, make more and bigger loans, and have significantly higher default rates.

Credit Technology

Among the most important assets of NGO credit programs is their lending technology, which is based on innovative credit contracts. These contracts

---

[27] Current legislation, of course, forbids institutions that are not part of the financial system to intermediate funds.

are generated during a borrower selection procedure that is based on the organization's own information about clients or on information offered by a specific group (such as community members or friends). Eight of the 16 NGOs with credit programs request some sort of guarantee. The guarantee concept is used more widely in these programs than in the formal sector, because NGOs often accept unconventional items (including small goods such as electric appliances and tools) as well as the more common guarantees (such as mortgages). The requirement for real guarantees is often combined with the use of solidarity groups, although this practice does not reduce the risk that members of the group may collude and decide not to repay.

Many NGOs preselect their borrowers based on either membership in a solidarity group or the moral endorsement of some social or productive institution such as a peasant community, producer group, or merchant organization. Credit is granted based on information that the group or members of the organization have about the credit applicant's capacity and willingness to repay. Eleven of the NGOs interviewed pointed out that they collect and use all the information they can get about their clients' credit history. However, many specialized NGOs said they do not concern themselves with collecting this type of information for members of solidarity groups.

These two mechanisms are the most widely used methods of selecting clients for NGO credit programs, but there is a fundamental difference between them. When solidarity groups are involved in the selection, they become liable for the individual loans. When they are not, liability rests solely with the individual borrowers. This distinction is important in matters of supervision and collection. Solidarity groups supervise and usually collect loans to their members. But the lender is responsible for supervising and collecting loans with only a social endorsement. In order to maintain a good relationship with the NGO, in practice many institutions that endorse loans also supervise them.

Nearly all of the NGOs pointed out that they discriminate between strategic defaults and other insolvencies. That is, the NGOs try to discover the cause of the delay in repayment. They take drastic collection measures only in cases of strategic defaults (generally by removing this client from the program) but try to refinance the debts of other insolvent debtors. This practice works because the programs are relatively small and adequate information flows between borrowers and lenders, either directly or indirectly (through solidarity groups and endorsing organizations).

Subsidies

The sustainability of NGO credit programs is often a matter of concern. Arguably these institutions survive and continue to operate only because they are highly subsidized. The subsidies may come from different sources, but most are from international donors. This issue is relevant to the question of whether the institutions can successfully become part of the formal financial sector and compete with other formal lenders. Can unsubsidized credit be extended to the social groups these organizations serve? If these social groups can be served only with the support of subsidies, formal lenders are unlikely to be able to cater to these clients. By the same token, if NGOs begin charging market rates, these borrowers will be cut off from credit.

This analysis compares NGOs to CMACs and CRACs, as these formal lenders serve similar borrower groups. The subsidy dependence index (SDI) suggested by Yaron (1992) was used for four NGOs in our sample, four CRACs and four CMACs (Table 9.7).[28] The SDI indicates how much lenders must increase their interest rates in order to cover all real costs and thus avoid all subsidies. The lower the SDI, the less dependent a lender is on subsidies, and the more sustainable the institution becomes. If the SDI equals zero the lender requires no subsidies. Institutions with a negative SDI are making a profit at current interest rates. Even if these lenders reduce their interest rates, their credit programs will pay for themselves.

The SDI takes into account three types of subsidies:

- Financial subsidies, which cover the difference between the interest on loans an institution grants and the interest the institution has to pay for its funding, multiplied by the total amount of loans received by the institution.

- Subsidized return to capital, or the difference between the opportunity cost of capital (using the prevailing interest rate on savings) and the institution's net profit, adjusted for inflation.

- Direct subsidies such as donations, direct subsidies for infrastructure, and software.

---

[28] Calculated using information for 1996 from Alvarado and Ugaz (1998).

Table 9.7. Credit by Sector, December 1997
(percent)

Type of bank	Agriculture	Cattle	Industry	Construction	Export	Consumer	Commerce	Other
Foreign banks	4.9	4.9	9.3	2.5	3.2	12.5	47.4	15.3
National banks	6.3	5.5	14.2	1.3	4.3	12.3	42.0	14.1
Total private banks	5.8	5.3	12.3	1.8	3.9	12.3	44.0	14.6
Public banks	34.4	3.8	19.2	0.0	1.6	17.3	20.2	3.6
System average	12.7	4.9	14.0	1.3	3.3	13.5	38.3	11.9

Source: Central Bank.

An institution wishing to reduce its dependency on subsidies can do so by making certain adjustments, which depend on the type of subsidy involved. An institution dependent on a high financial subsidy can increase its interest rate so the credit program can become self-sustaining. But an institution reliant on subsidized returns to capital needs to modify its portfolio.[29]

NGOs have high levels of subsidy dependence compared with the formal institutions. CRACs also rely on subsidies, though to a lesser degree than NGOs. But CMACs, which have more experience with credit programs, better management teams, and more sophisticated technology, do not depend on subsidies at all. CMACs are in fact the only lenders that work with small borrowers and are profitable. NGOs' reliance on subsidies keeps them from performing as well as CMACs.

Many NGOs have access to external credit and subsequently become dependent on financial subsidies. CMACs (and in this case all CRACs) do not receive financial subsidies from COFIDE.[30] In this sample of NGOs, two—J and O—receive large subsidies in the form of special loans from international agencies. Without this credit NGO O, for instance, would need to increase its current interest rate by 70 percent in order to break even. By comparison NGOs E and K do not use external credit and thus do not rely on financial subsidies.

All four NGOs have been receiving direct subsidies in the form of donations, using existing capacity to build up the credit program, or both. NGO K is the most dependent on this type of subsidy, which probably explains why this lender is the only one that is not considering the option of becoming a formal lender. CRACs and CMACs receive little in the way of direct subsidies. CMACs receive none, although they did receive significant subsidies during the 1980s from the German Agency for Technical Cooperation (GTZ).[31] For CRACs the only source of direct subsidies is the public sector, which has provided software and training for the managerial team.

---

[29] Costs of infrastructure such as software should be paid from the program itself. If they are counted as costs, however, the program's economic outcomes change significantly.

[30] Two CMACs receive limited concessionary funds from the nationwide federation. Even without these funds, however, these two CMACs would have to increase their interest rate by less than 2 percent to become self-sustaining.

[31] In the form of technology transfers (know-how), training for CMAC officials, and software.

This dependency on subsidies suggests that serving NGOs' specific target groups entails higher costs than working with more traditional clients. These high costs in turn may explain why banks are not interested in working with this segment of the population. Ultimately NGOs' heavy dependence on subsidies raises doubts about the ability of these informal lenders to become formal credit institutions.

One way NGOs can improve their situation is by making their portfolios more efficient. Efficiency in selecting a credit portfolio results in a low SDI. NGOs J and O have a negative subsidy, meaning that they are earning additional income from their credit portfolios. These two credit programs are very innovative in terms of their borrower selection technology and have solid management teams, much like CMACs. NGO O, which works in the Andean region, obtains higher capital returns than even the CMACs (including the Sullana CMAC, which is considered the best example of a formal lender working with small client groups). The credit technology this NGO uses is its most important asset. As shown above, CRACs have problems with their credit allocation and recovery procedures. Their high SDI levels reflect these difficulties, primarily their low returns to capital. These institutions could make more money leaving their resources in savings accounts in the banking system than lending it to their current portfolio.

Integrating Formal and Informal Lenders: Bank-NGO Coordination

Coordination between banks and NGOs allows commercial banks, which rely on conventional procedures in their credit operations, to access the technology of specialized informal intermediaries.[32] Bank-NGO coordination is the first effort at vertical integration between formal and informal lenders. For banks this coordination is a way to increase the number and type of borrowers. For NGOs it represents a way to obtain additional funding and to improve service to target groups.

The procedure works as follows. NGOs preselect borrowers using self-selected groups and present the potential borrowers as solidarity groups to the banks. The NGOs, which generally have a long-term relationship with the borrowers, prepare a technical file on each of the group's members, along

---

[32] Some CMACs, like that in Ica, also use these mechanisms as part of their farm portfolios.

with an analysis of the activity for which the loan will be used. The group also creates a guarantee fund, with each member contributing a certain amount. The bank combines this fund with a percentage of the loan and retains the sum in a common savings account for the group. The bank makes the final decision on the loan, although nearly all those who are preselected receive credit. The bank is responsible for loan recovery, but the NGO supervises the loan and receives a flat commission when the credit is delivered to the borrowers.[33]

These attempts at coordination have not been entirely successful, and a sizable number are no longer working, largely because of the way banks and NGOs became involved with each other. The terms of the coordination contracts were often not clear, and most of the benefits, costs, and risks were asymmetrically distributed. The contracts generated perverse incentives for NGOs in preselecting customers, gave banks only limited control, and increased principal-agent problems instead of reducing them. In turn banks have had incentives to break contracts and return to their traditional way of doing business.[34]

What Is Limiting Credit Expansion in Peru?

While the credit market in Peru has been growing, several factors limit its expansion. These include problems obtaining enough information to rate borrowers effectively and problems of judicial enforcement. Judicial enforcement is particularly hindered by the length of time and high costs involved in collecting debts through the courts.

Information Sharing and Borrower Selection

Peruvian lenders typically use risk assessments from private and public registers to select clients and determine the necessary reserves. Although these

---

[33] In the majority of cases this commission does not cover the NGOs' implementation costs. The NGOs are subsidizing borrowers (with funds from international agencies) and lenders.
[34] For more details regarding this problem, see Chaves (1993), González-Vega and Chaves (1996), and McDonald (1994).

registers are fairly modern and complete, the available information is often difficult to use. The main problems are:

- The information risk-rating registers provide is for individuals rather than loans, so that lenders cannot assess the performance of projects involving the same debtor. Furthermore, borrowers are classified according to their lowest rating. Thus some borrowers may have relatively high ratings for some projects, but these ratings are not available to potential lenders.[35]

- The information reflects only the borrower's current situation, not its history. Borrowers with no current or recent debts do not even appear in the rating register.

- The information shows only the debt and overdue balance but not any overdue amounts that have been paid.

- It is not clear how long records of bad debts are (or should be) kept.

- Decentralized institutions (CRACs, CMACs, and EDPYMEs) cannot find sufficient information about their credit applicants in risk-rating registers. The majority of the clients they work with have never had any connection with the formal credit system and generally have taken out only small loans (less than US$5,000).

- When a loan is refinanced, it is automatically classified as doubtful.[36] This situation makes lending more expensive. Banks have to increase their reserves, and debtors cannot change their ratings for a year.

Some intermediaries want to see the type of information that is available improved and expanded. Many are using alternative sources to supplement the information available from rating registers. Many intermediaries seek out information sources specific to the client. With farmers, for example, lenders turn to the former Banco Agrario or interview the stores where

---

[35] In the same way, since the worst rating remains on record for a period of at least a year, a debtor with a bad project or a liquidity problem cannot obtain funds for new projects until the rating rises, even if new projects are profitable.

[36] In exceptional cases the refinanced credit can be placed in the category "with potential problems" based on the payment capacity of each borrower.

potential clients buy inputs and sell their products. These techniques suggest that borrower selection has improved not only because of credit registers and other regulatory changes, but also because lenders have come to appreciate the value of collecting and utilizing several kinds of information about credit applicants.

Judicial Enforcement: Collateral Execution

The problems involved in recovering unpaid loans by liquidating guarantees stem from the legislation governing the process as well as from the judicial system itself. These problems affect the length and costs of legal proceedings and the seizure and liquidation of the actual guarantees. The relevant legislation (the Civil Trial Code) sets three significant limitations on the execution of guarantees:

- All processes must go through the judiciary. The legislation makes no provision for extrajudicial mechanisms such as arbitration.

- Prejudicial mechanisms are not allowed in the seizure of guarantees. A lender holding an expired loan contract endorsed with liquid guarantees such as shares or bonds cannot begin collecting on them without authorization from a judge.

- Judges have the power to regulate executions of guarantees. These lawsuits are "executive" processes that are, in theory at least, expedited. But while they should be faster and simpler than other types of lawsuits, judges have the power to require the lengthier procedure, which has many steps and allows for numerous appeals. Such cases are very common. For example, when borrowers claim that lenders have miscalculated the interest on a loan, judges institute the longer procedure.

The process of collecting loans that are in default involves many legal regulations. Castelar Pinheiro (1996) points out that the judicial enforcement system becomes less efficient as the number of legal procedures involved in the process increases. Corruption, which is widespread throughout the judicial system, exacerbates these problems. Unnecessary delays, lost documents, poorly trained judges, favoritism, and bribes are prevalent. Judiciary reform is currently under way and has already achieved improvements in some administrative procedures. But it has yet to eliminate or even reduce corruption.

The judiciary imposes further and serious limitations on the otherwise well-intentioned objectives of the enforcement process. First, it lacks specialized personnel and adequate facilities. The lack of trained personnel and dedicated courtrooms slow seizure proceedings considerably. In addition, the judiciary does not release information about collection procedures on a systematic basis. The excessive number of pending trials and the poor qualifications of many judges aggravate the problem even further. These types of weaknesses in judicial administration result in huge delays not merely in the procedures themselves but in efforts to interpret the credit contracts. The result is long and expensive trials, with intermediaries bearing the costs.[37] In response, intermediaries either demand more guarantees or bear these unpaid loans as losses. Both options are reflected in the cost of credit.

Measuring the length and costs of executions of guarantees is complicated by the sheer variety of contracts involved in seizure trials. Such variables as the loan amount, the type of guarantee involved, and the type of debtor help determine how long the process will last and what it will cost. Based on the situation in December 1997, Ortiz de Zevallos (1998) estimates that such processes average three years, and even then lenders recover only 30 percent of the loan's value. Ortiz de Zevallos goes on to calculate the amount banks lose on defaulted loans annually, arriving at a figure of around US$364 million. Some US$294 million of this amount is the interest that accrues during the judicial collection process. The other US$70 million reflects the costs of not being able to appropriate and sell the goods received as a guarantee and of delays in executing the guarantee. These losses amount to twice the judiciary's entire budget.

Based on these numbers, Ortiz de Zevallos estimates that current interest rates include an overcharge attributable to the inefficiency of the judicial system. This overcharge totals 12.34 percent of the rate in domestic currency and 20.4 percent in foreign currency. Thus, modernizing the guarantee execution system and other legal procedures could result in a substantial interest rate reduction.

---

[37] As reported and analyzed by Fleising and de la Peña (1996b).

Directions for the Future

The improved performance of Peru's financial system and the country's economic development allowed lending activity and total indebtedness to increase significantly during the 1990s. Two sets of factors have been instrumental in sustaining this debt expansion and opening the credit market to new groups of clients. The first of these is the institutional development and economic stability that grew out of the public sector reforms that were included in the economic structural adjustment program implemented in the early 1990s. The second is the new credit technologies—primarily information-sharing practices—that the private sector has developed to reach new clients without increasing the risk of strategic default.

The financial reforms adopted in the first half of the 1990s provided a relatively stable and modern environment, ensuring that the increasing indebtedness would not endanger the soundness of the financial system as a whole. The reforms opened up and liberalized the market and provided incentives for lenders to adopt innovative credit technologies such as information sharing and innovative rules for evaluating collateral. Despite a more open financial system, however, much of the increase in loans appears to have gone to traditional clients in the form of larger loans.

For lenders, reaching traditionally unserved or underserved clients is instrumental in enlarging the market and further diversifying loan portfolios. Most of the new clients are lower and middle-class urban individuals seeking small loans for consumption purposes, along with small entrepreneurs and microenterprises. To serve them, formal intermediaries have had to change their procedures and their credit technology, often by adapting procedures used by informal institutional lenders to the needs of the formal sector. This process has not always been successful or cheap, but it has allowed a number of private arrangements to develop that have improved borrower selection, credit monitoring, and recovery and made such lending viable according to market norms.

Both the institutional reforms and private arrangements to improve borrower selection procedures give information-sharing systems a central role. The new banking laws make the SBS responsible for providing information about clients of the financial system. To this end the SBS has developed its public rating register, which, together with the three private rating registers and informal institutional lenders such as department stores, has become a necessary source of information in any formal (and most informal) borrower selection procedures. The importance of these information-sharing systems has grown as telecommunications infrastructure development has reduced their costs.

Credit registers, however, do not include data on small and new clients. Given that these clients are becoming an increasingly significant part of the system, small intermediaries (formal and informal) catering to these clients have developed alternative solutions to their informational problems. These private arrangements reflect the first responses to the new institutional context and to a number of ongoing reforms, and in that sense they are still developing. However, their development is hindered by a number of factors, chiefly flaws in the design of information-sharing systems and the ineffectiveness of legal enforcement procedures (which translate into higher interest rates and higher transaction costs). Unfortunately, there is little hope of real improvement in the efficiency of the judicial system. But the new institutional context that has given rise to a range of responses from both formal and informal financial intermediaries has generated a shift toward more intensive reliance on information in lending. This information can be used to reduce the default rate—and thus avoid the need for judicial processes in the first place. This chapter has presented several examples of successful experiences that can be built on to create an effective, broad-based credit market with innovative institutions that effectively screens borrowers and minimizes defaults.

Bibliography

Aith, M. 1998. "The Judiciary's Impact on the Activities of Financial Institutions." In: A.C. Pinheiro, editor. *Economic Costs of Judicial Inefficiency in Brazil.* São Paulo, Brazil: Institute for Economic, Social, and Political Studies of São Paulo/Center for Social and Political Studies of São Paulo.

Alston, L.J. 1984. "Farm Foreclosure Moratorium Legislation: A Lesson from the Past." *American Economic Review* 74(3): 445-57.

Altman, E. 1984. "A Further Empirical Investigation of the Bankruptcy Cost Question." *Journal of Finance* 39(4): 1067-89.

Alvarado, J., and F. Ugaz. 1998. *Retos del financiamiento rural: Construcción de instituciones y crédito informal.* Lima, Peru: Centro Peruano de Estudios Sociales, Centro de Investigación y Promoción de Campesinado/Centro de Estudios Sociales Solidaridad.

Armendariz, B., and C. Gollier. 2000. "Peer Group Formation in an Adverse Selection Model." *Economic Journal* 110: 632-43.

Arnaudo, A.A., and M.P. Buraschi. 1998. "La normalidad de la cartera de préstamos de los bancos privados argentinos, 1993-97." *Estudios* 84: 3-11.

Arnott, R., and J.E. Stiglitz. 1991. "Moral Hazard and Nonmarket Institutions: Dysfunctional Crowding Out or Peer Monitoring?" *American Economic Review* 81(1): 179-90.

Arrow, K.J. 1962. "Economic Welfare and the Allocation of Resources for Invention." In: R.R. Nelson, editor. *The Rate and Direction of Inventive Activity.* National Bureau of Economic Research, Conference Series No. 13. Princeton, United States: Princeton University Press.

Avery, R., R. Bostic and K. Samolyk. 1998. "The Role of Personal Wealth in Small Business Finance." *Journal of Banking and Finance* 22(6-8): 1019-61.

Baird, D. 1991. "The Initiation Problem in Bankruptcy." *International Review of Law and Economics* 11(2): 223-32.

Balleisen, E. J. 1996. "Vulture Capitalism in Antebellum America: The 1841 Federal Bankruptcy Act and the Exploitation of Financial Distress." *Business History Review* 70: 473-516.

Baltagi, B. 1995. *Econometric Analysis of Panel Data.* Chichester, United Kingdom: John Wiley and Sons, Ltd.

Banco Central de la República Argentina (BCRA). 1997. *Informe Anual al Honorable Congreso de la Nación.* Buenos Aires, Argentina: BCRA.

Banco Central de Reserva del Perú. Various years. Nota Semanal. Lima, Perú: Banco Central de Reserva del Perú.

Bebchuk, L.A., and J.M. Fried. 1996. "The Uneasy Case for the Priority of Secured Claims in Bankruptcy." *Yale Law Journal* 105: 857-934.

Bebchuk, L.A., and R. Picker. 1998. "Bankruptcy Rules, Managerial Entrenchment, and Firm-Specific Human Capital." *Journal of Law and Economics.*

Becker, G.S. 1968. "Crime and Punishment: An Economic Approach." *Journal of Political Economy* 76(2): 169-217.

Bennardo, A., and M. Pagano. 2001. "Worthwhile Communication with Nonexclusive Lending." Salerno, Italy: University of Salerno. Unpublished manuscript.

Berger, A., and G. Udell. 1995. "Relationship Lending and Lines of Credit in Small Firm Finance." *Journal of Business* 68(3): 351-81.

Berglöf, E., and H. Rosenthal. 1998. "The Political Economy of American Bankruptcy: The Evidence from Roll Call Voting, 1800-1978." Paper presented at the annual meeting of the Midwest Political Science Association, Chicago, United States.

Berkovitch, E., I. Ronen and J.F. Zender. 1997. "Optimal Bankruptcy Law and Firm-Specific Investments." *European Economic Review* 41(3-5): 487-97.

Berkowitz, J., and M. White. 2000. "Bankruptcy and Small Firms' Access to Credit." Ann Arbor, United States: University of Michigan. Unpublished manuscript.

Besanko, D., and A.V. Thakor. 1987a. "Collateral and Rationing: Sorting Equilibria in Monopolistic and Competitive Credit Markets," *International Economic Review* 28(3): 671-89.

———. 1987b. "Competitive Equilibria in the Credit Market under Asymmetric Information." *Journal of Economic Theory* 42: 167-82.

Besley, T. 1995. "Savings, Credit and Insurance." In: J. Behrman and T.N. Srinivasan, editors. *Handbook of Development Economics.* Volume 3. Amsterdam, The Netherlands: North-Holland.

Besley, T., and S. Coate. 1991. "Group Lending, Repayment Incentives, and Social Collateral." Research Program in Development Studies 152. Princeton, United States: Princeton University.

―――. 1995. "Group Lending, Repayment Incentives and Social Collateral." *Journal of Development Economics* 46: 1-18.

Bester, H. 1985. "Screening vs. Rationing in Credit Markets with Imperfect Information." *American Economic Review* 75(4): 850-55.

Biais, B., and G. Recasens. 2001. "Corrupt Judges, Upwardly Mobile Entrepreneurs and Social Costs of Liquidation: The Political Economy of Bankruptcy Laws." Toulouse, France: Université de Toulouse. Unpublished manuscript.

Bianco, M., T. Jappelli and M. Pagano. 2001. "Courts and Banks: Effects of Judicial Enforcement on Credit Markets." CSEF Working Paper 58. *http://www.dise.unisa.it/WP/wp58.pdf.* Salerno, Italy: University of Salerno.

Bizer, D.S., and P. M. DeMarzo. 1992. "Sequential Banking." *Journal of Political Economy* 100(1): 41-61.

Bolton, P., and H. Rosenthal. 1999. "The Political Economy of Debt Moratoriums, Bailouts, and Bankruptcy." Research Network Working Paper R-370. Washington, DC: Inter-American Development Bank, Research Department.

Bolton, P., and D. Scharfstein. 1990. "A Theory of Predation Based on Agency Problems in Financial Contracting." *American Economic Review* 80(1): 94-106.

―――. 1996. "Optimal Debt Structure and the Number of Creditors." *Journal of Political Economy* 104(1): 1-27.

Borda, D. 1997. "Evaluación del Programa Global de Créditos a la Microempresa." Préstamo 707/OC-PR BID. Asunción, Paraguay: Central Bank of Paraguay, Technical Unit for the Execution of Microlending Programs. Mimeographed document.

Brock, P., editor. 1992. *If Texas Were Chile: A Primer on Banking Reform.* San Francisco, United States: Institute for Contemporary Studies Press.

Buera, F., and J.P. Nicolini. 1997. "Los Spreads de Tasas de Interés en Argentina." Buenos Aires, Argentina: Universidad Torcuato Di Tella. Mimeographed document.

Campos, L. 1995. *Costo del Dinero en el Paraguay, de la Administración Burocrática de las Tasas a su Liberalización: Efectos sobre el Mercado.* Serie Estudios No. 10. Asunción, Paraguay: Centro Paraguayo para la Promoción de la Libertad Económica y de la Justicia Social (CEPPRO).

Canals, J. 1996. *Bancos universales y diversificación empresarial.* Buenos Aires: Editorial Alianza.

Cañonero, G. 1997. "Bank Concentration and the Supply of Credit in Argentina." Working Paper 97/40. Washington, DC, United States: International Monetary Fund.

Carr, J.L., and G.F. Mathewson. 1988. "Unlimited Liability as a Barrier to Entry." *Journal of Political Economy* 96(4): 766-84.

Castelar Pinheiro, A. 1996. "Judicial System Performance and Economic Development." Ensaios BNDES 2. Rio de Janeiro: Banco Nacional de Desenvolvimento Econômico e Social and Agencia Especial de Financiamento Industrial.

————, editor. 1998. "Economic Costs of Judicial Inefficiency in Brazil." São Paulo: Institute for Economic, Social and Political Studies of São Paulo.

Castelar Pinheiro, A., and C. Cabral. 1998. *Credit Markets in Brazil: The Role of Judicial Enforcement and Other Institutions.* Rio de Janeiro: National Economic and Social Development Bank.

————. 1999. "Credit Markets in Brazil: The Role of Judicial Enforcement and Other Institutions." Research Department Working Paper R-368. Washington, DC, United States: Inter-American Development Bank, Research Department.

Catão, L. 1997. "Bank Credit in Argentina in the Aftermath of the Mexican Crisis: Supply or Demand Constrained?" IMF Working Paper 97/32. Washington, DC, United States: International Monetary Fund.

Centro Paraguayo para la Promoción de la Libertad Economica y de la Justicia Social (CEPPRO). 1994a. *Proyecto de Carta Orgánica del Banco Central del Paraguay: Comentarios Críticos y Propuestas.* Asunción, Paraguay: CEPPRO.

————. 1994b. *Proyecto de Ley General de Bancos, Financieras y Otras Entidades de Crédito: Análisis Crítico y Comentarios.* Asunción, Paraguay: CEPPRO.

————. 1996. *Informe Económico 1995.* Asunción, Paraguay: CEPPRO.

Chan, Y-S., and A.V. Thakor. 1987. "Collateral and Competitive Equilibria with Moral Hazard and Private Information." *Journal of Finance* 42(2): 345-64.

Chaparro, J. 1995. "El Financiamiento Rural en el Perú: Limitaciones y Perspectivas." Guelph, Canada: Ecological Services for Planning Ltd. Unpublished manuscript.

Chaves, R. 1993. "Diseño institucional de organizaciones: El caso de los bancos comunales." In: C. González-Vega, R. Jimenez and R. Quirós, editors. *Financiamiento de la microempresa rural.* San José, Costa Rica: Finca Costa Rica, Ohio State University, Academia de Centroamérica, and Fundación Interamericana.

Chong, A., and E. Schroth. 1998. "Cajas Municipales: Microcrédito y Pobreza en el Perú." Investigaciones Breves 9. Lima, Perú: Consorcio de Investigación Económica.

Clauretie, T.M. 1987. "The Impact of Interstate Foreclosure Cost Differences and the Value of Mortgages on Default Rates." *Journal of the American Real Estate and Urban Economics Association* 15: 152-67.

Clauretie, T.M. and T. Herzog. 1990. "The Effect of State Foreclosure Laws on Loan Losses: Evidence from the Mortgage Insurance Industry." *Journal of Money, Credit and Banking* 22(2): 221-33.

Coate, S., and M. Ravallion. 1993. "Reciprocity Without Commitment: Characterization and Performance of Informal Insurance Arrangements." *Journal of Development Economics* 40(1): 1-24.

Cooter, R., and T. Ulen. 1988. *Law and Economics.* New York: Harper Collins.

Cristini, M., R. Moya and A. Powell. 2001. "The Importance of an Effective Legal System for Credit Markets: The Case of Argentina." Research Network Working Paper R-428. Washington, DC, United States: Inter-American Development Bank, Research Department.

De Bondt, W.F.M., and R.H. Thaler. 1995. "Financial Decision-Making in Markets and Firms: A Behavioral Perspective." In: R. Jarrow *et al.*, editors. *Handbooks in Operations Research and Management, Volume 9: Finance.* Amsterdam, The Netherlands: Elsevier Science.

De la Cuadra, S., and S. Valdés. 1992. "Myths and Facts about Financial Liberalization in Chile: 1974-1983." In: P. Brock, editor. *If Texas were Chile: A Primer on Banking Reform.* A Sequoia Seminar. San Francisco, United States: Institute for Contemporary Studies Press.

Demirgüç-Kunt, A., and V. Maksimovic. 1998. "Law, Finance and Firm Growth." *Journal of Finance* 53(6): 2107-37.

———. 1999. "Institutions, Financial Markets, and Firms' Choice of Debt Maturity." *Journal of Financial Economics* 54(3): 295-336.

Detragiache, E., P. G. Garella, and L. Guiso. 2000. "Multiple versus Single Banking Relationships." *Journal of Finance* 55(3): 1133-61.

Domowitz, I., and T.L. Eovaldi. 1993. "The Impact of the Bankruptcy Reform Act of 1978 on Consumer Bankruptcy." *Journal of Law and Economics* 36(2): 803-35.

Domowitz, I., and E. Tamer. 1997. "Two Hundred Years of Bankruptcy: A Tale of Legislation and Economic Fluctuations." Economics Department, Northwestern University. Unpublished manuscript.

Economist. 1997a. "Adventures with Capital." January 25: 17-18.

———. 1997b. "Banking in Emerging Markets. A Survey." April 12. 343(8012): S1-S40.

———. 1998. "America Goes Bust." July 4: 85.

Edwards, S. 1995. *Crisis and Reform in Latin America: From Despair to Hope.* Washington, DC, United States: Oxford University Press.

Erb, B.C., R.H. Campbell and T.E. Viskanta. 1996. "Political Risk, Economic Risk, and Financial Risk." *Financial Analyst Journal* 52(6): 28-46.

Espina, A. 1998. "Sistemas Concursales y Eficiencia Económica: La Reforma Española y la Experiencia Comparada." *Hacienda Pública Española.*

Fabbri, D., and M. Padula. 2001. "Judicial Costs and Household Debt." Salerno, Italy: Università di Salerno. Unpublished manuscript.

Feinberg, J. 1986. *The Moral Limits of the Criminal Law, Volume 3: Harm to Self.* New York, United States: Oxford University Press.

Fleising, H.W., and N. de la Peña. 1996a. "Argentina: How Problems in the Framework for Secured Transactions Limit Access To Credit." Washington, DC, United States: Center for the Economic Analysis of Law. Mimeographed document.

———. 1996b. Peru: How Problems in the Framework for Secured Transactions Limit Access to Credit. Washington, DC, United States: Center for the Economic Analysis of Law.

Foundation for Latin American Economic Research (FIEL). 1996a. *Las pequeñas y medianas empresas en la Argentina.* Buenos Aires: Editorial Manantial.

———. 1996b. *La reforma del Poder Judicial en la Argentina.* Buenos Aires: Editorial Manantial.

———. 1999. "Los costos judicial y su impacto en las tasas de interés y el acceso al crédito regional." Background paper for the Argentine Central Bank Annual Report to the Congress. Buenos Aires, Argentina: FIEL. Mimeographed document.

Franks, J., K. Nyborg, and W. Thorous. 1996. "A Comparison of U.S., UK, and German Insolvency Codes." *Financial Management* 25(3): 86-101.

Freehling, W.W. 1989. *The Road to Disunion.* Vol. 1, *Secessionists At Bay, 1776-1854.* New York, United States: Oxford University Press.

Freixas, X. 1991. *El Mercado Hipotecario Español: Situación Actual y Proyecto de Reforma.* Madrid, Spain: Fundación de Estudios de Economía Aplicada.

Freixas, X., and J.C. Rochet. 1997. *Microeconomics of Banking.* Cambridge, United States: MIT Press.

Fudenberg, D., B. Holmstrom, and P. Milgrom. 1990. "Short-Term Contracts and Long-Term Agency Relationships." *Journal of Economic Theory* 51(1): 1-31.

Fuentes, J.R., and M. Basch. 1998. "Determinants of the Banking Spread in Chile." Research Network Working Paper R-329. Washington, DC, United States: Inter-American Development Bank, Research Department.

Fuentes, J.R., and C. Maquieira. 1999. "Institutional Arrangements to Determine Loan Repayment in Chile." Research Network Working Paper R-374. Washington, DC, United States: Inter-American Development Bank, Research Department.

Gale, D., and M. Hellwig. 1985. "Incentive-Compatible Debt Contracts: The One-Period Problem." *Review of Economics Studies* 52(4): 647-63.

Gavin, M., and R. Hausmann. 1996. "The Roots of Banking Crises: The Macroeconomic Context." In: R. Hausmann and L. Rojas-Suárez, editors. *Banking Crises in Latin America.* Washington, DC, United States: Inter-American Development Bank.

———. 1997. "Make or Buy? Appraches to Financial Market Integration." Working Paper 337. Washington, DC, United States: Inter-American Development Bank, Research Department.

Gertner, R., and D. Scharfstein. 1991. "A Theory of Workouts and the Effects of Reorganization Law." *Journal of Finance* 46(4): 1189-1222.

Goldstein, M., and P. Turner. 1996. "Banking Crises in Emerging Economies: Origins and Policy Options." Economic Paper 46. Basle, Switzerland: Bank for International Settlements, Monetary and Economic Department.

Gonzales de Olarte, E. 1998. *El Neoliberalismo a la Peruana: Economía Política del Ajuste Estructural, 1990-97.* Lima, Perú: Consorcio de Investigación Económica, Instituto de Estudios Peruanos.

González-Vega, C., and R. Chaves. 1996. "Diseño de intermediarios financieros exitosos: evidencia de Indonesia." *Debate Agrario* 23:113-33.

Gropp, R., J.K. Scholz and M.J. White. 1997. "Personal Bankruptcy and Credit Supply and Demand." *Quarterly Journal of Economics* 112(1): 218-51.

Grossman, S., and O. Hart. 1983. "An Analysis of the Principal Agent Problem." *Econometrica* 51(1): 7-45.

Hart, O. 1995. *Firms, Contracts, and Financial Structure.* Oxford, United Kingdom: Clarendon Press.

Hart, O., and J. Moore. 1988. "Incomplete Contracts and Renegotiation." *Econometrica* 56(4): 755-85.

———. 1994 "A Theory of Debt Based on the Inalienability of Human Capital." *Quarterly Journal of Economics* 109(4): 841-79.

———. 1998 "Default and Renegotiation: A Dynamic Model of Debt." *Quarterly Journal of Economics* 113(1): 1-41.

Hirsch, D. 1994. *Diversificación Agrícola.* Serie Propuestas No. 3. Asunción, Paraguay: CEPPRO.

History of Congress. Exhibiting a Classification of the Proceedings of the Senate, and the House of Representatives, from March 4, 1793; Embracing the First Term of the Administration of General Washington. 1843. Philadelphia, United States: Lea and Blanchard.

Holmstrom, B. 1979. "Moral Hazard and Observability." *Bell Journal of Economics* 10(1): 74-91.

———. 1982. "Moral Hazard in Teams." *Bell Journal of Economics* 13(2): 324-40.

Holmstrom, B. and P. Milgrom. 1990. "Regulating Trade among Agents." *Journal of Institutional and Theoretical Economics* 146(1): 85-105.

Inter-American Development Bank (IDB). 1996. *Informe sobre el Progreso Económico y Social en América Latina.* Washington, DC, United States: IDB.

IMF (International Monetary Fund). 1995. International Financial Statistics. Washington, DC, United States: International Monetary Fund.

———. 1998. "Paraguay—Selected Issues and Statistical Annex." IMF Staff Country Reports No. 98/15. Washington, DC, United States: International Monetary Fund.

Jackson, T.H. 1986. *The Logic and Limits of Bankruptcy Law.* Cambridge, United States: Harvard University Press.

Jaffee, A. 1985. "Mortgage Foreclosure Law and Regional Disparities in Mortgage Financing Costs." Working Paper No. 85-80. University Park, PA,
United States: Pennsylvania State University.

Jappelli, T., and M. Pagano. 1999. "Information Sharing, Lending and
Defaults: Cross-Country Evidence." University of Salerno Center for
Studies in Economics and Finance (CSEF) Working Paper 22 *http://
www.dise.unisa.it/WP/wp22.pdf* and Centre for Economic Policy Re-
search (CEPR) Discussion Paper 2184 *http://www.cepr.org/pubs/dps/
DP2184.asp.* Salerno, Italy and London, United Kingdom: CSEF/CEPR.
Forthcoming in *Journal of Banking and Finance.*

————. 2000. "Information Sharing in Credit Markets: The European Experience." University of Salerno Center for Studies in Economics and
Finance (CSEF) Working Paper 36 *http://www.dise.unisa.it/WP/
wp36.pdf.* Salerno, Italy: CSEF.

Kervyn, B. 1985. "Crédito en comunidades campesinas: Una experiencia en
el Cusco." Cusco, Peru: Centro Bartolomé de las Casas.

Kervyn, B., and R. Rojas. 1995. "Los Sistemas de Concesión de Crédito para
los Proyectos Agrícolas en Medio Rural." Informe Sintético de la Región
Andina Bolivia-Perú. Cusco, Perú: Centro Bartolomé de las Casas.
Manuscript.

Kroszner, R.S. 1998. "Is It Better to Forgive than to Receive? Repudiation of
the Gold Indexation Clause in Long-Term Debt During the Great
Depression." Chicago, United States: University of Chicago, Graduate
School of Business. Unpublished manuscript.

Kroszner, R.S., and T. Strattman. 1998. "Interest Group Competition and
the Organization of Congress: Theory and Evidence from Financial
Services Political Action Committees." *American Economic Review*
88(5): 1163-87.

La Porta, R. and F. López-de-Silanes. 1998. "Capital Markets and Legal Institutions." Cambridge, United States: Harvard University. Mimeographed
document.

La Porta, R., F. López-de-Silanes, A. Shleifer and R.W. Vishny. 1997. "Legal
Determinants of External Finance." *Journal of Finance* 52(3): 1131-1150.

————. 1998. "Law and Finance." *Journal of Political Economy* 106(6): 1113-
55.

Lazarte, J. 1996. "La situación de las cajas rurales de ahorro y crédito." *Debate Agrario* 24: 39-58.

Lohmann, S. 1992. "Optimal Commitment in Monetary Policy: Credibility versus Flexibility." *American Economic Review* 82(1): 273-86.

Manove, M., and A.J. Padilla. 1999. "Banking (Conservatively) with Optimists." *Rand Journal of Economics* 30(2): 324-50.

Manove, M., A.J. Padilla and M. Pagano. 1998. "Collateral vs. Project Screening: A Model of Lazy Banks." Center for Study in Economics and Finance (CSEF) Working Paper 10. Salerno, Italy: University of Salerno, Department of Economics *http://www.dise.unisa.it/WP/wp10.pdf.* CEPR Discussion Paper No. 2439. London, United Kingdom: Centre for Economic Policy Research. *http://www.cepr.org/pubs/dps/DP2439.asp.* Forthcoming in *Rand Journal of Economics.*

Maquieira, C. 1993. "Estimación de Costos Directos e Indirectos de Quiebra para Chile." Report prepared for Entel Chile. Santiago, Chile: Entel Chile. Mimeographed document.

Maquieira, C., and M.I. Sierralta. 1990. "El efecto de la devaluación en los retornos accionarios." *Paradigmas en Administración* 17:1-18.

Marthans, J.J. 1997a. "Hacia dónde va la política financiera peruana." *Entorno Económico* (September-October): 17-21.

―――. 1997b. "Reflexiones en torno a los mecanismos de información e inflexibilidad a la baja del costo del crédito." *Moneda* 101(February/ March): 61-66. Lima, Perú: Banco Central de Reserva del Perú.

McCoy, D.R. 1989. *The Last of the Fathers: James Madison and the Republican Legacy.* New York, United States: Cambridge University Press.

McDonald, B., Jr. 1994. "Credit Schemes for Microenterprises: Motivation, Design, and Viability." Washington, DC, United States: Georgetown University. Doctoral dissertation.

McKinsey Corporation. 1998. "Productivity—The Key to an Accelerated Development Path for Brazil." Washington, DC, United States: McKinsey Corporation.

Meador, M. 1982. "The Effect of Mortgage Laws on Home Mortgage Rates." *Journal of Economics and Business* 34(2): 143-48.

Melumad, N.D., and S. Reichelstein. 1986. "The Value of Communication Agencies." Research Paper 895. Stanford, United States: Stanford University, Department of Economics.

Ministerio de la Presidencia, Secretaría Ejecutiva de Cooperación Técnica Internacional. 1996. Directorio de organizacione no gubernamentales de desarrollo, ONGD-PERÚ. Lima, Perú: Ministerio de la Presidencia.

Monge-Naranjo, A. 1996. "On Financial Markets, Entrepreneurship and the Distribution of Wealth." Working Paper, Department of Economics, University of Chicago.

———. 1999. "Recursive Bank-Entrepreneur Relationships and the Aggregate Dynamics of Creation and Destruction." Chicago, United States: University of Chicago, Department of Economics. Unpublished doctoral dissertation.

Monge-Naranjo, A., J. Cascante and L. Hall. 2001. "Enforcement, Contract Design, and Default: Exploring the Financial Markets of Costa Rica." Research Network Working Paper R-429. Washington, DC, United States: Inter-American Development Bank, Research Department.

Moody's Investor Service. 1998. Report 33641. New York, United States: Moody's Investor Service, Inc.

Morris, F. 1997. "Un análisis crítico de la Ley General del Sistema Financiero y del Sistema de Seguros." *Moneda* 103(June/July): 52-55.

Myerson, R. 1979. "Incentive Compatibility and the Bargaining Problem." *Econometrica* 47(1): 61-74.

Noriega, J. 1997. Perú: Las organizaciones no gubernamentales de desarrollo (ONGD). Lima, Perú: Centro de Estudios y Promoción del Desarrollo.

North, D. 1961. *The Economic Growth of the United States, 1790-1860.* Englewood Cliffs, United States: Prentice-Hall.

———. 1981. *Structure and Change in Economic History.* New York, United States: W.W. Norton & Co, Inc.

O Globo. 1998. August 23, p. 37.

Ongena, S., and D.C. Smith. 2000. "Bank Relationships: A Review." In: P. Harker and S.A. Zenios, editors. *The Performance of Financial Institutions.* Cambridge, United Kingdom: Cambridge University Press.

Ortiz de Zevallos, G. 1998. "Nuevo contexto legal para el sistema de intermediación financiera." Lima, Perú: Instituto de Estudios Peruanos and Centro Peruano de Estudios Sociales. Unpublished manuscript.

Padilla, A.J., and M. Pagano 1997. "Endogenous Communication among Lenders and Entrepreneurial Incentives." *Review of Financial Studies* 10(1): 205-36.

———. 2000. "Sharing Default Information as a Borrower Discipline Device." *European Economic Review* 44(10): 1951-80.

Padilla, A.J., and A. Requejo. 2000. "The Costs and Benefits of the Strict Protection of Creditor Rights: Theory and Evidence." Research Network Working Paper R-384. Washington, DC, United States: Inter-American Development Bank, Research Department.

Pagano, M., and T. Jappelli. 1993. "Information Sharing in Credit Markets." *Journal of Finance* 43(5): 1693-1718.

Petersen, M.A., and R.G. Rajan. 1994. "The Benefits of Lending Relationships: Evidence from Small Business Data." *Journal of Finance* 49(1): 3-37.

Phelan, C., and R. Townsend. 1991. "Computing Multiperiod Information-Constrained Optima." *Review of Economics Studies* 58(5): 824-53.

Posner, R.A. 1992. *The Economic Analysis of the Law.* Boston, United States: Little, Brown and Company.

Powell A., A. Broda, and T. Burdisso. 1997. "An Analysis of Lending Interest Rates in Argentina: A Panel Interpretation of a Search Model with Bargaining." Buenos Aires, Argentina: Central Bank of Argentina. Mimeographed document.

Prescott, E., and R. Townsend. 1984a. "General Competitive Analysis in an Economy with Private Information." *International Economic Review* 25(1): 1-20.

———.1984b. "Pareto Optima and Competitive Equilibria with Adverse Selection and Moral Hazard." *Econometrica* 52(1): 21-46.

Rajan, R.G. 1992. "Insiders and Outsiders: The Choice between Informed and Arm's Length Debt." *Journal of Finance* 47(4): 1367-1400.

Rajan, R.G., and L. Zingales. 1998. "Financial Dependence and Growth." *American Economic Review* 88(3): 559-86.

Ramírez, G., and F. Rosende. 1992. "Responding to Collapse: Chilean Banking Legislation after 1985." In: P. Brock, editor. *If Texas were Chile: A Primer on Banking Reform.* San Francisco, United States: Institute for Contemporary Studies Press.

Rashid, M., and R. Townsend. 1994. "Targeting Credit and Insurance: Efficiency, Mechanism Design and Program Evaluation." ESP Discussion Paper Series 47. Washington, DC, United States: World Bank, Education and Social Policy Department.

Rogerson, W. 1985. "Repeated Moral Hazard." *Econometrica* 53(1): 69-76.

Rohrbough, M.J. 1968. *The Land Office Business: The Settlement and Administration of American Public Lands, 1789-1837.* New York, United States: Oxford University Press.

Rojas, J. 1996. "La reforma del sistema financiero peruano: 1990-95." *Boletín de Opinión* 25(April): 40-46.

———. 1997. "Tasas de interés, Spreads y Dolarización luego de la Reforma Financiera." *Moneda* 101(February/March): 44-48.

Romero, L. 1996. "Regulación y supervisión bancarias." *Boletín de Opinión* 25(April): 47-52.

Rothbard, M.N. 1962. *The Panic of 1819: Reactions and Policies.* New York, United States: Columbia University Press.

Rothschild, M., and J.E. Stiglitz. 1976. "Equilibrium in Competitive Insurance Markets: An Essay on the Economics of Imperfect Information." *Quarterly Journal of Economics* 90(4): 629-49.

Schmidt, R., and C.P. Zeitinger. 1994. "Critical Issues in Small and Microbusiness Finance." Frankfurt, Germany: Interdisziplinare Projekt Consult.

Schor, G. 1997. "Commercial Financial Institutions as Micro Lending Partners: Some Lessons of the Micro Global Program in Paraguay." Asunción, Paraguay: Internationale Projekt Consult GmbH. Mimeographed document.

Sherwood, R.M., G. Shepherd and C.M. de Souza. 1994. "Judicial Systems and Economic Performance." *Quarterly Review of Economics and Finance* 34(Special Issue): 101-16.

Shleifer, A., and R.W. Vishny. 1996. "A Survey of Corporate Governance." *Journal of Finance* 52(2): 737-83.

Smith, A. 1776. *The Wealth of Nations.*

Spear, S., and S. Strivastava. 1987. "On Repeated Moral Hazard with Discounting." *Review of Economic Studies* 54(4): 599-618.

Stiglitz, J.E. 1990. "Peer Monitoring and Credit Markets." *The World Bank Economic Review* 4(3): 351-66.

Stiglitz, J.E., and A. Weiss. 1981. "Credit Rationing in Markets with Imperfect Information." *American Economic Review* 71(3): 393-410.

Straub, S. 1998. "Evolución Macroeconómica del Paraguay 1989-97: Burbuja de Consumo y Crisis Financiera." *Revista de la CEPAL* 65: 119-32.

Straub, S., and H. Sosa. 1999. "Institutional Arrangements to Ensure Willingness to Repay in Financial Markets: A Case Study of Paraguay." Research Network Working Paper R-364. Washington, DC, United States: Inter-American Development Bank, Research Department.

Superintendencia de Banca y Seguros(SBS). Various years. "Información financiera mensual de las cajas municipales y cajas rurales." Lima, Perú: SBS.

———. Various years. "Información financiera mensual de banca múltiple, empresas financieras, empresas de crédito de consumo y entidades estatales." Lima, Perú: SBS.

Svensson, J. 1998. "Investment, Property Rights and Political Instability: Theory and Evidence." *European Economic Review* 42(7): 1317-1342.

Taylor, S.E. 1989. *Positive Illusions: Creative Self-Deception and the Healthy Mind.* New York, United States: Basic Books.

Thomas, J., and T. Worral. 1990. "Income Fluctuation and Asymmetric Information: An Example of Repeated Principal Agent Problem." *Journal of Economic Theory* 51(2): 367-90.

Townsend, R.M. 1979. "Optimal Contracts and Competitive Markets with Costly State Verification." *Journal of Economic Theory* 21(2): 265-93.

———. 1982. "Optimal Multiperiod Contracts and the Gain to Enduring Relationship under Private Information." *Journal of Political Economy* 90(6): 1166-86.

———. 1987. "Economic Organization with Limited Communication." *American Economic Review* 77(5): 954-71.

———. 1988. "Information-Constrained Insurance. The Revelation Principle Extended." *Journal of Monetary Economics* 21(2): 411-50.

———. 1993. *The Medieval Village Economy: Study of the Pareto Mapping in General Equilibrium Models.* Princeton, United States: Princeton University Press.

———. 1994. "Risk and Insurance in Village India." *Econometrica* 62(3): 539-91.

———. 1995. "Consumption Insurance: An Evaluation of Risk-Bearing Systems in Low-Income Economies." *Journal of Economic Perspectives* 9(3): 83-102.

Townsend, R.M., and R. Mueller. 1997. "Mechanism Design and Village Economies: From Credit to Tenancy to Cropping Groups." *Review of Economic Dynamics* 1(1): 119-72.

Trebilcock, M.J. 1993. *The Limits of Freedom of Contract.* Cambridge, United States: Harvard University Press.

Trivelli, C. 1998. Intermediación financiera en la agricultura en el Perú, 1994-1997. Documento de Trabajo 90. Lima, Perú: Instituto de Estudios Peruanos.

Trivelli, C., J. Alvarado and F. Galarza. 1999. "Increasing Indebtedness, Institutional Change and Credit Contracts in Peru." Research Network Working Paper R-378. Washington, DC, United States: Inter-American Development Bank, Research Department.

United Nations. 1995. *Monthly Bulletin of Statistics.* Volume 49. New York, United States: United Nations.

United States Bureau of the Census. 1975. *Historical Statistics of the United States: Colonial Times to 1970.* Washington, DC, United States: Government Printing Office.

Varian, H. 1990. "Monitoring Agents with Other Agents." *Journal of Institutional and Theoretical Economics* 146:153-74.

Velarde, J., and M. Rodríguez. 1996. "La reforma financiera en el Perú: 1990-94." *Boletín de Opinión* 25(April): 33-40.

Vicens, M. 1998. "El Crédito en la Argentina: Factores de Sobrecosto." In: Asociación de Bancos Argentinos, editor. *La Argentina en el Mundo: Convención Nacional de Banco 1997.* Buenos Aires: Asociación de Bancos Argentinos.

Weder, B. 1995. "Legal Systems and Economic Performance: The Empirical Evidence." In: W.H. Malik and M. Dakolias, editors. *Judicial Reform in Latin America and the Caribbean.* Technical Paper 280. Washington, DC, United States: World Bank.

White, H. 1980. "A Heteroskedasticity-Consistent Covariance Matrix and a Direct Test for Heteroskedasticity." *Econometrica* 48: 817-38.

Williamson, O.E. 1995. "The Institutions and Governance of Economic Development and Reform." In: M. Bruno and B. Pleskovic, editors. *Proceedings of the World Bank Annual Conference on Development Economics 1994.* Washington, DC, United States: World Bank.

World Bank. 1994. "How Legal Restrictions on Collateral Limit Access to Credit in Bolivia." Report 13873-BO. Washington, DC, United States: World Bank, Office of the Chief Economist, Latin America and the Caribbean Region.

――――. 1996a. *World Development Report.* Washington, DC, United States: World Bank.

――――. 1996b. "Paraguay. Principal Constraints to Private Sector Development." Report 15044-PA. Washington, DC, United States: World Bank, Country Operations Unit II, Country Department I, Latin America and the Caribbean Regional Office.

————. 1996c. "Paraguay: The Role of the State." Report 15044-PA. Washington, DC, United States: World Bank, Office of the Chief Economist, Latin America and the Caribbean Region.

Yaron, J. 1992. "Successful Rural Finance Institutions." World Bank Discussion Paper 150. Washington, DC, United States: World Bank.